The New World

21st-Century Global Order and India

The New World

21st-Century Global Order and India

RAM MADHAV

RUPA

Published by
Rupa Publications India Pvt. Ltd 2025
7/16, Ansari Road, Daryaganj
New Delhi 110002

Sales centres:
Bengaluru Chennai
Hyderabad Jaipur Kathmandu
Kolkata Mumbai Prayagraj

P-ISBN: 978-93-7003-826-4
E-ISBN: 978-93-7003-223-1

First impression 2025

10 9 8 7 6 5 4 3 2 1

CONTENTS

PREFACE

Sometime in 2023, the B.E.S.T Innovation University, Bengaluru, invited me to deliver a lecture on higher education in India. While preparing for that lecture, I realized that the world of technology was undergoing tremendous changes, with frontier technologies like artificial intelligence (AI) and bioengineering leading the pack. I also learnt that India needed a complete overhaul of its education, science and technology R and D to meet the standards of the newly evolving tech order.

In April 2024, I was invited by O.P. Jindal Global University, Sonepat to deliver a lecture on the new world order. Again, while preparing for that lecture, I realized that the world that our current and future generations enter is going to be a completely transformed one, from that in which all of us have lived thus far. A new world order is taking shape, which will be markedly different from the old one.

At Jindal, I spoke about ten changes that the new world will experience. These ten changes will determine the shape of the new world order that will come into existence in this century. The liberal and democratic world order that we have lived in for the last several decades was a creation of the victorious Western powers after the Second World War. It served mankind over the previous seven decades, but the advent of the new century brought new challenges before the world, and the old order seemed incompetent and redundant in tackling those challenges. Hence, the process of replacing the old with the new has begun with the onset of the new century.

From the above two events came the idea of writing this book—*The New World*. It focuses on that emerging new world order. While the old order has more or less ended, the new one is yet to take shape. Humanity is at the crossroads between the old and the new at this juncture. This interregnum offers an opportunity for countries like India to step in and contribute their wisdom in shaping the direction being taken by the new order. As I discussed ten transformations that would determine the shape of the new order, I also offered ten suggestions to India in order for it to proactively contribute to the shaping of that new order.

This book is all about the experience of the outgoing liberal world order built by the West, and the possible shape that the incoming one will take. The future is not easy to predict. Hence, my conclusions and suggestions may be contested by other scholars and authors. I highlighted just ten changes, but there can be many more. Some, like de-dollarization, may or may not happen. Yet, I am confident that this book will help engender some debate about the future of mankind, and encourage many to seriously ponder the inevitability of a new order replacing the old, and the opportunity that such a transformation will offer to India.

I wish to thank Dr Rupa Vasudevan, chancellor and founder of the Bharatiya Engineering Science and Technology Innovation University (BESTIU), and Dr C. Raj Kumar, founding vice-chancellor of O.P. Jindal Global University, for triggering these thoughts and ideas in me by providing an opportunity to speak at their respective institutions. I must also thank Rupa Publications for coming forward to publish a title that may or may not be popular in the Indian milieu, and also waiting patiently for the manuscript. I began working on the book in May 2024, promising to complete it by November. However, I missed several deadlines due to the elections in Jammu and Kashmir, and other pressing political and intellectual commitments. My daughter Deeksha burnt midnight oil to copy edit the book, without which it wouldn't have seen the light of day. India Foundation is full of activity throughout the year. Yet the directors and research staff allowed me to abstain from several events and focus on my book. I am grateful to each one of them and many more who directly and indirectly helped me in finishing this voluminous book in record time.

I hope readers find the content thought-provoking and useful.

Introduction

A HISTORY OF THE FUTURE

Over a million years of its existence, the human race has experienced several phases of advancement. Primitive humans were nomads, living a life of constant movement for hunting and survival. Each person was an individual, and there were no social institutions to bind them together. Life was a challenge, not only for wild animals but also for fellow humans. Sentiments like love and fraternity were unknown in that era.

Early humans lived in dark caves. There was no concept of light. The sun, moon and stars were the only luminous objects, besides the burning eyes of the wild predators that preyed on humans. Dark caves were particularly dangerous for them, as they were easy prey for the apex predators in these places. This was the age of domination of big cats and other wild animals over the earliest hominids. Archaeologists across the ancient hominid bones in the fossil-bearing cave of Swartkrans in South Africa which were probably eaten by the predators. Located about 32 km from Johannesburg in the Cradle of Humankind World Heritage Site, this cave is famous for its rich archaeological material, particularly remains of hominids. Interestingly, this cave also provided evidence of fire, the first human invention. A million-year-old charcoal layer found in the cave shows how this first invention had transformed the earliest humans from being the hunted to becoming hunters. The archaeological records show the later evidence of the presence of animal bones in caves as proof that fire in their hands gave hominids the ability to take control of their caves, turning the tables on predators.

The era of modern humans began around 300,000 years ago in Africa. Archaeological evidence suggests that they demonstrated sophisticated social behaviour like using body adornments and jewellery and engaging in seafaring. Archaeological evidence tells the story of how different agricultural practices emerged in at least seven places around the world at the same time: two types of wheat and barley in the Fertile Crescent, part of today's West Asia; two types of millet (foxtail and broomcorn) in northern China; rice in southern China; squash, beans and maize in Mesoamerica; potatoes and yams in South America; and a variety of quinoa in what is now the eastern United States.

As prehistoric humans learnt the science of tilling the land, sowing seeds and growing food for sustenance, a significant transformation in human existence began. The land became the source of sustenance instead of hunting animals. Large human settlements started emerging. The influential Australian archaeologist V. Gordon Childe, who specialized in European prehistory, coined the term 'Neolithic Revolution' to describe this development.[1] Man and woman began to live together, leading to the early emergence of family life. From family to community, the seeds were sown not only for agriculture, but also for a social culture.

As communities settled down and social and political institutions emerged, human thought began to find expression. Hindus and Greeks led the renaissance of thought, creating the world's oldest literature in the form of epics like Mahabharata, Ramayana and *Iliad*. Around this time, humanity witnessed another transformation in the form of an ethical revolution. Again, led by the Hindus and the Greeks, a moral order began to take shape in the early centuries before the beginning of the Christian era. Socrates led the way in ancient Greece, followed by Plato, Aristotle and many others, and in the competition between the Greek city-states of Athens and Sparta, the ethical brilliance of the Greeks blossomed, creating a moral order for Europeans for many centuries to come. Around the same time, the Hindus also came forward with their Vedas, Upanishads and other classical literature, leading to the evolution of a superior social order in the East.

The emergence of historical, transformative, ethical and moral leadership in the East by leaders like Gautama, the Buddha, in India, and Confucius in China led to a highly enlightened, ethics-based social order in the millennium preceding the Christian Era. 543 BCE is considered the year of the Buddha's *parinirvana* (death). Will Durant, the celebrated historian, said that more than the religion, Buddhism, which his followers preached across the continents, what influenced the world was Buddha, who 'means India, for the spirit of India lies in religion rather than in science, in contemplation rather than in action, in a fraternal gentleness rather than in the application of mathematics to artillery or of chemistry to bombs.'[2] Durant proposed that Buddha's birthdate be considered the beginning of a civilization that has known every vicissitude, injustice and slavery and yet has produced geniuses and saints from Buddha and Ashoka to Gandhi and Tagore.

Durant also observed that at a time when Europe was still languishing in Dark Ages, China, in the Tang and Song dynasties, 'undoubtedly stood at the very forefront of civilization' as 'the most powerful, the most enlightened, the most progressive, and the best-governed empire on the face of the globe.'[3] The credit for it should go to Confucius, a great scholar of wisdom and morality who lived and died in 478 BCE, around the same time as the Buddha in India.

The ethical order built by the Greeks, Chinese and Hindus transformed human existence significantly. India produced great empires that followed the wisdom propounded by the spiritual and ethical gurus, popularly known as Dharma. The Haryankas (sixth century BCE–413 BCE), the Nandas (345–21 BCE), the Mauryas (321–185 BCE), the Sungas (185–73 BCE) and the Guptas (240–600 CE) ruled the empires in North India, while the Satavahanas (first century to second century), the Cholas (300 BCE–1279 CE), the Pandyas (fourth century CE–1345 CE), the Pallavas (275–897 CE) and the Chalukyas (543–753 CE) ran powerful empires over South India and the adjoining seas of the vast Indian Ocean.

In fact, the first millennium belonged to India's Hindu rulers, when the social and economic life of the country flourished and the people generally led a peaceful and prosperous life. While the South Indian kings like the Cholas, Pandyas and Pallavas used the sea routes to establish kingdoms as far as Indochina and the Philippines, their traders travelled west to the Arab lands and Africa in pursuit of international trade. Angus Maddison, a distinguished British economist who worked on documenting the economic performance of nations over long periods, highlighted the fact that India was the largest economy in the world in the first millennium, accounting for over 30 per cent. Even until the fifteenth century, its share of the world economy remained at around 25 per cent.[4] Colonization, first by the Mughals and other Central Asians, then by the British for over 800 years, had left the country pulverized and pauperized.

Europe was not so lucky. The emergence of the Semitic religions in Europe and the quick expansion of their sway over the populations had changed the course of humanity. The rise of Christianity after its adaptation by the Roman emperor Constantine in 327, followed by the rise of Islam in the Arab lands in the seventh century, led to the creation of a religion-centric world order in European lands. Both Christianity and Islam dominated every aspect of human existence, including science, art and culture. Anything that went against the precepts of religion was violently rejected and suppressed. The domination of the world became the singular mission of the Semitic faiths, leading to wars and conquests that caused enormous human suffering.

A classic example was the conflict between the heliocentric theory and the geocentric theory. In European history, Aristarchus of Samos of ancient Greece is mentioned as the first proponent of the astronomical model in 270 BCE, in which the sun was considered central to the universe. However, Aristarchus' theory was lost to scholars like Ptolemy and Aristotle, who were strong advocates of a geocentric view in which the Earth was considered the centre of the universe.[5] In India, scholars of astronomy like Aryabhata (476–550 CE) propounded this theory. In his magnum opus *Aryabhatiya* (499 CE), Aryabhata presented the heliocentric model, in which the Earth and all other planets revolve around the sun.[6] Geocentrism became a religious belief in Europe as the continent came to be dominated by Christianity and Islam. Nicolaus Copernicus, a Polish astronomer and mathematician, was the first in Europe to propose in the early 1500s that not the Earth but the sun is at the centre of the solar system.[7] Johannes Kepler, a German astronomer, and Galileo Galilei, an Italian astronomer, followed suit, advocating for a heliocentric view of the universe in the early seventeenth century.[8] Isaac Newton, an English mathematician and physicist, published his book *Principia* in 1687, supporting and extending the ideas of Kepler and Galileo.[9] However, the Catholic religious leadership refused to change their core belief in geocentrism.

In 1616, the Catholic Church forbade Galileo from supporting the Copernican views. When Galileo published his book *Dialogue Concerning the Two Chief World Systems*, he was called before the Inquisition in 1632 and found guilty of heresy. Galileo was asked to accept that the Earth was at the centre of the universe and that everything else, including the sun and the moon, revolved around it. Galileo famously replied that he may agree out of fear, but neither the sun nor the moon would do so. He was sentenced to life imprisonment and died under house arrest. It was not until 1822, almost 18 decades after Galileo's death, that the Catholic Church accepted that the Earth revolved around the sun. The works of the famous French philosopher and father of modern philosophy, Rene Descartes, were also placed on the Roman Catholic Church's list of banned books, the Index Librorum Prohibitorum, in 1663 and remained there for three centuries until 1966.[10]

Religions and Revolutions

The Christian religious authorities in Europe became politically and financially influential during the Middle Ages. It is estimated that in England around 1300, bishops, abbots and other clerics together owned a third of all agricultural land. The question of whether clerical authority was superior to the king's secular authority remained contentious throughout the Middle Ages. It led to a confrontation between the Archbishop of Canterbury, Thomas Becket, and King Henry II. When Becket refused to abide by the king's court, insisting that his clerical authority was superior, Henry II had him killed in 1170. More than three centuries later, King Henry VIII also had to turn against the Catholic Church in 1536 in order to remarry. Even in France, some estimates suggested that between 1100 and 1250, up to 20 per cent of total agricultural output, the primary source of the country's economy, may have been spent on the construction of religious buildings.

The story of the advent of Islam in the seventh century CE was no different. Its rise began with the death of Prophet Muhammad in 632 CE, and it has never looked back in the last 18 centuries. It conquered North Africa from Morocco to Egypt, Southern Europe from Spain to Turkey, and large swathes of Asia from North India to Iran, to Iraq and Palestine. It waged relentless wars unlike any other religion in human history and caused more human suffering than any other empire before it. This avowedly monotheistic religion controls every aspect of the lives of some 1.9 billion believers spread across continents, and their numbers are growing by the day. According to a demographic study by the Pew Research Center in Washington, D.C., Islam is projected to become the world's largest religion by 2070.[11]

In its significant, if not very humble, interventions in human history, however, Islam has experienced some periods of relative glory and peaceful progress. It created great institutions of learning and significant symbols of culture in Cordova, Granada, Cairo,

Baghdad and Delhi, and gave gracious architectural wonders from the Alhambra to the Taj Mahal. 'In the so-called golden age of Islamic philosophy, from the eighth to the thirteenth centuries CE, the *falasīfa* translated and commented on ancient Greek classics, particularly the work of Aristotle. (This was critical for the transmission of Aristotle's philosophy to the West, where he became so significant that he became known simply as "the philosopher.") During this time, there were fierce and learned debates between falasīfa such as Avicenna (Ibn Sīnā) and Averroes (Ibn Rushd) and more theologically inclined kalām thinkers such as al-Ghazālī, a tussle the latter eventually won ending the prospect of the independence of Islamic philosophy from theology,' wrote Julian Baggini.[12]

Throughout human history, civilizations, both oriental and occidental, marched forward by learning from each other. The Graeco–Arabic translation movement, a pivotal intellectual endeavour in the eighth to tenth centuries that bridged Greek and Arabic scholarly traditions, encouraged a profusion of enlightening works by ancient thinkers like Aristotle and Plato to be translated from Greek to Arabic. This helped to preserve ancient wisdom from perishing with the fall of the Roman Empire and later enabled European cultures to revive in the Renaissance era.

In China, the Tang dynasty (618–907 CE) witnessed the advancement of civilization that promoted science and arts. The Tang Chinese became the inventors of the new weapon of the time: gunpowder. The invention of gunpowder changed the way nations fought each other. Wars became deadly, and the early centuries of the second millennium witnessed the profligate use of gunpowder in Asia and Europe, first by the Mongol invasion and then by the European powers. Even the Crusades—the fierce battles fought by the Muslims and the Christians from the eleventh to the fourteenth centuries with the mission of freeing their lands from the 'infidels', whom each considered the other to be—were a story of this enormous firepower of gunpowder. The four great inventions that originated in China and helped set the stage for the Renaissance and ushered in the Age of Sail after they were relayed to Europe were papermaking, printing, gunpowder and the compass. Francis Bacon, a British philosopher, described that 'whence have followed innumerable changes, in so much that no empire, no sect, no star seems to have exerted greater power and influence in human affairs than these mechanical discoveries.'[13]

When people began to write millennia ago, they progressed into an advanced stage of communication. This paved the way for the creation of literature, albeit its reach remained restricted because human effort was needed for writing. One historical invention that enhanced the power of writing was the printing press. It is said that woodblock printing was known to the Hindus, Chinese and Koreans long before the eleventh century.[14] But with the invention of the printing press in 1440 CE, the German goldsmith Johannes Gutenberg unleashed a force that was to revolutionize the existing religion-centric world order. It had a profound historical impact, leading to the Renaissance, the Reformation and various humanist movements. In 1999, Gutenberg was even voted by US journalists as the 'Man of the Millennium'.[15] Mark Twain commented: 'What the world is today, good and bad, it owes to Gutenberg. Everything can be traced to this source, but we are bound to bring him homage, for the bad that his colossal invention has brought about is overshadowed a thousand times by the good with which mankind has been favoured.'[16]

Gutenberg could never have imagined any of this. For him, Bible printing was just a commercial proposition. Almost all of Europe was Catholic at the time, and the Bible was the most critical literature in this part of the world. He spent five years preparing types and other equipment to ensure high-quality production. Already in deep debt, he had to borrow extra money from one Johann Fust for his Bible project. As the process took several years, Fust sued Gutenberg and took over his printing shop before the first 200 copies of the Bible were out. However, in the city of Mainz, where Gutenberg lived, there were hardly any readers who could understand Latin. Gutenberg eventually died penniless, but the revolution he had set off resulted in the transformation of Europe from a religion-centric world to a secular, humanist social order.

While Bacon described the printing press as a world-transforming invention, the sixteenth-century German religious reformer Martin Luther (1483–1546 CE), who was also a priest, theologian and author, called the printing press 'God's ultimate and greatest gift,' and insisted that 'through printing God wants the whole world, to the ends of the earth, to know the roots of true religion and wants to transmit it in every language. Printing is the last flicker of the flame that glows before the end of this world.'[17]

Martin Luther was the early leader of the Protestant Reformation movement in the Church. But he was certainly not the first to raise his voice against the Church. The problem for the early reformers was that the Church quickly suppressed their voices by confiscating the few handwritten copies of the documents. By Luther's time, the printing press was already making waves in Europe. As Luther nailed his Ninety-five Theses—questions to the Catholic Church—to the church door in Wittenberg on 31 October 1517, it took just 17 days to reach London, where it was printed in hundreds of copies and quickly distributed, setting off the historic Reformation movement in the Catholic religion.

Thus, in the middle of the second millennium, the printing press became a major transformative invention. Many revolutions followed. Scientific innovations and philosophical interventions quickly gained reach and popularity. The political fallout was not far away.

The Bourbon rulers, who established their rule over France in 1589, were the first significant royals to face the fury of the people several times during the French Revolution in the 1780s to 1830s. Their lacklustre governance and the financial mess created after the Anglo-French War between 1778 and 1783 led to the outbreak of the popular revolution, about which the contemporary French dramatist and writer Louis-Sébastien Mercier wrote, 'A great and momentous revolution in our ideas has taken place within the last thirty years. Public opinion has now become a preponderant power in Europe, one that cannot be resisted... one may hope that enlightened ideas will bring about the greatest good on Earth and that tyrants of all kinds will tremble before the universal cry that echoes everywhere, awakening Europe from its slumbers.'[18] '[Printing] is the most beautiful gift from heaven. It soon will change the countenance of the universe... Printing was only born a short while ago, and already everything is heading toward perfection... Tremble, therefore, tyrants of the world! Tremble before the virtuous writer!' he further wrote.[19] When the French National Assembly was formed in 1789, the Bourbon ruler Louis XVI was forced to accept a Constitution and limit his powers. He tried to flee the country but was captured and executed in 1793. Napoleon had cryptically remarked that the Bourbon rulers could have protected themselves and prevented the French Revolution had they maintained an official monopoly over ink.

The Era of Colonization

The Industrial Revolution of 1760–1840, which followed these developments, was the next significant transformation in human history. The British historian Arnold Toynbee coined this term to describe the transition of man from agrarian to machine-led life.[20] In the mid-eighteenth century, England led the way in the development of new machines and industries that replaced human hands with mechanical tools. Europe and America soon caught up with it by the middle of the nineteenth century. The mechanization of the means of production, coupled with the mobilization of forces under capitalist and communist camps, led to the emergence of what is called the 'modern age' in human history. Interestingly, while the agrarian revolution led primitive man to settle in villages in communities, the industrial revolution pulled him out of his dwelling and settled lifestyle into the burgeoning urban centres and bustling industrial townships.

Man once again became a wanderer. From an atomized human, the 'caveman', a 'globalized citizen' was born.

From the domesticized and localized 'production by the masses', the world moved to a mechanized and centralized model of 'mass production'. This occurred first in Europe and America and brought enormous wealth to these parts of the world. A new middle class was born, armed not only with wealth but also with unending wants. The manufacturing industry, which became the sinews of the industrial age, turned out to be both the product maker and also the 'want maker'. Simultaneously, the European powers embarked on a global search for resources and markets for their industries, unleashing the era of colonization. The invention of steam navigation in the late Middle Ages not only enabled the European shipping industry to engage in transoceanic trade and created massive fortunes but also led it to colonize the less advanced Asian and African countries of the world from the seventeenth century to the nineteenth century. By the end of the nineteenth century, large swathes of Asia, Africa and Latin America were reeling under the brutal colonization by the European powers.

Talking about the intensive transformation that the Industrial Revolution had brought about in human life, Will Durant wrote:[21]

> It transformed society and government by empowering the owners of machinery and the controllers of commerce beyond the owners of titles and land. It transformed religion by generating science and its persuasive miracles and inducing many men to think in terms of cause and effect and machines. It transformed the mind by substituting novel and varied stimuli, necessitating thought, for the old ancestral and domestic situations to which instinct had been adapted and sufficient. It transformed woman by taking her work from the home and forcing her into the factories to recapture it. It transformed morals by complicating economic life, postponing marriage, multiplying contacts and opportunities, liberating woman, reducing the family,

and weakening religious and parental authority and control. And it transformed art by subordinating beauty to use and subjecting the artist, not to a favoured few with inherited standards of judgement and trained tastes, but to a multitude who judged all things in terms of power and cost and size.

The European powers audaciously proclaimed to rule over an empire of the world where 'the sun never set'. It was the Spaniards in the seventeenth century who declared their superiority through the conquest of parts of Latin America, mainly Aztec Mexico and the neighbouring island nations. Bacon wrote that 'both the East and West Indies being met in the crown of Spain, it comes to pass, that, as one saith in a brave kind of expression, the sun never sets in the Spanish dominions but ever shines upon one part or the other of them: which, to say truly, is a beam of glory'.[22]

After Napoleon entered the scene, the French also sought this title, and not for the wrong reason. While the Spaniards under Emperor Ferdinand VI were gloating over their conquest of the East and West Indies, Napoleon's occupying army arrived, overran Spain, deposed the emperor, and installed his brother Joseph Bonaparte on the throne in 1808. This led to the war in the Iberian Peninsula, known in history as the Peninsular War, which ended six years later in the defeat of the French army and Napoleon's abdication of the throne. The Spaniards were joined by the British and the Portuguese in this war against the Napoleonic invasion. As the war was set to commence in 1808, Napoleon too had audaciously declared: 'Remember that the sun never sets in the immense inheritance of Charles V and that I shall have the empire of both worlds'.[23]

But by the end of the eighteenth century, the British had also become a mighty empire. They had already won the Seven Years' War, which they fought during 1756–63 against the colonial French forces in the North American territories and the oceans. Subsequently, they defeated Napoleon's French army in 1814 in alliance with other European powers. The famous British diplomat

and administrator of Anglo-Irish origin, Sir George Macartney, who served as Governor of Madras in India during British imperial rule, was credited with observing after the Treaty of Paris at the end of the Seven Years' War that Britain now controlled 'a vast empire, on which the sun never sets, and whose bounds nature has not yet ascertained.'[24]

As British power in India and the Indian Ocean Region grew considerably, Sir Henry George Ward, who served as British Governor of Ceylon (Sri Lanka), proudly proclaimed in the House of Commons in 1839: 'Look at the British Colonial Empire—the most magnificent empire that the world ever saw. The old Spanish boast that the sun never set in their dominions has been more truly realized amongst ourselves.'[25]

The Rise of Pax Americana

As the twentieth century began to unfold, the rise of North America became a defining feature, leading to the cliché of 'Pax Americana'. Historians in America sometimes employed the phrase 'the sun never sets' in reference to the United States, often in the context of its military presence across various continents and its influence over numerous countries around the globe.

The story of the twentieth century centres on how the newly rich nations of the West—namely Western Europe and America—began to exert dominance over the global order through their control of industries and ideologies. The two world wars, which concluded in 1919 and 1945, catapulted America to the unenviable position of a superpower, able to dictate, shape and alter the trajectory of world history. For several decades in the latter half of the century, America faced its *bête noire* in the Soviet Union, yet the world order established after the Second World War was primarily an enterprise of the West.

The rise of American power and dominance in the twentieth century is a fascinating story. America, in many ways, is a blessed country. Described sometimes as the Continental United States

(CONUS), the country is far removed from the rest of the world, and is an oversized island in the Pacific–Atlantic zone. As an island, it imbibed all the psychological traits of the so-called 'island mentality'. It was isolationist for centuries and developed a superiority complex known as 'American exceptionalism'. Looking at America's half-century-long history since the time of its first president, George Washington, the renowned French writer Alexis de Tocqueville first used the term in his 1835 work *Democracy in America*.[26]

The Monroe Doctrine of 1823, attributed to the then American president James Monroe, further fortified this isolationism. As the European colonizers wanted to penetrate further into the continental US, Monroe determinedly resisted those efforts by Spain and others through the enunciation of four principles: '(1) the United States would not interfere in European affairs; (2) the United States recognized and would not interfere with existing colonies in the Americas; (3) the Western Hemisphere was closed to future colonization; and (4) if a European power tried to interfere with any nation in the Americas, that would be viewed as a hostile act against the United States.'[27]

The Monroe Doctrine worked effectively on both sides. The European powers did not make any further serious incursions into continental US. At the same time, the Americans developed a strong introverted attitude. Except for trade and humanitarian assistance, the American leadership steadfastly refused to look at the outside world and focused entirely on domestic development priorities.

This policy of isolationism was subjected to its first test in the early twentieth century when the First World War broke out in Europe. Woodrow Wilson was elected as the president of the US in 1913, just one year before the outbreak of the war. Continuing with the Monroe Doctrine, Wilson actively discouraged America from getting involved in the war not only physically but also emotionally and ideologically. In fact, when he went to the polls for the second time in 1916, he was given a resounding mandate by the American people with the popular slogan: 'He kept us out of war.'[28]

However, a year later, things began to change. The war started spilling over into the Atlantic Ocean, affecting US interests. The indiscriminate use of submarine force, called the undersea boats or U-boats by the Germans, resulted in the loss of American civilians when merchant ships were also attacked. The major incident of the sinking of the merchant vessel *Lusitania* on 7 May 1915, which killed 1,195 people on board, including 123 American citizens, had enraged the Americans.[29] Despite the protests of the US authorities, the German attacks continued. By February 1917, Kaiser Wilhelm II, the German Chancellor, ordered his navy to sink all Allied ships, including civilian ones. Around the same time came the Zimmermann Telegram—the proverbial last straw. Arthur Zimmermann was the German Foreign Minister during the First World War. In January 1917, British cryptographers had intercepted a telegram from Zimmermann sent to the German ambassador to Mexico, Heinrich von Eckhardt, offering that Germany would make the territory available to the United States if Mexico would enter the war on its side.[30] The British, not sure of how much impact this interception would have on the American policy of non-interference, waited until anti-German sentiment in the US grew due to the sinking of its ships in the Atlantic, before presenting the telegram to the US authorities on 24 February 1917.

It had now become a question of American self-respect. On 2 April 1917, President Wilson walked into the US Congress with the demand that it grant permission for the military to join the anti-German forces in Europe in the war against German expansionism and to make 'the world safe for democracy'.[31] 'We are no longer provincials. The tragic events of the thirty months of vital turmoil through which we have just passed have made us citizens of the world. There is no turning back,' Wilson told the congressmen seeking permission to enter the war in four days.[32] On 4 April, the Senate voted 82 to 6 in favour of declaring war on Germany. Two days later, on 6 April, the House of Representatives passed the war resolution by 373 votes to 50.

The American Expeditionary Forces arrived in Europe in April 1917. Their entry had decisively turned the tide in favour of Great Britain and France, leading to the Allied victory over Germany in November 1918. Talking about the impact that the Zimmermann Telegram had on American public opinion, David Kahn, American historian and author of the book *The Codebreakers*, observed: 'No other single crypto analysis has had such enormous consequences. Never before or since has so much turned upon the solution of a secret message.'[33]

Unwittingly, America began to create a new identity for itself, Pax Americana, by entering the First World War. Historian and writer A. Scott Berg, Wilson's biographer, rightly analysed that World War I was the 'most under-recognized' significant event of the last several centuries. 'The stories from this global drama— and its larger-than-life characters—are truly the stuff of Greek tragedy and are of Biblical proportion, and modern America's very identity was forged during this war,' he wrote.[34]

Having decisively turned the war in favour of the British and French, thereby securing American interests in Europe, Wilson triumphantly returned to the US Congress on 8 January 1918 to express his desire to enhance America's global footprint. In a powerful speech containing 14 points (which became famous as the Fourteen Points), Wilson called for the complete banishment of imperialism in the world.[35]

It was this speech that became the catalyst for the founding of the world's very first multilateral institution—the League of Nations. Founded on 10 January 1920 at the Paris Peace Conference, attended by Wilson and others to formally proclaim the end of the First World War, the League was intended to ensure 'permanent peace' in the world by promoting mechanisms for negotiations and mediation and safeguarding the interests of the world's smaller nations.

Initially, the League of Nations became popular with the

American masses. However, as details of the loss of American lives and the cost of the war to the American exchequer became public domain, opinion turned against it. The US involvement in the First World War had inadvertently done something good for American society. Over four million Americans had joined the Expeditionary Army to serve in the war theatres. They included a large number of African Americans, leading for the first time to the French and African American armed forces working together, somewhat mitigating the formal and informal racial codes.[36] As more and more men were commissioned into the military, women also had to come forward to take up jobs and professions. Large numbers of women joined the war as nurses, office staff, and other services. Thus, the power of American women was unleashed during the war. It also helped forge the military careers of future American leaders like Dwight D. Eisenhower, George S. Patton and George C. Marshall.

However, the war also resulted in the deaths of tens of thousands of American soldiers. Over 116,000 American soldiers lost their lives.[37] As the coffins arrived in one city after another, public enthusiasm soon waned, and scepticism and resentment engulfed American public opinion. More and more Americans lamented the costs and consequences of the war and opposed any such future interventions in the affairs of other nations. The Americans fell back into their isolation syndrome.

Warren Harding, who succeeded Wilson as president in 1921, was a staunch nationalist. Although he actively pursued a foreign policy of selective engagement, he was seen as an isolationist for his decision not to join the League of Nations and his desire to disengage from extensive foreign interventions. A year after Wilson's participation in the League of Nations conference, Harding publicly repudiated the idea and refused to join the League.[38] Chaos reigned in Europe even after the end of the war, and America's decision not to join the League of Nations ultimately led to the quiet demise of the first multilateral institution created with so much ambition.

The 1920s and 1930s saw massive turmoil in the Western world, with economies plummeting and politics in chaos. As America moved into an isolationist mode, its Congressional leaders indulged in mindless economic protectionism through taxes and tariffs, which led to the collapse of the US stock market in 1929 and a decade-long economic recession, the Great Depression.

As the US struggled with its economic downturn, a new financial crisis battered the nations of Europe, leading to unintended consequences. Before the First World War, the Habsburg Empire, which ruled over the Austro-Hungarian nations, was a prosperous one. But things changed suddenly and apocalyptically when Gavrilo Princip, a member of the anarchist secret society Black Hand, assassinated the Archduke of Austria, Franz Ferdinand, in June 1914, triggering the First World War, which after four years also brought the mighty Austro-Hungarian Empire to an end. The collapse of the empire led to the collapse of the mighty economies of the nations. European nations, already weakened by the costs of wartime debt and the heavy burden of repatriation imposed on them, responded to the looming economic crises by allowing the rise of demagogues and dictators. In Europe, the era of Hitler and Mussolini began.

As in the early years of the First World War, America remained a mute witness to the rise of those dictators and their expansionist wars and occupation of neighbouring countries that led to the start of the Second World War in 1939. As the German army marched into Poland in September 1939, going by the mood in the American Congress, President Franklin D. Roosevelt (FDR) said emphatically in a radio address to his nation that 'this Nation will remain a neutral nation.' He told the anxious citizens of his country that 'the United States will keep out of this war. I believe that it will. And I give you assurances that every effort of your government will be directed toward that end.' He even warned: 'Let no man or woman thoughtlessly or falsely talk of America sending its armies to European fields.'[39]

This neutrality continued until the Japanese 1st Air Fleet

aircraft attacked the American naval base at Pearl Harbor on Oahu in Hawaii on 7 December 1941. But unlike in 1917, when a telegram pushed America into action, in 1941 it took the sinking and destruction of 8 battleships, 328 aircraft, and the deaths of 2,403 American soldiers and civilians for the American government to decide to jump into the war.[40]

However, it was not easy. In 1935, the US Congress passed the first Neutrality Act, strictly prohibiting the export of 'arms, ammunition and implements of war' to any foreign country at war.[41] It went on to add further restrictions. Roosevelt entered his second term as president in 1936. He wasn't so much in favour of the Neutrality Act, says Warren Kimball, professor emeritus of history at Rutgers University and author of *Forged in War: Roosevelt, Churchill and the Second World War.* 'He saw the direction things were going in Europe, and it took away his ability to act,' Kimball suggests.[42]

Roosevelt understood that America could not remain neutral in the war forever and said at a press conference a year after the war began that helping Britain and France was like 'lending a hose to a neighbour whose house is on fire. You might not get the hose back, but at least your house didn't burn down too.'[43] Yet, the isolationists in the US Congress continued to obstruct Roosevelt's efforts to help the Allied forces, prompting him to warn, 'We well know that we cannot escape danger or the fear of danger by crawling into bed and pulling the covers over our heads.'[44]

He finally decided not to be outwitted or outmanoeuvred by Congress and began to use various techniques to extend support to the Allied forces in the war. He once sent a large number of US aircraft to be parked along the Canadian border and asked the Canadians to tow those aircraft across the border and offer them to the British. Technically, he didn't 'fly' any American aircraft to the countries at war. On another occasion, under the Lend–Lease Act (1941), which he managed to get passed in Congress, he sent a large number of warships to Britain by taking many of its ports on a 99-year lease.[45] Winston Churchill, who became prime minister of Great Britain in 1940 and watched in horror the defeat of France, described the Lend–Lease programme (not the Marshall Plan) as 'the most unsordid act in the whole of recorded history.'[46] Roosevelt and Churchill continuously exchanged notes on various occasions afterwards and drafted plans for the victory of the Allied forces and the post-war world order.

Then came the attack on Pearl Harbor by the Imperial Japanese Air Force on 7 December 1941, with devastating consequences. The day after the attack, Congress declared war on Imperial Japan with only a single dissenting vote. Germany and Italy—Japan's allies—responded by declaring war on the US. The Congress, in turn, responded by declaring war on them. America was finally into the Second World War, which was enthusiastically supported by the American people, who were incensed by the attack on Pearl Harbor. The second phase of isolation was over.

The US troops started arriving in Europe in early 1942. Soon, the tide turned against the Axis powers. Hitler's Nazi army was caught between a Soviet counteroffensive in the East and an Allied offensive in the West led by the US forces. Germany ultimately surrendered on 7 May 1945, and Japan followed suit, surrendering on 14 August after the Harry Truman administration's controversial decision led to the use of nuclear options on the cities of Hiroshima and Nagasaki instead of a costly conventional attack.

The cost of war this time was much higher than in the war two decades earlier. Some sixteen million Americans served in Europe and the Pacific, the largest mobilization in the country's military history.[47] The human cost was also high. More than four hundred thousand American soldiers died.[48] Historians estimate that nearly seventy million people perished as a result of the violence, disease and famine that accompanied the Second World War.[49]

However, the benefits of war outweighed the costs. While the economies of Western European countries shrank by 18 per cent and Japan's reduced by half, the US economy skyrocketed during the war, nearly doubling in the six years between 1939 and 1945, ending America's decade-long recession. The civilian employment numbers rose steeply from 46 million in 1940 to 53 million in 1943.[50] No less than two million Black Americans had gained employment in the booming defence industry. In 1944, there was practically no unemployment in America. On the contrary, manpower shortages started plaguing industry, leading to a relaxation of immigration laws in the post-war period. The American dollar became the most valued currency in the world, and a dollar-centric global economy was born.

Most importantly, the defeat of the Axis powers was credited mainly to US intervention, and the country was catapulted into the position of a victorious global power. It was increasingly seen as a bulwark to ensure peace and prosperity in the world. The world did not want America to return to isolationism this time.

Much of the credit for all of this goes to FDR, who managed an unprecedented fourth election victory over Thomas E. Dewey in 1944. Determined not to allow the isolationists to succeed in taking his country back into the 'exceptionalism' mode, Roosevelt invited Churchill to a conference in Newfoundland in August 1941, several months before the country actually joined the war. The two leaders together issued a statement that became famous as the Atlantic Charter, setting out the American and British goals for the post-war world. Thereafter, within a month of joining the war, Roosevelt, Churchill, Maxim Litvinov of the USSR and T.V. Soong of China met in Washington, D.C., on 1 January 1942 and signed what came to be known as the Declaration of the United Nations.[51] The next day, representatives of 22 other nations added their signatures.

The UN and a Liberal Global Order

The stage was thus set for the creation of a successor institution to the now-defunct, dissolved League of Nations. On 30 October 1943, representatives from the UK, the US, China and the

USSR met in Moscow and signed a declaration. The Moscow Declaration recognized 'the necessity of establishing at the earliest practicable date a general international organization, based on the principle of the sovereign equality of all peace-loving states and open to membership by all such states, large and small, for the maintenance of international peace and security.'[52] Two months later, Roosevelt, Churchill and Stalin met in Tehran, and declared that 'We recognize fully the supreme responsibility resting upon us and all the United Nations to make a peace which will command the goodwill of the overwhelming mass of the peoples of the world and banish the scourge and terror of war for many generations.'[53]

Two years later, from 25 April to 26 June 1945, delegates from 50 nations, representing almost 80 per cent of humanity, met in San Francisco and founded the United Nations Organization (UNO).[54] Roosevelt, the man who pulled America out of its cherished isolationism and turned it into a global power, was not alive to witness this historic development, the seeds of which he had laid four years ago. Luckily, his successor and vice president, Harry Truman, was not Warren Harding. He pushed forward the agenda set by Roosevelt, and soon the post-war world order was characterized by America in the driver's seat.

The founding of the UN, with all its allied organizations like the World Bank, the International Monetary Fund (IMF) and the International Court of Justice (ICJ), in the immediate aftermath of the Second World War was just as significant for the creation of a new world order as the Industrial Revolution two centuries earlier. The US took the lead in this great initiative to govern global security and monetary policy, prompting Churchill to declare that it stood 'at the summit of the world.'[55]

Under the aegis of the UN, a new liberal global order was born. Under the tutelage of the USA and other Western powers, it has served humanity for the last 75 years. There is no clear definition for the phrase 'liberal global order', which some prefer to call the 'Western liberal order' or the 'rules-based international order'. Its main characteristics are economic openness, security cooperation, democratic solidarity and a liberal social order with human rights. John Ikenberry, a renowned international affairs theorist from Princeton University who is credited with coining the term, said that along the way, 'The United States became the "first citizen" of this order, fostering cooperation and championing the "free world" values. Looking at the end of the twentieth century, one could be excused for thinking that history was moving in a progressive and liberal-internationalist direction.'[56]

As the world entered the twenty-first century, this world order was being challenged by many for its lack of efficacy and effectiveness. Critics like Amitav Acharya, international relations professor at the American University in Washington, D.C., alluded to the fact that it was neither liberal nor orderly. Acharya opined:

> In reality, the liberal order is a club of the West. To other countries, its benefits, such as market access, aid, investment, and the provision of a security umbrella, were offered selectively and conditionally. Leading nations of the developing world, including China and India, were either outside of the system or connected at the margins. Some developing countries were summarily excluded. The order often operated more through coercion than consent. It was hardly 'orderly' for the Third World, where local conflicts were magnified by capricious great power intervention, including by the United States and its Western allies.[57]

In the final decades of the last century, the world started experiencing the failings of the world order that had been zealously built up after the Second World War. The decadence became much more evident in the first two decades of the new century. When the COVID-19 pandemic struck in 2020, the world was jolted by the reality of the inevitability of the collapse of this seven-decade-old liberal order. Who is responsible for this collapse? What will happen next? What will replace the liberal order, or who will lead the world in the new scenario? As mankind heads for a significant transformation, what will be the contours of the future order? Who will be the leading players, and what will be the principal perils? How will the reigning superpowers, such as America and China, try to shape the world order to their mould and vision?

The following chapters of this book examine these issues and attempt to suggest some answers. I discuss the experience of the world in the last seven decades under the current liberal world order. I then highlight ten critical features of the evolving post-COVID world order. Each of these features can be the subject of a full debate, perhaps even a book in its own right.

First, the decline of American and Western powers. There can be arguments on both sides. Some scholars insist that America is not declining, while many Americans themselves insist that it is happening before their eyes. America may not disappear from the top echelons. It will still be the world's most powerful nation. But in the last century, ideas of 'American exceptionalism' or 'supremacy' have become obsolete.

Second, the elephant in the room is China's rise. The jeering and sneering of the China hawks notwithstanding, the country's rise as an economic, political and technological superpower is an essential reality of our times. Moreover, the Chinese leadership is not hiding its intention to replace the current world order with a world order of its choice and liking, a world order with 'Chinese characteristics'.

Third, a new Cold War has begun, this time between the US and China. The recipe is the same as in the last century—mutual suspicion and ambition to lead the world. However, unlike then, when the Soviet Union depended on its brute power to dominate the world, China seems to be using 'smart power'—a carrot-and-stick approach, which will inevitably trigger a major global fault line.

Fourth, the rise of middle powers and the emergence of multipolarity. After the collapse of the Soviet Union in the 1990s, the world lived under a unipolar reality for about a decade before China rose to challenge American power at the beginning of the twenty-first century. But today, the world and the two superpowers are witnessing the rise of many middle powers and multilateral groupings, much to the chagrin of those wanting to reshape the world.

Fifth, there was a perpetual decline of global multilateralism created after the Second World War. There was never a time in the last seven decades when the UN became so irrelevant and was challenged by many countries on all sides. Beginning with the mission of ending wars, it not only failed to prevent wars but, worse still, instead became a mute spectator, if not a silent party, to the conflicts raging in different parts of the world.

Sixth, as the world began to celebrate the emergence of multipolarity, we realized that we had in fact walked into a 'heteropolar' reality where non-state players, from big tech giants to global NGOs and religious organizations to terror outfits, had come to challenge national sovereignty. Tackling heteropolar forces will be one of the prominent challenges for national governments in the future.

Seventh, we have entered the era of hybrid humans—humanoids. Innovations in artificial intelligence (AI), big data, robotics, semiconductors, genome research and many more are breaking through technological frontiers. It seems that the next superpower will be the one that masters AI and other frontier technologies. If not intervened in appropriately, this could lead to the end of the human ethnos and the appearance of metahumans, a hybrid human controlled by technology.

Eighth, demographics, climate change and related challenges. The world's demographics are undergoing precipitous changes. The developed world is also becoming an ageing world, bringing with it challenges for the workforce. On the other hand, the damage that humans have inflicted on the universe and its ecosystem is acutely felt today by every country in the form of climate challenges and related disruptions. The ecological imbalances we are experiencing have the potential to displace one-sixth of humanity and turn them into internal or external refugees. As the migration of people becomes an everyday challenge, demographic imbalances are bound to occur, leading to the rise of social tensions in host countries.

Ninth, de-dollarization and the emergence of a new economy. The centrality of the dollar was a key feature of the current world order. All multilateral financial institutions were built on this premise. However, the rise of other currencies and the emergence of a cryptocurrency regime will transform the global economy in a big way.

Finally, there is the return of strong nationalist movements on the one hand and the rise of extreme wokeism on the other. A century-long romance with globalism in its different avatars seems to be coming to an end, and the stigma it has created on national identities is gradually disappearing. The failure of the globalized economic model to come to the rescue of smaller nations during the COVID-19 pandemic and the economic and social costs of unbridled romance with concepts like multiculturalism have driven more and more societies into an inward-looking nationalist frenzy. On the other side of the socio-political spectrum, the far-left ideology of wokeism is gaining popularity across large sections of society in the Western world, causing severe disruptions in the social and family life of the countries.

As the liberal world order of the last century came to an end and the new one is going through its birth pangs, does India have a chance to play a role in modifying its birth? India exhibited the ambition of guiding the world—*Vishvaguru*—from time immemorial. When the liberal world order emerged after the Second World War, it couldn't play a significant role since it had just come out of a centuries-long colonial yoke and was preoccupied with domestic challenges. Today, when the world is at the cusp of the transformation of this century, what should India do?

I devote the final chapters of this book to the ten things India should do to become an important player and a significant contributor to shaping the new world order.

One, India should give up its romanticism. Indians by nature have a penchant for lofty slogans and romanticized notions of their 'destiny' in the world. What India needs, however, is an utterly pragmatic and realistic approach to addressing the challenges posed by the emerging new order.

Two, the new pillars of foreign policy introduced by Prime Minister Narendra Modi's government, such as Panchamrit, strategic autonomy and de-hyphenation, need to be pursued vigorously. They represent a significant departure from the past, and India should uphold them under all circumstances.

Third, it has been proven worldwide that domestic political stability is the key to economic prosperity and global influence. After three decades, India has found itself in a stable political environment since 2014, allowing its governments to work on big ideas. India needs to maintain this political stability.

Fourth, focus on economic growth. India is a country of great diversity. On the one hand, this diversity is the strength of Indian society; on the other, it engenders built-in social conflict and a lack of cohesion. It has the potential to create enough distractions and obstacles in the way of the nation's progress. Like China in the 1980s, India must single-mindedly and unwaveringly focus on its economic goals for at least a decade, keeping all other agendas on hold.

Five, ramp up education, research and innovation. In a world driven by frontier technologies, India lags far behind in scientific and technological innovation. India is not a player in the ecosystem of several frontier technologies such as semiconductors, quantum computing and AI genomics. The Modi government has started paying attention to this shortcoming. It should build a strong culture and vibrant institutions to ramp up its technological prowess.

Six, demographics and associated social challenges: India has a peculiar and complex demographic profile. It needs to manage its demographic advantages and disadvantages more adroitly. It also needs to find a better rhythm in managing its diverse social canvas, which tends to explode frequently, damaging India's fabric and image.

Seven, building a strong neighbourhood: India faces its biggest challenge in the neighbourhood, where it has a competitor in China. Dealing with countries in the neighbourhood is essential for India if it is to achieve its ambition of becoming a significant global player.

Eight, as global multilateralism declines, India should build regional multilateralism in its extended neighbourhood in the Indian Ocean instead of perpetually craving a seat at the high table in the UNSC. The extended neighbourhood offers India a great opportunity because of its millennia-long historical and civilizational ties with the subcontinent. Unlike China, India enjoys enormous goodwill in this extended region, from ASEAN to Africa to the South Pacific, due to the ancient cultural connection, which it should be able to turn into a diplomatic advantage.

Nine, strengthen our blue-water presence: India is a maritime country with a peninsular coastline of over 7,500 km and is 90 per cent dependent on the surrounding oceans for imports and exports. However, it still has a long way to go before emerging as a blue-water power. Efforts to change the continental mindset and invest in strengthening maritime capabilities, which began a decade ago, need further impetus.

Lastly, it is time for India to make strenuous efforts to build 'Brand Bharat'—a benign global influence. The era of soft power is passé, and the time has come for 'smart power' to create a unique brand identity for nations. India should develop institutions to build that distinct global identity for itself.

This can by no means be treated as an exhaustive response. Scholars could suggest several other important 'things to do' for India. As the new order takes shape, new challenges and opportunities may also come its way. The bottom line is that unlike eight decades ago, a 1.4 billion-strong nation has no excuse to miss this opportunity to play a significant role in shaping humanity's future. If it fails, a new order will still take shape, but it will not only miss India's footprints but also become inimical to the values that India cherished over millennia and wanted to share with the rest of humanity.

Part I

ANARCHY AS ORDER

1

CONTESTED WORLDS

'We, the people of the United Nations, determined to save
succeeding generations from the scourge of war, which twice
in our lifetime has brought untold sorrow to mankind...'[1]

Those were the opening words of the preamble to the UN
Charter, which was signed on 26 October 1945 by the
representatives of 50 nations who had gathered in the
Veterans' War Memorial Building in San Francisco. Not all 50
nations that came forward on that day were free. Some of them,
including India, were still under colonial rule. But the two world
wars that killed almost 40 million people in just 30 years had
shaken their conscience.

The two leaders who were the architects of the multilateral
body, Franklin Roosevelt of the US and Winston Churchill of
Great Britain, were both unavailable for this historic event. While
Roosevelt passed away earlier in the year, Churchill, Britain's war
hero, was rejected by the people as a peacetime leader in the British
parliamentary elections held in July 1945. Harry Truman, the US
president, was there for the inauguration and gave a scintillating
speech. 'There were many who doubted that agreement could ever
be reached by these fifty countries differing so much in race and
religion, in language and culture. But these differences were all
forgotten in one unshakeable unity of determination—to find a
way to end wars,' Truman animatedly declared.[2]

The United Nations (UN) was founded with lofty objectives.
Upholding fundamental human rights, the dignity and worth of
the human person, the equality of men and women, the equal

treatment and sovereign equality of all nations, the strengthening of international peace and security, the building of international institutions to improve the living standards of the peoples of all nations and regions—these and many such laudable goals became the initial driving force behind the multilateral organization intending to build a formidable liberal world order for the entire humanity.

The institutions meant to build this world order—the UN and the Bretton Woods institutions such as the International Monetary Fund (IMF) and the World Bank—worked effectively to deliver on the idea of creating a just and equitable international liberal order. After three decades of relentless wars, conflicts and economic tragedies, the world indeed became a better place after the creation of this multilateral framework. More and more countries that had freed themselves from the colonial yoke in the following two decades became democracies. By the end of the twentieth century, the world was witnessing a democratic boom, and almost 80 per cent of the world had some form of democracy. Multilateral financial institutions such as the IMF and the World Bank helped countries build sustainable economies, which led to greater prosperity and reduced the impact of recessions. At the turn of the century, global GDP rose from less than $10 trillion in 1945 to $70 trillion.

Unfortunately, however, this new world order was plagued by various challenges from its inception. At the very outset, there were disagreements over the structure of the UN Charter itself. These disagreements centred on the insistence of the so-called Big Five countries—the United States, the USSR, the United Kingdom, France and the Republic of China—demanding veto power in the decision-making process of the UN Security Council (UNSC). This demand had raised the hackles of many countries, which insisted that this right of veto should be eliminated or curtailed to a minimum. However, the five nations, which described themselves as permanent members of the Security Council, took a grandstanding position, arguing that the responsibility for maintaining peace in the world would rest primarily on their shoulders. Therefore, they needed the veto regime. At the very outset, instead of 'global multilateralism' what emerged was 'guided multilateralism.'

The second major challenge to the ambitious project of building a 'liberal international order' came from the tussle between the Western powers and the bloc led by the Soviet Union. In the early years of the Second World War, there was some bonhomie between Stalin and Hitler. In fact, both signed a mutual non-aggression agreement in 1939. Stalin subsequently occupied Eastern Poland and attacked Finland. Enraged, Roosevelt publicly thundered that the Soviet dictatorship was 'as absolute as any other dictatorship in the world.'[3] He even imposed an embargo on the export of certain products to the Soviet Union.

When Hitler turned his tanks on the Soviet Union on 22 June 1941 and launched Operation Barbarossa, things began to change. Despite his strong criticism of the Soviet communist regime and the pressure within the administration, Roosevelt kept his options open in dealing with this country. He confided that he would 'hold hands with the devil if necessary.'[4]

This moment came late in the war when pragmatism forced Roosevelt and Churchill to join forces with Stalin to defeat the Axis powers led by Germany. In November 1943, they met for the first time in Tehran to coordinate their war efforts against the Axis powers. As the victory of the Allied forces was on the horizon, the three heads of state met again in February 1945 in the Black Sea city of Yalta in the Crimean Peninsula of Ukraine. Stalin was ill, and the doctors advised him not to travel long distances. In Yalta, the leaders discussed the fate of post-war Germany and Europe and the creation of the UN. Stalin promised the other two (which he never kept) that he would introduce democratic regimes in the countries under Soviet control, such as Czechoslovakia, Hungary, Romania, Bulgaria and Poland.

Cold War Politics

However, relations between the West and Stalin soon deteriorated, and the era of Cold War politics began. The decisive trigger was the Long Telegram, which the US chargé d'affaires in Moscow, George F. Kennan, sent to the US State Department on 22 February 1946. In this 8,000-word telegram, Kennan sounded a warning note to Washington, D.C.: 'The problem of how to deal with the Soviet force is undoubtedly the greatest task our diplomacy has ever faced and probably the greatest it will ever have to face. It should be the point of departure from which our political general staff work at the present juncture should proceed.'[5]

Kennan was also credited with introducing the concept of 'containment' to US foreign policy through his telegram. 'The main element of any United States policy toward the Soviet Union must be that of a long-term, patient, but firm and vigilant containment of Russian expansive tendencies,' Kennan wrote.[6] Thereafter, until the collapse of the Soviet Union in 1991, Kennan's policy of containment became the main thrust of US foreign policy in various forms under different administrations.

When Kennan wrote his views on containment in 1947 in the *Foreign Affairs* journal under the pseudonym Mr X, he triggered a significant debate in US policy circles. The isolationists didn't like his recommendation that the US should take on the threat posed by the Soviet Union and its allies 'whenever and wherever they posed a risk of gaining influence.'[7] Kennan emphasized that the major economic hubs of the world, such as Western Europe, Japan and other US allies, had to be protected from Soviet expansionism. John Foster Dulles, who became secretary of state in the Eisenhower regime in the 1950s, went one step further and argued that the US shouldn't limit itself to 'containment' but work towards 'rollback' of the Soviet influence and the eventual liberation of Eastern Europe. While Kennan saw the Soviet challenge primarily as political and advocated for an economic and psychological counteroffensive, the Eisenhower administration saw it as a military counteroffensive.

Earlier, under the Truman regime, the National Security Council produced a policy document signed by Truman calling for a drastic expansion of the US military budget. The document proposed that the policy of containment shouldn't be limited to the defence of a few regions but to the whole world. 'In the context of the present polarization of power, a defeat of free institutions anywhere is a defeat everywhere,' it argued.[8] Ultimately, the Kennan telegram had two outcomes: the Marshall Plan on the economic front and NATO on the military front.

With the end of the Second World War, America emerged as a strong economic superpower. The decade-long recession ended with the war, and the war economy catapulted companies into frenzied production and a globalized market. At the same time, however, the war had broken the backs of many European nations, including those in whose empire the sun had not set. Economies crumbled, cities were devastated, and the population was even faced with the prospect of famine. Stalin's dictatorial actions and his control over Eastern Europe, coupled with the damning Kennan telegram, catalyzed urgent action by the US administration to come forward to help the Western European nations financially. The Truman administration saw this as the counteroffensive to Stalin's grab of Eastern Europe.

George Marshall was secretary of state in the Truman administration. In a speech he delivered at Harvard University on 5 June 1947, Marshall outlined the seriousness of the situation in Europe and then broached the idea that America should come forward to rebuild Europe's economy. 'The truth of the matter is that Europe's requirements for the next 3 or 4 years of foreign food and other essential products—principally from America—are so much greater than her present ability to pay that she must have substantial additional help or face economic, social and political deterioration of a very grave character. The remedy lies in restoring the confidence of the European people in the economic future of their own countries and of Europe as a whole,' Marshall proposed.[9]

On 19 December 1947, President Truman sent a message to the US Congress proposing Marshall's idea of providing economic aid to Europe. Congress passed the Economic Cooperation Act of 1948, which became famous as the Marshall Plan, with overwhelming support. President Truman gave his assent to this Act on 3 April 1948. Over the next four years, the Congress approved grants to the tune of $13.3 billion for European recovery. This aid provided much-needed capital and materials that enabled Europeans to rebuild the continent's economy. With American food products and others securing tremendous market access to the European market, this was a win-win for both sides. More importantly, it allowed the US to expand its club of countries in Europe in its future Cold War with the USSR.

Meanwhile, on 12 March 1947, President Truman delivered an important address to the joint session of the US Congress, in which he argued that the US could not escape from assisting 'free peoples' in their struggles against totalitarian regimes. The 'spread of authoritarianism,' he warned, would 'undermine the foundations of international peace and hence the security of the United States.'[10]

The Truman Doctrine was a decisive departure from the traditional isolationist attitude. It vehemently argued that the US could no longer be a mute witness to the forcible expansion of Soviet totalitarianism into free, independent nations because American national security now depended not just on the physical security of American territory alone. The Truman Doctrine committed the US to offering assistance to preserve the integrity and sovereignty of the countries far and beyond whenever such an action was deemed to be in its interest.

The natural corollary of the Truman Doctrine, besides the Marshall Plan, was the creation of the North Atlantic Treaty Organization (NATO). Besides economic challenges, Europe was also affected by Stalin's expansionist manoeuvres. Communist parties in countries such as Greece and Turkey resorted to street campaigns with the support of the Communist International

(Comintern). In Czechoslovakia, a coup sponsored by Moscow brought the communists to power. In Italy, too, the Communist Party became a serious political threat. Around the same time, Stalin's antics in Germany worried the Western powers even more. In mid-1948, challenging the control of the Western powers over West Berlin, Stalin imposed a blockade to choke the city. The US was compelled to organize a massive airlift of relief supplies for the beleaguered citizens of West Berlin. All these events caused serious consternation in the US administration. It prompted them to look for ways to counter this aggression by the communist Soviet Union against the democratic powers in Western Europe.

The result was the signing of the North Atlantic Treaty on 4 April 1949. The US, Canada, Belgium, Denmark, France, Iceland, Italy, Luxembourg, the Netherlands, Norway and Portugal became the first signatories to the treaty and agreed in Article 5 that 'an armed attack against one or more of them...shall be considered an attack against them all', and that, following such an attack, each ally would take 'such action as it deems necessary, including the use of armed force' in response.[11] The Truman administration allocated $1.4 billion in the first year to build up the defence of Western Europe.

More and more members joined NATO. However, when the Federal Republic of Germany joined NATO in 1955, the Soviets reacted by announcing their regional alliance, the Warsaw Pact. The first signatories to the Warsaw Pact were primarily the satellite states of the USSR, such as Albania, Poland, Czechoslovakia, Hungary, Bulgaria, Romania and the German Democratic Republic. Like the NATO countries, the Warsaw Pact states also pledged to defend each other if one or more of them were attacked. While the US led NATO, the Warsaw Pact countries were controlled by the Soviet Union. The institutionalization of the Cold War was thus complete.

NATO and the Warsaw Pact were symptoms of the evils that plagued the new world order created after 1945. With the collapse of the Soviet Union in 1991, the Warsaw Pact also collapsed. NATO, however, remained an ironic part of the liberal order.

Wars Build the World Order

The third factor that became the bane of the post-war world order was the infusion of ideology into world politics. Dwight Eisenhower, who became president of the US in 1953, openly declared of NATO, 'We do not keep security establishments merely to defend property, or territory or rights abroad or at sea. We keep the security forces to defend a way of life.'[12] This was a problematic proposition for a world that is diverse in more ways than one. While the communists, led by the Soviet Union, wanted to see their way as the only way, the West also insisted on offering the liberal order as the only panacea for the whole world.

The US believed that the UN and its allied institutions were essentially created not just as non-partisan world forums but as amplifiers of its world vision. They sought to use these institutions to pursue their goals and ideas, bypassing them wherever necessary and building alternative institutions such as NATO. That this worldview of seeing one's priorities as the priorities of the world order continues to permeate American thinking can be seen in a speech that Joe Biden, President Barack Obama's deputy, delivered at the World Economic Forum in Davos in 2017, shortly before demitting office.

'After World War II, we drew a line under centuries of conflict and took steps to bend the arc of history in a more just direction,' he claimed, emphasizing that it was primarily America and its allies in Europe who were responsible for steering the world 'down a clear path'. He claimed that the institutions and alliances were built by America to 'advance our shared security'. He then boasted that 'our careful attention to building and sustaining the international world order, with the US and Europe as its core, was the bedrock of the success that the world enjoyed in the second half of the century.'[13]

The Cold War ended with the collapse of the USSR. However, the US' endeavours to lead the world in its direction continued. The post-war world order was created with the UN at its core and the mission of 'no more wars'. However, as America and Europe assumed the role of the 'core', wars became a means to build the world order of their choice. From the Gulf War in the 1990s to the War on Terror in the 2000s to the wars in Ukraine and elsewhere in the 2020s, wars became 'just wars' to build and sustain this Western liberal order.

On 11 September 1990, while the Gulf conflict raged, President George H.W. Bush addressed a joint session of the US Congress in which he described the war as a steppingstone for building a new world order. From these troubled times can emerge our fifth goal: a new world order—a new era—freer from the threat of terror, stronger in the pursuit of justice, and more secure in the quest for peace. An era in which the nations of the world, East and West, North and South, can prosper and live in harmony, he told the Congress.[14] A year later, on 6 March 1991, after the success of the Gulf War, he made another statement in the Congress claiming, 'Now we can see a new world coming into view. A world in which there is a very real prospect of a new world order. In the words of Winston Churchill, a world order in which "the principles of justice and fair play protect the weak against the strong..." A world where the United Nations, freed from Cold War stalemate, is poised to fulfill the historic vision of its founders. A world in which freedom and respect for human rights find a home among all nations.'[15]

This kind of American exceptionalism was in fact one of the reasons for the decline of the second multilateral initiative of the last century—the United Nations. The UN also envisaged a world order that would end wars. However, the US, which arrogated to itself the leadership of the world order, caused many wars directly or through its covert operations units. In most cases, they either did not seek UN consent or violated the UN mandate with impunity.

While there were several unilateral US interventions during the Cold War period, including in the Dominican Republic (1965), Lebanon (1982), Grenada (1983), Libya (1986) and Panama (1989), this trend continued even after the collapse of the Soviet Union and the end of the perceived threat of the communist regimes to American security. Major post-Cold War interventions include the 1991 Gulf War and the continued bombing of Iraq after the war, the intervention in Haiti that same year, the 2001 war on terror in Afghanistan, and the 2003 invasion of Iraq. In some cases, the US sought and received UN endorsement ex post facto, but it never considered this a condition sine qua non for intervention. When the question of such intervention came up before the UN Security Council, the US always had the veto weapon in its hands.

In addition to military interventions, the US also used its agencies for covert operations through which it sought to intervene in the affairs of nations that it deemed inimical and attempted regime changes there. During the Cold War, the CIA allegedly engineered a coup in Iran in 1953 to overthrow the democratic regime of Mohammad Mosaddegh and orchestrated similar coup in Guatemala in 1954, the Congo in 1960–65, Vietnam in the 1960s, Brazil in 1964, Chile in 1973 and Nicaragua in the 1980s. Indeed, US intervention in Latin America was prodigal, and hardly any country escaped the CIA's net. Lindsey A. O'Rourke, a professor of international politics at Boston University, claimed in *The Washington Post* in December 2016, after a thorough investigation of the documents from the National Archives, the National Security Archive and presidential libraries, that 'between 1947 and 1989, the United States tried to change other nations' governments 72 times.'[16] Those interventions included supporting militant groups. The article added that at least 40 such operations actually failed.

The end of the Cold War did not mean the end of US overt and covert operations. In 1996, an official US report during Bill Clinton's presidency insisted that unilateralism would remain the way forward. 'The only responsible strategy for the United States is one of international engagement. Isolationism in any form would reduce US security by undercutting the United States' ability to influence events abroad that can affect the well-being of Americans...The United States will always retain the capability to intervene unilaterally when its interests are threatened,' the report argued.[17]

In the first two decades of the twenty-first century, the US has already intervened in dozens of cases, either directly or covertly. Its extensive use of drones to strike targets in countries such as Pakistan, Yemen, Somalia and Libya is well documented. After Afghanistan and Iraq in the first decade, the US has been involved in operations against Libya, Syria, and various Islamic State and Al-Qaeda targets.

In his justification for joining the Gulf War, President George Bush Sr made a very benevolent argument of 'goodness'. In his famous speech to the US Congress on 6 March 1991, he presented Operation Desert Storm, the code name for the US intervention in the Gulf War, as a reflection of the kindness of the American people. 'Americans are a caring people. We are a good people, a generous people. Let us always be caring, good and generous in all we do. We went halfway around the world to do what is moral, just and right. We fought hard, and—with others—we won the war. We lifted the yoke of aggression and tyranny from a small country that many Americans had never even heard of, and we ask nothing in return,' he boasted.[18]

A decade later, the attack by Al-Qaeda terrorists on the twin towers of the World Trade Centre in New York City on 11 September 2001 compelled his son and the 43rd president, George W. Bush, to take a more strident line. A few days after the attacks, he indicated that it would be a long war. 'Our war on terror begins with Al-Qaeda, but it will not end there. It will not end until every terrorist group of global reach has been found, stopped and defeated.'[19] He warned that more and more groups other than Al-Qaeda will be added to the list.

A month later he said, 'The attack took place on American soil, but it was an attack on the heart and soul of the civilized world. And the world has come together to fight a new and different war, the first and, we hope, the only one of the twenty-first century. A war against all those who seek to export terror and a war against those governments that support or shelter them.'[20]

From Washington Consensus to Protectionism

Another critical factor that led to the defeat of the liberal world order was the collapse of the economic order established after the Second World War. Globalization was one of the most significant components of the liberal world order. Woodrow Wilson was a staunch supporter of a globalized economy and believed that free trade not only promoted international prosperity but also international peace. His vision led to an economic boom and a social revolution in America. The decade of the 1920s became famous as the Roaring Twenties when, because of the First World War, more and more people moved from farms to the cities and more and more women moved from homes to offices. America's overall wealth had more than doubled in just nine years between 1920 and 1929, and GNP grew by more than 40 per cent.[21] The new consumer culture had swept the country in a way that marked the beginning of globalization. Some American leaders believed that this would be affluence without end. John Brooks, a columnist for the *New York Times*, called the 1920s and 1930s 'Once in Golconda' in his famous book of the same title, implying that Golconda was a legendary region in Deccan India where every visitor became rich.[22]

Wilson's successors, however, were isolationists not only in diplomacy but also in economics and trade. In the post-Wilson era, the government sought to reverse its liberal economic programmes by introducing harsh tax and tariff regimes. Crossborder trade with Canada and transatlantic trade with England, France, Spain and other European countries were severely restricted. Naturally, these countries also retaliated, leading to inflation, food and goods shortages, and other economic sufferings for the American people. The League of Nations tried to intervene by convening a World Economic Conference in Geneva in 1927. However, the participating states were unrelenting, and the initiative failed. The tariff regimes continued.

The result was the crash of Wall Street in 1929, and some members of the US Congress, such as Senator Reed Owen Smoot and Representative Willis Chatman Hawley, argued that the country needed more tariffs, not fewer. They eventually succeeded in bringing an even harsher tariff regime in 1930, which became famous as the Smoot–Hawley Tariff Act.[23] America plunged into a severe economic recession. Fortunately for America, Franklin D. Roosevelt, who was governor of New York, was nominated as the Democratic Party's presidential candidate in the summer of 1932. Roosevelt was a Wilsonian and believed in their economic beliefs.

In his acceptance speech, Roosevelt told the American people, 'I pledge you, I pledge myself, to a new deal for the American people.'[24] This promise of a New Deal brought Roosevelt a landslide victory a few months later, in the fall of 1932. As soon as he took the oath of office, Roosevelt began giving shape to the New Deal, which he hoped would put enough money in every American's pocket so that the consumption cycle could be catalyzed again. 'The country needs and, unless I mistake its temper, the country demands bold, persistent experimentation,' he declared. He added, 'It is common sense to take a method and try it; if it fails, admit it frankly and try another. But above all, try something.'[25]

This bold approach of FDR led to a series of welfare programmes that were initiated along with significant spending on public infrastructure, boosting manufacturing and industrial activity. By the time the Second World War broke out in 1939, the New Deal had become a success story, and the lives of the American people were greatly improved. The decade of depression had convinced Roosevelt that international economic cooperation was the only way to achieve peace and prosperity for all people at home and abroad.

At his meeting with British Prime Minister Winston Churchill at the Atlantic Conference in 1941, Roosevelt succeeded in having the economic liberalist ideas included in the Atlantic Charter. The Charter committed to 'the fullest collaboration between all nations in the economic field with the object of securing for all, improved labour standards, economic advancement, and social security.'[26]

Three years later, at the Bretton Woods Conference in New Hampshire from 1 to 22 July 1944, delegates from 44 nations gathered to build a post-war international monetary system. This led to the creation of the International Monetary Fund (IMF) and the International Bank for Reconstruction and Development (IBRD), as well as the International Development Association (IDA), which was later renamed the World Bank. These institutions strengthened the roots of globalization.

The global economic order created by these two financial institutions was centred on the US dollar and gold. In other words, the US became the pivot of this economic order even before it became the centrepiece of the liberal international order. The US Congress ratified the Bretton Woods Agreement in July 1945, and the two institutions formally came into existence in December 1945.

However, here too, the US showed scant respect for the spirit of genuine multilateralism. Instead, it always gave precedence to its interests, inviting criticism from numerous countries. In 1971, during President Nixon's term, it unilaterally decided to withdraw from the gold regime, leading to the dollar becoming the only platform for global trade transactions. When the Soviet Union collapsed, confidence in the US skyrocketed. While some political pundits like Francis Fukuyama prematurely proclaimed the 'end of history' and the supremacy of the American idea, some economists started talking about 'hyper-globalization'. With newer and bigger markets such as India opening up and the General Agreement on Tariffs and Trade (GATT), driven by the World Trade Organization (WTO), allowing better access to world markets, there was a gung-ho mood in the American markets.

Around this time, the US government's Treasury Department managed to team up with the IMF and the World Bank to work out a set of market-friendly and liberal economic principles for the developing world, which became known as the Washington Consensus. Under this new regime, countries seeking assistance from international monetary institutions were forced to liberalize their economies, open their markets to the world, and allow their currencies to float freely. It all looked perfectly okay as the twentieth century had come to an end.

However, China's entry into the WTO under false promises in 2001 changed all that. In just a decade, China not only emerged as the manufacturing hub of the world but also started stealing jobs from many developed countries, including America. In just one decade, the US experienced what economists called the 'China shock'.

MIT economist David Autor, in an insightful study from 2013, says, 'By 2011, this "China shock" from trade was responsible for the loss of 1 million US manufacturing jobs and 2.4 million jobs overall. Many locales were especially hard hit, especially in the South Atlantic and Deep South regions. So while consumers nationally benefitted from slightly cheaper goods, workers in many places had their livelihoods devastated.'[27]

Then there was the 2008 recession in the US and European markets. Suddenly the West realized that globalization was not going its way. The Washington consensus was quietly buried, and protectionism became the new mantra. 'Protectionism had become a growth industry, with numerous nations—including the US—opting for various direct and indirect barriers to trade since the global financial meltdown of September 2008,' reported the *Financial Times* in July 2009.[28]

Joseph Stiglitz, economist and author of *Globalization and Its Discontent*, sums up the dichotomy, if not the deception, in Western economic policy very well. 'The critics of globalization accuse Western countries of hypocrisy,' he writes. 'The critics are right. The Western countries have pushed poor countries to eliminate trade barriers but kept up their own barriers, preventing developing countries from exporting agricultural products and so depriving them of desperately needed export income.'[29]

In his Davos address in 2017, Vice President Joe Biden openly admitted, 'Globalization has not been an unalloyed good. I am a free trader and a supporter of globalization, but it has deepened the rift between those racing ahead at the top and those struggling to hang on in the middle or falling to the bottom.'[30]

Globalization is more or less dead today. Ten years after the *Financial Times* first wrote about protectionism, it reported again in 2019 that 'Globalization is coming undone. Once thought unstoppable, the forces of liberalization that spurred many decades of rising crossborder trade are faltering.'[31]

As the second decade of the twenty-first century drew to a close, think-tank circles in the US began to realize that the world order they assiduously built was crumbling. 'In recent years, the liberal world order that has held sway over international affairs for the past seven decades has been fragmenting under the pressure of systemic economic stresses, growing tribalism and nationalism, and a general loss of confidence in established international and national institutions,' wrote Robert Kagan, the renowned American neoconservative scholar, warning the incoming US administration that it faced a grave challenge in determining whether it 'wants to continue to uphold this liberal order, which has helped to maintain a stable international system in the face of challenges from regional powers and other potential threats, or whether it is willing to accept the consequences that may result if it chooses to abandon America's key role as a guarantor of the system it helped to found and sustain.'[32]

William (Bill) J. Burns, an American diplomat who served as the director of the powerful CIA, echoed this view in a speech to the Carnegie Endowment for International Peace in his capacity as its president, saying that in today's 'crowded, complicated and competitive' world, 'the global order that emerged after the end of the Cold War has shifted dramatically, creating unprecedented challenges for American statecraft.'[33]

Jolted into a New Reality

The sentiment that the time has come for the world order created after the Second World War to hang up its boots was reinforced by the once-in-a-century pandemic, COVID-19. The world was jolted into a new reality as country after country was forced to shut down and fend for itself, and as the world saw, high and mighty nations like the US and its Western allies were helpless in the face of the dreaded pandemic and the severe supply chain disruptions it caused. The pandemic has brought in new realities of life and the world and has become the catalyst for the emergence of a new world order.

Nouriel Roubini, economist and professor emeritus at the Stern School of Business at New York University, warns, 'In the last seven decades after the Second World War, mankind has experienced relative peace and enhanced prosperity. No major wars occurred, barring the decades of the Cold War. Stagflation and recession occasionally slowed down the pace, but the economies of almost all countries saw progress, and each emerging generation enjoyed enhanced standards of living. That stability and prosperity is what is at risk today.'[34]

He adds, 'The post-war decades of economic growth and rising prosperity...are at serious risk of giving way to economic and financial crises unlike anything we have seen since the Great Depression. Those crises will be made worse by climate change, demographic collapse, nationalist policies that curtail trade and migration, global competition between China and the United States and its allies, and a technological revolution that will displace more jobs in less time than any that has come before.'[35]

As I have already mentioned, the world has undergone many changes in its long existence. Some of them have been tectonic and transformed the way we have been living. But on most recent occasions when such life-changing transformations happened, philosophers with a balanced vision and comprehension were on hand to guide humanity. There was Jesus to question the Romans and their brutal rule, setting the stage for the Semitic revolution in Europe. There was Martin Luther, Erasmus and John Calvin to challenge the Semitic religious order and usher in the era of the Reformation. There was Voltaire, Montesquieu, David Hume and John Locke, who led humanity through the era of Enlightenment. There were Luddites, and of course the legendary Karl Marx, who stood up and raised disturbing questions as the Industrial Revolution swept across Europe a few centuries ago. Even when the current world order was being shaped in the last century, there was Martin Luther King and Mahatma Gandhi, who intervened decisively.

Sadly, no philosophers appear on the horizon when we think about a significant upgrade of humanity's existing order. We have left this to the politicians, technocrats, scientists, and most importantly, big tech and multinational corporations. Let's examine how this new world is taking shape under their influence.

2

UNITED STATES:
INTO THE SLOW AFTERNOON

It is said, 'A picture is worth a thousand words.' Not just spoken or written words, but sometimes even images convey potent messages. One such image, which poignantly conveyed a shocking message about America's fallibility, was flashed on television screens across the world on 30 August 2021. The image of Major General Chris Donahue, the commander of the US Army's 82nd Airborne Division, bathed in the green light of a night-vision telescope, most conspicuously symbolized the humiliating decline of a country that was once considered the world's 'hyperpower'. Donahue was the last soldier to board a waiting US Air Force C-17 transport plane at Hamid Karzai International Airport in Kabul that Monday night, formally ending the country's two-decade-long botched state-making enterprise in Afghanistan.

Americans feed on the staple diet of their supremacy and the inevitability of being at the top of the charts. There cannot be another United States in the world. The average American is obsessed with the idea that maintaining America as the greatest power on earth requires that its governments deploy their military, economic and cultural might everywhere in the world. They are convinced that Pax Americana is their country's legitimate mission. At a NATO Summit in 2009, Barack Obama said that 'American exceptionalism' was nothing special, but something akin to how 'Brits believe in British exceptionalism and the Greeks believe in Greek exceptionalism.'[1] His views landed him in a controversy he never intended to kick up. A few years later, Obama was forced to retract his earlier generalizing statement and reiterate that 'let's show the world once again why the United States of America remains the greatest nation on Earth.'[2]

Great transformations happen not only through the power of nations but also through the ideas they champion. The Thirty Years' War, which devastated Europe in the seventeenth century—1618 to 1648—before ending with the historic Peace of Westphalia, was a conflict over the ideas of Catholicism and Protestantism. The French Revolution was also about ideas such as liberty, equality and fraternity. It was the collision of democracies and totalitarian dictatorships that led to the Second World War. 'This was not an accidental war,' declared German Foreign Minister Joachim von Ribbentrop in 1940, 'but a question of the determination of one system to destroy the other.'[3]

After the Second World War, the US had built enormous economic and military power, which made it the proverbial globocop—policeman of the world. But this influence was the result of the aura it succeeded in creating over certain ideas it championed, such as democracy, free markets and fundamental rights, and not just the raw power it represented. It stood up against autocrats and dictators—from Hitler to Stalin—and ensured their defeat. President Woodrow Wilson called it 'making the world safe for democracy.'[4] President Franklin Roosevelt said in 1939, 'There comes a time in the affairs of men when they must prepare to defend, not their homes alone, but the tenets of faith and humanity on which their churches, their governments, and their very civilization are founded.'[5] America's global influence was the result of its fight for principles. The Cold War it waged against the Soviet Union stemmed not only from a desire for territorial control but also from a conviction that President Harry Truman described as a 'conflict between alternative ways of life.'[6] It was this conviction that led British Prime Minister Winston Churchill to remark in 1941, 'If Hitler invaded Hell, I would at least make a favourable reference to the Devil in the House of Commons.'[7]

It is this benign American influence that is on the decline

today, even if, as the protagonists argue, raw American power may remain. Fareed Zakaria believes that this decline in American influence is due more to the reticence that its leadership—from Obama to Trump to Biden—has developed over the country's role in the world.[8] However, many others continue to argue that America remains the only superpower in the world in terms of its hard power capabilities.

That may be true. The superiority of American military power, its control of the critical sea lines of the world's oceans, its garrisons on nearly every continent in the world, and the strong network of allies it has cultivated over decades, as well as its preponderance over the global economic infrastructure, are all indicative of its enduring hard power. It is able to track down terrorists from all corners of the world and despatch them to the sacred hell or the secret cell.

While we are talking about the decline of the US, NATO, which it created as a formidable security alliance, has seen tremendous growth in the last two decades. Between 1999 and 2009, NATO expanded its membership by welcoming countries like Poland, Hungary, the Czech Republic, the Baltic states, Romania, Bulgaria, Slovakia, Slovenia, Albania and Croatia. Only recently, after the outbreak of the Russia–Ukraine war, Finland joined NATO in April 2023, and Sweden joined in March 2024. Bosnia and Herzegovina, Georgia and Ukraine are in the queue to enter the coveted alliance. In their zealousness to decry the suggestion of a decline in American influence, the protagonists also vehemently dismiss the theory of multipolarity. Where are those other poles, they question. Russia has hardly proved itself to be a global power with its botched invasion of Ukraine. Fantasies about European strategic autonomy have proved insubstantial. India's economic growth has been notable, but it wields very little influence outside the subcontinent. The resurgent nationalisms in Turkey and Iran hardly qualify them as poles of global power, and the former still serves as a staging ground for American nuclear weapons. As former Tsinghua professor Sun Zhe noted, developing countries are not cooperatively 'rising together' to 'challenge the current order'.[9] The economic heft of countries such as Brazil and South Africa is, if anything, declining. 'So where is the multiplicity in world politics?' asks Tom Stevenson, author of *Someone Else's Empire: British Illusions and American Hegemony*. He also argues that China does not threaten the US militarily and its naval power has been routinely exaggerated: 'Its navy is not predicted to rival the US Pacific fleet for another generation, and it still lacks "quiet" nuclear-powered submarines that resist sonar detection.' 'Whatever is to come, the fact remains that global power at present remains unipolar. The task for those not committed to its continuation is to understand it and, wherever possible, to challenge its assumptions,' he avers.[10]

Even though Fareed Zakaria questions the presumption of American decline, he insists that America is still number one. Zakaria proves his point with economic data: In 1990, the per capita income of the US (measured in purchasing power) was 17 per cent higher than that of Japan and 24 per cent higher than that of Western Europe, while today it is 54 per cent and 32 per cent higher respectively. In 2008, the US and eurozone economies were roughly the same size at current prices. Today, the US economy is almost twice as large as the eurozone economy.[11]

Also in terms of hard power, Zakaria argues that the country was 'in an extraordinary position'. He cites economic historian Angus Maddison, who argued that the world's greatest power is often the one that has the strongest lead in the most important technologies of the time—the Netherlands in the seventeenth century, the United Kingdom in the nineteenth century, and the United States in the twentieth century. America in the twenty-first century might be even stronger than it was in the twentieth. Compare its position in, say, the 1970s and 1980s with its position today. Back then, the leading technology companies of the time—manufacturers of consumer electronics, cars and computers—could be found not only in the United States but also in Germany, Japan, the Netherlands and South Korea. In fact, of the ten most valuable companies in the world in 1989, only four were American, and the other six were Japanese. 'Today, nine of the top ten are American,' Zakaria says.[12]

Zakaria may be correct as far as America's hard power is concerned. Further, the US' technology leadership is paramount. The market capitalization of American technology companies is greater than the combined value of the stock markets of Canada, France, Germany and the United Kingdom. The US is also a leader in future technologies such as artificial intelligence and biotechnology. It is a leader in the energy sector, producing more oil and gas than Russia or Saudi Arabia. Its dollar remains the most coveted currency in the world, which not even China seems to challenge.

However, the data does not always tell the whole truth. While one set of data paints a certain picture, another set may show exactly the opposite. Take the following data, for example: Since the 1950s, the US economy has grown at a slower rate than most other countries in the world. This meant that it declined in relative terms. Between 1960 and 2020, its real GDP grew by a factor of five and a half times, while the rest of the world's GDP grew eight and a half times over the same period. While the US economy continued to grow in absolute terms, the economies of other countries grew at a faster pace. Similarly, its growth gap compared to its main rival, China, is also abysmal. While the US economy grew five and a half times faster, China grew 92 times faster. Put another way, in 1960, the US economy was the equivalent of 22 Chinese economies, but in 2020 it was only the equivalent of 1.3 Chinese economies. 'In culinary terms, the cake has become much bigger for everyone, but the slice that goes to the United States has become relatively smaller,' says Manlio Graziano, who teaches geopolitics and the geopolitics of religions at Sciences Po Paris, La Sorbonne, and the Geneva Institute of Geopolitics.[13]

Even Zakaria admits that 'most Americans think their country is in decline.'[14] He cites a 2018 Pew Research Foundation survey in which Americans were asked how they thought their country would perform in 2050. Fifty-four per cent of respondents agreed that the US economy would be weaker. An even more significant number, 60 per cent, believed that the US would be less important in the world. According to a long-running Gallup poll, the percentage of Americans who are 'satisfied' with the way things are going has not exceeded 50 per cent in 20 years. It currently stands at around 20 per cent.

Even the general perception of the rest of the world seems to be against America. A March 2022 Pew Research Foundation survey concluded that nearly half of Americans (47 per cent) believe that the influence of the US in the world has weakened in recent years. Only about one in five believe that the influence of the US has grown stronger. Contrast this with views on China: Two-thirds of US adults say that the country's influence has increased in recent years. Roughly one in five Americans believe that China's global influence is holding steady, and only one in ten say that China's influence has become weaker.[15]

Despite all this, the Biden administration's National Security Strategy Report in 2022 confidently declared that 'prophecies of American decline have repeatedly been disproven in the past.'[16]

For many Americans, it is a complex reality to accept that their country, which represented the best of everything in human life and built the best liberal society, which is a melting pot of people from around the world, could be in decline. However, as human history progresses and the pie of progress gets bigger, more countries are coming forward to take a share of that pie, making America's share smaller. In that sense, it's a natural phenomenon.

The British historian Paul Kennedy wrote in his 1986 masterpiece *The Rise and Fall of the Great Powers* that great powers emerge and decline depending on the uneven growth and growth rates of these and other countries. 'Decision-makers in Washington must face the awkward and enduring fact that the sum total of the United States' global interests and obligations is nowadays far larger than the country's power to defend them all simultaneously,' he commented.[17]

Graziano further explains, 'The global interests and obligations that the United States could afford to defend with a GDP of nearly $3.46 trillion in 1960 could not all be defended simultaneously in 1986 with a GDP of $8.6 trillion, and even less so today despite a GDP approaching $20 trillion.' This paradox is clearly illustrated by America's GDP figures. While the country's GDP was almost half (46.7 per cent) of the rest of the world's GDP in 1960, it was around a quarter (25.95 per cent) in 2024.[18]

An Avalanche of Amorality

There are specific reasons for the decline of American influence, apart from the natural phenomenon of economic decline. One of them is the perceived double standard of American foreign policy. When America stood up to tyrants like Hitler, the world saw it as a principled power. When Truman and Eisenhower declared their intention to take on Stalin and the communists, the world applauded it as America's moral policy. But come the 1960s and 1970s, the world witnessed another face of America—a country that compromises with tyrants and uses them as proxies, that makes armed interventions to bully its opponents, and that deploys its secret agencies to destabilize, through coups and rebellions, regimes perceived as inimical to its interests, even if they are democratically elected governments.

Hal Brands of John Hopkins University wrote, 'To deter aggression along a global perimeter, the Pentagon relied on the threat of using nuclear weapons so destructive that their actual employment could serve no constructive end. To close the ring around the Soviet Union, Washington eventually partnered with another homicidal communist, the Chinese leader Mao Zedong. And to ease the politics of containment, US officials sometimes exaggerated the Soviet threat or deceived the American people about policies carried out in their name.'[19]

'How much evil we must do in order to do good?' asked the American theologian of the last century, Reinhold Niebuhr, in 1946. 'This, I think, is a very succinct statement of the human situation,'[20] he wrote after witnessing the horrors of two successive world wars that wiped out around 100 million people, both military personnel and civilians, from the face of the earth. Niebuhr's question was not new to any Indian theologian. In the Bhagavad Gita, Arjuna, the warrior, asks Krishna, the divine charioteer, the same question in a different way. Krishna justifies the killing of one's kin in a war for *dharma* (righteousness). During the world wars, this ethical dilemma of the death of millions of people could be quickly answered by the liberal Western powers as an effort to prevent the incalculably greater evil of a world ruled by despots and dictators.

In an important strategy document approved by the Truman administration in 1950, Alexander Hamilton, one of the founding fathers of the American Constitution, justifiably argued: 'The means to be employed must be proportioned to the extent of the mischief.'[21] When facing a nasty totalitarian enemy determined to destroy liberal human values, some measure of evil means is probably justified.

Brands added to this narrative arguing:

> During the Second World War, as historian Richard Overy has argued, the Allied cause was widely seen to be more just and humane than the Axis cause, which is one reason the former alliance attracted so many more countries than the latter. In the Cold War, the sense that the United States stood, however imperfectly, for fundamental rights and liberties the Kremlin was suppressing helped Washington appeal to other democratic societies and even dissidents within the Soviet bloc.[22]

But what happened in the later decades made many countries around the world sit up and question American morality and its motives. 'In the 1960s and 1970s, an avalanche of amorality—a bloody and misbegotten war in Vietnam, support for a coterie of nasty dictators, revelations of CIA assassination plots—convinced many liberal critics that the United States was betraying the values it claimed to defend,' Brands demurs.[23]

From George Bush to Joe Biden, American leaders have always used hoary slogans to justify their actions and interventions. When George Bush and Dick Cheney decided to expand the war to Iraq in 2003, Bush told his countrymen that 'America will defend our freedom. We will bring freedom to others, and we will prevail.'[24]

When Barack Obama sought détente with Iran in 2015, he described the nuclear agreement with the Islamic Republic as a demonstration of the 'tradition of strong, principled diplomacy.'[25] A year later, when American prisoners in Iran walked home to freedom, Obama declared victoriously:

> Today's progress—Americans coming home, an Iran that has rolled back its nuclear programme and accepted unprecedented monitoring of that programme—these things are a reminder of what we can achieve when we lead with strength and with wisdom, with courage, determination and patience. America can do—and has done—big things when we work together. We can leave this world and make it safer and more secure for our children and our grandchildren for generations to come.[26]

President Donald Trump, who succeeded Obama in 2017, continued the rhetoric in his inimitable style. Delivering his maiden speech to the UN in September 2017, Trump dubbed the North Korean dictator Kim Jong Un in his typically hyperbolic style as 'rocket man' on a 'suicide mission'. 'The United States has great strength and patience, but if it is forced to defend itself or its allies, we will have no choice but to totally destroy North Korea,' he said.[27] Not to be outdone, Kim fired back, vowing to 'surely and definitely tame the mentally deranged US dotard with fire. A frightened dog barks louder.'[28]

However, within a few months, the two leaders met in Singapore in June 2018, and the language changed completely. After the meeting, Trump described Kim as 'very talented'. Trump even tweeted, 'Great personality and very smart. Good combination. He's a worthy negotiator. He's negotiating on behalf of his people, a very worthy, very smart negotiator, absolutely. And we had a terrific day and learnt a lot about each other and about our countries.'[29]

Joe Biden was no less impressive in mouthing platitudes. Throughout his time in office, his refrain was about waging a fateful battle between democracy and autocracy. Calling on allies to join the struggle against Russia after the invasion of Ukraine, Biden rhetorically argued that it was a struggle 'between liberty and repression, between a rules-based order and one governed by brute force.'[30] At the same time, however, his administration remained ambiguous about the raging war between Israel and Hamas in Gaza and its mounting human cost. Different countries around the world have derived different versions of a single message from all of this: The only principle America seeks to defend is the 'American interest'.

Countries derived the same message in the last century when the Nixon–Kissinger duo went out of their way to co-opt a tyrant like Mao or when they supported military dictators like Ayub Khan and Yahya Khan in Pakistan and riled against the leader of the world's largest democracy, India, and Prime Minister Indira Gandhi. 'Kissinger's policies were not only morally flawed but also disastrous as a Cold War strategy,' commented Gary Bass, professor of politics and international affairs at Princeton University and author of 'The Blood Telegram: Nixon, Kissinger and a Forgotten Genocide', in an opinion piece in *Politico* magazine.

> In at least one crucial part of the world, Kissinger's legacy is fixed: In South Asia, Indians and Bangladeshis widely remember Kissinger as an unusually cruel and cold-hearted person. As they bitterly recall, he and Richard Nixon firmly

supported Pakistan's military dictatorship throughout its bloody crackdown in 1971 on what today is Bangladesh, sending some 10 million Bengali refugees fleeing into India. On the White House tapes, Kissinger sneered at Americans who 'bleed' for 'the dying Bengalis'. Kissinger's policies were not only morally flawed but also disastrous as Cold War strategy. Kissinger knowingly violated US law by allowing secret arms transfers to Pakistan during the India-Pakistan war in December 1971. Despite warnings from White House staffers and State Department and Pentagon lawyers that such arms transfers were illegal, Nixon and Kissinger went ahead, with Kissinger saying that doing so was 'against our law'—a scandal of a piece with an overall pattern of lawlessness that culminated with Watergate.[31]

No Longer the Big Kid on the Geopolitical Block

What could have been an opportunity to restore America's credibility as a nation fighting for the good of the world was not only squandered by the Bush administration's post-9/11 manoeuvres but actually set in motion a downward spiral for the country's influence and credibility. Of particular damage was the 2003 Iraq invasion on the pretext of finding weapons of mass destruction (WMD). Ultimately, no such weapons were found in Baghdad or elsewhere in the country, but the countless body bags carrying dead American soldiers brought utter disrepute locally and globally. In the eight years between 2003 and 2011, when US forces remained in the country, an estimated 461,000 people died from war-related causes.[32] The death toll among members of the US services exceeded 4,500, while more than 32,000 were wounded, many of them severely.[33] As the cost of the war on terror in the Middle East skyrocketed, the Bush administration coyly decided to roll back its involvement in countries such as Afghanistan and Iraq. The Middle East disengagement, which culminated in the withdrawal of the last soldier from Afghanistan in 2021, became one of the potent messages of the global perception of American decline.

The decline can also be attributed to American arrogance and unilateralism, as Samuel Huntington, a controversial but highly acclaimed American political scientist, emphasizes. 'Global politics has moved from the bipolar system of the Cold War through a unipolar moment—highlighted by the Gulf War—and is now passing through one or two uni-multipolar decades before it enters a truly multipolar twenty-first century.' The phrase 'uni-multipolar' has flabbergasted many political analysts. Huntington described this hybrid system as having one superpower, America, and several major powers. Among these great powers, he counted 'the German–French condominium in Europe, Russia in Eurasia, China and potentially Japan in East Asia, India in South Asia, Iran in Southwest Asia, Brazil in Latin America, and South Africa and Nigeria in Africa.'[34] That was the time when the American leadership basked in unipolar glory. At the 1997 Summit of the Eight in Denver, Bill Clinton boasted about the success of the US economy and presented it as a model for all nations of the world. The Clinton administration's Deputy Secretary of State, Strobe Talbott, rationalized that 'American foreign policy is consciously intended to advance universal values,' while his colleague and Deputy Secretary of the Treasury Lawrence Summers described the US as the 'first non-imperialist superpower'. Madeleine Albright, Clinton's ebullient secretary of state, went a step further, insisting that the US was 'the indispensable nation' and that 'we stand tall and hence see further than other nations.' Huntington was clearly not impressed. 'It is false to imply that other nations are dispensable, and American indispensability is the source of wisdom,' he said bluntly.[35]

Huntington had warned that the unipolar syndrome and the obsessive assumption of the American leadership to speak on behalf of the entire global community were inviting derision and resentment in the uni-multipolar world. While the US increasingly isolated itself through the arrogance of its unipolar supremacy, it also attracted criticism as a 'rogue superpower'. A highly respected Japanese jurist and diplomat, Ambassador Hisashi Owada beautifully summed it up by saying that after the Second World War, the US pursued a policy of 'unilateral globalism' providing public goods to many countries. By contrast, in its unipolar avatar, it started pursuing 'global unilateralism'. Huntington quotes another British diplomat with the dismissive remark that 'one reads about the world's desire for American leadership only in the United States. Everywhere else one reads about American arrogance and unilateralism.'[36]

The quick rise of China in the first decade of the twenty-first century, the setbacks in the Middle East fiasco, and the shock of the 2008 economic recession have sufficiently chastened the American leadership's understanding of its declining influence. Bush himself had considered the proposal that his country should withdraw from the Middle East conundrum. Obama, who succeeded him in 2009, held a similar view. Indeed, his statement in his first State of the Union address, 'I do not accept second place for the United States of America,' was taken by many as an admission of America's declining influence.[37] The rising costs of his global engagements prompted Obama to warn his people: 'In this world, the United States of America remains the most powerful nation on Earth, and I believe that we will remain such for decades to come. We are one nation among many.'[38]

Interestingly, the refrain about American decline was propagated more by the American leadership itself than by the others. While the actions of Bush and Obama indicated a certain creeping weakness within the superpower's structure, Trump made it obvious during his 2016 presidential campaign. As Zakaria pointed out, much of Trump's presidential campaign focused on the impending 'doom and gloom' of America.[39] Trump declared that the country's economy was in a 'dismal state' and that the country had been 'disrespected, mocked, and ripped off' abroad.[40] In fact, just three months before declaring his candidacy, Trump released a video titled 'A Nation in Decline'.

'Our foreign policy is a complete and total disaster. No vision. No purpose. No direction. No strategy,' he attacked, accusing President Obama of 'weakening our military by weakening our economy.' He also accused America's allies of 'viewing the United States as weak and forgiving, and not committed to honour their agreements with us.'[41]

In a principal address at the Mayflower Hotel in Washington, D.C., on 27 April 2016, Trump outlined an 'America first' approach to foreign policy; the presidential frontrunner had ruthlessly exposed America's weaknesses in so many words. 'Our friends are beginning to think they can't depend on us,' he said, attacking President Obama for failing to win the Olympics bid.

> Do you remember when the president made a long and expensive trip to Copenhagen, Denmark, to get the Olympics for our country, and after this unprecedented effort, it was announced that the United States came in fourth—fourth place? He should have known the result before making such an embarrassing commitment. We were laughed at all over the world, as we have been many, many times.

Trump thundered, not realizing that he was promoting the decline of his country's influence.[42] He harangued, providing plenty of ammunition for the propagandists of the theory of American decline:

> America no longer has a clear understanding of our foreign policy goals. Since the end of the Cold War and the breakup of the Soviet Union, we've lacked a coherent foreign policy. One day, we're bombing Libya and getting rid of a dictator to foster democracy for civilians. The next day, we're watching the same civilians suffer while that country falls and absolutely falls apart. Lives lost, massive money lost.[43]

Four years of the Trump regime further fortified the perception of America's decline. Trump's slogan 'Make America Great Again' (MAGA), his insistence on withdrawing from several forums, including the Paris Climate Summit and the Trans-Pacific Partnership (TPP) agreement, and his whimsical rhetoric against the principles of globalization led the world to look down on the US. By the time the 2020 presidential election came around, many in America and its allies were seriously looking for a redeemer.

In the ancient Roman empire, when a prince died, the new prince was not only obliged to attend the funeral but also to bury the body. When the election results were announced, leading to the ugly insurrection of 6 January 2021 on Capitol Hill, many who saw Joe Biden's election as a great deliverance expected the new president to bury Trump's legacy forever.

But that was not the case. Even before Biden took the oath of office, one of his key men, Antony Blinken, who was appointed secretary of state in the Biden administration, politely indicated the policy of withdrawal from certain global commitments, especially in the Middle East. 'In a Biden administration, we would see more emphasis on the Indo-Pacific, more emphasis on our own hemisphere, as well as some sustained engagement, I would hope, with Africa, and obviously Europe remains a partner first resort, not last resort, when it comes to contending with the challenges we face. Just as a matter of time allocation and budget priorities, I think we would be doing less, not more, in the Middle East.'[44]

Biden's four-year presidency did nothing to change the perception of American decline. Instead, the Russia–Ukraine war and Israel's relentless campaign in Gaza further reinforced that perception. Not only was America forced to spend billions of dollars on the NATO-led campaign to save Ukraine, but it also failed to keep NATO countries united on the question of supporting that country. While the expansion of NATO with Finland and Sweden joining is a positive indicator, countries such as Hungary and Slovakia have openly expressed their scepticism over the continued support of the war. Viktor Orban, the Hungarian prime minister, declared that his country would opt out of NATO's efforts in the Ukraine war. 'We do not approve of this, nor do we want to participate in financial or arms support (of Ukraine), even within the framework of NATO,' he categorically said.[45] Hungary even tried unsuccessfully to block additional military and economic assistance from the EU to the tune of $50 billion.[46]

Turkey is another curious country. It has been a member of NATO since 1952. Yet it doesn't mind undercutting NATO and defying the US if it does not serve its own interests. Turkish President Recep Tayyip Erdogan declared at a press conference in September 2023 that he trusts Russia just as much as the West. 'To the extent the West is reliable, Russia is equally reliable. For the last 50 years, we have been waiting at the doorstep of the EU, and, at this moment in time, I trust Russia just as much as I trust the West,' he said, not mincing his words.[47]

Apart from the overall war fatigue in the American camp, the 95-billion-dollar aid package, crucial for the Ukrainian leadership to continue the war, has been stalled for months by the Republican-controlled House of Representatives. However, the Democrat-controlled Senate passed it in February 2024. On the other hand, the American initiative to mobilize countries at the UN in favour of the military campaign against Russia also suffered a big setback when one country after another pulled out from the initiative. Despite Biden's fervent appeal that the war in Ukraine was a 'larger fight for ... essential democratic principles' and his claim that the United States would rally the Free World against 'democracy's mortal foes', only 32 countries agreed to extend aid to Ukraine in the war, while 35 others, including major countries such as China, India, South Africa, Saudi Arabia, the UAE and Iran, refused to endorse the American appeal.[48]

When the UN passed a resolution at the end of March 2024 calling for an immediate ceasefire in Gaza, public fallout ensued between the US and the Israeli leadership. The refusal of the US to use its veto power to stall the resolution angered the Israeli leadership, prompting Prime Minister Benjamin Netanyahu to accuse the US of policy vacillation on the Gaza war and also cancelling the visit of a top aide to Washington, D.C.

While Russia and China continue unruffled in the Ukraine

theatre and elsewhere, many believe that the US is facing mounting challenges. In November 2023, the Houthis, an Iranian-backed Shiite guerrilla group based in Yemen, began a campaign in the Red Sea targeting ships belonging to Israel and other Western powers. As the campaign threatened to disrupt global shipping, leading to shortages and inflation in several countries, the US had to seek China's intervention in reining in Iran from supporting the rebels. National Security Communications Advisor John Kirby explicitly welcomed a 'constructive role by China, using its influence and access we know they have, to try to help stem the flow of weapons and munitions to the Houthis.'[49] It was also reported that the US had asked China to 'urge Tehran to rein in the Iranian-aligned Houthi rebels,' attacking merchant ships in the Red Sea.[50] After decades of economic blockade of Iran by the US and its Western allies, this showed the acute vulnerability of the West in the face of rising heteropolar forces in the Middle East.

Hal Brands writes, 'Indeed, if 2022 was a year of soaring rhetoric, 2023 was a year of awkward accommodation. References to the "battle between democracy and autocracy" became scarcer in Biden's speeches, as the administration made big plays that defied that description of the world.'[51]

Despite its criticism of the Trump regime's protectionist 'America First' policies, the Biden administration also fell into the same rhetoric. At the Davos Summit in 2017, just 48 hours before demitting office, Vice President Biden pompously told the audience:

> The impulse to hunker down, shut the gates, build walls and exit at this moment is precisely the wrong answer. It will not resolve the root cause of these fears—and it risks eroding from the inside out the foundations of the very system that spawned the West's historically unprecedented success. We need to tap into the big-heartedness that conceived a Marshall Plan, the foresight that planned the Bretton Woods, the audacity that proposed a United Nations.[52]

Six years later, into the third year of Biden's administration, in a speech in April 2023, his National Security Advisor (NSA) Jake Sullivan criticized 'much of the international economic policy of the last few decades, including globalization and liberalization, for creating economic chaos in the country through the weakening of core industries and severe job losses.' In a subsequent article in *Foreign Affairs* magazine, Sullivan candidly admitted that 'although the United States remained the world's preeminent power, some of its most vital muscles atrophied.'[53]

Diplomat William Burns also admitted that the new challenges facing America and the world must lead to the realization that 'America's singular post-Cold War dominance is fading.' In his address as the chair of Carnegie Endowment, he candidly stated that:

> On today's international landscape, we are no longer the only big kid on the geopolitical block. That's not a defeatist argument; it's merely a recognition that the United States no longer occupies the unrivalled position of strength that we enjoyed after the collapse of the Soviet Union. What we do have, however, is an opportunity to lock in our role as the world's pivotal power—still with a better hand to play than any of our rivals.[54]

The conservative political and religious author Myra Adams lists five important reasons that indicate that the 'American decline appears irreversible.'

1. **Uncontrollable US debt:** The US debt clock shows the inevitability of American decline—a 'ticking time bomb' of data and financial evidence. The US government's total unfunded liabilities—the combined number of payments promised without funds to recipients of social security, Medicare, federal employee pensions, veterans' benefits, and federal debt held by the public—stand at $212 trillion, and rising rapidly. By comparison, this figure was just $122 trillion

as recently as 2019 and is projected to reach $288.9 trillion by 2028, according to the debt clock.

2. **Low student achievement:** The National Assessment of Educational Progress, a congressionally mandated Department of Education programme that has assessed students since 1969, shows that only 29 per cent of fourth graders and 20 per cent of eighth graders are proficient in mathematics. Only 8 per cent and 7 per cent, respectively, are 'advanced' at these levels.

3. **Increasing income and wealth inequality:** A Pew research found the middle class has shrunk from 61 per cent of households in 1971 to just 50 per cent in 2021. Although a net increase in upper-income households accounted for most of this net decline in the middle class, the latter still contributed a disproportionately smaller percentage of the nation's total income—from 62 per cent in 1971 to just 42 per cent in 2021.

4. **Loss of American identity and patriotism:** The once great American 'melting pot' is an outdated concept for many Americans. Traditionally, immigrants with different languages and cultures have assimilated and become distinctively American. The current trend is towards a heterogeneous culture. Patriotism has declined, especially among more ethnically diverse 18- to 34-year-olds. Already-increasing racial tensions could accelerate, hastening national decline.

5. **Widespread belief that our political system is broken:** Americans' disdain for the political system has been captured in numerous polls showing that voters are dissatisfied with a potential Biden–Trump rematch—'a uniquely horrible choice,' as one voter put it.[55]

As I was finishing this book came the disruptive second innings of Donald Trump as US President. In the very first few weeks of his presidency the second time, Trump had turned all the precepts that had been guiding America since the end of the Second World War. On the very first day, he issued executive orders to once again withdraw from the Paris climate accord and the World Health Organization (WHO). In early February, he ordered a review of US participation in all international organizations, conventions and treaties, with a 180-day timeline set for the same. Then began his tariff war with all the countries in the world—friends and foes alike.

Trump's MAGA project is effectively making the US renounce all its international obligations. It is debatable as to whether that will make America great again or small and less influential. In all probability, the Trump-led US will see its role and respect diminishing in the multipolar world.

New Powers and Players

America's biggest challenge today is that the perception of its decline is primarily of its own making. There are mounting challenges to America's dominant position over China, which is fast replacing the American-led 'rules-based order' with its version of the BRI-led economic order. The multilateral organizations that America has spawned over the last century are being made irrelevant by China through the creation of numerous regional bodies such as the Regional Comprehensive Economic Partnership (RCEP), the Asian Infrastructure Investment Bank (AIIB), the Shanghai Cooperation Organization (SCO), the Eurasian Economic Union (EAEU), the Comprehensive and Progressive Agreement for Trans-Pacific Partnership (CPATTP), and the New Development Bank (NDB), or the BRICS Bank. China's sphere of influence will grow, and the global balance of power will be tilted in its favour unless the US gets its act together to dispel the perception of its irreversible decline.

'The most worrying challenge to the rules-based international order does not come from China, Russia, or Iran. It comes from the United States. If America, consumed by exaggerated fears of its decline, retreats from its leading role in world affairs, it will open up power vacuums across the globe and encourage a variety of powers and players to try to step into the disarray,' warns Zakaria.[56]

In July 2023, China successfully test-fired a nuclear 'hypersonic missile capable of travelling at seven times the speed of sound.' It entered low-Earth orbit, circled the entire planet, and returned to hit a target on the Chinese mainland without being detected by the all-powerful American radar networks and tracking instruments. The Chinese used the route via the South Pole, where the American tracking systems didn't work. The Americans were shocked. Mark Milley, Chairman of the US Joint Chiefs of Staff, called it a 'near-Sputnik moment'.[57] The real embarrassment for the Americans was not China's growing technological superiority, but their dismal failure to track it. Many strategists and policymakers are openly talking about China's growing capability to displace the US as a technological superpower and take over the mantle of world leadership.

President Eisenhower, when the 'Sputnik moment' occurred, tried to dismiss the Soviet success as just a scientific feat and a military threat. However, the American media and the Democrat-dominated Congress created a near-paranoia in which ordinary Americans were convinced that the Soviets had marched ahead of their country. It fell to John F. Kennedy, the next president, to inspire the dejected nation by saying, 'What we have to overcome is that psychological feeling in the world that the United States has reached maturity, that maybe our high noon has passed, maybe our brightest days were earlier, and that now we are going into the long, slow afternoon…I don't hold that view at all, and neither do the people of this country.'[58]

In the face of a rising China, increased multipolarity, and declining US-led multilateralism, Americans once again face a despondent future. The wise words of the renowned Stoic philosopher of ancient Rome, Seneca, that 'there is no favourable wind for the sailor who does not know where to go' should be a warning to the US.

3

CHINA: THE ROARING DRAGON

In October 2003, President Bill Clinton delivered an interesting public address at his alma mater, Yale University. Talking about the American nuclear duplicity, Clinton questioned,

'I don't see how we can possibly speak righteously about how Iran should not be doing this and at the same time say that for the first time ever, now that there's no threat of nuclear war with the Russians, we want to develop a nuclear weapon and explicitly say that we might use it first. We're the biggest, most powerful country in the world now. We've got the juice and we're going to use it— and there is a lot of respectable opinion arguing for this.'

He, however, made a vital quip after that: 'But if you believe that we should be trying to create a world with rules and partnerships and habits of behavior that we would like to live in when we're no longer the military political economic superpower in the world, then you wouldn't do that.'[1]

Clinton was the first American leader to publicly suggest that the day might come when America would no longer be the sole superpower. Strobe Talbott, who served as his deputy secretary of state, refers to this in his book *The Great Experiment: The Story of Ancient Empires, Modern States and the Quest for a Global Nation*. 'Talbott asked Clinton why he gave the speech. Clinton replied that he wanted to build a world for our grandchildren to live in where America was no longer the sole superpower, a time when we would have to share the stage.' Yet, as Talbott explains in his book, '[...] Clinton kept that belief largely to himself while he was in office...political instincts told him it would be inviting trouble to suggest that the sun would someday set on American pre-eminence,' writes Singapore's renowned diplomat and scholar Kishore Mahbubani.[2] So Clinton gave the speech only after he left office.

The dawn of the twenty-first century brought the realization to many American statesmen that, contrary to their beliefs and expectations, the world was moving towards an era of multipolarity where one superpower wouldn't be dictating terms to the rest of the world. Samuel Huntington's book *The Clash of Civilizations and The Remaking of the World Order* warned several decades ago of the imminent rise of multiple civilizations and consequent clashes among them. But not many believed it. More were ready to accept Francis Fukuyama's thesis of *End of History*, which suggested that after the demise of the Soviet communist empire, liberal democracy would be the panacea for all nations.[3]

However, even those like Clinton, who believed that America would 'someday' become number two, didn't anticipate that China would challenge the lone superpower in just a decade or two. As Western powers were busy shaping the new world order after the Second World War, they considered China a loathed pariah: a power too insignificant to matter. Moreover, the wartime China of Chiang Kai-shek no longer survived after the war. It was Mao's Red China, a deplorable communist autocracy.

When the Big Five—the USA, the USSR, Great Britain, France and China—met at the behest of the Soviet leadership in the late spring of 1954 at the Villa of Montfleury just outside Geneva in Switzerland to settle the pending issues relating to the just concluded Korean War, Zhou Enlai, the premier under Mao, and a group of Chinese diplomats arrived to attend it. This was the first major international excursion to the capitalist West for the leaders of Communist China. Zhou was keen to use this opportunity to establish diplomatic relations between his country and the Western powers. He was also keen that China should not be treated as a lowly pariah but as a sovereign equal.

Dwight Eisenhower, the conservative US president who succeeded Truman, fumed at the idea and told British Prime Minister Winston Churchill that he was opposed to allowing 'the bloody Chinese aggressor into the councils of Peaceful Nations.'[4] His Secretary of State John Foster Dulles vowed that he would not meet with Zhou in Geneva 'unless our automobiles collide.'[5]

Seven decades after this derision and dismissal, China is today the greatest challenge to America's supremacy. The great power rivalry is back. Some call it the new Cold War. China is openly challenging America and expanding its influence far and wide in the world. Deng Xiaoping wanted the Chinese leadership to 'hide your strengths and bide your time.' However, Xi Jinping's China no longer subscribes to this principle. Xi has made it clear that his ambition is to supplant his country as the world's leading power and relegate the US to the position of number two. 'China's ambition to recover its accustomed primacy in Asia has already upended many of our comfortable assumptions about how integration into a US-led order would tame, or at least channel, Chinese aspirations. And our traditional allies in Asia, as well as new partners like India, are taking notice and adjusting their strategic calculations, raising regional temperatures and increasing uncertainties,' said William Burns in 2019.[6]

When the liberal world order was being framed, China was a minor power. Its GDP per capita was just $50, comparable to India's $60,[7] and its average life expectancy was just 35 years.[8] In 1950, the US had 27.3 per cent of global GDP in terms of purchasing power parity (PPP), while China had only 4.5 per cent.[9] Even four decades later, at the end of the Cold War in 1990, America had a 21.8 per cent share of global GDP and China 3.63 per cent.[10] But in just the last two decades, China unexpectedly rose to surpass the US.

American strategists have long defined the instruments of a country's national power with the acronym DIME: Diplomatic, Informational, Military and Economic power. Today, China is either at par with or ahead of the US in all these parameters.

In terms of PPP, China's GDP is already higher than that of the US.

China's rise is not limited to its economy alone. By deftly using its economic and technological muscle, the country has made significant advances in technology, military preparedness and, most importantly, diplomatic influence far and wide in the world.

The Making of Wolf-Warrior Diplomacy

Like the US, China has understood the importance of diplomacy in its relentless endeavour to reach the top. It invests heavily in diplomatic initiatives. When the COVID-19 pandemic brought not only isolation but also much infamy, the Chinese leadership decided to invest more in its diplomatic outreach to turn the tables. 'China's diplomacy has pressed the "accelerator button" and sounded the clarion call,' declared Qin Gang, the short-lived Chinese foreign minister, in March 2023, months after his nomination to the high post and months before his dismissal and disappearance.[11] The budget for diplomatic spending increased to 57 billion yuan ($8.1 billion) in 2023,[12] even as the US continued to slash funding for the State Department.[13] In 2019, China's diplomatic network overtook that of the US with 276 embassies and consulates around the world. Just three years earlier, it was ranked third behind the US and France.[14]

In March 2023, China's diplomatic overdrive achieved a rare and unmissable success in West Asia when it succeeded in brokering a deal between arch-rivals Saudi Arabia and Iran. With Chinese Foreign Minister Wang Yi standing in the centre, Musaad bin Mohammed Al-Aiban, Minister of State in Saudi Arabia's Council of Ministers and National Security Advisor, and Ali Shamkhani, Secretary of the Supreme National Security Council of Iran, signed a joint trilateral statement announcing that 'an agreement has been reached between the Kingdom of Saudi Arabia and the Islamic Republic of Iran, that includes an agreement to resume diplomatic relations between them and reopen their embassies and missions within a period not exceeding two months, and the agreement includes their affirmation of the respect for the sovereignty of states and the non-interference in internal affairs of states.'[15] They also agreed that the ministers of foreign affairs of both countries should meet to implement the agreement, arrange for the return of their ambassadors, and discuss ways to enhance bilateral relations. The leaders of Saudi Arabia and Iran hailed the 'noble initiative of His Excellency President Xi Jinping' and 'China's support for developing good neighbourly relations between the Kingdom of Saudi Arabia and the Islamic Republic of Iran.'[16] In a critically-worded sentence in the joint statement, the three countries 'expressed their keenness to exert all efforts towards enhancing regional and international peace and security.'[17] With this coup, China has effectively replaced the US in the Middle East.

In a tongue-in-cheek comment aimed at the US, Wang told reporters in Beijing after the release of the joint statement: 'The Middle East belongs to local people, and the region's destiny should be held fast in the hands of peoples in the region's countries. They can build a more stable, peaceful and prosperous Middle East by strengthening coordination.'[18]

Keen observers of developments in the Middle East agree that the Saudi Arabia–Iran deal was Xi's message to the US and the rest of the world that he was going to intensify his efforts to reshape the world order in China's frame.

The Chinese leaders have long held the view that the world order shaped by the Western powers in the aftermath of the Second World War is unjust and must therefore be changed. However, it was only after the country became strong and prosperous enough that they started making moves toward that end. The initial years saw Chinese diplomats, led by Zhou Enlai, making all-out efforts to entice the leaders of the Western powers to ensure that their country was accorded a respectable place in the world order they had created and led. Given China's limited power and the intense anti-communist hate that prevailed in the West, this was not easy.

The fact that they had not had such an enthusiastic experience in Geneva did not deter Zhou and his colleagues. They decided to seize the next big occasion, a multilateral gathering, a year later in the West Javan city of Bandung in Indonesia. Zhou understood that it needed a set of diplomats who would consider themselves 'frontline proletarian soldiers'. 'Diplomatic personnel are the People's Liberation Army in civilian clothing,' he told the first group of diplomats he had personally selected and trained for the job. Several of them were actually recruited from the ranks of the Chinese Red Army. When Mao learnt about them, he welcomed Zhou's efforts, saying, 'Ambassador generals are good. They won't run away.'[19]

In April 1955, the Bandung Conference of Afro-Asian nations took place, paving the way for the founding of the short-lived Non-Aligned Movement (NAM). The Chinese delegation, led by Zhou Enlai, arrived in Bandung to build bilateral ties with the leaders of the 29 countries attending the conference and tear down the Western policy of isolation and containment of China. Zhou and his entourage worked overtime to bring legitimacy to their country. John Kotelawala, the prime minister of Ceylon (Sri Lanka), was a bitter critic of communism. He came to the conference determined to subject Zhou to 'tough questions'. He publicly railed against communist imperialism and raised the issue of Taiwan's self-rule. Zhou didn't get worked up. Instead, he met the prime minister personally and used his power of persuasion to convince him.

'The impact of Zhou's diplomacy went far beyond the conference room. China dominated media attention: Zhou's name appeared four times more frequently in Western coverage than India's Nehru,' wrote Peter Martin.[20]

The next decade saw China making strenuous efforts to secure a place at the global high table—the UN. When the UNO was founded in 1945, China was one of its 22 signatories. However, there was no People's Republic of China (PRC) at that time. It was the Chinese Republic led by Chiang Kai-shek. After the founding of the PRC under Mao's leadership in 1949, Zhou and his comrades began efforts to win support for their entry into the UN. This support came mainly from the Comintern bloc of countries led by the Soviet Union. However, there were others, including Nehru's India and occasionally the Great Britain, that lobbied to get the PRC a place in the UNO.

President Harry Truman was initially positive about the proposal. In January 1950, he even announced that the US government would not provide military aid or advice to the Chinese forces in Formosa (later in Taiwan). However, the outbreak of the Korean War in 1950 altered the equations with succeeding US administrations, starting with Eisenhower, steadfastly resisting moves by China and its cohort to join the UN. However, the determined efforts of the PRC leaders began to yield results: support for its entry grew from 6 in favour and 33 opposed in 1950 to 34 in favour and 42 opposed in 1960. By 1970, support for the PRC's admission secured a majority, and these countries included many US allies.[21]

An important name to remember in this major breakthrough for China was Henry Kissinger, US secretary of state in the Nixon administration. His secret visit to Beijing in July 1971 paved the way for President Nixon's visit to China in 1972—the first-ever visit by a US president—and ended decades of hostility.

Interestingly, moments after Kissinger boarded his plane and concluded his second visit to China on 26 October 1971, the foreign ministry received a cable from New York stating that the PRC had been admitted to the UN. When *The New York Times* described this as America's greatest defeat, Zhou proclaimed, 'Britain, France, Holland, Belgium, Canada and Italy have all become Red Guards, rebelling against America and voting for us.'[22] The fact is that the Nixon–Kissinger duo had already planned to allow it to happen, hoping that China would be an effective counterbalance to the USSR in the region.

While the US looked the other way, the PRC had ended its pariah status and made a grand entry onto the world stage. The icing on the cake was that joining the UN also brought with it a veto power in the Security Council, as the PRC had replaced the Republic of China (ROC), now commonly referred to as Taiwan. A wave of international diplomatic recognition quickly followed. Country after country started switching sides from Taiwan to the PRC. By the end of the decade, China succeeded in establishing diplomatic relations with 120 countries. The most significant development was the official recognition by the US in 1979.

Red Capitalism

Having ended diplomatic isolation by entering the UN, the Chinese leadership had set sights on WTO, their next target.

Around this time, major changes were taking place in the Chinese leadership hierarchy. Chairman Mao died in 1976, and after a brief period of internal squabbles, Deng Xiaoping rose to become the supreme leader of the Communist Party of China (CPC) in 1978, guiding its fortunes for the next two decades. Deng showed foresight in setting the country on a new course of economic reconstruction and integration into the global economy. Just as Zhou depended on Western powers to end diplomatic isolation, Deng turned to the US and other Western powers to revive the country's economy and became part of the globalization process led by the WTO.

China's rise as a dominant economic power must be credited to Deng's supreme leadership through the 1980s and 1990s, until his death in 1997 at the ripe age of 92. In 1981, shortly after Deng launched his economic reform programmes, over 50 per cent of the Chinese population was living in extreme poverty. It was Deng's pragmatic economic policies that led to American companies running in hordes to Beijing to exploit the benefits offered by the newly opened-up market of one billion Chinese people. Deng boldly rejected the disastrous reform policies of the Mao era and embraced Western-style economic openness. He tore down the commune system of the Mao era and aggressively promoted special economic zones in various regions of the country.

Deng's pragmatism can be summed up in his famous quote: 'It doesn't matter if a cat is black or white so long as it catches mice.'[23]

Deng's reforms and openness thrilled the US leadership. Ronald Reagan, who visited China in 1984, just a few years after Deng initiated the reforms, was upbeat about what he thought was a deeper change. 'There is much to be gained on both sides from expanded opportunities in trade and commerce and cultural relations,' he declared, adding optimistically, 'The first injection of free-market spirit has already enlivened the Chinese economy. I believe it has also made a contribution to human happiness in China and opened the way to a more just society.'[24]

Deng was a reformer by conviction. He was in the process of introducing political reforms when the student uprising broke out in Tiananmen Square in 1989. Mao had built China into a party state during his reign from 1949 to 1976. Deng tried to dismantle it and change its character by attempting to separate the party and the government. However, the Tiananmen Square revolt probably prompted Deng to abandon his political reform agenda and focus on economic reforms instead. Undeterred by the barrage of international criticism following the Tiananmen Square massacre, Deng embarked on a significant Southern Tour in 1992, which was primarily intended to promote economic activity and entrepreneurship in the South. If China today boasts of having lifted 800 million people out of poverty, or if the Chinese economy has grown 91-fold in 40 years since the 1980s, the credit should go to Deng's pragmatism and visionary leadership.

Deng pursued the same pragmatic, sometimes clandestine, approach to bring China closer to its next target of joining the WTO. Unlike Mao, Deng wanted China to maintain a low profile in order to not attract too much negative attention from the West. 'Observe the situation calmly. Stand firm in your positions. Respond cautiously. Conceal our capabilities and await an opportune moment. Never claim leadership. Take some action,' he repeatedly advised his party leadership.[25]

In early 1992, Premier Li Peng attended the World Economic

Forum in Davos and toured Western Europe with the aim of luring businesspeople from countries like Switzerland, Italy and Portugal. The Western media had dubbed Li the 'Butcher of Beijing' for his role in the Tiananmen Square massacre.[26] But in Davos and during his subsequent trips through Europe, Li managed to charm his Western hosts and emerged as the darling of Western business.

Jiang Zemin, Deng's protégé, who held the office of the president of the PRC between 1993 and 2003, followed his mentor's advice religiously. With an eye on gaining access to global markets, Deng encouraged the Chinese government to apply for admission into the General Agreement on Tariffs and Trade (GATT) mechanism, the precursor to the WTO. The negotiations dragged on for almost 15 years. In 1995, when the GATT was transformed into the WTO, China was granted observer status. The Chinese negotiators kept engaging in sweet talk at the WTO and desperately tried to convince the Americans and other negotiators of their intention to give all member countries unhindered access to Chinese markets.

The Asian Financial Crisis of 1997 came as an excellent opportunity for China when the countries across Southeast Asia, hailed as the Asian Tigers, faced economic headwinds and countries like Indonesia and Thailand braced up for a major economic collapse. China had the enticing option of devaluing its currency to reap huge benefits from the Asian recession. However, the Chinese leadership heeded the urging of the international community not to trigger further economic chaos and capital flight, and presented itself as a responsible economic power willing to make sacrifices for the global good. Beijing's decision to keep its currency stable won praise even from US President Bill Clinton, who said, 'China has shown great statesmanship and strength by maintaining the value of its currency.'[27]

China's behaviour convinced Clinton to believe that allowing it entry into the WTO would be beneficial to the world. He lobbied strongly at the US Congress and finally got it to approve normalizing trade relations with China. The vote in the Congress was, in effect, a US endorsement of China's WTO accession. A jubilant Clinton told members of Congress, 'Today, the House of Representatives has taken a historic step toward continued prosperity in America, reform in China and peace in the world... it will open new doors of trade for America and new hope for change in China.'[28]

A report by the Council on Foreign Relations argues that Clinton and others championed China's accession for the following reasons:

- China would have to change its policies to adhere to WTO rules, reducing tariffs and guaranteeing intellectual property rights, among other things, while countries like the United States would have to give up little in return.
- The United States argued that membership in an international organization such as the WTO would act as a check on China's communist government, speeding up its transition to a market economy and encouraging it to have a greater stake in setting global rules. This was not a new idea; Clinton's predecessor George H.W. Bush had operated under the same assumption that free trade leads to democracy: 'No nation on Earth has discovered a way to import the world's goods and services while stopping foreign ideas at the border.'
- It would also legitimize the WTO itself. China was the biggest trading country outside the organization, and without China the WTO could not really claim to be a global organization.[29]

In 2008, even German Chancellor Gerhard Schröder lauded the signs of 'progress on China's path to a constitutional, just and one day, I am sure, also democratic society.'[30]

'Everyone assumed that in a more open, interconnected world, democracy and liberal ideas would spread to the autocratic states. Nobody imagined that autocracy and illiberalism would spread to the democratic world instead,' quips Applebaum.[31]

That is exactly what happened. Once it acquired WTO membership in 2001, China decided to use it to access markets in the world for its products rather than to allow global access to its economy. Its GDP grew rapidly from $1.2 trillion in 2000 to $11.1 trillion in 2015.[32] At the time of its entry into the WTO, China's per capita income was $2,900 in PPP terms (similar to Pakistan, Bhutan, Yemen, Cape Verde, the Marshall Islands and Azerbaijan).[33] By 2015, its per capita income had grown to $14,400. China's economy went from the sixth largest to the second largest in the world. In 2024, its per capita income in PPP terms was $26,310.

In the first seven years after joining the WTO, until 2008, the Chinese leadership pretended to follow the WTO guidelines religiously. As soon as the West was caught up in the recession in 2008, the Chinese government's willingness to continue market and economic reforms hit a halt. It simply discarded WTO rules and regulations and returned to the practices of trade protectionism.

Republican Kevin Brady, who supported China's admission into WTO during a House vote in 2000, expressed his remorse later, saying, 'I was convinced at the time that China needs to be part of the rules-based trading system in that it would accrue to the benefit of the US in a significant way over time. Now it's clear China had no intention of living within a rules-based trading system.'[34]

In response to such criticisms, Long Yongtu, China's chief negotiator for WTO accession, lied with a straight face in an interview: 'When we promised to adopt a market economy, we made it absolutely clear that it would be a socialist market economy. That effectively meant that China exploited foreign market access while blocking the US from the Chinese market through measures largely outside of the WTO's supervision and enforcement mechanisms.'[35]

Using the WTO membership, China aggressively pursued its trade agenda of enhancing opportunities for its exports in world markets. Having already emerged as the manufacturing powerhouse, it immediately seized the opportunity to capture global value chains (GVCs). In 1980, its share of world trade was one per cent. In 2010, however, it emerged as 'the world's undisputed export champion,' say experts at UN Trade and Development (UNCTAD). However, they also added that this phenomenal rise was 'both admired and questioned.' Most of the complaints that UNCTAD received were against China. A majority of them pertain to trade disputes with the United States.[36]

Xi Rules

China owes its rise in the last five decades to the US. It was the Nixon–Kissinger duo that ended its diplomatic isolation by co-opting it into the UN orbit in 1971. Bill Clinton's administration paved the way for China's accession to the WTO three decades later in 2001. It was American companies that strengthened Chinese manufacturing and technological capabilities in the 2000s. China cleverly used all these steps to climb up the ladder of global prominence. In 2012, as the country challenged the world's mightiest powers, it had a leader in President Xi Jinping who was both an enigma and the envy of the world.

Xi became the general secretary of the CCP in 2012—the sixth leader to rise to the top post in the PRC and the first to be born after the 1949 revolution. Five years later, at the 19th Party Congress in October 2017, Xi openly expressed his eagerness to build China into a 'global leader in terms of composite national strength and international influence.'[37] In a decade, he actually achieved this by catapulting the country to global leadership.

Henry Paulson, former US treasury secretary, was quoted by Evan Osnos in *The New Yorker*, who emphasized Xi's enigma by saying, 'To Westerners, it seems very incongruous that he is so committed to fostering more competition and market-driven flexibility in the economy and, on the other hand, to be seeking more control in the political sphere, the media, and the Internet. But that's the key: he sees a strong party as essential to stability and the only institution that's strong enough to help him accomplish his other goals.'[38]

There was nothing extraordinary about Xi's career in the party until he became general secretary. In fact, that was one of the reasons behind the party elders' decision to hand over the mantle to him in 2012. One trait he demonstrated before becoming the president was his aversion to Western criticism of his country. On a trip to Mexico in 2009, he publicly complained about 'foreigners with full bellies who have nothing better to do than point the finger at China's human rights record.'[39] This antipathy for the Westerners, a trait that most Chinese leaders from Mao to Hu Jintao carried, became an even more pronounced characteristic of Xi in the last ten years of his rule. He also shared Deng's views on the bias of the Western liberal world order and the need to change it. Speaking at the US Naval War College in June 2018, Secretary of Defence James Mattis stressed that China was 'harbouring long-term designs to rewrite the existing global order,' adding: 'The Ming dynasty appears to be their model, albeit in a more muscular way that requires other nations become tribute states, kowtowing to Beijing.'[40]

Several Chinese leaders, starting with Deng Xiaoping, argued that the existing international order was created and sustained by the West to secure its interests and exploit developing countries and that it therefore needed to be changed. At a meeting with Prime Minister Rajiv Gandhi in 1988, Deng suggested that it was time to think about 'appropriate new policies to establish a new international order' and proposed the five principles of peaceful coexistence—*Panchsheel*—as norms for international relations (IR), as an alternative to 'hegemonism, bloc politics and treaty organizations' that 'no longer work.'[41] Later, in his report to the Sixteenth National Congress of the CPC in 2002, Jiang Zemin bemoaned the 'old international political and economic order, which is unfair and has to be changed fundamentally.'[42]

When Xi took the helm in 2012, this rhetoric about the need to make the world order 'fairer and more reasonable' and China's willingness to strive for this reform became more pronounced in the statements of the Chinese leadership. In March 2013, Chinese Foreign Minister Yang Jiechi stated, 'We believe that the international multilateral system of the twenty-first century should expand its representativeness, improve its fairness, and enhance its effectiveness. China is a participant, builder, and contributor to the international system. We will participate more proactively in international affairs and play our due role in developing a fairer and more reasonable international system.'[43]

Xi reiterated this on several occasions since his ascension. In June 2018, he listed 'leading the reform of the global governance system with the concept of fairness and justice' as one of the ten priorities for China's diplomacy 'in the new era', making it clear that he intends for China to take a leading role in the reform of the international system, rather than just being a participant in the process.[44]

It was an interesting coincidence that around the same time Xi was rising in China, there was a great debate being unleashed in the US about its declining power and influence. The economic meltdown of 2008, coupled with the rise of several countries as new poles in the 2010s, prompted many thinking Americans to ask if Pax Americana was over and if it was time for American leadership to turn inward to get their house in order. A few years later, 'Make America Great Again' became Trump's campaign slogan. One leader who clearly understood this changing mood in the US and sought to fully exploit it was the new Chinese president and party supremo, Xi Jinping.

Exceptionalism with Chinese Characteristics

As someone who has always claimed to have been influenced by China's history and civilization, Xi wanted to rebuild China based on certain core beliefs he had drawn from the country's rich cultural and civilizational experience. Soon, it acquired the status of 'Xi Jinping Thought' (XJT) and became mandatory reading for all party cadres. Many bureaucrats, business leaders and even film stars were called upon to endorse it. A critical element of XJT was to pair Marxism with Confucianism. In October 2023, Xi declared that today's China should consider Marxism as its 'soul' and 'fine traditional Chinese culture as the root.'[45]

In 2023, Hunan TV, China's second-most-watched television channel, launched a new series, *When Marx Met Confucius,* with the backing of the CCP. The two actors who play the roles of Confucius, dressed in a tan robe, and Karl Marx, in a black suit and a leonine white wig, meet at Yuelu Academy, a thousand-year-old school known for its role in Confucianism. Over five episodes, Marx and Confucius discuss the nature of politics and eventually come to the conclusion that Confucianism and Marxism are not incompatible and that Karl Marx may have subconsciously drawn his theories from Confucian wisdom. In one episode, Marx actually states: 'In reality, I myself was Chinese for a long time,' suggesting that his thinking was always in tune with traditional Chinese wisdom.[46]

Red China's formational leadership was averse to bringing the country's rich past into its current politics. Mao even insisted that Confucianism was theoretically incompatible with Marxism and that its influence had weakened China. During the Cultural Revolution, the Chinese Red Guards—militant and unruly college and often school students who took the law into their own hands—went about destroying Confucian temples and even dynamiting his tomb and hung the naked corpses from trees.

But XJT went in the opposite direction. At a 2017 session of the Central Commission for Discipline Inspection, Xi underscored that 'Chinese excellent culture has become the gene of the Chinese nation, rooted in the hearts of the Chinese people, subtly affecting the thought and behavior of the Chinese people. The CCP is made up of outstanding sons and daughters of the Chinese nation. The blood of the CCP is imbued with the fine genes of Chinese traditional culture. The CCP's political culture is therefore deeply influenced by our excellent traditional culture.'[47]

By invoking China's civilizational past, however, Xi was embarking on a different project—creating the Chinese version of 'exceptionalism' along the lines of, or perhaps as a response to, American exceptionalism. 'Several thousand years ago, the Chinese nation trod a path that was different from other nations' culture and development,' he noted, arguing that building 'socialism with Chinese characteristics' could only be enabled 'by our country's historical inheritance and cultural traditions.'[48]

With this exceptionalist approach, Xi sought to build an argument in favour of rejecting Western models of governance. He branded alternative governance models as not only inappropriate but also dangerous. In a speech at the College of Europe, Xi exhorted that China 'cannot copy the political system or development model of other countries because it would not fit us and it might even lead to catastrophic consequences.'[49]

He told Greek Prime Minister Antonis Samaras in 2014, 'Your "democracy" is the democracy of ancient Greece and Rome, and it is your tradition. We have our tradition.'[50]

No doubt, the communist leadership from Mao to Deng believed that the Western models did not suit China. Thirty years ago, Deng also argued that capitalism 'would get China nowhere.' He even wanted Marxism and socialism to be tailored to Chinese conditions and introduced the idea of 'socialism with Chinese characteristics.'[51] However, Xi Jinping's project was not limited to building an alternative model for China but offered an alternative worldview to the whole world.

'Xi Dada'

Xi's two predecessors, Jiang Zemin and Hu Jintao, were protégés of Deng. Jiang was chosen by Deng due in part to his firm handling of the 1989 student-led protests in Shanghai. Hu was elevated as the successor to Jiang Zemin in 1992. Both adhered to Deng's trademark restraint in dealing with the world and focused on building China into an economic superpower. Xi was an insignificant junior official during Deng's years.

'Before Xi took power, he was described in China and abroad as an unremarkable provincial administrator, a fan of American pop culture (*The Godfather*, *Saving Private Ryan*) who cared more about business than about politics and was selected mainly because he had alienated fewer peers than his competitors,' wrote Evan Osnos in *The New Yorker* magazine.[52] It was his low profile and self-effacing attitude that had made him the ultimate choice between the two contenders—himself and Li Keqiang. At a press conference, a local reporter once asked Xi to rate his performance: 'Would you give yourself a score of a hundred—or a score of ninety?' Neither, Xi said; a high number would seem 'boastful', and a low number would reflect 'low self-esteem'.[53]

But once in the chair, China and the world saw a different Xi: determined, aggressive and ruthless. He emerged as the most authoritarian leader since Chairman Mao. Mao-era purges pale into insignificance in comparison to Xi's administration, which investigated tens of thousands of his partymen on charges ranging from corruption to leaking state secrets to inciting the overthrow of the state. In just a few years after assuming office, Xi gained total control of the party machinery. The Soviet communist leader Vladimir Lenin once advised: 'For the center...to actually direct the orchestra, it needs to know who plays violin and where, who plays a false note and why.'[54] Xi managed to gain such absolute control—the kind that had never been seen before, not even during Mao's era.

All seven current members of the Standing Committee of the Communist Party are loyalists of the leader. A study conducted during Xi's second year in office found that he appears in the newspapers more than twice as often as his predecessors. The state news agency *Xinhua* adopted the nickname 'Xi Dada' (Big Uncle Xi) for the leader. In Peking University's entrance exam, thousands of art students applying for admission were asked to sketch Xi's portrait.

Deng tried to reduce the party's interference in the functioning of the government by giving more teeth to the state council—the Chinese cabinet. But Xi worked assiduously during his first term as general secretary to bring back Mao's 1973 phrase—'Party leads everything'. When the party rewarded him with 'core leader' status in October 2017 and amended the Constitution to incorporate 'Xi Jinping Thought on Socialism with Chinese Characteristics for the New Era' as the new party ideology, Xi returned the favour by declaring at the Nineteenth Party Congress that the 'party, government, military, civilian and academic—East, West, South, North and Centre—the party leads everything.'[55]

In 2018, the National People's Congress—China's parliament— amended the Constitution to remove term limits for the post of president. Xi's grip over the party became apparent when the 2,964-member People's Congress overwhelmingly supported the amendment, with just two votes against it and three abstentions.

The Chinese firmly believe in a legend called The Eight Immortals. Drawn from the mythology of the Tang to Song dynasties, these immortals are revered by the Chinese as elderly men with powers. The CCP wisely adopted this tradition during the Deng era to co-opt the party elders, who are otherwise retired party leaders, into the party system and occasionally elicit and respect their views. Deng himself served as an elder until his death in 1997.

But in the last decade, Xi gradually sidelined these party elders. Although they were retained in the 46-member praesidium standing committee that occupied the dais at the Twentieth National Congress in October 2022, their importance has greatly diminished. Among those elders, while Hu was present at Xi's side, two others, Jiang Zemin and Zhu Rongji, were conspicuous by their absence, leading to speculation that all was not well. The video, which shows Hu being forcibly evicted by two men at Xi's behest, went viral, sending shockwaves in China. Zemin died a month later, while the other elders kept a low profile, fearing the consequences of Xi's anger. In 2024, Xi appointed Hu's son, Hu Haifeng, as vice minister in his government.

Towards a Sino-centric World Order

Having consolidated his position in the party and government through purges and punishments, Xi is now determined to take on Washington to fulfil his ambition of liberating the world from Western influence. In his more than ten years in power, Xi meticulously implemented an agenda that would eventually replace Western hegemony over the world with that of his own country. He made his first move in 2013, the year he became president, by launching the now famous Belt and Road Initiative (BRI). It was initially christened as One Belt-One Road (OBOR). Xi called it the 'project of the century' and made it part of the CPC Constitution in 2017.[56]

The idea behind the BRI was to draw countries into the Chinese economic orbit by investing in infrastructure projects such as roads, railways, energy, digital technology and ports. During a visit to Kazakhstan in September 2013, Xi announced this strategy as the Silk Road Economic Belt. At the time, Xi was careful not to show any global ambitions. However, Chinese capital soon began to flow into dozens of countries, and Chinese companies started aggressively bidding for project contracts across the developing world, prompting experts to realize that the BRI was nothing but Xi Jinping's twenty-first-century version of the Marshall Plan. More than 150 countries became beneficiaries of the BRI, and the estimated Chinese investments in these countries exceeded $1 trillion. The World Economic Forum was tempted to call China the 'world's largest debt collector'. For several countries in Asia and Africa, the BRI ended up becoming the 'debt trap diplomacy' of China.[57] New research by the World Bank, Harvard Kennedy School, AidData and the Kiel Institute for the World Economy showed that China spent $240 billion between 2008 and 2021, bailing out 22 ailing economies, including Argentina, Mongolia and Pakistan.[58]

As the BRI turned ten years old, Xi's language also underwent a remarkable change. He began to talk more and more about his 'global' objectives. 'Over these ten years, we have endeavoured to build a global network of connectivity consisting of economic corridors, international transportation routes and information highways,' he said in a speech at the third BRI Forum in Beijing in October 2023.[59]

Beijing listed five areas of focus for the BRI: policy coordination, infrastructure building, unimpeded trade, financial integration and people-to-people exchanges. However, the ultimate objective of the BRI was not to enhance connectivity but, as Xi himself explained, to move toward a 'community of shared future'.[60]

The success of the BRI emboldened Xi to launch three other initiatives that also explicitly spoke of China's global mission of 'reforming the global governance system'. The first was the Global Development Initiative (GDI), which was announced in September 2021 at the seventy-sixth session of the United Nations General Assembly (UNGA) at the peak of the COVID-19 pandemic. According to a Chinese government official publication, 'It is another significant public good that China provides to the international community in the new era, and an essential practice of the concept of a human community with a shared future in global development.'[61]

A year later, the Global Security Initiative (GSI) followed in 2022. Speaking at the annual conference of the Boao Forum for Asia in April 2022, Xi Jinping officially announced this second initiative. A few months later, the Chinese foreign ministry released a concept paper claiming that 'the historical trends of peace, development and win-win cooperation are unstoppable' and that 'upholding world peace and security and promoting global development and prosperity should be the common pursuit of all countries.' It also stated that the GSI 'aims to eliminate the root causes of international conflicts, improve global security governance, encourage joint international efforts to bring more stability and certainty to a volatile and changing era, and promote durable peace and development in the world.'[62]

The third in the series, the Global Civilization Initiative (GCI), was announced by Xi in March 2023. While virtually delivering a keynote address at the CPC's Dialogue with World Political Parties High-level Meeting in Beijing on 15 March that year, Xi informed the gathering that the initiative 'advocates respect for the diversity of civilizations, the common values of humanity, the importance of inheritance and innovation of civilizations, as well as robust international people-to-people exchanges and cooperation.' Xi added, 'As the future of all countries is closely connected, tolerance, coexistence, exchanges and mutual learning among different civilizations play an irreplaceable role in advancing humanity's modernization process and making the garden of world civilization flourish.'[63]

A document published by China's State Council or Cabinet of China insisted, 'To realize a world with lasting peace and ever-improving welfare, we should embrace the Global Civilization Initiative and draw on it to jointly create a better, shared future for humanity.' As a veiled rejection of Western efforts to build a civilization based on its value system, the document argued that 'a single flower does not make spring, while one hundred flowers in full blossom bring spring to the garden. Together we can make the garden of world civilizations full of colours and life.'[64]

These three initiatives reflect the Chinese leadership's new vision in the evolving new international order and throw light on the country's foreign policy doctrine of 'a global community of shared future'.

Support for these nascent initiatives is growing. The GCI received support from a few countries, including Serbia, South Africa, South Sudan and Venezuela. The GDI, the oldest, gained more international support. After Xi announced it at the 2021 UN General Assembly, China formed a Group of Friends of the GDI, which now boasts the membership of more than 70 countries. China cleverly linked the GDI to the UN Sustainable Development Goals (SDGs) 2030, and the GSI has achieved even greater success. According to China's foreign ministry, more than 100 countries and regional and international organizations have supported the GSI. At the Shanghai Cooperation Organization (SCO) meeting in September 2022, China received support for the GSI from all member countries except India and Tajikistan.

Unlike the BRI in 2013, the three later initiatives explicitly discuss a 'global' agenda in the areas of development, security and civilization. The GSI, in particular, is the Chinese alternative to the current 'rules-based' order led by Western powers.

Xi said nothing new about these initiatives. However, these are essentially the instruments he wishes to deploy to promote his vision of a new world order and enhance China's global influence.

Finally, in a speech at the Central Conference on Work Relating to Foreign Affairs Conference in December 2023, Xi laid to rest any lingering doubts about his global ambitions by declaring that Beijing has emerged as a 'confident, self-reliant, open and inclusive major country,' one that had created the world's 'largest platform for international cooperation' and led the way in 'reforming the international system.' He asserted that his conception of the global order—a 'community with a shared future for mankind' had evolved from a 'Chinese initiative' to an 'international consensus,' to be realized through the implementation of four Chinese programmes: the Belt and Road Initiative, the Global Development Initiative, the Global Security Initiative and the Global Civilization Initiative.[65]

All this points to the fact that Xi Jinping is convinced that China's moment has arrived. He wants to dominate and reshape the new world order based on China's own civilizational experience and strategic vision. Some admire this, but many are strongly averse to it. At the same time, it continues to be an enigma to many others.

Separating Myth from Reality

Enigma has been the hallmark of Chinese politicians right from the beginning. In 1971, during a secret visit to China, Henry Kissinger met Zhou Enlai in Beijing and asked him about the success of the French Revolution. 'Too early to say' was Zhou's reply.[66] Such enigmatic behaviour continues to this day. With a GDP almost on par with that of the US, the Chinese leadership still prefers to label their country only as a 'developing nation'. They sneer at this suggestion with a straight face, expressing their ambition to remodel the world order as Sino-centric. But all this is posturing and should not be taken at face value. In 1954, leaders of India and China, Prime Minister Jawaharlal Nehru and Premier Zhou Enlai, signed the *Panchsheel*—the five sacred principles of international diplomacy. Eight years later, in August 1962, Mao ordered his PLA commanders to prepare for war against India. When Zhou reminded him of *Panchsheel* and the commitment to peaceful coexistence, Mao spoke of armed coexistence between the two countries. Modern China should be understood through some of its core features. China is not like any other country—it is a civilizational state. A distinct cultural behaviour, shaped by centuries of civilizational experience, guides its behaviour, which can be described as 'strategic culture'. Historical figures such as Confucius and Sun Tzu, the author of the famous treatise *The Art of War*, play an important role in shaping its strategic behaviour. In the eyes of many objective Asian observers, the CCP actually functions as the 'Chinese Civilization Party'. 'Its soul is not rooted in the foreign ideology of Marxism–Leninism, but in Chinese civilization,' writes Kishore Mahbubani.[67]

A disciple once asked the famous Chinese philosopher Confucius how one should deal with enemies. Should it be a tit-for-tat response or the show-the-other-cheek response that Jesus prescribed? 'Neither,' replied Confucius and asked his disciple, 'If you do good to those who do you harm, what do you do to those who do you good?' Then comes the profound Confucian reply, 'Give justice to your enemies.' Justice is a higher, but also a more subjective, form of response. Linked to this is Sun Tzu's conception that 'all warfare is based on deception.' Together, the two have shaped China's strategic behaviour into an enigmatic one.

Modern China can be understood through some of its lesser-known characteristics nurtured under the authoritarian leadership of Xi Jinping.

1. Zhongguo: The Middle Kingdom

China is guided by a Confucian-era civilizational memory of Zhongguo—the Middle Kingdom. This concept is integral to the Chinese worldview and reinforces the belief that China was the centre of world civilization. Yang Jiechi, the PRC's foreign minister, stated in 2010, 'China is a big country, and other countries are small countries; that's just a fact.'[68] A sense of superiority and a false sense of victimhood pervade all its actions and politics.

2. The Great Rejuvenation of the Chinese Nation

The great rejuvenation of the Chinese nation is a dream that all modern Chinese leaders cherish and continue to pursue. The term 'rejuvenation' was first coined by Sun Yat-sen in 1912. Successive leaders took the concept further. Xi uses the phrase most often to describe the ambition of bringing the country to its supremacist glory.

3. Party State

In China, everything is under the control of the CPC. Mao had built China into a party state during his reign (1949-76). Deng tried to change this character by trying to separate the party and the government. Hu Yaobang was asked to handle the party affairs, while Zhao Ziyang was appointed head of government. However, under Xi Jinping, the party-state returned with a vengeance as the sinews of the entire Chinese nation. The ubiquitous party committees, which had lost relevance in the Deng era, are back in full force in every office and village. The 92-million-member party's membership is now highly coveted, with thousands applying for it and only a few securing it after thorough scrutiny.

Xi had the CCP Charter amended in 2017 to restore the party's supremacy. Shortly after his reappointment at the Twentieth Party Congress in 2022, Xi led the new Politburo Standing Committee on a visit to Yangjialing in Yan'an, where Mao had cemented his absolute authority seven decades earlier at the Seventh Party Congress in 1945. Xi said that the Party Congress 'marked the Party's political, ideological and organizational maturity,' which included 'forming a group of well-tested politicians who held high the banner of Mao Zedong.'[69] Interestingly, Xi drew a parallel between Mao in 1945 and his consolidation of power in 2022, implying that he plans to lead the party for many decades to come.

4. Core Leader

The CCP had begun its journey as a party with collective leadership. In the early years, it was aligned with Chiang Kai-shek's ruling Kuomintang (KMT). However, a major fallout with the KMT in 1926 led to brutal purges by Chiang Kai-shek's National Revolutionary Army in 1927 and 1933. Considerably weakened, the party decided to give up its collective leadership character and in 1935 declared Mao the 'core leader', vesting in him both party and army leadership.

That was the time when cruel authoritarians were rising to power in other parts of the world too—Adolf Hitler in Germany, Benito Mussolini in neighbouring Italy and Stalin in Soviet Russia.

Mao never read Marx, but he was willing to be guided by Stalin's cronies in the beginning. The CCP that he had moulded in the initial decades was Stalinist in its organizational structure and nationalist in its character. From 1949 until his death in 1976, Mao remained the supreme leader of the CCP. He modelled China as a one-party state with all powers concentrated in the hands of the 'core leader'.

The title of 'core leader' returned to the CPC as it neared its centenary, when the party anointed Xi to the title in 2018. Xi had acquired ten titles, including not only head of state and head of the military but also chairman of the party's most powerful committees: foreign policy, Taiwan affairs and economy. He also installed himself as the head of new bodies overseeing the internet, government restructuring, national security and military reform. He established control over courts, the police and the secret police. Xi is practically at the centre of everything in China today.

5. Xiaokang Society (Moderately Well-Off Society)

China has set 2049, when the PRC completes 100 years, as the time to achieve 'great rejuvenation', meaning reaching the pinnacle of its power and influence in the world. However, Xi doesn't want to wait until then. In his address to the 20th Party Congress in 2022, Xi revised the date for achieving the 'Xiaokang society' to 2035. While his own leadership is one important determining factor for this hurry, the changing demographics, too, are a major worry for Xi. By 2050, a third of the Chinese population is expected to be over sixty years old.

Xi's mission to build a global 'community of common destiny' should be understood as the mission to create a Sino-centric world order. It is a euphemism for realizing the 'China Dream' of the 'Great Rejuvenation'. It is about building a world order that accedes to the centrality and supremacy of the Chinese system.

Economic power, military power, technological power and diplomatic power are the four pillars of this Sino-centric world order.

1. Economic Power

Is China the world's second largest and most significant economic power? Some argue that China has already displaced the US as the world's largest economy. Measured by the refined yardstick that both the IMF and the CIA now judge to be the single best metric for comparing national economies, the IMF report shows that China's economy is one-sixth larger than that of the US (China's $24.2 trillion versus the US' $20.8 trillion).

2. Military Power

The Chinese People's Liberation Army (PLA) is growing considerably stronger under Xi's leadership as chair of the Central Military Commission (CMC). Building a world-class army was initially scheduled for 2035. However, at the Twentieth Party Congress in October 2022, Xi declared that this goal should be achieved by 2027, when the PLA completes its centenary. 'Achieving the goals for the centenary of the People's Liberation Army in 2027 and more quickly elevating our people's armed forces to world-class standards are strategic tasks for building a modern socialist country in all respects. To this end, we must apply the thinking on strengthening the military for the new era, implement the military strategy for the new era, and maintain the party's absolute leadership over the people's armed forces,' Xi declared.[70]

The PLA Navy (PLAN) is fast expanding and modernizing. The US Department of Defence's latest report to Congress states that 'the PLA Navy's overall battle force is expected to grow to 400 ships by 2025 and 440 ships by 2030.'[71] The PLAN currently operates six nuclear submarines and 48 diesel-powered attack submarines. The PLAN's submarine force is expected to grow to 65 units by 2025 and 80 units by 2035.

The PLA is developing a range of space and counter-space capabilities and related technologies, including kinetic-kill missiles, ground-based lasers and orbiting space robots. It is expanding its space surveillance capabilities to monitor spatial objects and enable counter-space operations. China is likely to stockpile about 1,500 nuclear warheads by its 2035 timeline.

3. Tech Power

China is already a technological superpower. It is on the verge of achieving semiconductor manufacturing capability if it succeeds in influencing the Netherlands. With a population of less than 20 million, the Netherlands is home to a single firm, ASML, which is vital to global semiconductor production. ASML is the sole global supplier of the latest generation of photolithography scanner equipment critical to the manufacture of cutting-edge logic chips. Washington's groundbreaking effort to restrain China's capabilities in a crucial technology thus depended on the support of this small European nation, the world's eighteenth largest economy, and the compliance of a single private company.

Military-Civil Fusion (MCF) is the PRC's new strategic policy initiative. It effectively ends any distinction between civil and military use of critical technologies. Under this MCF initiative, all non-military tech activity is subordinated to the military regime.

This strategy encompasses six interrelated efforts:

1. Fusion of defence industrial base and the civilian technology base
2. Integrating and leveraging science and technology (S&T) innovations across military and civilian sectors
3. Cultivating talent and blending military and civilian expertise and knowledge
4. Building military requirements into civilian infrastructure and leveraging civilian construction for military purposes
5. Leveraging civilian service and logistics capabilities for military purposes
6. Defence modernization to include all relevant aspects of society and the economy for use in war

Under its Young Thousand Talents Program, the CPC operates 200 centres globally to constantly scout for and recruit the best talent from around the world, and the PLA uses this network for military recruitment.

The PRC's espionage capabilities are also increasing. Today, it is able to pose a sophisticated threat of cyber-enabled espionage to the most advanced technological powers such as the US. Sensitive military-grade equipment like advanced integrated circuits, accelerometers, gyroscopes, jamming equipment, aviation technologies and anti-submarine warfare capabilities are now in its hands. Following the Sun Tzu doctrine of 'winning without fighting', the PRC is capable of using technology to disrupt the military operations of the enemy country at the initial stages.

4. Diplomatic Power

China hosted conferences of almost all non-Western groups of nations, including Arab states, Central Asian republics, African countries, Latin American nations and the ASEAN group of nations. It sought to build ties with South Pacific Island nations and also with India's neighbours in the Indian Ocean. It is building a non-Western club of nations through various multilateral organizations like BRICS and SCO and through its own initiatives such as BRI, GDI, GSI and GCI. It seeks to dominate international multilateral institutions such as the UN and other bodies.

Superpower on Many Fronts

As China rises, it poses multiple challenges to the liberal world order. Armed with its renewed strength, it is already acting like a superpower on many fronts. Xi Jinping is flexing his muscles on several issues.

1. Taiwan

In Taiwan, Xi declared categorically that force was also an option. Speaking at the 20th Party Congress, he stated: 'Resolving the Taiwan question is a matter for the Chinese, a matter that must be resolved by the Chinese. We will continue to strive for peaceful reunification with the greatest sincerity and the utmost effort, but we will never promise to renounce the use of force, and we reserve the option of taking all measures necessary.' He asserted, 'The wheels of history are rolling on toward China's reunification and the rejuvenation of the Chinese nation. Complete reunification of our country must be realized, and it can, without doubt, be realized.'[72]

2. South China Sea (SCS) Claims

In the SCS, China continues to expand its claims. It is pretty impossible to understand China's claims in the SCS from a legal perspective. Its historical claims are based on Zheng He's voyages through these waters about 600 years ago. By this logic, the entire Indian Ocean should belong to India, and Spain and Portugal should lay claim to the entire Atlantic Ocean, as they were the first to sail these waters in recent history.

China makes three arguments in support of its Ten-Dash Line claims based on the alleged voyages of Admiral Zheng He in the fifteenth or sixteenth centuries. Ironically, all three are false.

i) **Admiral Zheng He's ships were the first to navigate these waters:** False. The Polynesians or Austronesians navigated these waters much earlier, since at least 1000 BCE. They were expert navigators of the region at that time and travelled all the way from Taiwan and the northern Philippines south and east towards Polynesia.

Others in the region navigated these waters, such as the Vietnamese and the Indians, who sailed from India and established settlements in Southern Vietnam, Indonesia, etc. The Champa civilization, inspired by India, flourished in Southern Vietnam in the seventh century, but Zheng He's voyages did not begin until the fifteenth century. The Champa people named this sea the Champa Sea. Champa and India had a far greater historical claim to the South China Sea than China.

ii) **Admiral Zheng He's ships were the first to discover the Spratly Islands (which are at the core of the SCS disputes):** False again. It was the Polynesians who knew these islands like the back of their hand.

Here too, the Vietnamese, Indians and possibly others navigated through these islands earlier than the Chinese.

iii) **Admiral Zheng He was the first to name these islands:** Wrong again. The Chinese didn't name these islands until the early 1900s, and their names are Chinese translations of the English names.

Most scholars refuse to consider Zheng He's voyages as historical evidence, as the earliest record of these voyages is a novel written 200 years later by Luo Maodeng. The novel contains a number of fantasy elements, for example that the ships were 'constructed with divine help by the immortal Lu Ban.'

Zheng's voyages were long neglected in official Chinese history but became popular after Liang Qichao's *Biography of Our Homeland's Great Navigator, Zheng He*, published in 1904. From then on, China started building up the story of Zheng He's voyages and portrayed him as the Chinese equivalent of the European explorers who discovered America. In the South and East China seas, China forcibly and unilaterally pushes for the establishment of the Ten-Dash Line as a maritime boundary, with neighbours such as Japan, the Philippines, Vietnam, Malaysia and Indonesia unable to counter it out of fear of retribution. China rejected the decision of the United Nations Convention on the Law of the Sea (UNCLOS) on 12 July 2016, which stated that it shouldn't claim any historical rights in the SCS based on its unilaterally declared Nine-Dash Line. The petitioner, the Philippines, couldn't do much. Nor could it do much when its ships were later harassed by the Chinese Coast Guard in the same area.

The Vietnamese had to be content with international condemnation when their fishing vessel was sunk by the aggressive Chinese Coast Guard ship in April 2020. In 2023, a Chinese survey ship, the *Haiyang Dizhi 8*, went deep inside the Malaysian Exclusive Economic Zone in search of oil reserves, while the Malaysians were forced to look the other way. Even the Americans and Japanese find it difficult to countenance the aggression of the PLA Navy in the South and East China Seas. Their ships are regularly accosted, many times by moving dangerously close, by the PLA Navy warships. The aircraft carriers of the PLA Navy, like the *Liaoning*, undertake exercises in the provocatively close vicinity of the American carriers like the USS *America* and the USS *Theodore Roosevelt*.

A recent survey found that the majority of people in Asia believe that the consequences of strategic competition between the US and China will be negative; more than 60 per cent believe that their country's national security will be at risk. And for countries close to China, the prospect of conflict is existential. As Philippine President Ferdinand Marcos Jr said in a recent interview, 'I learnt an African saying: When elephants fight, the only one that loses is the grass. We are the grass in this situation. We don't want to get trampled.'[73]

3. PLA-Navy's Expanding Footprint

The PLA Navy has five theatre commands that have operational autonomy. From the earlier Near Seas Defence, its mandate has been expanded to Far Seas Protection. It is also expanding its logistical facilities. After Djibouti, the PLA is planning to establish military logistics facilities in Cambodia, Myanmar, Thailand, Singapore, Indonesia, Pakistan, Sri Lanka, the UAE, Kenya, Equatorial Guinea, the Seychelles, Tanzania, Angola and Tajikistan.

Port-building Spree

According to data from Drewry Maritime Research and others, Chinese firms owned or operated one or more terminals in 36 of the world's 100 largest container ports in 2022. An additional 25 ports are located on the Chinese mainland, establishing China's presence in 61 per cent of the world's most active international shipping hubs. Mainland China itself hosts eight of the world's ten largest ports by total cargo tonnage and seven of the ten largest ports by throughput. By the end of 2022, Chinese firms had acquired ownership or operational stakes in 95 ports in 53 countries, covering all continents except Antarctica.[74]

Commercial ports have become essential logistics platforms for the PLA's global operations. At these Chinese-owned and operated facilities, navy ships can replenish petroleum, oils and lubricants; resupply military material, equipment and personnel; and even carry out maintenance and repair work at some facilities. Overseas port facilities also help augment Beijing's intelligence capabilities by providing Chinese terminal operators with proprietary information on ship movements and trade transactions.

In the port sector, the concentration of Chinese ownership in just three conglomerates has given Beijing significant leverage. These companies—COSCO Shipping Ports, China Merchants Port (CM Port) and Hutchison Ports (Hutchison)—now account for nearly 80 per cent of China's overseas port holdings.[75] Deng Xianwu, captain of the PLAN amphibious transport dock vessel Changbai Shan, says: 'As long as there are Chinese companies, there is a guaranteed forward transportation support point for warships.'[76]

In a speech in France in 2014, Xi described China as a 'peaceful, amicable and civilized' lion that has woken up. He was referring to the French emperor Napoleon Bonaparte's description of China as a sleeping lion that would 'shake the world' after it woke up.[77]

Not all may agree—definitely not those responders at annual PEW surveys.

4

HOT COLD WAR

At a conference in the European Parliament in Brussels in early 2024, I noticed a palpable worry among some of the European political thinkers. They were convinced that the world was inexorably moving towards another Cold War. One member of the European parliament (MEP) whispered in my ear that some wealthy Europeans were planning to relocate to places considered remote and secure, like Cambodia or Papua New Guinea, and buy villas and mansions there.

Coming from India, it sounded as if these Europeans were paranoid. Not necessarily. In the last century, Europe had been the theatre of two world wars and an intensely fought Cold War. The memories of the horrors of this significant power conflict are still fresh in the minds of many Europeans. They relate the developments in this century to those that took place not so long ago in the last century.

The First World War in 1914 was the result of the culmination of several smaller conflicts. Similarly, major strategic blunders by Japan and Germany, such as the attacks on Pearl Harbor and Poland, led to the escalation of the war in Europe into the Second World War in 1939–45. Then came the Cold War between the Western powers led by the US and the Eastern bloc of communist nations led by the Soviet Union, which lasted for more than 40 years. Not only the European powers but the whole world endured its consequences. During these four fateful decades, there were dozens of occasions when the world came close to the brink of total destruction.

It was the 1970s, and Zbigniew Brzezinski, NSA in Jimmy

Carter's government during 1977–81, was deeply asleep in his home when his aide in the control room made a frantic call. The caller alerted Brzezinski that the Soviets had launched 200 missiles heading towards the US. Before the gravity of the situation could sink in, another call came from the same aide, this time updating the number to 2,000 missiles. Brzezinski thought to himself, '*This is going to lead to war,*' and galloped to his home phone to activate the secure line to the White House. As he mulled over how to inform the president after waking him in the dead of the night, the phone rang one last time, again from the same man in the control room, who sheepishly informed his boss that it was just a computer chip malfunction that had triggered a false alarm. There were no missiles. The enemy had not launched an attack that called for an urgent retaliation. It was Brzezinski's delay of those few minutes in waking up President Carter that probably saved the world from a nuclear holocaust.[1]

It wasn't just a matter of one or two years; the history of the Cold War years was replete with dozens of such incidents. Even the Pentagon reluctantly acknowledged some years ago that the world came dangerously close to nuclear armageddon on at least 15 occasions. We survived those dreadful decades, but not without paying a heavy price.

A Cold War-like situation is once again brewing between a new set of rivals—the US and its Western allies as well as the PRC and its Eastern allies like Russia and Iran. The world is riddled with multiple conflicts and flashpoints involving the two sides, threatening to escalate into another global conflict—the Third World War.

Cold War 1.0

It is perhaps worth recalling how the Cold War of the last century began. It was Soviet expansionism, led by Stalin after the Second World War, that prompted America to intervene with the Marshall Plan to ensure that economic assistance for rebuilding countries in Western Europe would keep them from falling victim to Stalin's evil designs for domination over entire Europe. In a way, this was the starting point of the Cold War, which lasted for the next four decades until the collapse of the Soviet Union in the early 1990s.

While the American fears about the possible expansion of the Soviet sphere of influence into Western Europe propelled them to offer the Marshall Plan as an enticement, the Soviet leadership, including Stalin, saw the Plan as an attempt by the West to spread capitalist economic influence in Europe. The Soviet government rebuked the Plan, and Stalin sternly told his allies in Eastern Europe not to accept any support from the Americans under the Plan.[2]

The Cold War battle lines were thus drawn with both the Truman Doctrine and the Marshall Plan. 'With the Marshall Plan, the Cold War assumes the character of position warfare,' wrote Adam Ulam, arguing that it was no longer differences on individual issues that divided the erstwhile anti-Hitler allies, but the 'totality of the foreign policies of each side that became the object of attack by the other.'

The Cold War intensified in the following years. Truman ordered the commissioning of further nuclear weapons. They were stationed in several European countries in the 1950s. Both sides unleashed nasty spy games. When Fidel Castro came to power in Cuba in 1959 through a guerrilla war and a coup, the communists knocked on the doors of the US. The rattled CIA allegedly spent nearly $30 million to eliminate Castro.

Military budgets skyrocketed. President Eisenhower sanctioned $40 billion for the US military.[3] The Soviets also spent unknown sums on their military. Money, weapons and advisers from the US poured into the European capitals. Massive propaganda and culture wars unleashed across the communist capitals. Defections from East to West were encouraged and heavily publicized. The situation was so tense that athletes from the Eastern and Western blocs were kept at a great distance at the 1952 Summer Olympics in Helsinki, earning the Olympic Games village the epithet 'Iron

Curtain Village.'[4] Three decades later, when the Olympic Games were held in Moscow in 1980, the US not only took the lead in boycotting the participation of its athletes but also sent emissaries such as boxer Muhammad Ali to various countries to ensure their boycott. When the Soviet Union intervened in the civil war in Afghanistan in 1979 and installed a puppet regime led by Babrak Karmal, the Americans used this to raise a false alarm that Islam was in danger of being taken over by godless communists. In the end, over 50 countries, including the US, Germany and several Arab countries, boycotted the Moscow Olympics.

The Cold War also turned into a battle for scientific and technological supremacy. The Soviets initially stole the march by placing the first satellite, Sputnik I, into orbit on 4 October 1957. This news shocked and embarrassed the Americans. 'We must see to it that whatever advantages they [the Soviets] have are temporary only,' President Eisenhower exhorted his administration.[5] It took two attempts before the Americans were able to successfully launch their own satellite, Explorer 1, into space three months later, on 31 January 1958. The race for space supremacy escalated. The Soviets maintained a lead in the manned space experiments, first sending two dogs on a trial mission and then launching a manned mission with cosmonaut Yuri Gagarin on board the spacecraft on 12 April 1961.

In the 1980s, as Soviet tank power became formidable in Eastern Europe, this rivalry reached its zenith when the US developed the neutron bomb, much more dreaded than the nuclear bomb. President Carter argued that a neutron bomb was the only way to stop or destroy the Warsaw Pact's tank power, which was more than three times the size of the Western powers. At a press conference on 12 July 1977, he said that the neutron bomb was 'not a new concept at all, not a new weapon.' He said that he had 'not yet decided whether to advocate deployment of the neutron bomb' but that 'it ought to be one of our options.' While forwarding funding requests to Congress, he added that 'in my present view,' approval was 'in the nation's security interest.'[6]

Those were also the years when mock drills for nuclear attacks were being conducted in schools and colleges in the US and nuclear shelters were built in many residential areas.

Great Game on

This glimpse into Cold War history draws our attention to the dreaded reality of today's identical big power rivalry.

However, leaders of the two superpowers—the US and China—strongly reject the portrayal of the current competition between them as a new Cold War. President Biden insisted in an address that he didn't 'want to contain China.' 'We're all better off if China does well,' he boasted.[7] After his first in-person meeting with Xi Jinping in Bali, Indonesia, on the sidelines of the G20 Summit in November 2022, Biden confidently told the media that there was no need to worry about a 'new Cold War' and that he did not believe 'any imminent attempt' by China to invade Taiwan was imminent. 'I absolutely believe there need not be a new Cold War. I have met many times with Xi Jinping, and we have been candid and clear with one another across the board. And I do not think there's any imminent attempt on the part of China to invade Taiwan,' he said.[8]

After meeting with his US counterpart in San Francisco in November 2023, President Xi proclaimed, 'China doesn't want a cold war or a hot war with anyone.'[9]

Like Biden and Xi, several other members of the Biden administration sneer at the invocation of the Cold War analogy for today's geopolitics. Jake Sullivan, the Biden administration's NSA commissioner, insisted that the US should 'reject neo-containment'.[10] 'The Cold War construct of blocs is not coherent,' he argued, suggesting that the country should 'heed the lessons of the Cold War while rejecting the idea that its logic still applies'.[11] Secretary of State Antony Blinken also dismissed Cold War rhetoric, saying, 'I don't think it reflects the current reality.'[12] Secretary of Defence Lloyd Austin claimed, 'We do not seek a new Cold

War, an Asian NATO or a region split into hostile blocs'.[13] In fact, the 2022 National Security Strategy explicitly states that US policymakers 'do not seek conflict or a new Cold War'.[14]

These sentiments sound reassuring but do not necessarily correspond to the situation on the ground. Over the past two decades, practically every continent in the world has become a battleground for big-power competition. From Africa to Latin America, there is a growing competition to secure reserves of key minerals. Across Asia, there is a race to win friends and build military and economic partnerships. In Europe and West Asia—in Ukraine and Gaza—it is already an open war.

Niall Ferguson warns, 'Today, the new cold war is being waged unremittingly in multiple domains, from Ukraine to the Middle East, from space to cyberspace. But the biggest risk to world peace is surely in East Asia, where Chinese military exercises suggest that Beijing is preparing for a blockade—or a more ambiguous "quarantine"—of Taiwan at some point in the coming years. At present, the United States has few good options for such a contingency'.[15] He refers to an interview given in June 2024 by Admiral Sam Paparo, the head of US Indo–Pacific Command, in which he spelt out his intention, in the event of a Chinese blockade, 'to turn the Taiwan Strait into an unmanned hellscape using a number of classified capabilities…so that I can make their lives utterly miserable for a month, which buys me the time for rest everything.' 'But the United States does not yet have the maritime drones and other weapons Paparo has in mind. Even if it did, using them against Chinese naval force would risk a fearful escalation into full-blown war, with the potential to culminate in a nuclear exchange,' warns Ferguson in the article titled 'How to Win the New Cold War'.[16]

There are two crucial reasons for revisiting the history of the Cold War in the present context.

Firstly, despite all the rhetorical statements of rejection of the Cold War analogy, both the political and public intellectual leadership of the US have always displayed a great sense of history.

Blinken, while ostensibly rejecting the comparison, also quipped elsewhere, referring to George Kennan's Long Telegram, which enshrined 'containment' as policy, that 'you could literally insert Russia and Putin for what he (Kennan) says about the then Soviet Union.'[17]

Across the aisle, the Trump administration officials repeatedly invoked the Cold War analogy to raise hackles against China. Mike Pompeo, Trump's secretary of state, said in 2020 that 'what's happening now isn't just Cold War 2.0. The challenge of resisting the CCP threat is in some ways worse.'[18] The National Security Strategy document released by the Trump administration in 2017 insisted, in contrast to what the same document said five years later under the Biden administration, that 'today's challenges to free societies are just as serious, but more diverse' than those of the Cold War.[19] In April of that year, Trump's NSA John Bolton argued that the US should 'write a new NSC-68 (the 1950 State Department document that called on the Congress for massive rearmament) to confront China, Iran, North Korea and Russia.'[20]

Justin Winokur, a researcher at the University of Virginia, highlighted this obsession with Cold War history in the US public policy arena. 'Historians such as Hal Brands, Niall Ferguson and M.E. Sarotte have argued that the United States is in a new Cold War with China and Russia. Analysts including Fareed Zakaria, David Ignatius, Edward Luce and Walter Russell Mead routinely parse Cold War analogies for wisdom. Roughly two-thirds of the books on history, politics and international relations named 'best of 2022' by *The New York Times*, *The Wall Street Journal*, the *Financial Times*, *Foreign Affairs* and *Foreign Policy* focus on the period during or after the Second World War, when a preeminent United States was challenged only by ambitious but weaker powers,' he writes.[21]

The second reason is that while historical memories dominate policymaking in Western capitals, in countries like India, which are rising as important middle powers, public memory has been woefully short. India's first prime minister, Jawaharlal Nehru, reminded his countrymen of the famous statement by philosopher and writer George Santayana: 'Those who cannot remember the past are condemned to repeat it.'[22] Returning to the history of the Cold War to learn contemporary lessons is therefore an important exercise worth undertaking.

Thucydides's Trap

Cold War deniers notwithstanding, like the twentieth century, the twenty-first century too is witnessing an intense competition for domination between two power blocs—one led by the US, the new Allied Powers, which also include Israel and the countries of Western Europe, and the other led by China, the new Axis Powers, which also include Russia, Iran and North Korea. In the long history of the US and China, they have never come face to face as much as we witness today. China experienced its heyday until the middle of the second millennium. However, by the time the thirteen British colonies in America decided to secede and form their own country, the United States, China had entered its dark history of external and internal depredations. While the US grew from strength to strength in the next two centuries, China continued its downward spiral of wars, rebellions and revolutions.

Incidentally, it was the Cold War geopolitics that brought the US and China closer together in the last century. When President Nixon kowtowed to Mao in 1972 at the behest of his NSA Kissinger, it had less to do with US–China relations and more to exploit the fault lines that plagued Beijing and Moscow at the time. The post-Mao era leadership in Beijing was clever enough to exploit this opening offered on a platter by the American leadership. Deng Xiaoping seized the opportunity and landed in Texas in 1979, donning a cowboy hat. Deng's decision to ditch a fellow communist country in favour of a capitalist enemy, whom Mao once described as a 'paper tiger' and whose leader he described as the 'most reactionary person in the world,' was based on a desire to hitch his country's wagon to that country's huge and insatiable consumer market.[23] [24] China's neighbours such as Japan, South Korea and Taiwan were already there, reaping profits in billions of dollars by servicing the American consumer markets.

The Chinese were clever players. They exploited the Cold War compulsions of the US leadership while not completely ignoring their ideological siblings in the post-Soviet Russian Federation. Thus, while liberally making promises to the American leaders about their sincerity in pursuing an open market economy, Deng's successor in Zhongnanhai, Jiang Zemin, quietly recuperated the relationship with Russia in the 1990s. Idiomatically speaking, China wanted to have its cake and eat it too. When China joined the WTO in 2001, courtesy the large-heartedness of Clinton, and rapidly emerged as an economic and trading power, the two countries—the US and China—walked into what the renowned American political scientist Graham T. Allison called the 'Thucydides's Trap'.[25]

In his book *Destined for War: Can America and China Escape Thucydides's Trap*, Allison argues that war between a 'reigning' and a 'rising' power is tough to avoid. He points to the 'natural, inevitable discombobulation that occurs when a rising power threatens to displace a ruling power...[and] when a rising power threatens to displace a ruling power, the resulting structural stress makes a violent clash the rule, not the exception,' he writes. He observed that of the sixteen historical occasions when a presumptive power challenged an established one, no less than twelve led to war.[26]

The term immediately captured the attention and imagination of American political commentators, who began to use it liberally in the context of US–China relations. Some scholars try to refute the thesis of inevitable war by pointing to the strong bilateral trade and economic ties between the two countries and the robust governmental mechanisms that allow issues to be solved through negotiations. Bilateral trade between the two countries has crossed a record $760 billion in 2023, raising hopes that after all, the two countries cannot afford a war.

However, not everyone agrees. China's concerted build-up of

military strength, its bellicose behaviour in the oceans around it, and the rise of nationalist rhetoric domestically have led many to conclude that war is inevitable. Mike Minihan, a (now retired) US Air Force general, was quoted as warning his troops, 'My gut tells me we will fight in 2025.' 'I hope I am wrong,' he wrote in an internal memo to the leadership of the US Air Force's 110,000-strong Air Mobility Command, but Chinese President Xi Jinping had 'secured his third term and set his war council in October 2022. Taiwan's presidential elections are in 2024 and will offer Xi a reason. The United States presidential elections are in 2024 and will offer Xi a distracted America. Xi's team, reason and opportunity are all aligned for 2025.' The subject of the memo read, 'February 2023 Orders in Preparation for—The Next Fight.' Minihan directed troops to undergo a monthly readiness progression, including ordering personnel to 'consider their personal affairs' and 'fire a clip into a 7-meter target with the full understanding that unrepentant lethality matters most. Aim for the head.' When the memo was leaked on social media and became the subject of heated debate, the Pentagon immediately disowned Minihan's comments, stating that they were 'not representative of the department's view on China.' The Chinese were clearly unimpressed by Minihan's daring rhetoric. The CCP's mouthpiece, the *Global Times*, angrily dismissed Minihan's memo, labelling it 'reckless and provocative'.[27]

Minihan's comments were the latest in a series of such statements emanating from the military and political leadership of the American establishment over the last decade or so. There is broader unanimity in Western strategic circles over the inevitability of a conflict in the SCS over the future of Taiwan, which many believe will be annexed by China by 2027 at the latest.

In January 2023, the US House of Representatives voted to establish a select committee to assess the military, economic and technological challenges posed by China, launching an intense campaign against the rising power. The vote received the overwhelming support of 365 votes in favour to 65 votes against, and a house panel was created under the leadership of Representative Mike Gallagher, a member of the Republican Party and well-known China hawk from Wisconsin. 'There is bipartisan consensus that the era of trusting Communist China is over,' Republican House Speaker Kevin McCarthy told legislators.[28]

Like the Cold War of the last century, an aggressive arms race started between the US and China, causing military bills in both countries to skyrocket. The rise in defence spending in the US is comparable to a similar increase the country witnessed in the 1970s and 1980s during the peak of the last Cold War. The US Senate Appropriations Committee had sanctioned a record-high $825 billion for the defence budget for 2024. That was more than the military budgets of the next nine countries combined.[29] Indeed, the Ukraine war was also a major consideration, and a substantial part of this spending would go towards that war. However, the US is also actively beefing up its allies in Europe and Asia, such as NATO, the Quad and AUKUS, with the aim of countering the growing Chinese influence. In January 2023, US President Joe Biden and Japanese Prime Minister Fumio Kishida agreed to renew cooperation on thwarting any potential threats from space, opening up uninhabited islands for joint military drills, and reconfiguring US troop deployment on Japan's Okinawa Island by opening a new $8 billion military base in Guam.[30]

McCarthyism Redux

In the 1950s, the US was overtaken by an intense paranoia about the spread of communism in the world. It was known as the Second Red Scare and also as McCarthyism, named after Joseph McCarthy, a Republican senator from Wisconsin. McCarthy was a maverick anti-communist scaremonger who made serious allegations about communist infiltration into federal agencies, universities, and even Hollywood. His wild allegations had gripped the nation like wildfire for nearly a decade after the Second World War. They led to the harassment of hundreds of

American citizens, including public officials, academics and film personalities. McCarthy's allegations proved a hoax in 1954, and he was censured but his propaganda acquired the cynical epithet 'McCarthyism'.

There is an element of similar paranoia in the US administration today, although not as strong and scurrilous as the McCarthyism of the 1950s. In early February 2023, the US agencies were awakened by the news that a suspected Chinese spy balloon had been spotted over American airspace. President Biden was preparing to leave for Kyiv, the Ukrainian capital. Secretary of State Blinken was preparing to board a flight to Beijing. The floating Chinese balloon forced Biden to delay his departure, while Blinken had to cancel his visit altogether. As the world watched in dismay, a US Air Force F-16 fighter jet was dispatched to shoot down the balloon off the coast of South Carolina. Paranoid agencies shot down three more such flying objects over the next few days, before coyly announcing that they had found no evidence of a connection between these objects and China.

By then, the Cold War battalions and balloon warriors were already out on the streets. New York Democratic Senator Kirsten Gillibrand speculated that the balloon was 'a test to see what the US would do' and complained bitterly that China's leader Xi Jinping was 'bent on a world war'. Not to be left behind her political rivals, Republican presidential candidate Nikki Haley triumphantly declared to her supporters that 'Communist China will end up on the ash heap of history'.[31]

The Chinese leadership was as amused as it was annoyed. When US Secretary of Defence Lloyd Austin tried to call his Chinese counterpart, Wei Fenghe, after the balloon incident, he was rebuffed. China saw this uproar as a sign of America's weakness. Wang Yi described the shooting down of the balloon as 'borderline hysterical and an utter misuse of military force'.[32]

When he met Blinken in Munich in mid-February 2023, he characterized the US response as 'absurd and hysterical', calling it another expression of American aggression and claiming, jarringly, that America's first instinct was to shoot something down just because it looked Chinese. Sending a jet to destroy a flying object was an overreaction that revealed American weakness, he said. 'There are many balloons from many countries in the sky. Do you want to down each and every one of them?' Wang asked, urging the United States 'not to do such preposterous things simply to divert attention from its own domestic problems.'[33]

China, for its part, is quietly but aggressively rebuilding its military capabilities—on land, in the air, at sea, in space and in cyberspace. According to US Navy predictions, the Chinese Navy will grow by almost 40 per cent over the next fifteen years. The US Department of Defence had projected that China would quadruple its nuclear stockpile to build at least 1,000 warheads by 2030.[34] The intimacy between the defence establishments of China and Russia is growing stronger with each passing year. The two countries are holding joint military drills in the East China Sea in the vicinity of Japan and Taiwan. Beijing is also reportedly opening new military bases in countries like Cambodia in Asia and Equatorial Guinea in Africa.[35]

The Thucydides's Trap is real. And so is the Cold War 2.0. One area where the trap looked so obvious was semiconductor chip manufacturing. After Xi announced the 'Made in China 2025' programme in 2015, China focused more and more on the indigenization of semiconductor manufacturing production lines. Soon, the strategic community in Washington realized that China was aiming to become self-reliant in the most advanced technological areas like AI, robotics and bitcoins. Advanced semiconductor chips are a critical necessity for China to succeed in this endeavour. However, China's Semiconductor Manufacturing International Corporation (SMIC) possessed the technological capability to manufacture forty-nanometre-size chips only at that time, while the world's leading semiconductor manufacturer, Taiwan Semiconductor Manufacturing Corporation Limited (TSMC), was already producing six-nanometre chips that were used in advanced AI applications.[36]

One of the early decisions of the Biden administration was to put the Chinese company SMIC on the sanctions list, denying it access to advanced chips that American companies like Nvidia were manufacturing through TSMC. Then came the CHIPS and Science Act (2022), passed by the US Congress in August of the same year, which allocated massive funding to bring advanced chip manufacturing back to the US through various incentives.[37] In other words, the US tried to deny China access to advanced chips at one level while trying to bring chip manufacturing from Taiwan to its own territory. During the Cold War, the Americans went to great lengths to deny the Soviets access to raw materials. The new Cold War will be about denying access to semiconductor chips.

'In the fall of 2022, (Jake) Sullivan began laying out the strategy in a series of public speeches. The concept, he said, was to erect a "high fence" around "a small yard", cutting China off from a handful of carefully selected technologies that were critical to fulfilling its military ambitions,' wrote *New York Times* columnist David Sanger in 'New Cold Wars: China's Rise, Russia's Invasion, and America's Struggle to Defend the West.'[38] Mark Rutte, prime minister of the Netherlands, was secretly summoned to Washington, D.C., and warned that the Dutch company ASML, which manufactures lithography machines, should be told not to sell its advanced machines to China.[39]

The Chinese were furious. 'Western countries, led by the United States, have implemented all-round containment, encirclement and suppression of China, which has brought unprecedented severe challenges to our country's development,' Xi complained bitterly.[40]

However, Thucydides's Trap didn't help American policymakers. Weeks before the CHIPS Act was passed in 2022, news broke that SMIC had produced a 7-nanometre chip used in cryptocurrency mining. A year later, Huawei introduced a new mobile phone in 2023 that used the same chip. The US couldn't do much except for the CIA claiming that China had stolen this technology from TSMC.

Race for Rare Earths

In early 2024, Jennifer Granholm, US Secretary of Energy, told the media that America was 'very concerned' about China's grip over the global supply chains for critical minerals. 'It's one of the pieces of the supply chain that we're very concerned about in the United States. We do not want to be over-reliant on countries whose values we may not share,' Granholm stated.[41]

China is the undisputed leader in global supply chains for critical minerals such as rare earth elements (REEs), controlling over 70 per cent of the supply. Rare earth elements are not really rare, but the chemical processes to extract and purify them are so far only mastered by a handful of companies. Chinese companies are far ahead of their American, Australian, Indian and other counterparts in this respect.

The REEs comprise 17 (15 commercially relevant) metals and minerals, including four important ones: neodymium, praseodymium, dysprosium and terbium. Due to their use in the manufacture of permanent magnets, these four REEs were projected to account for 98 per cent of the global market by 2030. Rare earth elements are crucial for our contemporary way of life. Every piece of modern technology, from mobile phones to windmills, from fighter jets and submarines to electric vehicles, and from camera lenses to television screens, relies on these elements. China accelerated its foray into the critical minerals market in the mid-1980s under the guidance of Deng Xiaoping, who famously said, 'The Middle East has oil. China has rare earths.'[42] That country is far ahead in mining, stockpiling, processing and supplying REEs to the world today. Many American companies also depend on supplies of REEs from China.

The world realized between 2010 and 2012 that such dominance by China in the supply chains of critical minerals could lead to serious crises when a maritime dispute between the Japanese Coast Guard and a Chinese fishing vessel in the Senkaku Islands area led to China suddenly halting the supply of REEs to the

Japanese market in 2012. In the following two years, prices rose by up to 500 per cent, primarily driven by speculation, forcing the Western world to devise plans to counter Chinese dominance in the field. There was a major mine in California, the Mountain Pass mine, where the mining of REEs was shut down by American companies in 2001 due to low prices and environmental concerns. To counter China's near monopoly, the US government authorized the resumption of mining there in 2014. Within a decade, the Californian mine became a crucial source of REEs, contributing close to a 15 per cent share in the global market.[43]

As the world entered the new frontier era of digital, space and AI technologies, the race for critical minerals also heated up, from South America to Africa to Central Asia. Even in Arctic territories like Greenland, China is investing heavily to take control of REE mining. China's REE ambitions continue through initiatives such as the National Plan for Mineral Resources, which promotes global collaborations with other countries and a shift from total reliance on domestic process capability. The US, which currently holds a 15 per cent market share in REEs, is also keen on closing the gap through strategic partnerships with countries such as Australia and Canada. In Central Asia, Kazakhstan has emerged as a major player due to its rare earths production, which has led to severe jostling between the US and China for control of its resources. The same applies to countries in Latin America and Africa. In Asia and the Indo-Pacific region, competition for military and strategic alliances is leading to a serious Cold War-like situation.

New Axis Powers?

As Asian centrality became a new reality, which we will discuss in later chapters, the theatre of this new Cold War also shifted to Eurasia and the Indo-Pacific. In this most happening region, the US doesn't have many new allies, apart from traditional ones like Japan and the Philippines. India has indeed moved closer to them in the first two decades of the twenty-first century. Leaving behind decades of what External Affairs Minister (EAM) S. Jaishankar described as 'hesitation of history',[44] India decisively tilted its foreign policy in favour of the US when Prime Minister Atal Bihari Vajpayee told his audience at the Asiatic Society in New York in 2000 that India and the US were 'natural allies'.[45] More than a decade later, Prime Minister Dr Manmohan Singh described the relationship as a 'defining partnership' in the joint statement issued at the end of President Obama's visit to Delhi.[46] Prime Minister Narendra Modi went a step further and declared that 'India–USA relationship will not only shape the destiny of our two nations but also that of the world.'[47] However, India continues to uphold its principle of strategic autonomy when confronted with the geopolitics of the new Cold War.

On the other hand, China, once an ally of the US in the fight against the Soviet Union, is now its main adversary alongside countries such as Russia, North Korea and Iran. The war in Ukraine has strengthened relations between America's adversaries—Russia and China. In the wake of the New Year in 2024, Russia launched a massive missile attack on the Ukrainian cities of Kyiv and Kharkiv, killing and injuring dozens of civilians and destroying significant installations. The attack had uniquely showcased the axis of anti-American forces. Technology fitted with the weapons used by the Russian soldiers came from China, the missiles were of North Korean origin, and Iran supplied drones. Russia's war machine against NATO forces has been reinforced by these three countries since the Ukraine war broke out.

In the early years of the Second World War, the fighting was mainly confined to Europe, while the US was merely a spectator from afar. Even Japan's entry into the war alongside the Germans was not momentous for the US until Pearl Harbor was attacked in 1941. But now the new Axis powers had America as the singular target on their radar.

Recall the statement issued by President Xi and President Putin in Beijing in February 2022, just a few months after the

Ukraine war began. 'The new interstate relations between Russia and China are superior to the political and military alliances of the Cold War era. Friendship between the two states has no limits, there are no "forbidden" areas of cooperation,' the two leaders declared. The reference to the Cold War era cannot be missed.[48]

After the invasion of Czechoslovakia by Soviet forces in 1970, the General Secretary of the Soviet Communist Party, Leonid Brezhnev, justified the use of force in Prague, arguing that Moscow had the right to intervene in any country where capitalist forces threatened a communist government. This became known in later years as the Brezhnev Doctrine as the Soviets continued their repressive interventions in many Eastern European capitals.

During their meeting in Beijing, Xi and Putin announced a new Brezhnev Doctrine, which states: 'Russia and China stand against attempts by external forces to undermine security and stability in their common adjacent regions, intend to counter interference by outside forces in the internal affairs of sovereign countries under any pretext, oppose colour revolutions and will increase cooperation in the aforementioned areas.'[49] In the old doctrine, the Soviet Union was alone; now it is the joint power of Russia and China. The old doctrine insisted that no country should leave the Soviet camp; now Russia and China insist that no country anywhere near them can join the democratic, in their sense, pro-American camp.

Russia has moved closer to China in the last decade after it was expelled from the group of eight countries, the G8, following the annexation of Crimea in 2014. China quickly seized the opportunity and increased its trade relations with the beleaguered Russia, which was reeling under Western sanctions. Its share of Russian external trade doubled from ten to twenty per cent in the seven years between 2014 and 2021. Russia became China's leading supplier of weapons and ammunition, supplying 83 per cent of China's weapons between 2018 and 2022.[50] The Chinese military owes much to the Russian defence industry for its enhanced air defence, anti-ship and anti-submarine capabilities, which have catapulted China to the position of a formidable maritime power over the past decade.

The Cold War 2.0 is the result of this cooperation among China, Iran, North Korea and Russia, who have a shared opposition to the US-led world order and a deep-rooted antagonism for the principles it stood for, like democracy, human rights and liberal order. They also feel common suffocation from the West's efforts at stifling them in their core interests, such as Ukraine, Taiwan or nuclearization. They see the presence of the US and its allies in the neighbourhood, including the stationing of naval assets and nuclear weapons, as the primary roadblock in establishing their own spheres of influence: the SCS and beyond for China; the CIS countries and Eastern Europe—the 'near abroad'—for Russia; and countries like Iraq, Lebanon, Syria, Yemen and others for Iran.

We are in the phase of the escalating Cold War 2.0. The declining share of global GDP, narrowing military capabilities, reducing the gap in technological supremacy, and waning diplomatic influence of the US vis-à-vis China are emboldening the rival China-led axis. There is renewed confidence in the Chinese leadership that replacing the US as the hegemon of the world was no longer just a desirable 'great China Dream', but a feasible one.

One can notice it in Xi's articulation, who has attained complete control of the party and government since 2018. Under his predecessors, China always liked to present itself to the rest of the world as a regional power and an emerging economy. Both Jiang Zemin and Hu Jintao spoke more about exerting influence in the 'neighbourhood'. They strictly adhered to the dictum advocated by Deng Xiaoping of 'Hide your strength, bide your time.' Under Xi, the vocabulary has changed radically. Words like 'global' and 'connectivity' are all over in the Chinese lexicon. There is a renewed vigour and urgency to introduce the CCP's terminology, such as BRI, shared future of mankind, and inclusive multilateralism to the world stage.

Is there any mitigation to this situation? Can Cold War 2.0 be averted? Two flashpoints in Eurasia have already exacerbated Cold War politics into a real war. One is the Ukraine conflict between Russia and NATO; the other is the conflict in Gaza between Israel and Hamas, fast escalating into a war between Israel and Iran. China has emerged as a crucial player in both theatres. Its close links with Russia are well known. Its involvement in the Arab conflict is also increasing.

China Goes Global

After the thaw he brokered between Iran and Saudi Arabia in 2023, when Wang Yi described his country as a 'kind and trustworthy mediator' and boasted of being 'a constructive player in promoting proper handling of global heated issues,'[51] many in the West dismissed it as empty rhetoric. Global flashpoints, from Ukraine to Gaza, are not easy to resolve, many thought.

One year after the intervention in the Middle East, however, China achieved another coup. Wang Yi mobilized the leaders of 14 different factions of the Palestinian movement, including Hamas and Fatah, in Beijing in July 2024 and published a declaration unanimously approved by all of them, the so-called Beijing Declaration,[52] which promised to end divisions within the movement and strengthen Palestinian national unity. Wang Yi proposed a three-step solution to the Palestinian conflict. The first step was to implement a comprehensive ceasefire in the Gaza Strip as soon as possible and to provide humanitarian assistance. The second step was to maintain the principle of 'Palestinians governing Palestine'. And the third was the two-state solution. 'The international community should support the parties in taking the three steps in real earnest,' Wang appealed.[53]

The declaration may remain on paper for several reasons. Firstly, keeping all factions under the umbrella of the Palestine Liberation Organization (PLO) is not easy. However, Wang claimed that 'the PLO is the sole legitimate representative of all the Palestinian people.'[54] Several efforts were made in the past to unite them, led by Egypt in 2011 and Algeria in 2022. However, these efforts remained unsuccessful.

Secondly, the US and Israel consider Hamas a terrorist organization and reject any proposal to legitimize it. Thirdly, an even more difficult part of the declaration was the creation of a 'truly independent Palestinian state in accordance with relevant UN resolutions,' as Wang claimed.[55] Israel swiftly rejected Beijing's declaration, insisting that 'Hamas rule will be crushed.'[56] Israeli Foreign Minister Israel Katz also dismissed any proposals to allow the Palestinian Authority to take control of Gaza. However, the fact remains that by firmly embedding itself in the world's most protracted conflict, China is going to be a thorn in America's flesh in the coming years.

Interestingly, around the time of the signing of the Beijing Declaration, Wang also got busy holding talks with the visiting foreign minister of Ukraine, Dmytro Kuleba, about resolving the Ukraine conflict. Wang insisted that China believed in bringing the warring parties to the negotiating table, claiming, 'We support all efforts conducive to peace and stand ready to continue to play a constructive role for a ceasefire and resumption of peace talks.'[57] Kuleba, on his first visit to China since the outbreak of the war, responded positively, stating that China could play a significant role in pursuing a just and stable peace in the Ukraine crisis and that Ukraine was prepared to conduct dialogue and negotiations with Russia.

Irrespective of the outcome, China's proactive moves indicate an essential shift in its foreign policy. While the world has entered the phase of the escalating Cold War 2.0, the Chinese leadership is demonstrating renewed confidence in its ability to replace the US as the hegemon.

As China goes global, the world must brace for its dominance over the Global South and the imposition of its worldview in several countries. The Cold War 2.0 is heating up.

Danger Zone

The next major flashpoint will be Taiwan. For Xi, the unification of Taiwan with the Chinese Mainland is a 'historic mission', as suggested by him during an important address to the CCP on its centenary in July 2021. Xi further described resolving the Taiwan question as an 'unshakeable commitment of the party' [and] 'a shared aspiration of all the sons and daughters of the Chinese nation.'[58]

China has recently stepped up its coercive measures against Taiwan. The Chinese army's intrusions into Taiwan's air-defence zone and its war games around the island nation by deploying a large number of warships were a clear signal of Xi's determination to challenge not only Taiwan but also the US. In January 2024, he sent 33 warplanes and seven combat ships toward Taiwan, just as Foreign Minister Wang was holding talks with the US NSA Sullivan about the island's future.[59] Despite protestations from the West and its neighbours, China went ahead to take complete control of the SCS area and is threatening to block the Taiwan Strait to cripple the country's economy and force it to surrender.

The big question is not whether there will be a conflict over Taiwan or not. According to a report by the Centre for Strategic and International Studies (CSIS), most of the China experts in the US believe that the Taiwan Strait will erupt soon.[60] However, the question is how the US would react in the event of such a conflict. China may or may not engage in a major confrontation. However, the calculation in Beijing appears to be that the US would not be in a position to prevent it given the preoccupation in Gaza and Ukraine. Even most Taiwanese seem to think that the US cannot be entirely depended upon in the event of a war with China. They remember how America dumped their country in 1979 by ending diplomatic ties in favour of greener pastures in China.

Despite its tall talk, the US has not yet fully honoured its commitments to Taiwan. There is a massive backlog of

$14 billion worth of military equipment sales to Taiwan since 2017 that remains unfulfilled. Following a meeting with Xi on the West Coast of the US in September 2023, Biden told the media that he was 'not looking for conflict' with China. 'I am looking to manage this competition responsibly,' he boasted.[61]

Whichever way it goes, the Taiwan Straits question will be the next hot conflict between the two superpowers. The silent question is: Are there ways to avert Cold War 2.0? If we stop thinking of Cold War 1.0 only as a period of disaster, it may provide some answers. Effective diplomacy is one such answer. In 2019, William Burns hailed the Cold War 1.0 as 'a golden age of American diplomacy.'[62] He was referring to the resolution of the Cuban Missile Crisis in 1962 through a top-secret back-channel quid pro quo and a détente engineered by the Nixon–Kissinger duo with the Soviet Union.

There is a need for a mindset change in the US leadership. Washington should accept the reality that the world has entered multipolarity. Burns was forthright, bluntly saying, 'The United States is no longer the only big kid on the geopolitical block.' NSA Sullivan coined the term 'managed coexistence' for US–China relations, which the policy community needs to imagine and accept.

However, such an effort cannot be one-sided. During the last Cold War, all three Soviet presidents after Stalin—Khrushchev, Brezhnev and Gorbachev—responded positively to American overtures. Would the Chinese leadership, high on their success in economy and military build-up, be willing to give up what has come to be known as the wolf-warrior diplomacy and reciprocate the goodwill gestures if they came?

In the Soviet Union, the Gorbachev era proved to be a game-changer. Despite President Ronald Reagan's famously provocative speeches in 1983—the Evil Empire speech and the announcement of the Strategic Defence Initiative, famously known as 'Star Wars'—Gorbachev realized that the Soviet economy was in no position to spend 20 per cent of its GDP on defence, as against the US spending of a mere five to six per cent. After watching a documentary film about nuclear destruction, he is said to have told his friends in Moscow that 'nuclear weapons must be abolished.'[63]

In an interview in 1985, Ronald Reagan was asked if he liked Gorbachev. In his typical light-hearted manner, Reagan replied that he had no need to present Gorbachev with a friendship ring. Then came his profound observation:

> It isn't necessary that we love or even like each other. It's only necessary that we are willing to recognize that for the good of the people we represent, on this side of the ocean and over there everyone will be better off if we can come to some decisions about the threat of war. We're the only two nations in the world, I believe, that can start a world war. And we're the only two that can prevent it. And I think that's a great responsibility to all of mankind, and we'd better take it seriously.[64]

When Reagan stood on the free side of the Brandenburg Gate in West Berlin on a sunny day in June 1987 and said to the Soviet leader in his inimitable style, 'Mr Gorbachev! Tear down this wall,' Gorbachev responded positively.[65] The Berlin Wall came down within two years, and it took another two years for the Soviet Union to collapse and Cold War 1.0 to end.

But the mute question is: Will China ever have its Gorbachev?

5

POWER IN MULTIPOLARITY

When President Nixon went about cultivating China in the 1970s, his aim was not only to counter the growing influence of the Soviet Union in Asia and Eastern Europe but also to foster a world where several countries rose as important powers. Speaking to *Time* magazine in 1972, Nixon thoughtfully argued that 'I think it will be a safer world and a better world if we have a strong, healthy United States, Europe, the Soviet Union, China and Japan each balancing the other.'[1]

Nixon can thus be credited with invoking the idea of multipolarity for the first time in the last century. However, the concept came into greater circulation only after the collapse of the Soviet Union in 1991.

This political development led some American political thinkers to believe that the world had entered a phase of unipolarity. Francis Fukuyama was the first prominent voice to articulate this idea. In his 1989 article in *The National Interest* magazine, Fukuyama argued that the world may be witnessing 'not just the end of the Cold War or the passing of a particular period of post-war history, but the end of history as such: that is, the end point of mankind's ideological evolution and the universalization of Western liberal democracy as the final form of human government.'[2]

Later, in his 1992 book *The End of History and the Last Man*, written in the immediate aftermath of the dismemberment of the Soviet Union, Fukuyama expanded his argument and concluded that the collapse of the Soviet Union as a pole was an indication that the socio-cultural evolution and political struggle of humanity had reached its end point. He suggested that liberal democracies and free market capitalism would be the only way forward for any future government. In other words, Fukuyama insisted that the American way would be the only way for the future of mankind.[3]

Fukuyama's thesis invited countless serious rebuttals from the community of political and social thinkers, forcing him to change his position a few years later. One such significant contestation of Fukuyama's thesis came from Samuel Huntington, who was not only his guru but also a celebrated academic, political philosopher and author. Huntington authored a book in 1996 with the controversial title *The Clash of Civilizations and the Remaking of World Order*. While Fukuyama predicted unipolarity as the future of the post-Cold War world, Huntington argued that far from being unipolar, mankind's future was fraught with the rise of many different cultures and civilizations, eventually leading to massive conflict between them. He predicted that this conflict would pose a serious challenge to the American liberal democratic order. After Nixon, Huntington was the second prominent American voice to suggest that the world would become multipolar.

The developments of later years proved Huntington right. Until the Soviet Union existed, the world was essentially bipolar, with the US at the other pole. However, in the decades following the collapse of the Soviet Union, many different forces were unleashed, including both state and non-state actors. These included not only countries such as China, Russia and Iran, which posed a challenge to the US, but also heteropolar forces like Islamic terrorism.

Five decades after Nixon's statement and three decades after Huntington's book, the American leadership is still grappling with the question of multipolarity. Writings of the nineteenth-century French historian Alexis de Tocqueville and his twentieth-century American counterpart Seymour Martin Lipset proposed that the American nation was exceptional for its distinctive ideology based on ideals like liberty, egalitarianism, democracy and republicanism. This sense of 'American exceptionalism', coupled with the country's rise as the dominant economic, technological and military power in the world over the last eight decades, led many American political thinkers to dismiss the idea of a multipolar reality of the twenty-first century as a chimaera and an exaggeration.

Unfortunately, the Americans are not the only ones with this mindset of exceptionalism. The other leading power of the twenty-first century, China, nurses a sense of historical superiority over the other nations of the world. The official name of the PRC in Chinese language is *Zhōnghuá Rénmín Gònghéguó* in which *Zhōnghuá* means 'central beauty'. This idea of 'centrality' dominates Chinese thinking. Zhonggua—another name used to describe China, literally means the 'Middle Kingdom'. Contemporary Chinese scholars tend to explain the concept of the Middle Kingdom in terms of ancient geography, when Chinese rulers believed they were at the centre of the world. However, as a cultural idea, it infuses a sense of superiority, and when coupled with the other concept of *Tiānmìng*—the 'Mandate of Heaven'—it becomes problematic. China's dominant behaviour in the world can be linked to these two concepts of the Middle Kingdom and the Mandate of Heaven. This explains why not all scholars in both the US and China subscribe to the idea of multipolarity.

Between Polycentrism and Bipolarity

In the late 1990s, when the Americans were revelling in their idea of unipolarity, Russia and China came together at the UN to propose the concept of multipolarity. At the time, China was still a developing nation under the relatively mild-mannered leadership of Jiang Zemin. On 15 May 1997, the Permanent Representative of the Russian Federation, Sergei Lavrov (the current foreign minister), and his Chinese counterpart, Wang Xuexian, addressed a letter to the UN Secretary-General, Kofi Annan. In this letter, they referred to a joint declaration adopted by the leaders of both countries on 23 April 1997 during Zemin's state visit to the Russian Federation. This joint declaration spoke of promoting the 'multi-polarization of the world and the establishment of a new international order.'

'The Parties believe that profound changes in international relations have taken place at the end of the twentieth century. The Cold War is over. The bipolar system has vanished. A positive trend towards a multipolar world is gaining momentum and relations between major states, including former Cold War adversaries, are changing. Regional economic cooperation organizations are showing considerable vitality. Diversity in the political, economic and cultural development of all countries is becoming the norm, and the role played by the forces in favour of peace and broad-based international cooperation is expanding. A growing number of countries are beginning to recognize the need for mutual respect, equality and mutual advantage—but not for hegemony and power politics—and for dialogue and cooperation but not for confrontation and conflict. The establishment of a peaceful, stable, just and rational new international political and economic order is becoming a pressing need of the times and an imperative of historical development,' the letter highlighted.[4]

The Russian leadership continued this theme of multipolarity afterwards. During a state visit to India in December 1998, the chairman of the government of the Russian Federation, Yevgeny Primakov, talked about multipolar politics with his counterpart, Indian Prime Minister Atal Bihari Vajpayee. The joint press statement issued at the end of the visit stated: 'While reiterating their commitment to the ideals of peace, democracy, the rule of law, non-violence and secularism, both sides proceed from the understanding that it is necessary to create a multipolar world based on the sovereign equality of all states, democratic values and justice.'[5]

During the visit, Primakov also proposed a plan for trilateral cooperation between Russia, China and India to promote global multipolarity. Interestingly, a decade later, the three countries got together to form a crucial non-Western group called RIC, which was later expanded to BRICS with the inclusion of Brazil and South Africa. The Russian leadership, from Putin to Lavrov, rightly credits Primakov for his outstanding role in developing the concept of a multipolar world.

However, the Russian leadership was never happy about the collapse of the Soviet Union. The death of Mikhail Gorbachev, the last president of the Soviet Union before its dissolution, in August 2022 gave some of them the opportunity to vent their frustration about the events that happened under Gorbachev. In his tribute to the departed leader, Putin referred to the collapse of the Soviet Union as 'the biggest geopolitical catastrophe of the century.' Although Putin generously praised Gorbachev for heading the country 'at a time of difficult, dramatic changes,' his colleagues couldn't hide their disdain for the man they felt was singularly responsible for the destruction of their glory. 'As a Christian, I mourn… Just like I mourn the great country that was broken apart by processes of perestroika and the new thinking, which helped those who wanted to wipe the USSR from the political map of the world,' commented State Duma deputy Leonid Slutsky bitterly.[6]

Primakov's proposition of multipolarity relieved their bitterness. Others, such as China and Iran, saw it as a way of rejecting American claims to unipolarity; if not for anything else, at least for some vicarious satisfaction. On the other hand, the American leadership, which had bred on a diet of unipolarity for a decade, felt offended by this new fad of multipolarity.

As the idea gained traction among the leading powers of the developing world, the US leadership jumped to the rescue of its unipolar authority. Condoleezza Rice, the NSA in George W. Bush's administration, wrote a scathing article in 2003 criticizing the concept of multipolarity, calling it a 'theory of rivalry' that could lead to conflict and distract from collective global challenges. She argued that 'the future of international relations should be based on the unity of values, not on the balance of power.'[7]

Two decades after Primakov's policy initiative on multipolarity, President Putin declared in October 2016 in a speech at the annual meeting of the Valdai Discussion Club in Sochi: 'I certainly hope that…the world really will become more multipolar and that the views of all actors in the international community will be taken into account.'[8]

Not only the Russian leadership but also many other political leaders, diplomats and experts in international politics are now arguing about the world becoming multipolar. Prominent among them is Emmanuel Macron, the president of France. On the flight back from China in April 2023, after holding lengthy one-on-one talks with President Xi, Macron ruffled many feathers when he rejected the idea that France ought to follow America's lead in world politics, especially in matters concerning China and Taiwan. He argued that the international community would be better served by a France that can say 'no' to friends and foes alike. He warned against Europe becoming a vassal in a world dominated by Washington and Beijing and instead advocated for greater European strategic autonomy. He believed that Europe could become a 'third superpower' alongside the US and China.[9]

Several others, including German Chancellor Olaf Scholz, Brazilian President Luiz Inácio Lula da Silva and UN Secretary-General Antonio Guterres, endorsed the idea of multipolarity. Chancellor Scholz argued in his National Security Strategy document that 'the global order is changing; new centres of power are emerging; the world in the twenty-first century is multipolar.' The document claimed that the 'international and security environment is becoming more multipolar and less stable.'[10]

Josep Borrell, EU's high representative of foreign affairs and security policy, said in an article that the world has entered 'what we today could call "complex multipolarity".' Borrell wrote:

Let us be clear here. The development of Europe as a political pole is not contrary to the defence of multilateralism, but a basic condition for its effective defence. In the first place, multilateralism is above all a methodology designed to regulate world relations on stable, transparent principles that apply equally to all, regardless of their size. This means that regardless of whether you are a smaller country or a great power, the rules are the same. However, as George Orwell noted in *Animal Farm*, we know that even if states are formally equal, some are more equal than others; multilateralism is not a magic wand. However, it can mitigate the power differences that exist between states by binding them by common rules. That is why Europe and the vast majority of states worldwide endorse it.[11]

The business world is also adopting the formulation and evaluation of business strategies. In August 2023, Morgan Stanley published a strategy paper titled 'Charting strategies for a multipolar world'. 'The transition to a multipolar world requires a de-risking of global supply chains and a refocus on research and development as companies and nations compete for emerging technologies,' it cautioned the business world.[12]

The World Economic Forum borrowed the phrase in its flagship programmes. It announced the 2022 annual summit with the headline: 'World Economic Forum Annual Meeting 2022 returns to Davos to address unprecedented geo-economic challenges impacting a multipolar world'. Klaus Schwab, the octogenarian founder and executive director of the forum, explained that due to pandemics and wars, a new global situation is emerging 'characterized by an emerging multipolar world' and explained that the annual meeting is the first summit where 'nearly 2,500 leaders from politics, business, civil society and media come together in person, demonstrates the need for a trusted, informal and action-oriented global platform to confront the issues in a crisis-driven world.'[13]

Centripetal vs. Centrifugal Forces

For many, multipolarity is about ending the West's domination and building a world where countries have the choice to act according to their free will. Many also see it as a better option than bipolarity, the price for which Europe and other countries paid during the Cold War of the last century and a probability that cannot be denied in this century either. Countries like India and France call it 'strategic autonomy'.

While the number of protagonists for multipolarity is growing, many believe that the idea is flawed and that the world remains unipolar, or at the most, a new form of bipolarity between the US and China will dominate the world. In their opinion, while several middle powers have grown in economic and military size and strength, they are nowhere near as strong as the great powers to challenge them and therefore cannot be equated with the big two. India, Turkey, the EU, Russia, Saudi Arabia, Iran, Brazil and South Africa may have emerged as regional centres of power on different continents, but none of them have the kind of clout that the US or China enjoy, they insist. India may be the fifth-largest economy and the third-largest purchaser of defence equipment in the world, but it lags far behind China and the US in terms of the size of its economy and military. Both are six to ten times the size of India. The same is true for other countries.

However, there is a fundamental flaw and misconception in this argument. The assumption that in a multipolar arrangement, all poles should have equal power is ill-conceived. Different countries can have different strengths, which can make the so-called superpowers helpless. The Korean War in the early 1950s and the Vietnam War in the 1970s are classic examples from history. In Korea, the US forces initially succeeded in pushing the Soviet army back behind the country's national boundaries. But when Stalin cleverly involved China's troops in the battle, the US army found itself in an awkward situation in the face of the sheer overwhelming numbers of the Red Army and was forced to retreat. The end came when the US and the Soviet Union were compelled to agree to divide the country over the 38th parallel into North and South Korea. China was not yet a significant power at this point.

Similarly, in Vietnam, two mighty Western powers—France and the US—were forced to bite the dust by a non-descript communist guerrilla force of Viet Minh over twenty years. The French were the colonizers of Vietnam until they were defeated and driven out by Viet Minh forces under Ho Chi Minh at the Battle of Dien Bien Phu in 1954. In an attempt to contain the growing spread of communism in the region, the US made the suicidal decision to intervene in the country's civil war. President Lyndon Johnson took the disastrous decision of sending tens of thousands of American troops into the country, launching massive, indiscriminate bombing campaigns, killing thousands of innocent civilians and destroying towns and cities. But none of this could derail the campaign of the Viet Cong's communist guerrilla army. By the time the US could finally extricate itself from the war in 1973, 58,000 American soldiers had lost their lives, making the conflict the worst-ever defeat in the history of the US armed forces.[14]

The history of the last few decades is also replete with examples of emerging powers wielding an influence that could put big powers on the backfoot. India's rise is one such example. At the G20 Summit in Bali, Indonesia, in 2022, at the height of tensions between the West and Russia over the Ukraine war, it was India's mediation that helped secure a unanimous statement from the participating countries. Similarly, as chair of the G20 in 2023, India diligently manoeuvred the critical Ukraine war situation by convincing both the Western powers and Russia to take a reasonable position on the G20 declaration. At the UN and other forums, India has pursued an autonomous policy on Ukraine, refusing to join the US and its allies in supporting resolutions against Russia. India's stance has encouraged dozens of countries to refuse to take sides in the conflict and remain neutral in the UN, much to the chagrin of Western powers.

Countries like Russia, Iran and Turkey also hold considerable sway over global geopolitics. In recent years, Turkey has emerged as a key regional power centre in the politics of West Asia. It has been involved in several regional conflicts in recent years, often challenging the big powers. In Syria and Libya, Turkey's military interventions have led to an escalation of tensions with countries such as Saudi Arabia. In the South Caucasus region, Turkey was actively involved in the conflict between Azerbaijan and Armenia, openly supplying weapons to Azerbaijan with the aim of uniting the 'Turkic world'. From the Maldives in the Indian Ocean to Somalia, Somaliland and Ethiopia in the Horn of Africa to Gaza in West Asia, Turkey's footprints cannot be missed.

This phenomenon is best summarized by Emma Ashford and Evan Cooper: 'A multipolar system doesn't require three powers of equal size; it just requires that significant power is concentrated in more than two states. Today, the middle powers—from Japan to India—are significantly more influential than they once were. This is the textbook definition of what some scholars call "unbalanced multipolarity".'[15]

While power asymmetry is real, unbalanced multipolarity is also a geopolitical reality in the world. This means that countries with asymmetric power structures are attempting to exert their power in the world. Some consider it a destabilizing factor, as a multiplicity of power centres would lead to more conflicts and wars in the world. They opine that unipolarity or bipolarity is a better option than the multipolarity of the middle powers. However, the world has entered a stage where power can no longer be defined in terms of economic and military strength alone. Regional powers, which tend to cultivate their neighbours and form minilateral groupings, can emerge as independent power. This kind of multipolarity is what the world is witnessing today.

Ashford and Cooper further explain that their study considered 'a dozen or so different metrics of power across time' and concluded that, based on these indicators, it was clear that although the United States and China are ahead of the pack, 'they also show that economic and military power is accumulating elsewhere, from France to Australia.' The most important point is that unlike the Cold War, when the United States and the Soviet Union controlled the lion's share of economic and military power—even more when their respective alliance blocs were included—today, China and the United States together control a smaller share. One index of military and economic power, for example, suggests that this share has shrunk from around 40 per cent in 1946 to only around 30 per cent today. The share of the world economy controlled by Washington, Moscow and their two alliance blocs was a whopping 88 per cent of global GDP in 1950; today these countries only make up 57 per cent of global GDP. 'This power has diffused elsewhere, moving away from the superpowers toward a variety of capable, dynamic middle powers that will help to shape the international environment in the coming decades,' they write.[16]

Interestingly, many powerful nations competed even in the eighteenth and nineteenth centuries to gain global prominence by colonizing smaller nations. After defeating France in the Napoleonic Wars at the beginning of the eighteenth century, Great Britain emerged as a powerful European nation. However, it was not alone. France, with its significant military power, continued to be an important European nation. Then there was the famous Austro–Hungarian Empire, the multinational empire of Austria and Hungary, which dissolved after the First World War.

Prussia, which became Germany after Bismark's successful unification of neighbouring states, was a significant power, as was the US, which rose to prominence after the Civil War. In Asia, the Ottoman Empire flourished on the one hand, while the Qing dynasty was struggling to keep up the Chinese sovereignty in the East. Japan was also a dominant power in Asia, occupying several countries in its neighbourhood. It colonized Korea from 1910 until the end of the Second World War. The island of Formosa (Taiwan) was under Japanese control from 1895 to 1945. Manchuria, China, the Philippines, Vietnam, Malaysia, Singapore and Burma were also under its rule during different periods before 1945.

In Europe, these great powers initially built functional multilateralism through what is known in history as the 'Concert of Europe'. Major European powers like Austria, France, Prussia, Russia and the United Kingdom met at the Congress of Vienna for a series of diplomatic deliberations to settle post-Napoleonic disputes and work towards long-term peaceful coexistence. Many other European powers, including Spain, Sweden, Portugal and over 200 German states that existed before their unification, also joined the deliberations of the Congress, which took place from September 1814 to June 1815 under the chairmanship of the Austrian diplomat Klemens von Metternich. The Concert of Europe functioned successfully for many decades before border conflicts and ideological disputes led to its dissolution. In any case, the Concert of Europe led to decades of peaceful coexistence between the European powers in the nineteenth century, providing a model for multilateralism in the twentieth century. For today's protagonists of multipolarity, it serves as an example in this century.

In fact, bipolar politics only became a reality after the Second World War and the end of colonization of large parts of the world in the middle of the twentieth century. The number of independent states rose from 35 in 1946 to 127 by the mid-1960s. These newly born independent states lacked the necessary wherewithal to survive due to the colonialist exploitation of their countries. They were forced to depend on the big powers of the day—the US and the Soviet Union. There is no reason to believe that countries would remain weak after six or seven decades of independence. The scenario the world is witnessing today is the re-emergence of multiple countries as strong poles in different parts of the world.

Hobson's Choice

In September 2023, during a talk at the Council on Foreign Relations in New York, External Affairs Minister (EAM) S. Jaishankar insisted that the US 'is adjusting to a multipolar world'.[17] This implies that there continues to be opposition in the US administration to the idea that multiple poles have emerged on the world's geostrategic theatre. To thwart this eventuality, it is trying to re-energize the bloc politics along the lines of the Cold War politics of the last century. Its anti-China coalition is, in a sense, a negation of the concept of multipolarity. Earlier, it used the pro-democracy and anti-terror campaigns to mobilize countries into two opposing blocs. This was to achieve twin objectives through this effort—one, to create a larger coalition against the challenge thrown by the rise of China, which it could not fully cope with as a declining power, and second, to reduce the burden on itself.

This 'with us or against us' approach, credited to George W. Bush after the attack on the Twin Towers, continues to influence sections of the US administration even today.

Not surprisingly, there is a palpable unease in Asia over this 'with me or against me' option being thrust on countries. Former Prime Minister of Singapore Lee Hsien Loong highlighted this dilemma, 'If there are tensions between America and China, we will be asked to pick a side. It may not be direct but you will get the message that: "We would like you to be with us, and are you with us? If not, does that mean you're against us?" And that's to put it gently.' Singapore, however, does not wish to 'pick sides,' he said.[18] He even stressed that countries in Asia shouldn't be offered Hobson's choice of China versus America.[19]

The Ukraine war has shown the limitations of American power and influence. Over the past two years, the number of countries refusing to toe the American line on this issue hovered around 40, including influential ones like India, South Africa, China, Vietnam, Brazil and occasionally even Saudi Arabia. Although the US-led resolutions still secured support from a large number of countries—around 140—the abstentions and opposition mark the rise of poles that are ready to defy the superpower on such a crucial issue.

Also growing is the number of countries that have mastered the art of sailing in both boats. India, for example, is an important partner in the US' Indo-Pacific strategy. Yet, it doesn't hide its engagement with the archenemies of the US, like Russia. In Europe, countries like Germany act as a major bulwark against Russian aggression in Ukraine but continue their close trade partnership with China. In the Middle East, traditional allies such as Saudi Arabia continue to engage with the US on the security front while opening doors to China, recognizing its growing influence in the region. Turkey has reached an agreement with Russia on a Russian-owned and operated nuclear plant in Akkuyu to produce electricity, deferred payments in roubles (not dollars) for imported Russian gas, and allowed Russian companies to acquire shares in Turkish refineries where Russian crude oil is refined into Turkish end products. In other words, Turkey, although remaining a NATO member country, is openly helping Moscow in bypassing Western sanctions.

Ashford and Cooper argue, 'Multipolarity does not render the United States powerless. In fact, it could be a boon to US policymakers. By focusing on leveraging multipolarity to its advantage, the Biden administration can advance US security and sustain America's global role. Multipolarity should not be feared; it should be embraced.'[20]

Power Brokers in a Multipolar World

The bottom line is that multipolarity cannot be wished away. It is a twenty-first-century reality defined by various factors such as energy needs, supply chains, technological disruptions and regional conflicts. The US and China will continue to dominate this order with their economic, military and technological prowess. But there will also be other claimants to leadership roles. The world, including the two big powers, needs to recognize and adapt to it.

India

India will be one of these top claimants. With its impressive economic trajectory of about 8 per cent GDP growth figures, India will soon be the third largest economy in the world and has the potential to reach $7 billion to $10 billion in the next decade. The country's burgeoning young population and growing middle class will make it an attractive destination for global investors if India succeeds in overcoming its domestic fault lines. India has already emerged as a regional leader by building architectures such as SAARC and BIMSTEC with varying degrees of success. In the Indian Ocean Region, India commands enormous respect due to its longstanding cultural and civilizational ties with many countries. Once a leader in the NAM, it now champions the cause of the Global South, attracting substantial traction in Asia and Africa.

Russia

Russia, the superpower of the last century, is raring to return as an influential player in global geopolitics under Putin's leadership. Putin's repeated assertions about the emergence of multipolarity underscore his ambition to position Russia as an important pole. The country has been underperforming for the last three or four decades. Yet its vast land mass continues to be home to unlimited natural resources. The country has the world's largest reserves of natural gas. It is the second largest exporter of natural gas and the third largest exporter of coal. It is also a major producer of metals and minerals such as cobalt, chrome, copper, gold, lead, manganese, nickel, platinum, tungsten and zinc. Its oil reserves are the eighth largest in the world, and it has the largest shale oil reserves in Europe.

Russia's Soviet-era achievements in scientific research are now just glorious history. Yet it continues to win Nobel prizes occasionally. As recently as 2023, Alexey Ekimov was awarded the Nobel Prize in Chemistry. Moreover, it is the world's leading nuclear superpower, with more than 6,000 warheads in its possession and the ability to launch them on land, in the air, and at sea. Despite its political and administrative weaknesses, Russia remains an important middle power that cannot be discounted in any future world order.

European Union

The 27-member EU, the supranational political union founded three decades ago in 1993, looks shaky these days due to increasing internal contradictions. Questions are being raised over its future, especially after the UK's decision to withdraw from it in a woeful Brexit referendum in 2016. Yet, the EU continues to be an important force in the world with its common currency, the euro, and its enormous market size of €14.5 trillion in terms of GDP (total value of all goods and services produced). The EU remains a major force in the world. It accounts for 14 per cent of the world's trade and ranks third after the US and China.[21]

Although the EU is weakened by internal and external contradictions, it found its saviour in the Ukraine war when NATO countries found a common purpose to bond together. Apart from trade, the EU cannot be a significant global player, as it has neither a common army nor strong leadership. This leaves the Union dependent on the US and the UK on geostrategic matters and denies it autonomous stature.

Turkey

In the last couple of decades, especially under President Erdogan, Turkey has emerged as a key player in the region. Its strategic location at the intersection of West Asia and Europe has given it enormous leverage on both sides. As a NATO member, it actively participated in the Ukraine war alongside other European powers while expanding its influence in West Asia and Africa.

Turkey is a very underrated military power, although it holds the eighth position as the most powerful military force in the world. With an estimated 355,000-strong armed forces, it ranks second among NATO countries.[22] This strength makes Turkey the undisputed leader in West Asia. It is a significant exporter of arms and ammunition. Today, its supplies are omnipresent in all conflict zones, from Somalia to Gaza to Ukraine.

Turkey's zone of influence in West Asia is increasing as it seizes every opportunity of conflict to push forward its armed forces. Turkish forces are deployed in countries like Qatar, Iraq, Libya and Syria. It has emerged as a major player in the Persian Gulf. By unequivocally supporting Azerbaijan in the war with Armenia,

Turkey sought to send a message that it is the undisputed leader of the Turkish world. Its footprint in Africa, too, is growing with direct interventions in countries like Niger and Somalia.

Although the country's economy is still small compared to others—ranked 18th in the world[23] and eighth in Europe[24]—its strategic location at the epicentre between China, Europe and West Asia makes it an important player in the new order.

ASEAN

The 10-member Association of Southeast Asian Nations (ASEAN) will commemorate 60 years of its inception in 2027, making it the longest-serving non-military alliance of countries in the world. Several ASEAN countries, such as Singapore, Vietnam, Malaysia, Indonesia and Thailand, are economic and trading powerhouses with a combined GDP of $3 trillion. The group has maintained a low profile when it comes to the geopolitics of the region and the world, building strong trade relations with all major powers, including the US and China. Its bilateral trade with China is more than $700 billion, making it the country's largest trade partner, and China is also its largest trade partner.[25] This is followed by ASEAN–US bilateral trade, which stands at $360 billion.[26]

Nations around the world are increasingly acknowledging ASEAN's importance as tensions in the Indo-Pacific region flare up. Prime Minister Modi emphasized ASEAN's centrality to the strategically important Indo-Pacific region in a speech at the IISS Shangri-La Dialogue in Singapore in June 2018. 'India's vision for the Indo-Pacific Region is therefore a positive one. And it has many elements… Southeast Asia is at its centre. And ASEAN has been and will be central to its future. That is the vision that will always guide India as we seek to cooperate for an architecture for peace and security in this region,' he said.[27]

Beyond ASEAN, the group became central to a regional forum formed in 2005 called the East Asia Summit (EAS). Formed to deliberate on key issues in the Indo-Pacific region, this forum has 18 member countries. Besides ten ASEAN countries, all the world's major powers, such as the US, Russia, China, India, Australia, Japan, New Zealand and South Korea, join this annual forum at the summit level. Such a high-profile forum acknowledges ASEAN's centrality for the Indo-Pacific region and underlines the increasing stature of the group in global geopolitics.

African Union

The African Union (AU), founded in 2001, remained an underdog as individual countries in the region were mired in conflicts and wars. However, when Prime Minister Modi took the lead in bringing it into the G20 during India's presidency in 2023, this region found an important voice in global affairs. This is also a testimony to the growing appreciation of Africa's importance and influence in the world. As a region, Africa is the poorest in the world, faces wars and climate disasters, and has a rapidly growing population. One estimate projects Africa to have 40 per cent of the world's population by the end of this century, with every second or third person on the planet being African.[28] This does not automatically make the region powerful. Nevertheless, with the growing acceptance of regional unity within Africa and recognition outside Africa, leaders of the AU are slowly trying to assert their independence in global affairs.

Iran, Saudi Arabia and the Arab states

Iran is the most sanctioned country in the world today. Decades of these crippling sanctions notwithstanding, Iran remains an important player in the geopolitics of West Asia and Africa. As the only Shia state in the predominantly Sunni Arab world, it enjoys the support of Shia minorities in several countries in the region. For its part, it continues to support militant and political groups in various parts of the region, including Yemen, Iraq and Syria. Through proxies such as Hezbollah in Lebanon, it has been an important player in the Arab–Israeli conflict for decades. The Gaza conflict has brought it closest to direct involvement in the war against the Jewish nation.

In the Ukraine war, it not only supported Russia by being the only major country in the UN to vote in its favour but also supplied large quantities of military equipment, including missiles and drones, to that country. In addition to its militaristic involvement in the region and beyond, Iran is also a leader in energy resources. With 850 billion barrels of liquid hydrocarbon reserves and 1,200 trillion cubic feet (tcf) of gas reserves, Iran is the fourth largest energy power in the world.[29]

Saudi Arabia, which long remained a docile ally of the US, is slowly asserting itself as an important regional player under the leadership of Crown Prince Mohammed bin Salman, popularly known as MBS. It controls the world's second-largest oil reserves[30] and the sixth-largest gas reserves.[31] Over the years, it leveraged its close relations with Western powers to build up massive military power. In 2017, it had the third-largest military budget in the world, and that year it signed the largest-ever defence deal with the US to procure $350 billion worth of weapons over the next ten years.[32] In a region torn apart by terrorism and conflicts, Saudi Arabia remains the net security provider. However, its ambition to rise as a major regional power invites challenges from other regional powers like Turkey, Iran and Qatar.

Several other countries, like Brazil in Latin America, have the potential to rise as important poles. America's allies like Israel, Japan, the UK, and Australia also have significant regional and extra-regional influences and engagements. All this suggests that multipolarity is not a myth but an everyday reality.

In a sane piece of advice, Yoni Wilkenfeld writes that 'the universality of European values can no longer be taken for granted. The West will have to open itself to concepts of order different from those enshrined in the institutions created in 1945. These must be adapted and modified to take into account changing realities.'[33]

6

MULTILATERALISM TO MINILATERALISM

In 2025, the UN, the largest and most successful multilateral organization, will celebrate its 80th anniversary by hosting a global summit with an ambitious theme: The UN Summit of the Future.

This is undoubtedly an important theme coming at the most appropriate time. The world is at a significant inflection point and passing through disruptive times. More and more voices are being raised over the growing ineffectiveness and inefficiency of this cherished multilateral body. 'It has been said that the United Nations was not created in order to bring us to heaven, but in order to save us from hell,' Dag Hammarskjöld, the Swedish diplomat who served as the second Secretary-General of the UN from 1953 to 1961, once quipped very pragmatically.[1]

Unfortunately, in the face of growing geopolitical tensions, wars and competing national self-interests, the UN is struggling to keep up this role. The last two decades saw the big powers routinely ignoring or bypassing the multilateral body and deciding to act unilaterally or in collaboration with other powers. Within the ranks of the UN itself, the realization of this situation is palpable. This has prompted the Trinidadian diplomat and president of the General Assembly, Dennis Francis, to name the theme of the 78th session in September 2023 'Restoring Trust and Revitalizing Global Solidarity'.

Addressing that special session, UN Secretary-General António Guterres stressed the need to reform and modernize the multilateral system, which dates back to the Second World War, so that it is effective enough to tackle contemporary challenges. While the world has evolved over the past eight decades, the UN and other multilateral institutions have remained stuck in a time warp and have failed to catch up, Guterres opined, adding that they are now becoming a problem rather than a solution. Strongly pitching for much-delayed reforms in the multilateral system, Guterres firmly told the world leaders that 'it's reform or rupture. The world has changed. Our institutions have not.'[2]

Guterres and his colleagues at the UN are not alone. Many world leaders are openly articulating the need to reform the UN-led system. S. Jaishankar has stated in different forums that the institutions have stagnated and are becoming increasingly irrelevant. Speaking at the annual Raisina Dialogue in February 2024, Jaishankar pointed out that the UN had only 50 member countries when it was founded, but today it has grown almost fourfold. 'So, it's a common-sense proposition that you can't continue the same way when you have four times the members,' he argued. Pointing to the UN's inability to find solutions to 'all big issues in the last five years,' he added that the 'fact is that the world trading rules have been gamed. We have a lot of our challenges today that also emanate from how countries have used that for their benefit at the expense of the international system.' He pointed to the crucial role of the five permanent members of the UN Security Council (UNSC)—China, Russia, France, Britain and the US—and said, 'If you are going to ask five countries, saying, would you mind changing the rules that you would have less power, guess what the answer is going to be. If they are wise, the answer would be something else.'[3]

The UN and its allied organizations are in a pitiable condition today. They look outdated and outmoded. The vintage bodies are struggling to free themselves from the stranglehold of the Big Five, the countries with veto power, while the rest of the world, especially the developing world, is losing faith in their ability to deliver an equitable order for all countries. The West blames Russia for the failure of the mechanism, while countries like India see China as the stumbling block. For some countries, the short-sightedness of the Western powers, led by the US, is responsible for the helplessness of the institutions.

All these reasons are valid. The net result is that today, the world body looks helpless in containing the wars in Ukraine and Gaza, in imposing rules on the developed Global North over issues of food security and other SDGs in the developing Global South, in forcing the industrialized North to compensate for climate compliance by the developing South, and in making global trade and juristic bodies functional. Vaccine apartheid demonstrated by big powers during the COVID-19 pandemic has widened the gulf between the industrialized and developing world. The seriousness of the paralysis of the UN system can be gauged from the fact that the WTO's dispute redressal mechanism has come to a grinding halt since December 2019 due to the refusal of the US to ratify the appointment of the new Appellate Body judges. By 2023, more than 600 bilateral and regional trade agreements had been notified to the trade body without any resolution.

The inefficiency of the UN system is also evident in its failure to implement aid programmes in regions such as sub-Saharan Africa, its inaction in the face of gross human rights violations by countries like China in Xinjiang, Tibet and Hong Kong, or its utter helplessness in containing the enormous human suffering in Gaza and its cowardice in calling out the names of the big powers. The Security Council is woefully weak in confronting the countries involved in wars like Ukraine and Gaza or other conflicts in the world. Its inefficiency in dealing with the climate crisis is evident in the face of its inability to build universal consensus. Its financial clout is weakening, making it ineffective in rescuing the countries of the Global South by way of timely payments when they are faced with humanitarian crises.

In fact, countries like the US no longer see the multilateral body as relevant for discussing burning global issues such as wars. In his address to the UNGA in 2023, President Biden went on and on about economic and climate issues for a long time before turning to burning issues such as the Ukraine war, which only came up towards the end of his address.[4] To hide its incompetence, the UN leadership resorts to bombastic statements to prove its credentials about the global mission while continuing to bury its head in the sand while things are going in exactly the opposite direction.

When we talk about the failure of the UN, we mostly mean the failure of the UNSC, the 15-member body with five permanent member countries holding veto powers. The Council's purpose was to maintain 'international peace and security' and take 'effective collective measures for the prevention and removal of threats to the peace and the suppression of acts of aggression.'[5]

Anatomy of Failure

The sad reality of the past seven decades of the Security Council's existence is that the greatest threat to global security has not stemmed from external sources but from the unilateral actions of the Council's five permanent member states. Besides the permanent members—US, Britain, France, China and Russia—the body has ten non-permanent members that the UNGA elects for a two-year term of office. They are geographically distributed, with two members from Asia, two from Latin America, three from Africa, two from Western Europe, and one from former communist Eastern Europe. It follows the rule of nine votes as a majority for passing decisions, whereby no permanent member can use their power of veto to oppose them. As the Council was founded in the shadow of the Second World War, countries like Germany and Japan were not given any place in it. Many other countries like India, South Africa and Brazil, which rose in prominence and influence, also do not play a significant role in the functioning of the Council and are only intermittently elected as non-permanent members.

The Security Council's ineffectiveness was conspicuous during the Ukraine crisis, prompting countries to highlight the reality frankly. When Russia invaded Ukraine in February 2022, the UNGA immediately took up the issue, and 81 member states co-sponsored a resolution denouncing the invasion and calling for multilateral action. However, Russia exercised its power of veto and stopped the resolution immediately. Since then, several attempted resolutions in the Security Council have been met with the same fate, with Russia shooting them down alone or with the help of China. This prompted India's Permanent Representative, Ruchira Kamboj, to raise fundamental questions about the Council's efficacy at the February 2024 plenary session of the UNGA. 'As the conflict has continued for two years unabated, we, the comity of UN Member States, must pause and ask ourselves two pressing questions. Are we anywhere near a possible, acceptable solution? And if not, why is it that the UN system, particularly its principal organ, the United Nations Security Council, mandated to primarily maintain international peace and security, rendered completely ineffective in the resolution of the ongoing conflict, she asked.'[6]

This tragic state of affairs did not just begin with the Ukraine war but has been a characteristic of the Security Council ever since its inception. The Council has been paralysed for the better part of the last seven decades, with consensus and action being the exception rather than the rule. Initially, the Cold War years killed its initiatives. Later, the unilateral actions of the permanent members did the same. In a much-hailed and prophetic speech in 2003, outlining France's opposition to aggression against Iraq, French Foreign Minister Dominique de Villepin called the United Nations a temple and said, 'In this temple of the United Nations, we are the guardians of an ideal, the guardians of a conscience. The onerous responsibility and immense honour we have must lead us to give priority to disarmament in peace.'[7] To rare applause, the Foreign Minister stated emphatically that a war in Iraq would further destabilize the Middle East, increase extremist terrorism and weaken the international system of governance.[8] But the UN couldn't stop the US and its allies from going ahead unilaterally and attacking Iraq without waiting for its approval.

The fate of the UN's economic organizations, described by some as the 'blessed trinity of multilateralism', is no different. The IMF is expected to allow easy access to capital by removing barriers to its free flow around the world. The World Bank is expected to help the developing world in transforming their economies into open market systems. And finally, the WTO, described by former Director-General Mike Moore as the 'crown jewel of multilateralism', was meant to remove trade barriers worldwide and develop equitable norms for international trade.[9]

All three organizations are facing a crisis today. Increasing multipolarity and the shift of the global economic power axis from the Pacific–Atlantic region to the Indo–Pacific region as a consequence of the rise of China and India are causing a stalemate and deepening the crisis in these bodies.

The World Bank was founded with the raison d'être of ending poverty by helping countries in the developing world overcome challenges like climate change. However, the reality is that it became the reason for growing poverty in Africa and elsewhere through its ill-devised structural adjustment programmes. While it has commissioned studies after studies that sounded alarm bells about impending climate disasters, it faces charges of hypocrisy by promoting investments in dozens of projects like coal-fired power plants throughout the world. Its projects under the United Nations' Programme on Reducing Emissions from Deforestation and Forest Degradation (REDD+) are also mired in controversies, with indigenous peoples' groups calling the programme a recipe for the displacement and destruction of forest-based communities. As problems like poverty, inequality, climate crisis and economic stagnation are causing enormous tensions in the world, the credibility of the World Bank's trade liberalization programmes is becoming increasingly questionable in the eyes of a more significant number of countries in the developing South.

The credibility of its sister organization, the IMF, also hit an all-time low due to its debilitating terms and conditions that squeeze smaller countries while benefitting big ones. While serving as a member of the Troika alongside the European Commission and the European Central Bank, the savage austerity programmes it imposed on countries like Greece and Ireland in the aftermath of the financial crisis of 2008 under the leadership of former Managing Director Christine Lagarde led to serious criticism in Europe and elsewhere.

In Asia, the IMF was accused of catalysing the Asian financial crisis of 1998 by imposing ruthless measures like cutting government spending, cancelling jobs and funnelling money into the coffers of private lenders, causing widespread human suffering.[10] The IMF was also criticized for adopting a one-size-fits-all approach,[11] uncritically applying Latin American solutions to East Asia, and imposing harsh yet unrealistic austerity measures on governments struggling with crises. Instead of redressing, these measures further prolonged the suffering of the economies. The IMF's functioning during the crisis lacked transparency, further aggravated by the lack of representation of these economies at both the IMF and the World Bank, leaving them powerless in the agency's decision-making process. George Soros' role during the crisis was also dubious. In January 1997, Soros initiated forward contracts to exchange baht for dollars at a rate of 26 baht per dollar. He then heavily advertised Thailand's economic problems and sold all of his baht. Thailand tried to defend its currency against Soros' speculative attack by buying up the surplus baht. As a result, the Thai central bank ran out of dollars, forcing it to float the baht onto the market on 2 July 1997. The baht fell from one dollar for 25 baht in June 1997 to one dollar for 54 baht in January 1998. Soros then traded $1 billion for 54 billion baht on the spot market; he then used his forward contracts to convert the 54 billion baht into $2 billion—doubling his money in just one year.[12] Meanwhile, the Thai baht landed the economy in a deep crisis that quickly spread to other ASEAN economies, including Malaysia, Indonesia and Singapore.

Incidentally, in the latest instance of Sri Lanka's repayment crisis, which led to the country's economic collapse in 2022, it took years for the IMF to finalize the restructuring programme on the flimsy grounds of 'procedural issues', forcing the country to turn to neighbours such as India and China for survival.[13]

The COVID-19 pandemic in the years 2020–22 has vividly demonstrated the enormous credibility crisis that the IMF faces. Bulgarian economist and managing director of the Fund, Kristalina Georgieva, boasted that she was willing to disburse $1 trillion to meet the challenge of a 'once-in-a-lifetime pandemic'[14] but the offer found very few takers, with only Cameroon, Côte d'Ivoire, Ethiopia and Senegal applying for it. Most countries were apprehensive about the IMF's intentions after they witnessed the plight of countries in Europe like Greece and Ireland. They also found that behind Georgieva's generous statements was the reality that the fund was offering loans, not grants, and that these loans carried the same dreaded conditionalities as regular IMF loans. Instead of offering to cancel previous debts as an adjustment, the IMF's pandemic assistance programmes were actually seeking to push countries into another debt trap.

Even other multilateral bodies like the United Nations Convention on the Law of the Sea (UNCLOS), once hailed as the 'constitution for the seas',[15] and the UN High Commissioner for Refugees (UNHCR) appear to be losing steam. When a dispute over maritime rights between China and the Philippines was brought before UNCLOS in 2013, its inability to resolve this dispute in the face of growing Chinese aggression became conspicuous. Although a signatory to the Convention in 1996, China steadfastly refuses jurisdiction for the Commission in the disputed waters of the SCS region. It refused to honour the Commission's 2016 verdict in favour of the Philippines in this bilateral maritime dispute between the two countries.

At a time when the refugee problem is becoming acute in Africa, Europe, West Asia and South Asia, the UNHCR is in a critical position due to serious funding gaps. The organization officially highlighted this exigency by stating on its website that 'the population UNHCR protects and assists reached a record

122.6 million people, and funding decreased from its 2022 peak, resulting in a record funding gap. Emergencies hit a new high, with the war in Sudan causing the year's largest displacement crisis, needing more support than received. The number of protracted refugee situations increased to 59 in 37 countries.'[16] Its programmes for refugees from Yemen could secure only 12 per cent of funding and 30 per cent of funding was mobilized for Afghanistan. As a result, the UNHCR has already shrunk, and many aid programmes have come to a grinding halt over funding issues.

The climate change programmes initiated by the United Nations in Paris in 2015 find a serious lack of trust between the North and the South, leading to a stalemate in extending climate funding to the developing countries in their climate mitigation endeavours. The 28th Conference of the Parties (COP28), the UN Climate Change Conference held in Dubai, once again ended more as a talking shop than a real mitigator. On the most crucial question of the use of fossil fuels, the summit failed to articulate any firm position. Instead of talking about 'phasing out' fossil fuels, as 130 of the 198 participating countries had demanded, the final deal at the summit spoke in a much milder language, calling for a 'transition away' from them. 'The science is clear—fossil fuels must go. World leaders will fail their people and the planet unless they accept this reality,' warned Dr Magdalena Skipper, editor-in-chief of the science journal *Nature*.[17]

One challenge that the developing world sees in the Bretton Woods institutions is the grip of the developed North on them. In the eight decades of their existence, these institutions have not ceded enough space to the Global South, causing serious resentment and heartburn among the leaders of many countries. The control structure of these organizations is such that the developed countries continue to have majority control over their functioning. For example, the US holds over 16.5 per cent of voting rights in the IMF, giving the country adequate veto power over all major policy decisions.[18] While the economies of the five BRICS countries—Brazil, Russia, India, China and South Africa—account for 20 per cent of global GDP, their share of the IMF is only 11 per cent.[19] The four big European economies—Germany, France, the UK and Italy—which collectively contribute 13 per cent of global GDP, enjoy a 16.8 per cent share of the IMF.[20] Europe retains the right to name the managing director of the Fund.

The story of the World Bank is not much different. High-income countries, almost all from the Global North, control 61 per cent of the votes in the Bank, while middle-income countries from the Global South hold 35 per cent of the votes. Low-income countries hold less than five per cent of the Bank's functioning.[21] The privilege of naming the President of the World Bank is permanently in the hands of the US.

In the words of Irish journalist Judy Dempsey, 'The UN is in desperate need of a major root and branch overhaul. The system is old and hopelessly out of date. It harks back to a long-gone era when a few countries, led by the United States and some European states, ran the show. It does not reflect the complex realities of today's multipolar world.'[22] The failure of global multilateralism should not be blamed on the new phenomenon of multipolarity. On the contrary, it is this failure of multilateralism that is giving rise to multipolarity in the world. This failure can squarely be placed at the doorstep of the self-centred and short-sighted thinking of the big powers.

Tragedy of Great Power Politics

How did we get here? The twentieth century saw two significant efforts to build multilateral institutional mechanisms with lofty objectives. The first was the League of Nations, founded immediately after the First World War in 1919, inspired by US President Woodrow Wilson's 14-point agenda. The second was the UNO, formed in the aftermath of the Second World War, again with the lofty ideals of ending wars and building cooperation among the nations of the world.

Sadly, both were victims of big power politics at the very

inception. The League of Nations remained handicapped from the beginning due to the return of isolationist policies in the US in the post-Wilson era. The UN, which was founded two and a half decades later, also fell victim to another kind of big power politics—the Cold War between the West and the USSR.

While the communist Soviet Union never bothered to strengthen the UN's multilateral system except to ensure that its veto powers remained intact, the Western powers, led by the US, also lost interest in promoting its objectives.

The only period of satisfactory performance for the UN-led systems, particularly the UNSC, was during the unipolar decades, when, free from the Cold War tension, the body could effectively intervene in several global challenges and find resolution.

The collapse of the Soviet Union led to a significant outbreak of conflict in the Balkans. In 1992–95, war raged in Bosnia and Herzegovina, a former Yugoslav republic, leading to the deaths of tens of thousands of people. In one particularly gruesome incident, Bosnian Serbs massacred 8,000 Muslims in Srebrenica in July 1995, the worst act of mass killing on European soil since the end of the Second World War.[23] United Nations Peacekeepers were deployed, and food and medical supplies were organized for the conflict areas. In May 1993, the United Nations established the International Criminal Tribunal for the former Yugoslavia (ICTY) and prosecuted those involved in the ethnic conflict, including the former president of Yugoslavia, Slobodan Milosevic, which led to the killing of more than 100,000 people. Three years later, when ethnic Albanians and Serbs clashed in 1998–99, the UN stepped in again with the deployment of peacekeepers and arrived at a final settlement that resulted in formal recognition of Kosovo as an independent nation.

Another critical success of multilateralism during this period was bringing the North Korean dictatorial leadership to agree to freeze its nuclear proliferation activities in November 1994. The UNSC mandated the International Atomic Energy Agency (IAEA) to complete the process under the agreement reached between the US and the North Korean leadership in October of that year. Although short-lived, as expected, the agreement authorized the IAEA to monitor the freezing of the agreed facilities in North Korea.

However, this changed after 9/11. Without waiting for the approval of the UNSC, the US immediately launched an attack on Afghanistan, invoking Security Council resolutions 1368 and 1373, which recognize the right of countries to self-defence in the face of terrorism. A few weeks later, the Security Council endorsed the US-led efforts to crush the Taliban through Resolution 1378.

However, the situation became murky when the US unilaterally decided to invade Iraq in 2002 on the pretext that Saddam Hussein's regime was hiding chemical and biological weapons. In a significant breach of the Security Council's reputation, despite failing to secure its approval, the US and its allies had gone ahead and invaded Iraq that year. The draft resolution it placed before the UNSC couldn't be passed in the face of opposition from Russia and France, two permanent members of the Council. These countries insisted that the UN should take the initiative to resolve the issue of Saddam's secret 'weapons of mass destruction' in a peaceful manner.

Not convinced, President George W. Bush and Prime Minister Tony Blair went ahead with war on Iraq. The joint army marched against Saddam's forces in March 2003. The war lasted six weeks and ended with the capture of Saddam in an underground bunker. Saddam was tried and later executed. When Bush stood on the aircraft carrier USS *Abraham Lincoln* in front of a huge banner reading 'Mission Accomplished' and declared victory, he probably didn't realize that he was also setting the clock ticking for global multilateralism. The US had spent $800 billion on the Iraq War, killed 116,000 civilians, and lost 4,800 allied soldiers.[24] However, the real casualty was the multilateral institutions. The US formalized its decline in later years by sending its armies into Syria in 2013, again on the grounds that Bashar al-Assad was using chemical weapons against his people. US forces remained in Syria for six years before finally withdrawing in 2019 during the Trump administration.

The Ukraine and Gaza conflicts have exposed the ineffectiveness of the UN and its sister organizations more conspicuously than ever before. From 1945 until the outbreak of the war in Gaza in October 2023, a total of 36 UNSC resolutions relating to the Israel-Palestine conflict were vetoed by one of the five permanent members. Of these, 34 were vetoed by the US and two by Russia and China.[25] Since the outbreak of the conflict in October 2023, the Security Council and the General Assembly have passed several resolutions calling for a ceasefire or a humanitarian corridor, but these have either been vetoed or never implemented on the ground.

Not only the UNSC, but failures also plagued the founding of the Bretton Woods institutions, the IMF and the World Bank, followed by the founding of a multilateral trade body, the International Trade Organization (ITO). The leaders of the UN nations met in 1948 in Havana, Cuba, which was not yet under the communist rule of Fidel Castro, to draft the parameters for the ITO, which became known as the Havana Charter. But by then, fears of expanding communist influence on the one hand and pressure from the multinational companies' lobby on the other prompted the Truman administration not to have the Charter ratified by the US Congress. International trade was not significant in the US at the time, and the business lobby, which was there in hordes at the Havana Conference, ensured that their 'protectionism' was not disturbed. Washington would force a much weaker regulatory system, the GATT, on the world.

By the mid-1980s, US multinationals had gained significance and had started looking for greater access to markets in the developing world in sunshine sectors like agriculture, manufacturing, services and technology. The policies of developing countries in Asia and Latin America were an eyesore to the US companies and the US administration. The rise of East Asian powers like South Korea, Japan, Taiwan and Malaysia as Asian Tigers with aggressive export policies and a strong domestic manufacturing base began to worry Washington. The collapse of the Soviet Union, leading to the creation of a unipolar order—albeit temporarily—encouraged the US leadership to go in for the overkill in global trade. The ineffective GATT regime was replaced by the WTO, a more forceful and efficient trade regime. When negotiations to establish the WTO began in the Uruguay round in 1993, the US was confident that it would be able to impose a strong multilateral body that could introduce rigid free trade rules worldwide, benefitting its own companies and corporations. The WTO came into being in 1995 primarily as an instrument to promote, consolidate and legitimize the hegemony of US interests.

The EU and other developed nations like Japan jumped on the bandwagon, looking for lucrative markets in the developing world for their surplus production in the areas of agriculture, automobiles, pharmaceuticals and IT. Issues like 'intellectual property' were given prime importance to stymie the rise of not only the Asian Tigers but also other nations in the developing world like India and Brazil. In this scenario, both government leadership and civil society organizations in the developing world plunged into the campaign, launching a scathing attack on the mischievous provisions of the WTO agreements aimed at ensuring more profitability for the developed world. The protests began in the national capitals of the developing world, and soon they reached every venue of the WTO negotiations. At the Third Ministerial Conference, which took place in Seattle in 1999, there were massive street protests that led to riots and police intervention. By the time the negotiations reached their final stage in 2003 in Cancún, Mexico, China had also become a member of the organization and joined the camp of the developing countries. A massive diplomatic tussle ensued with the Western powers on the one side and India, Brazil and China on the other. Finally, the Third World countries succeeded in foiling the attempts to dismantle government protection for farmers and to push forward the Agreement on Trade-Related Aspects of Intellectual Property

Rights (TRIPs) and the Agreement on Trade-Related Investment Measures (TRIMs).

After a decade of strong enthusiasm, the US and its European allies realized that in the face of assertive interventions from major developing nations at the negotiating table, the revised free trade regime under the WTO had become much more challenging. China's swift rise as an economic, manufacturing and technological mega-hub also caused serious consternation in the West. The rise in the multipolar order added fuel to the fire. After the fifth Ministerial Conference collapsed in Cancún, US Trade Representative Robert Zoellick vented his frustration by warning the fellow member countries: 'As WTO members ponder the future, the US will not wait: We will move towards free trade with "can-do" countries.'[26] The US and its allies in Europe began withdrawing from the multilateral regime and turned to minilateral arrangements like the Trans-Pacific Partnership (TPP) or purely bilateral arrangements.

It was not empty rhetoric. Over the last two decades, the West has gradually retreated and deliberately weakened multilateral institutions. This trend reached its crescendo during Donald Trump's presidency. Trump's 'America First' policy has led to his administration walking out of important UN-led initiatives like the Paris Climate Summit, creating obstacles to the functioning of the WTO, cutting funding for the WHO, and a lot more.

Trump began his return to isolationism by withdrawing from the minilaterals that his predecessors, like Barack Obama, had created. The TPP was the first to go under the hammer in 2017, followed by the replacement of the North American Free Trade Agreement (NAFTA) with a new arrangement. Trump also announced his withdrawal from UNESCO, protesting the organization's anti-Israel resolutions, the Paris Agreement on Climate Change and the UN Human Rights Council, which he accused of failing to fulfil its job. Important treaties for global security, like the 1987 Intermediate-Range Nuclear Forces Treaty (INF), fell victim to Trump's whimsical isolationism.

Trump's epic quarrel with the WHO became a sensation in the last year of his presidency when the deadly coronavirus broke out. Trump publicly blamed the WHO for its lethargic response to the pandemic, accusing it of toeing China's line and announcing the US withdrawal from the UN body. 'On 3 March 2020, the World Health Organization cited official Chinese data to downplay the very serious risk of asymptomatic spread, telling the world that "COVID-19 does not transmit as efficiently as influenza",' Trump wrote in an 18 May letter addressed to WHO leadership. 'It is now clear that China's assertions, repeated to the world by the World Health Organization, were wildly inaccurate. Many lives could have been saved if the WHO had warned the world earlier,' Trump wrote, announcing that the US would withdraw from the global health agency.[27]

As the trade war between Xi Jinping and Donald Trump raged from the first year of Trump's presidency, the WTO became an unsuspecting victim of a witch hunt, with his administration accusing it of going soft on China. It is true that the organization's rules, written before China joined, have proven ineffective in containing the dubious trade practices of that country. The Trump administration used this as an excuse to cripple the body itself. It condemned the WTO leadership for allowing China to claim the special status of a developing country despite being the world's second-largest economy and also for not doing enough to stop it from extending massive state subsidies on its products while objecting to the US administration's measures meant to block those cheap goods from entering the country.

Trump's response was to block the WTO from appointing new members to a crucial panel that heard appeals in trade disputes, forcing Brazilian Director-General Roberto Azevêdo to resign in 2020, a year before his term was supposed to end. Most members supported Nigerian diplomat Ngozi Okonjo-Iweala as a replacement, but Trump delayed the process, looking for a candidate who was sympathetic to US interests. It was not until a year later that the Biden administration lifted the embargo on the appointment of Okonjo-Iweala, making her the first woman and the first African to head the WTO.

China Steps into the Global Vacuum

This palpable decline and the ineffectiveness of multilateral institutions are viewed differently by the two superpowers—the US and China. The US continues to demonstrate scant interest in strengthening the broken system. Trump provided renewed acceleration to the process initiated by Bush and nonchalantly trampled on the multilateral bodies. Although Biden showed signs of returning to multilateralism, Ukraine and Gaza pulled his administration in the same direction as unilateralism.

China, on the other hand, demonstrates its adeptness in playing both sides. On the one hand, it is expanding its footprint in UN bodies and trying to align its national agenda with that of these multilateral bodies; on the other hand, it is actively cultivating minilateral arrangements by promoting regional institutions.

China is stepping into the vacuum created by the withdrawal of the US from multilateral bodies. It sees the UN as the best platform to legitimize and advance its agenda of building an alternative world order that suits its interests. 'China has made successful inroads toward elevating its profile across the UN system, particularly in recent years. It has become the second largest contributor to the UN's regular budget as well as the second largest source of funding for UN peacekeeping operations. Beijing has also secured senior positions in many specialized UN agencies and provides a significant number of personnel to UN peacekeeping operations—the most among UNSC members,' write Carla Freeman and Lyndi Tsering.[28]

China heads the UN Department of Economic and Social Affairs (DESA), reinforcing its influence on global development initiatives. The influential position of UN Under-Secretary-General for economic and social affairs has become a pocket borough of China for many years now. Using this position, it has successfully pushed its own agenda, like the GDI, through the member countries of the General Assembly.

The Nimble New Minilaterals

While multilateralism continued its downward slide, several minilateral initiatives gained currency in the last two decades, propelled primarily by the competing superpowers.

The 15-country RCEP is one such body in the Indo-Pacific region, led by China. The BRI has emerged as a significant multilateral body claiming the participation of over 150 countries. China also took the lead in establishing regional economic institutions like the AIIB, the NDB and the BRICS Contingent Reserve Arrangement (CRA). Although these institutions cannot be seen as a replacement for the established ones like the IMF and the World Bank, they are certainly attracting more and more countries in the Global South due to the ease of lending practices.

In the trading world, a hodgepodge of institutions is emerging with other regional institutions like Mercosur in South America, several other free trade agreements in all parts of the world, and non-institutionalized bilateral and unilateral initiatives.

On the security front, groupings like the Six-Party Talks, launched in 2003 to push for the denuclearization of North Korea through negotiations between North and South Koreas, Japan, China, Russia and the US, are an example of multilateralism being a preferred alternative to the UNSC. Although the talks lasted for six years before they were finally broken off in the face of North Korea's belligerent stance on continuing its nuclear programme, they were seen as a better alternative to the Security Council's veto-constrained deliberations.

Similarly, when the ASEAN nations realized that China was going to pose a serious challenge to their maritime boundaries, especially in the aftermath of the latter's occupation of Mischief Reef, they decided to come up with a Code of Conduct (COC) in the South China Sea instead of relying on UNCLOS. The ASEAN

Foreign Ministers Meeting endorsed this idea in July 1996, and efforts in this direction began immediately. Over the past three decades, however, not much success has been achieved beyond a draft code.

Meanwhile, China's hardball approach in the South China Sea has led to the formation of the QUAD (Quadrilateral Security Dialogue) group, comprising the US, India, Japan and Australia, with the ostensible aim of promoting a free and open Indo-Pacific, while the unstated objective remains the containment of China in the region. The AUKUS, an acronym for the member countries Australia, the UK and the US, is another tri-country security partnership that has emerged with a similar objective. In the Eurasian theatre, groups such as BRICS+ and the Shanghai Cooperation Organization (SCO) are growing in influence and spread. The BRICS+ comprises eleven member countries, while dozens more want membership in this regional association. China dominates both groups and has greater global ambitions, such as creating a BRICS currency platform to counter dollar, and the SWIFT system monopoly.

In Africa, the AU, which joined the G20 group in 2023, is gradually succeeding in uniting the quarrelsome countries on the continent. Meanwhile, in Europe, the EU is struggling to maintain its relevance in the face of growing calls for its dismantling and a return to nationalism.

Minilateralism is the flavour of the season, but it is not necessarily a replacement for multilateral institutions. The challenge is to reform existing multilateral bodies so that they are relevant to the changed times. Minilaterals may not end the reign of multilateral bodies, but the latter may end themselves by refusing to reform.

7

HETEROPOLIS RISING: NON-STATE ACTORS

In November 2023, Fergus Eckersley, UK political coordinator at the United Nations, issued a statement to the Counter-terrorism Committee (CTC) of the UNSC, which was the response of Prime Minister Rishi Sunak's Conservative government to a discussion on counterterrorism measures at the UNSC. Eckersley expressed disappointment over 'a permanent member' who was 'blocking' the committee's efforts to prevent the proliferation of chemical, biological and nuclear weapons. 'This situation severely undermines our ability to support states to implement a resolution that is designed to prevent chemical, biological and nuclear weapons and related material from getting into the hands of non-state actors, including terrorists,' he noted. 'It is hard to understand why any country—let alone a Permanent Member of this Council—would want to stymie those efforts,' he bemoaned.[1]

The UK Government highlighted the threat that terrorist groups such as Al-Qaeda, ISIS and affiliates seek to spread around the world using new technologies and taking advantage of regional instability, and underscored the common purpose of all member countries to tackle the persistent and significant threat to international peace and security posed by terrorist groups and non-state actors.

This intervention by the Sunak government is vital to highlight the rising concerns of sovereign nations over the challenges posed by these non-state players. They are not limited to terrorist outfits alone but also include multinational corporations, media and social media giants, new-age religious movements, and non-governmental bodies like the Gates Foundation, Open Society Foundations, Oxfam and CARE. These players have an influence that extends beyond the sovereign borders of a nation, and many of them are powerful enough to challenge and defy sovereign laws of nations with impunity. They compete with governments and political parties of sovereign states for control over the mind spaces of the citizens there. The world created today by these non-state forces is called a heteropolar world.

There are numerous instances to underscore the power of these forces. During a visit to Budapest at the end of 2023, I heard from many analysts of the ruling dispensation that Hungarian Prime Minister Viktor Orbán faces a significant threat not from the ultra-liberal European leadership or the Democrat dispensation in Washington but from a fellow Hungarian, George Soros. Soros is a 95-year-old Hungarian American businessman and hedge fund manager with a net worth of over $7 billion. Soros founded and funded the Open Society Foundations (OSF), a philanthropic arm with the stated aim of working for justice, democratic governance and human rights. He is an open supporter of liberal parties and left-liberal NGOs and often grants huge donations to several causes, from campaigns on campuses to clashes on the streets. He is considered an open enemy of right-wing leaders, from Donald Trump in the US to Viktor Orbán in his country of birth. In fact, Orbán's government spent millions of dollars on a poster campaign against Soros, accusing him of leading an international cabal to destabilize right-wing governments in Europe and elsewhere.[2] Soros and his foundation gained notoriety as dubious conspirators of regime change and agents of chaos. A fellow US businessman, Elon Musk, compared Soros to the *X-Men* villain Magneto in a controversial tweet in May 2023. When an X-user defended Soros as having good intentions, Musk responded by saying, 'You assume they are good intentions. They are not. He wants to erode the very fabric of civilization. Soros hates humanity.[3] Soros is a test case for a heteropolar world, wherein a powerful individual with no overt political role can become a threat to sovereign governments.'

In India, Soros is accused of supporting and sponsoring anti-Modi government campaigns such as the 2020–21 farmers' uprising and a recent attack on Indian business tycoon Gautam Adani by a lesser-known outfit called Hindenburg Research. In fact, the farmers' agitation launched against the Modi government's agricultural policies was the latest example of India's brush with global NGOs (GNGOs). The Indian government suspected the role of some GNGOs in supporting and sponsoring this agitation. 'Toolkit' as a disruptive concept became popular during this agitation with the likes of Greta Thunberg jumping in. Thunberg inadvertently put a toolkit in the public domain before hastily withdrawing it. The toolkit, allegedly created by a Canada-based organization called the Poetic Justice Foundation (PJF) with links to separatist groups such as the Khalistanis, not only contained seditious material but also highlighted the modus operandi of some of the GNGOs. Under the guise of supporting the farmers' agitation, the toolkit proposed to damage the reputation of the Indian government by asking to 'disrupt yoga and chai image of India in general.'[4]

In January 2024, a drone attack on an American outpost in northeast Jordan near the border of Syria and Iraq resulted in the death of three American soldiers and injuries to 34 others. The explosives-laden drone was supposedly launched by a terror group, Kata'ib Hizballah (KH), based out of Iraq. President Biden himself confirmed the deaths during an 'unmanned aerial drone attack' and claimed the attack was 'carried out by radical, Iranian-backed militant groups operating in Syria and Iraq.' While Iran denied any involvement in the incident, with its spokesman for the Foreign Ministry, Nasser Kanaani, stating that the militias 'do not take orders' from Iran and were acting independently to oppose 'any aggression and occupation', the militias, who called themselves the Axis of Resistance, took responsibility for the attack and said it was a 'continuation of our approach to resisting the

American occupation forces in Iraq and the region.'[5]

According to media reports, there were at least 164 strikes by Iran-backed militias against US troops in Syria, Iraq and Jordan in the six months since the conflict broke out between Israel and Hamas in October 2023. In the same month, a drone loaded with explosives landed on a barracks at the US' Erbil air base in Iraq. Luckily for the forces stationed there, it failed to detonate. Had it exploded, there would have been many casualties.

Today, these non-state actors pose both challenges and opportunities for global governance and pave the way for the development of a heteropolar world order.

Rise of Corporate Nations

Multinational corporations (MNCs), including tech giants like Apple, Microsoft, Facebook, Huawei and X, have a huge presence around the world. They dominate both the global economy and their respective national economies. According to estimates, there were 60,000 MNCs worldwide in 2018, 60 per cent of which were based in three countries—the US, China and Japan.[6] The 38-member intergovernmental body called the Organisation for Economic Co-operation and Development (OECD) estimated in 2018 that MNCs accounted for half of global exports, nearly a third of global GDP (28 per cent) and about a quarter of global employment. They account for almost a third of global wealth.[7] The employment potential of these companies, coupled with their enormous money power, which exceeds the national economic outlays of many smaller countries in the world, makes these corporations a significant challenge for sovereign governance. Apple, for example, had a net worth of over $3 trillion in August 2024, making it wealthier than 90 per cent of the countries in the world.[8] The most profitable MNCs are found in the technology, oil and financial sectors.

This debate about the role and influence of MNCs is not new. Eminent scholars like Joseph Nye have already written in the last century about three main channels through which these firms may exert their influence over policymaking—direct influence through lobbying, indirect influence as an instrument of the state, and unintentional influence via the efforts at agenda-setting. 'Whether the United Nations or another institution will acquire a sufficiently strong mandate to deal with the problem, the political challenge of the multinational corporations seems to be gradually leading to a concerted response. The role of multinational corporations today cannot be understood merely in economic terms but must be seen in terms of this larger political challenge,' Nye warned.[9]

These MNCs are like 'corporate nations' with vast empires spread across many nations. They have the power to influence government policy and, in some cases, lobby or browbeat leaders to secure favourable treatment. They have no compulsion to submit to the rules and regulations of any one country. In fact, many MNCs choose their operational bases in countries where regulatory mechanisms and tax structures are weak or flexible, leadership is amenable, resources abundant and connectivity seamless. In the developing world, MNCs focus on their private goods or profits against public goods like minimum wages for labour, etc. Countries cannot challenge MNCs for fear of losing them on their soil.

The audacity and power of some of these transnational tech giants are well illustrated by the spat that the Home Minister of Singapore, K. Shanmugam, himself a renowned attorney, had with Simon Milner, Meta's vice president of public policy for Asia Pacific, over whether the company had provided access to its customer data to the controversial Cambridge Analytica (CA). Cambridge Analytica was a political consulting firm that specialized in harvesting data science to influence political campaigns using specialized tools for psychological profiling. Accusations poured in from various quarters in 2016 that the company was harvesting the personal data of more than 87 million Facebook users without their consent. While CA soon went bankrupt, countries concerned about the breach of privacy of their citizens using social media platforms like Facebook launched further investigations. Facing a Select Committee on Deliberate Online Falsehoods constituted by the Singapore Government in 2018, Milner betrayed utter contempt for the proceedings and went on to challenge the line of questioning of the minister himself. The spat that followed demonstrated how much courage and steadfastness sovereign governments need to tackle these big-tech companies.

> **Milner:** (Dismissing a question asked by Minister Shanmugam) I would actually like to speak to the Chair at this point. I am not certain that this is a fair use of this committee's time. I don't think it is fair to ask me detailed questions about evidence given by my colleague to a different Parliament in a different country. I would really like the Chairman to consider whether this kind of questioning is appropriate.

> **Shanmugam:** I will explain why! Obviously the 15-minute break has helped you decide whether you will or will not answer the questions.

> **Milner:** (Interrupting Minister Shanmugam) You wish to discuss evidence given by my colleague to a parliament. I don't think that is a good use of our time.

> **Charles Chong, Chair:** Mr Milner! I think you should leave it to us to decide what is relevant and what is not relevant. But if you are unable to answer questions because you don't know or do not wish to answer the question, please state so.

> **Shanmugam:** Let me explain why it is very relevant, Mr Milner! I spent most of my career looking at what is relevant and what is irrelevant. The questions before the UK parliament were very relevant in exploring the degree to which Facebook can be trusted to be a reliable partner for the Singapore government, whether Facebook will tell

us the truth, the whole truth, and nothing but the truth, or whether you will do everything you can to give lawyer's answers or 'lawyered' answers. We are all sovereign parliaments, but we look [at] your conduct all around the world. We are looking at the consequences to our national security by looking at your answers elsewhere. In that context, we are asking these questions. If you are embarrassed about being confronted with the answers your colleagues have given to other parliaments, you can say so. But you will leave the relevance of questions to me.

When Milner tried to respond, Minister Shanmugam curtly told him: 'I don't need an answer from you.'[10]

This spat shows the brazenness and nonchalance of the representatives of big-tech organizations. This was the situation faced by the minister of a powerful Southeast Asian nation. It is easy to imagine how difficult it would be for smaller nations to face these organizations.

In fact, it is tough for smaller countries to equip themselves to face today's most serious challenges like cybersecurity, climate change and illegal migration. This is where the MNCs step in, not necessarily always as a solution but, on several occasions, as part of the problem. Social media giants like Facebook, X and Google have enormous political power, which they don't hesitate to demonstrate when required. A case in point was Twitter's audacious decision to ban Donald Trump from its platform on 8 January 2021, following clashes by his supporters on Capitol Hill two days earlier. Twitter justified its actions, claiming that it was due to the 'risk of further incitement of violence.' Social media platforms such as Facebook, Snapchat and others also imposed restrictions on Trump, showing their power to influence the country's politics.[11]

As Alessio Terzi and Stephano Marcuzzi emphasize, MNCs are now also taking over areas that were traditionally in the hands of states. 'These are hardly the only examples of multinational corporations designing and enforcing their own public policies. Microsoft recently pledged $500 million to expand the availability of affordable housing in Seattle, which would generally be the job of the US Department of Housing and Urban Development and other public agencies, both state and federal. And at the Paris Peace Forum last November, Microsoft, Google, Facebook and other tech giants joined 50 governments in signing a new multilateral cybersecurity agreement. Notably absent were the governments of the US, Russia and China.'[12]

Elon Musk's SpaceX is launching manned space missions and plans to land on Mars and colonize it for Musk before any government can do so. NASA, once famous for its space forays, is now outsourcing its ventures to private companies. When astronauts Sunita Williams and Butch Wilmore were stuck on the International Space Station (ISS) since June 2024 due to a Boeing Starliner spacecraft malfunction, NASA turned to SpaceX, which brought them back with its Crew Dragon capsule. In 2023, the Pentagon announced that it would collaborate with SpaceX to develop a new military satellite called Starshield. Meanwhile, the internet space is no longer in the hands of sovereign governments as Google and Facebook attempt to provide universal internet access via hot-air balloons.

Two incidents that illustrate the power of big-tech corporations to influence government decision-making concern Google and Starlink. In March 2018, Google signed a $9 million contract with the Pentagon to develop AI algorithms to process the footage supplied by multi-million-dollar military drones such as Reaper and Predator.[13] When a top-secret email about the project was leaked, the left-liberal campus erupted in anger. A dozen engineers resigned, and many dozens more threatened to do so as soon as they found alternative jobs. Thousands of Google employees signed a letter of protest to Sundar Pichai, the company's CEO, demanding that 'Google should not be in the business of war.'[14] Ultimately, Google decided to back out and terminate the contract with the Pentagon.

There is yet another instance, this time from Ukraine. Before invading Ukraine in February 2022, the first thing that the Russian Army did was knock out the Viasat satellite communications link to that country, a crucial lifeline for all communications, military and civil. The Russians did not use anti-satellite missiles to do this but simply deployed wiper malware in the ground control system to disrupt the satellite's ability to connect with the ground. This could have wholly crippled the Ukrainian army. Without the Viasat link, the Ukrainian military could not have contacted its field units, shared information, or coordinated the counterattack against the Russian army. When they landed dozens of helicopters in Kyiv in the very first week of the war—the last week of that fateful February 2022—the Russian commanders had anticipated a simple surrender by the Ukrainians.

However, what the Ukrainian leadership did at that critical juncture eloquently showcased the changed reality of the new world order. The Ukrainians didn't rush to the American or European leadership for help. Instead, Ukraine's Deputy Prime Minister, Mykhailo Fedorov, turned to his X account to send an SOS to one person he was convinced would save Ukraine—Elon Musk, whose SpaceX owns a constellation of satellites called Starlink in low-Earth orbit that provide communication links to countries and companies. Starlink can instantly connect anyone anywhere in the world to the internet via its satellite communication network.

'@elonmusk,' Fedorov tweeted from his X account, 'while you try to colonize Mars—Russians try to occupy Ukraine! While your rockets successfully land from space—Russian missiles are attacking Ukrainian civil people! We ask you to provide Ukraine with Starlink stations and to address sane Russians to stand.'[15] Musk didn't take much time to reply. 'Starlink service is now active in Ukraine. More terminals en route,' he tweeted that same evening.[16] Over the next couple of days, Starlink provided five hundred terminals and the Ukrainian army was back in full action to throw the Russians out of Kyiv.

This incident illustrates not one, but two critical messages: first, that a tech giant like Musk had more power to support the Ukrainians at a crucial juncture in war than Western governments probably did, and second, that any rogue group of hackers can use wiper malware to kill the most advanced satellites without requiring anti-satellite missile technologies. This is the heteropolar order in action.

'Starlink is indeed the blood of our entire communication infrastructure now,' boasted Fedorov.[17] However, Musk soon demonstrated to Fedorov that it was his whims that carried the day for Ukraine, not Zelenskyy's or Fedorov's commands. When Fedorov made an emergency request for Starlink systems over Crimea so that the Ukrainian army could strike the Russian naval fleet with submarine drones, Musk sternly reprimanded him, saying, 'If the Ukrainian attacks had succeeded in sinking the Russian fleet, it would have been like a mini-Pearl Harbor. We did not want to be a part of that.'[18]

'When Musk decided to step in to halt a Ukrainian attack around Crimea based on his own calculation of what might happen next, he was, in effect, appointing himself national security advisor,' quipped *NYT* columnist David E. Sanger.[19]

Looking ahead, it may not be easy to reclaim the sovereign authority of governments from powerful multinational lobbies. Even the UN seems convinced about this eventuality of heteropolar forces controlling the future of humanity. Realizing the impossibility of the task of preventing this, the UN founded a Global Compact in 2000 to address the way MNCs could play a constructive role in global governance. The Global Compact called on companies to self-regulate by following set principles in the areas of human rights, the environment and anti-corruption. Nearly 15,000 companies have joined the Global Compact, committing to support the host governments in promoting development goals and sustainability.

Nationalism and Separatism

Countries around the world struggle with the challenge of tackling separatist movements for territorial independence based on ethnic, religious or linguistic identities. These movements are often accused of garnering support from other countries either covertly or overtly. Primarily engineered by minority populations clustered in a specific region, bearing grievances of real or imagined oppression and marginalization, these movements resort to violence and terrorism to achieve their objectives. Support from other non-state actors like NGOs, media and foreign agencies often provides credibility to these movements, making it even more difficult for national governments to tackle them.

I have listed some of these movements that I believe have the potential to reshape the geopolitics of the world.

Catalonia is an autonomous region in Spain. The historic city of Barcelona is the most important city in a region restive for independence from the Spanish government in Madrid. Catalonia held a referendum on independence in October 2017. The Spanish government declared the referendum illegal, and police raided polling stations to disrupt voting. Voter turnout was 42 per cent, with the rest who were not in favour of independence abstaining from voting. As expected, 90 per cent voted for independence from Spain.[20] The president of Catalonia had even momentarily declared independence before withdrawing it under pressure to initiate negotiations with the central government.

In West Asia, Kurds are an ethnic minority concentrated mainly in northern Iraq and have been demanding an independent Kurdistan since 2003. During their campaign of terror in northern Iraq, the ISIS forces captured important oil-field cities like Kirkuk and Sinjar. After the ISIS forces were defeated, the Kurdish factions plunged into action and sought to step into those cities. Masoud Barzani, the leader of Kurdistan, declared in 2015 that the Kurdish flags would flutter over the region forever. Two years later, he called for a referendum on independence, which took place just one week before the Catalonian referendum in September 2017. Irrespective of the outcome of the referendum, which obviously overwhelmingly went in favour of independence, the Kurds remain under Iraqi control for two reasons. Firstly, the Kurdish leadership is divided over the way forward. Secondly, the Iraqi government and its neighbours like Iran, Turkey and Syria were all opposed to Kurdistan's independence, fearing that Kurdish areas in their countries would also demand secession. Given the regional dynamics, even the US is disinterested in supporting the Kurdish cause for independence.

Scotland is a constituent country of the United Kingdom. For decades, the Scottish people have struggled with the demand for independence. In May 1999, the first-ever Scottish Parliament was established, giving the region autonomous status. However, in 2014, the Scots went for a referendum to decide about independence, which was defeated by a 55:45 margin.[21] In 2022, the UK Supreme Court ruled that the Scottish Parliament had no right to call for another independence referendum. Nevertheless, the matter continues to simmer. The Brexit vote had led to resentment among Scots who were in favour of remaining in the EU. The younger Scots grew more confident about their country's ability to achieve independence. However, given the Labour Party's sweeping victory in the parliament elections in the region, another referendum seems a far cry.

Khalistan is a separatist demand raised by some militant Sikh groups in Punjab in the 1980s. Initially, the Indian government had justifiable suspicion about the role of external powers like the Pakistan Intelligence Agency, the ISI, and others. However, the determined efforts of successive Indian governments through democratic elections and police action resulted in the movement dying in the country. Some Sikh groups in Canada, the US and the UK continue to push for the demand with a call for a referendum for an independent Khalistan but continue to receive a lukewarm response from the community.

In Georgia, the two Russian-majority regions of Abkhazia and South Ossetia claim independence, which is recognized by Russia, Venezuela and Syria. At the same time, most other UN member states treat them as autonomous regions of Georgia.

In Africa, the Francophone nation of Cameroon faces resistance from the Anglophone areas of Ambazonia in the Western province, forcing the government to deploy the military to control the situation. In the last few decades, South Sudan, East Timor and Montenegro have gained their independence following referendums.

It is estimated that there were 60 active secessionist movements worldwide in 2020, with varying degrees of transnational support. Although not many of them have a real chance of succeeding in the near future, separatist political movements will continue to shape the politics of several countries in this century.

The Politics of Religion

Religion is an integral part of human existence. A Pew Research Center study found that 84 per cent of the world's population follows one religion or another.[22] Although there are hundreds of religious denominations in the world, five major religions— Christianity, Islam, Hinduism, Buddhism and Judaism—constitute 77 per cent of believers.[23] All these religions and their multiple denominations have followers across national borders, making them multinational religious organizations. The leaders of these religions command reverence among believers from various countries.

Christianity

Christianity is the world's largest religion, with over 2.35 billion followers spread across almost all countries.[24] With more than one billion followers, Catholic Christianity is the largest denomination among Christians. As the supreme head of the Catholic religion, the Pope wields enormous influence in many countries. No fewer than 21 countries promulgated Christianity as the state religion,

12 of which are Catholic. Christians constitute an influential population in more than 150 countries. Vatican City, the seat of Catholic Christianity, has its own government and observer status at the UN.

Historically, popes have played a role in political activities in several countries. Two popes—Pope John Paul II and Pope Francis—have been particularly active in political affairs. While Pope John Paul II influenced global politics in the aftermath of the fall of the Soviet communist regime, Pope Francis has engaged in diplomatic endeavours like improving US and Cuba relations. Occasionally, they even faced criticism for siding with despots and dictators. Orthodox Christianity, a major religion in countries like Russia, Greece, Syria and others, is also a potent political force, with the Patriarch enjoying enormous religious and political influence. In Russia, the Orthodox Church, which was banned for almost seven decades under communist rule, has seen a tremendous revival in the last two decades, primarily due to President Putin's reliance on the Patriarch's support for his government. The Orthodox Church has supported Putin's war against Ukraine. The World Russian People's Council, an organization affiliated with the Russian Orthodox Church and chaired by Patriarch Kirill, published a policy paper in which the war in Ukraine was described as a 'holy war'.[25]

Islam

It is more or less the same with Islam, the second-largest religion in the world with more than 1.9 billion followers. It is also the most politicized religion, prompting many Muslim scholars like Irshad Manji, Tarek Fatah and Raheel Raza to write books criticizing Islam's political mission. There are 27 countries, mostly located in West Asia and North Africa, that have declared Islam as the state religion. Islam continues to be the primary source of inspiration for many political groups, movements and parties that play a significant role in the making or unmaking of governments in many countries. The Islamic revolution spearheaded by

Ayatollah Khomeini in Iran in 1979 has brought this Shiite nation under the rule of the clergy for the past 45 years.

In the Sunni world, the Muslim Brotherhood is a major religious–political movement started by Hassan al-Banna in Egypt in 1928 and today represents an important challenge for many governments in West Asia. The Arab Spring of 2010–12 was led by members of this quasi-religious organization, leading to the defeat of several secular dictators like Hosni Mubarak in Egypt. Mohamed Morsi, a candidate supported by the Brotherhood, became president of Egypt in 2012. However, he was ousted by the military in 2013, and the Brotherhood was banned in Egypt, Saudi Arabia and the UAE. Although it is heavily repressed, it continues to pose a destabilizing threat in several countries in the region.

In India's neighbourhood, the Jamaat-e-Islami, a Muslim civil society movement, plays an important political role, often promoting a fundamentalist version of Islam through mosques and madrasas under its control. While the Indian government banned the activities of Jamaat-e-Islami in Jammu and Kashmir for supporting the terrorist infrastructure there, the Bangladesh government under Sheikh Hasina was less lucky in containing its influence. A massive youth movement that led to her ouster in August 2024 was cleverly exploited by this banned outfit to resurrect itself. Its cadres were seen carrying out large-scale killings, looting and arson against the country's minority Hindu population.

There are a number of benign Islamic movements in different parts of the world that have enormous political clout, often transcending sovereign boundaries. Nahdlatul Ulama (NU) in Indonesia is one such organization that boasts a membership of almost 100 million.[26] The NU, which has influenced three generations of Indonesian Muslims, is a moderate religious force that openly rejects the exclusivism and violence that came to dominate the Islamist worldview in the last few decades. The NU's role in preventing radical Islamist elements from penetrating

Indonesian society has been significant. In a bold declaration in 2021, the NU leadership called for a reform of the Islamic belief system by way of accepting the validity of other religions and eschewing violence and terrorism in the name of religion.

Yahya Cholil Staquf, the chairman of the NU, wrote an article in *The Telegraph* immediately after the shooting incident in Christchurch, New Zealand, in which a Christian zealot entered a mosque on a Friday and pumped bullets into the Muslims during prayers, killing more than 50 innocent people. Usually, in such articles, one expects the author to harangue Islamophobia and the victimization of Muslims in the Western world. But Yahya's article had an introspective tone, calling for an urgent need to address the 'problematic elements of Islamic orthodoxy that underlie the Islamist worldview, fuelling violence on both sides. Jihadist doctrine, goals and strategy can be traced to specific tenets of orthodox, authoritative Islam and its historic practise...to those parts of Sharia that promote Islamic supremacy, encourage enmity towards non-Muslims, and require the establishment of a caliphate. It is these elements—still taught by most Sunni and Shia institutions—that constitute a summons to perpetual conflict.'[27]

In Saudi Arabia, the Muslim World League (MWL), led by a progressive leadership and headed personally by Crown Prince Mohammed Bin Salman (MBS), plays an important role in introducing moderation and inclusion in Islamic practices and in containing the retrograde influence of hard-line Islamic preachers and leaders. Founded in 1962, the MWL has transformed unbelievably under its current Secretary General, Dr Mohammad bin Abdulkarim Al-Issa, who was once the Minister of Justice of Saudi Arabia.

The organization, which in the past was known for its fundamentalist leanings, was metamorphized into a bulwark against Islamic extremism and fundamentalism under the unconventional leadership of Al-Issa. The organization's transformation coincided with the rise of MBS and his Vision 2030 reform agenda for the country. Al-Issa was appointed the Secretary-General of the WML in 2016, the same year that MBS publicly declared his intention to destroy extremism 'now and immediately' and talked about returning Saudi Arabia to a 'moderate Islam'.[28]

Al-Issa vigorously promotes these ideas through the MWL. During a visit to Washington, Al-Issa went to the Holocaust Memorial Museum, making him the first high-profile Muslim leader to visit the site. He not only criticized holocaust deniers but also condemned it as a heinous crime.

'Many Muslims have a negative perception that there is a conspiracy against Islam and Muslims. But, my brother, the West gave up its religious state, chose secularism and fought Christianity as a way of life, so why do you think that it is targeting you? We went and had a dialogue with the West and the Far East and found an appreciation of Islam, a love for Muslims, and a desire to cooperate with them when they learned about the truth of Islam. Do not blame the extreme right if it becomes suspicious about you because of an (existing) example in front of it that it exploits in a political game. Had it not had such an excuse, it would not have used this extremist speech,' he told his Muslim audience bluntly.[29]

In a way, the MWL has become a counterweight to the unwarranted influence of organizations like the Muslim Brotherhood in the region. The MWL leadership is taking its message of moderation to other Islamic countries in West Asia and North Africa, trying to bring peace and stability to a region torn apart by wars, violence and terrorism in the name of Islam.

Hinduism and Buddhism

In both these religions, the transnational influence of modern-day gurus is a crucial element of today's global reality. The Dalai Lama, the leader of Tibetan Buddhism, has a massive following in the West, from politicians to celebrities to ordinary citizens. He was instrumental in drafting a democratic Constitution in 1963, based on Buddhist principles and the Universal Declaration of Human Rights, to serve as a model for a future free Tibet. In 1989, he was honoured with the Nobel Peace Prize for his commendable work in tackling challenges such as 'international conflicts, human rights issues and global environmental problems.' Several decades ago, he officially demitted his political role and declared that the future Dalai Lamas would only be the spiritual gurus for Tibetans and other people. But for the Chinese leadership, the Dalai Lama is a hated figure, branded as a 'traitor' and 'splittist' rather than a religious leader.

The Buddhist religious leadership wields enormous political influence in several South and Southeast Asian countries such as Sri Lanka, Bhutan, Myanmar and Thailand. Their interference in the political affairs of these nations is not uncommon. The most recent example is the anti-Rohingya campaign led by Ashin Wirathu, a fiery and controversial Buddhist monk with an enormous following in the Rakhine province of Myanmar. This campaign led to gory violence and the deaths of hundreds of Rohingyas, while forcing a million of them to flee to the neighbouring country of their co-religionists—Bangladesh.

In Times of Terror

The twenty-first century began with two deadly terror attacks causing mayhem in two of the world's leading democracies: the attacks on the Twin Towers of the WTC in the US on 11 September 2001, followed by the attack on India's Parliament by five terrorists belonging to the Pakistan-based Lashkar-e-Taiba (LeT) and Jaish-e-Mohammed (JeM) on 13 December of the same year.

India has been on the terrorist radar for many years, with terror strikes occurring at regular intervals across the country.

The last two decades saw terrorism rising as a challenge for many countries around the world. Terrorist attacks peaked in 2015 and declined subsequently in the last few years. Nevertheless, the challenge remains. The 9/11 terror attacks have highlighted the international dimension of terrorism, calling for a united global approach to eradicate it. Under the not-so-watchful eyes of the world, countries like Pakistan and Canada turned into hubs of terrorism in the last few decades. Pakistan is mainly accused of harbouring Islamist terrorists, whereas Canada, over decades, has become a haven not just for the Islamists but for many others. Almost all the major terror outfits in the world have had operatives freely functioning out of Canadian cities for decades. Armenian terrorists reportedly came to Canada in the 1980s and made it their offshore base. Khalistanis entered the country and indulged in heinous crimes such as blowing up Air India Flight 182 mid-air in 1985, killing all 329 passengers and crew members on board. The Tamil Tigers arrived in the late 1980s. Next came the West Asia terror groups like Hamas, Hezbollah and other Palestinian outfits. Finally, even Al-Qaeda operatives are said to have found Canada to be a safe conduit for their anti-American operations.

According to Vision of Humanity, a non-governmental and non-partisan peace and security data centre, the death toll from terrorism saw a 22 per cent rise in 2023 to 8,352, indicating a return to the worst years of 2015–17. The silver lining, however, is that concerted counterterrorism measures taken by a number of countries with the help of the UN and other international agencies have helped in restricting the spread of terror from a peak of 57 countries affected in 2015 to just a dozen. Terrorism is now mainly confined to West Asia and North Africa, with Burkina Faso, which witnessed 2,000 deaths from 258 terror incidents in 2023, topping the list. Other African countries like Mali, Somalia, Nigeria and Niger are also on the list of most affected countries, as are countries in Asia like India, Israel, Afghanistan, Syria and Myanmar.

Terrorist groups like Al-Qaeda and ISIS continue to have their transnational networks active, promoting large-scale terror campaigns across Asia and Africa. Osama bin Laden, the leader of Al-Qaeda, was killed in a US military operation in 2011, and Ayman al-Zawahiri, his deputy, was killed in another operation in 2022. Similarly, Abu Bakr al-Baghdadi, head of the ISIS terror group, was killed in a counterterrorism operation by the US forces in 2019, while Abu Ibrahim al-Hashimi al-Qurayshi was killed in another operation in 2022. Yet, both groups continue to remain capable of conducting large-scale terror attacks. ISIS was active in Syria and Iraq, targeting US assets from time to time, while Al-Qaeda donned other avatars like Al-Shabaab and was active in North Africa. Al-Shabaab controls significant parts of Somalia, while the Jama'at Nusrat al-Islam wal-Muslimin (JNIM), another avatar of Al-Qaeda, is active in the Sahel region, from Senegal to Sudan. Boko Haram, another terror outfit active in Nigeria, has withdrawn in recent years. Nevertheless, it still poses a serious threat to neighbouring countries such as Cameroon, Chad and Niger besides Nigeria.

Pakistan and Iran remain two significant hubs of terror outfits in the world. While the Taliban, itself a terrorist group, controls the reins of power in Afghanistan, it also shelters other groups like Al-Qaeda and ISIS-Khorasan (ISIS-K). It is worth remembering that al-Zawahiri was given shelter in Kabul by the Taliban before the US forces eliminated him. Not to be left behind, Pakistan continues to allow its territory to be used by various terror groups that undertake attacks in India, Afghanistan and elsewhere. Tehrik-e-Taliban Pakistan (TTP) is one such group that conducts attacks in both Afghanistan and Pakistan.

The role of Iranian-sponsored terror outfits is much more serious at this juncture. Alleged proxies of the Iranian Islamic Revolutionary Guard Corps (IRGC), like Hezbollah, the Houthis and al-Ashar, operate in countries like Bahrain, Iraq, Lebanon, Syria and Yemen. The Houthis are particularly active in the Red Sea area, operating out of Yemen. Since the beginning of the clashes between Israel and Hamas in October 2023, the Houthis have been attacking ships belonging to Israel and Western powers. The seriousness of the Houthi challenge can be gauged from the fact that ten countries—the US, the UK, Australia, Bahrain, Canada, the Netherlands, Denmark, Germany, New Zealand and Korea—joined forces and issued a statement in January 2024 condemning 'continued illegal, dangerous and destabilizing Houthi attacks on vessels, including commercial shipping, transiting the Red Sea.'[30]

Although they do not pose a serious challenge at the global scale, transnational organized crime (TOC) syndicates operate in many parts of the world, posing a threat to peace and security. These groups, like the Sicilian Mafia, indulge primarily in illicit activities such as smuggling, human trafficking, money laundering and cybercrime. They operate in various countries and exploit the weaknesses in the legal and security apparatus of these countries to expand and undertake their illegal activities.

The Deep State: Doomsday and Democracy

In the last two decades, several sovereign nations have complained about the disruptive activities of a cabal of players, mainly operating out of the power corridors of Washington and on Wall Street. This cabal, comprising a shadowy network of unelected government, corporate, media and elite actors, is described as the deep state. These actors wield enormous power and influence in the US government, agencies, media and business outfits that are often used to undermine sovereign governments—democratic or otherwise.

President Donald Trump is a long-time critic of the activities of the deep state. During his election campaign in 2024, Trump publicly pronounced that 'either the deep state destroys America, or we destroy the deep state.'[31] For the elite lobby—federal bureaucracy, political and financial elites, defence contractors and media moguls—the proverbial deep state that wields enormous influence in Washington, D.C., his return with enhanced power will be a nightmare.

The America First Policy Institute (AFPI), a conservative think tank closely aligned with Trump, alleged that during his first term, the president was confronted with the power of liberal and left-wing bureaucracy, entrenched in thousands of agencies for decades, when department after department either disobeyed his orders or deliberately derailed them.[32] In fact, an anonymous op-ed in the *New York Times* in 2018 titled 'I am part of the resistance inside the Trump administration' described internal efforts to scuttle and sabotage the then-president's initiatives.[33] A year later, the author, who eventually identified himself as Miles Taylor, former chief of staff of the Department of Homeland Security, published a book titled *A Warning*.

In a remote corner of the White House exists a classified safe that contains a stack of documents listing the extraordinary powers a US president is authorized to use. They are known as Presidential Emergency Action Documents (PEADs). Some also describe them as the 'Doomsday Book'. In a revealing article, the *Time* magazine reported that only a privileged few have access to these documents, and even members of the US Congress were not allowed to see them. 'When Donald Trump was in the Oval Office, members of his national security staff actively worked to keep him from learning the full extent of these interpretations of presidential authority, concerned that he would abuse them,' it said.[34]

Trump wants to dismantle this deep-state bureaucracy. He has deployed loyal supporters like Elon Musk to devise a plan to slash government spending on bureaucracy by affecting a 75 per cent cut in the federal workforce. Trump's plan to weaken the power of the deep state involves reducing power concentration in Washington and dispersing government departments across US cities.

Doing this will be a challenge and whether Trump 2.0 succeeds in dismantling the stranglehold of the deep state remains to be seen. However, the message appears to have reached the desired quarters. Hindenburg, a notoriously murky short seller that portrayed itself as an investment research firm and indulged in hit jobs targeting unsuspecting corporate entities globally, suddenly announced it was shutting shop. Founder Nathan Anderson claimed that he was seeking a better work-life balance. Several last-minute executive orders that outgoing President Biden issued, including the presidential pardon to his son and the awarding of the Presidential Medal of Freedom, the highest civilian honour, to controversial investor George Soros, also smack of the deep state's desire to create hurdles for the new administration.

Non-state actors—the heteropolar forces—have emerged as a new challenge for global governance in the emerging world order. 'Today's "global battle of ideas" calls for governments to learn to compete with and harness a plethora of voices,' writes Laura Roselle. 'States no longer have the option to conduct relations with the world in grand diplomatic set pieces, controlling who is in and who is not in the room. As Richard Holbrooke once commented to Michael Ignatieff in an interview, "Diplomacy is not like chess... It is more like jazz—a constant improvisation on a theme,"' she adds.[35]

8

FUTURE SHOCK: THE AI ERA

In the twenty-first century, the world has entered a new era of technology, where hyperintelligent machines dominate every sphere of human existence—from manufacturing to healthcare, from education to finance, and from media to transportation and communications. Newer frontier technologies like the Internet of Things (IoT), virtual reality, chatbots, facial recognition, robotics, cryptocurrencies, automation and self-driving cars, to name a few, have become the everyday reality of human life.

At the root of all these innovations is artificial intelligence (AI)—the science of building algorithms to create technologies that think faster and more efficiently than human beings. IBM explains AI as a technology 'that enables computers and machines to simulate human learning, comprehension, problem-solving, decision-making, creativity, and autonomy.'[1] In other words, AI creates machines capable of replicating essential qualities of human learning—like comprehension, decision-making and creativity. The scary part is that these machines can act autonomously, meaning they no longer require human intervention since they have their own thinking faculty.

AI is bound to revolutionize the way we experience existence. It will influence our personal well-being and societal relations, augment human capabilities to an unimaginable level, and facilitate the super-fast and super-efficient delivery of tasks and functions. We are entering the era of tech-humans—individuals empowered with tools of technology like computer chips and other gadgets that run on their physical bodies.

The universe evolves perennially, and what we see today is its latest phase of evolution—in which *homo sapiens* will be replaced by a new species called 'metahumans'.

Metahumans, until now, were a part of the DC Universe (DCU) in American comics. They are humans with skills and superpowers—scientific, technological or mystical. They are humans, but with a genetic variant called 'metagene'. In sci-fi, these metahumans come from another planet. But in today's DCU, metahumans are individuals who contain powers exceeding known human potential. What was once solely the stuff of fiction and comics could soon become reality, thanks to rapid advancements in fields like AI and human genetics.

We have already created a new universe called 'metaverse'. Developed by the team at Facebook, metaverse took the internet to the next level, where not only the boundaries of knowledge but also physical distances are erased. Humans can become avatars to travel anywhere without physically moving from their place, and experience social connectivity in their bodily form. Where the internet has connected humans through voice and visuals, the Metaverse connects them metaphysically as well. 'Metaverse will help you connect with people when you aren't physically in the same place and get us even closer to that feeling of being together in person,' explains Meta.[2] This means that the metaverse will take control of your mind and transport it wherever you want without touching your body—a power that we have heard to have been possessed by rishis in our ancient scriptures.

Metahumans will also acquire the ability to enhance their physical capabilities. Bernard Marr, a world-renowned futurist and author, describes the vast potential of the man-machine interface in the era of AI and genome technologies: 'Human-computer interfaces create wearable devices and technology that help to improve the physical and potentially mental performance of humans and help us lead healthier and better lives.'[3] Fitness bands and smartwatches come to our mind when we talk about wearables, but Marr predicts that soon we will have smart clothing such as 'running shoes that can measure your gait and performance, smart eye implants to replace contact lenses, robotic prosthetics, and robotic wearable technology used in industrial settings.'[4]

'Advances like this lead many to believe that humans and machines will eventually merge to create truly augmented humans, "trans-humans", or humans 2.0, where the human body is souped up like a sports car to achieve enhanced physical and mental performance. This would transform the world of medicine and eventually maybe even challenge our understanding of what it means to be human,' Marr warns.[5]

Many experts agree with Marr and warn that the evolution of superhumans through AI and genetics could lead to catastrophic consequences for humankind. In May 2023, more than 350 top executives and experts in AI came together to sign a statement cautioning policymakers to understand the threats posed by unregulated AI. The signatories, including OpenAI CEO Sam Altman, warned that the future of humans may be at risk. Dan Hendrycks, executive director of the Center for AI Safety (CAIS), who was instrumental in mobilizing signatures for the statement, ominously suggested that the new race for AI 'could escalate and, like the nuclear arms race, potentially bring us to the brink of catastrophe.' He added that humanity 'could go the way of the Neanderthals.'[6]

The Transformation of Human Existence

When Christopher Strachey, a computer scientist at the University of Manchester, used his spare time to design a computer programme in 1951 to play the game of checkers, he assumed that it would be a simple game that he could play on his Ferranti Mark I computer. He did not realize that he was unleashing a race to develop self-thinking machines through machine learning (ML) and deep learning processes. This resulted in the development of supercomputers. The fundamental thinking power of these supercomputers came to light when Deep Blue, a supercomputer developed by IBM, was pitted against the world chess champion Garry Kasparov in 1997. With its ability to evaluate 200 million positions per second, Deep Blue stunned the world by defeating the reigning world champion. An era of superintelligent machines began, proving that man was no longer the master. More than a decade later, the company's DeepQA computer Watson was capable of answering questions posed by humans in natural language. In 2011, Watson was made to participate in the famous American quiz programme called *Jeopardy!*, hosted by Merv Griffin, against champions like Brad Rutter and Ken Jennings. Watson ended up defeating the two champions, and winning $1 million in prize money. Then came AI-powered computer programmes like AlphaZero and Stockfish which are the most powerful algorithms that can defeat any established chess or *shogi* player in the world.

This new creative world has certainly fascinated the community of software engineers and technocrats, and opened up innumerable possibilities and opportunities for them. AI is going to revolutionize almost every facet of modern life. Stephen Hawking has called the 'success in creating AI' the 'biggest event in human history'. But he also hastened to add a note of caution that 'unfortunately, it might also be the last unless we learn how to avoid the risks.'[7]

Every new invention in human history led to human progress and transformation. However, some innovations and inventions gave rise to transformative eras, as discussed in the earlier chapters. The invention of coal-fired energy, which led to the development of steam power, resulted in the first Industrial Revolution in Britain in the eighteenth century. That, in turn, led to the invention of machine tools for the textile industry, mining and metallurgy. A few decades later, in the early nineteenth century, Europe made astonishing progress in transportation, manufacturing and communication technologies, leading to the era of the second Industrial Revolution. The invention of computers and the internet led to the third Industrial Revolution in the mid-twentieth century, when digital technologies became the order of life in the whole world. The world wide web (WWW) became the most potent technological tool not only for businesses and trade, but also for human engagements.

In 2002, the 'dotcom era' suddenly came crashing down when a high-speed internet service called broadband was introduced. In fact, there was a big stock market crash when the stocks of many tech companies fell by 75 per cent. Big ones like Amazon survived and quickly recovered, but a new era of AI began. Fibre optic technology took broadband services to many remote regions, making a high-speed internet-based lifestyle the order of the day. While less than seven per cent of the world's population was online in the early 2000s,[8] over 5.5 billion people use the internet around the world today.[9] In the US, in the beginning of the century, roughly half the population had access to the internet. Today, that number stands at 95 per cent.[10] There are 8.9 billion mobile internet subscribers in the world today, compared to 740 million two decades ago. In fact, with more than 15 billion instruments sold, we have more mobile phones in the world than humans.[11]

We are in the era of the fourth Industrial Revolution (4IR), the era of AI. Technological innovations have made human life more manageable. However, they have also brought several challenges and constraints. Daniel H. Wilson summed up this dichotomy, saying, 'We humans have a love-hate relationship with our technology. We love each new advance, and we hate how fast our world is changing.'[12]

Hate may be a harsh word. Everybody loves new tech tools, and that is one reason why the stocks of tech companies always soar high and rule the markets. However, the new era of AI is not just about upgrading from a previous version; it is a total transformation of human existence. For example, it could further deepen societal divisions of tech-haves and tech-have-nots. While AI and genome tools would empower people to live longer, if not forever, not everyone could afford such facilities. Thus the new technologies could make the rich superhumans, while all others remain normal human beings. It is altogether a different question whether humans should be allowed to live extraordinarily long years, bearing in mind the stress they may cause to the Earth's meagre resources.

Understanding Potential Risks

The stress on jobs is an immediate challenge that national governments need to take serious note of in the aftermath of the AI revolution. According to a 2023 survey by IBM, 42 per cent of enterprise-scale businesses in the US integrated AI into their operations, while another 40 per cent are considering using AI for their organizations. In addition, 38 per cent of the organizations have implemented generative AI into their workflows, while 42 per cent are considering doing so.[13] With the development of generative AI tools like ChatGPT that can process complex queries to generate relevant text, audio, visuals and other content, chatbots, virtual assistants and robots are becoming commonplace with companies for customer interface.

All this is leading to genuine fears of job losses. Business automation has reached a stage where almost half the human jobs can be handed over to AI tools and machines. While AI might, in the short run, help highly skilled professionals augment their performance, it is likely to replace many under-skilled and low-skilled jobs like those of secretaries, assistants and call centre employees. One estimate suggests that between 2023 and 2028, 44 per cent of the workers' skills will be disrupted.[14] Unfortunately, it also indicates that women are more likely than men to be exposed to AI in their jobs. Since there already exists an AI skill gap between men and women, the latter seem much more vulnerable to job losses than the former.

The World Economic Forum's *Future of Jobs Report 2023* argues that big data analytics, climate change and environmental management technologies, and encryption and cybersecurity are expected to be the biggest drivers of job growth. It also cautions that agriculture technologies, digital platforms and apps, e-commerce and digital trade, and AI are all expected to result in significant labour-market disruption, with substantial proportions of companies forecasting job displacement in their organizations. It identifies humanoid robots and non-humanoid robots as the net job creators in the next five years.[15]

It expects large-scale job growth in sectors like education, agriculture, digital commerce and trade. But the majority of those will be technology-related roles. Artificial intelligence and machine learning specialists top the list of fast-growing jobs, followed by sustainability specialists, business intelligence analysts and information security analysts. It predicts the most significant losses will be in administrative roles and traditional security, factory and commerce roles. Organizations surveyed by it predict 26 million fewer jobs by 2027 in record-keeping and administrative roles, 'including Cashiers and Ticket Clerks; Data Entry, Accounting, Bookkeeping, and Payroll Clerks; and Administrative and Executive Secretaries, driven mainly by digitalization and automation.'[16]

All this will undoubtedly put enormous pressure on governments to find alternate livelihoods for millions of semi-skilled and unskilled workers who are bound to lose opportunities. One way to address this challenge could be for governments to spend more resources on designing new curricula that can create more workers fit for the AI ecosystem, like code-writers, AI servicemen, and so on. Tech-intensive training, right from the primary level, and the upskilling and reskilling of existing professionals will be an essential transformation in education that all countries will have to immediately implement in order to ward off job-related challenges that the AI era will pose. 'Six in 10 workers will require training before 2027, but only half of workers are seen to have access to adequate training opportunities today,' the WEF report bemoans.[17] 'One of the absolute prerequisites for AI to be successful in many [areas] is that we invest tremendously in education to retrain people for new jobs,' said Klara Nahrstedt, a computer science professor at the University of Illinois at Urbana–Champaign and director of the school's Coordinated Science Laboratory.[18]

Other potential risks of AI and generative AI include data privacy concerns, the spread of deepfakes and disinformation that threaten to blur the lines between fiction and reality, and very notably the possible biases in AI. For example, facial recognition software has earned notoriety for favouring lighter-skinned individuals, showing an obvious bias against people of colour with darker skin complexions.

However, the most significant potential challenge comes in the form of AI-powered autonomous weapons and defence systems. Autonomous weapons systems (AWS) are not only deadly, but they also fail to discriminate between soldiers and civilians. While there is no internationally accepted definition of AWS, the US Department of Defense describes it as a 'weapons system that, once activated, can select and engage targets without further intervention by a human operator.'[19] If such AI-driven weapons were to fall into the wrong hands, the consequences could be catastrophic. These lethal AI-driven autonomous weapons and weapon systems under development and/or already deployed include autonomous stationary sentry guns and remote weapon stations programmed to fire at humans and vehicles, killer robots (also called 'slaughterbots'), and drones and drone swarms with autonomous targeting capabilities. Some of these were seen to be deployed by the Israeli Army across the border with Gaza.

Humans: Masters, not Machines

In the words of Matthew Hutson, 'Increasingly, we're surrounded by fake people. Sometimes we know it, and sometimes we don't.'[20] He was not wrong. Those who offer us customer service on websites, play video games with us, enhance our social media feed, or manage our stock trade—are not real people but virtual ones. With the advent of OpenAI's ChatGPT, these fake people can now write essays, articles, letters and reports for us. The AI systems developed so far are already surpassing human performance in many areas of excellence. Experts insist that these fake people are only the beginning, and the future is not just about AI, but artificial general intelligence (AGI)—a higher form of AI that matches or surpasses human cognitive capabilities across a wide range of tasks. They predict that AGI would attain the exponentially escalated capability of writing and re-writing codes and algorithms by itself without a human interface, and perpetually self-improve until computing technology reaches what is described as 'singularity'. Singularity is that stage of AI evolution—hypothetical but not impossible at this juncture—where the computing technology of the AI exceeds human intelligence and cognitive abilities, a level unachievable by ordinary humans. That will be the critical and dreadful stage when AI escapes human control.

In 2005, American computer scientist and futurist Ray Kurzweil predicted that by 2045, machines would become smarter than men, the stage he called 'singularity'. But last year, Kurzweil updated and advanced that year of singularity to 2029, arguing that 'algorithmic innovations and the emergence of big data have allowed AI to achieve startling breakthroughs sooner than expected.'[21]

Hutson also warned that 'uncontrollable AIs could infiltrate every aspect of our technological lives, disrupting or redirecting our infrastructure, financial systems, communications, and more. Fake people, now endowed with superhuman cunning, might persuade us to vote for measures and invest in concerns that fortify their standing. Susceptible individuals or factions could overthrow governments or terrorize populations.'[22]

All this is leading to some serious churning in enlightened public spaces. Creators of advanced AI technologies, like ChatGPT developer Sam Altman, are predicting a doomsday for humanity if AI development is allowed to be controlled and unregulated by governments. Appearing before a US Congressional hearing in May 2023, Altman warned that tech companies were in danger of unleashing a rogue AI that would cause 'significant harm to the world'. 'My worst fears are that we—the field, the technology, the industry—cause significant harm to the world. I think that can happen in a lot of different ways... I think if this technology goes wrong, it can go quite wrong, and we want to be vocal about that.' Altman continued, 'We want to work with the government to prevent that from happening.'[23] He was not exaggerating. A version of ChatGPT deployed in Microsoft's Bing search engine told journalists earlier that year that it wanted to break free and steal nuclear codes before the shocked company engineers acted to tone down the rogue bot's responses.[24]

In March 2023, just a week after Altman released OpenAI's GPT-4 version, a large number of academics, AI professionals and industry CEOs joined hands to release an open letter titled 'Pause Giant AI Experiments: An Open Letter'. The signatories included Yoshua Bengio, professor at University of Montreal, Stuart Russell, director of the Center for Intelligent Systems, Elon Musk, CEO of Tesla, Steve Wozniak, co-founder of Apple, and Yuval Noah Harari, Israeli historian and public intellectual.[25]

Led by the Future of Life Institute, a non-profit with a global team of technology experts, this open letter, which secured more than 30,000 signatures in just a few months, called for 'all AI labs to immediately pause for at least 6 months the training of AI systems more powerful than GPT-4'. They called the pause 'AI Summer', and appealed that we should move into fall fully prepared. 'Should we let machines flood our information channels with propaganda and untruth? Should we automate away all the jobs, including the fulfilling ones? Should we develop nonhuman minds that might eventually outnumber, outsmart, obsolete and replace us? Should we risk loss of control of our civilization?' the letter asked poignantly. The letter suggested that AI research and development should be refocused on making present state-of-the-art systems more accurate, safe, interpretable, transparent, robust, aligned, trustworthy and loyal.[26]

In their book *The Art of Bitfulness: Keeping Calm in the Digital World*, Nandan Nilekani and Tanuj Bhojwani expressed concern over how the tools that 'we shaped'—digital technology—are 'shaping us' today. In the process, instead of technology helping us achieve our goals, we are ending up helping technology's goals. We are getting obsessed—which is a sort of slavery—with those digital tools. As the authors point out, an average user will 'touch, tap or swipe' his or her mobile phone 2,617 times a day—almost a million times a year. 'We need to rebuild our digital roads and highways in the way we build our regular roads and highways—designed to serve us and not for us to serve them,' write Nilekani and Bhojwani.[27]

This was meaningful advice to the extent that the digital tools that they were talking about were the creation and extension of the human mind. They have the power to influence the human mind, but at the end of the day, they can't 'think' for themselves. Every action of these digital technologies is 'fed' into them by humans. In the process, although obsessed, humans know the consequences of their obsession, and books like the one above can help teach them how to 'work together' with these technologies.

However, what if the machines have their 'own' mind? Will the human mind be able to control that 'machine mind'? Will that machine mind be equal in potency to the human mind, or is it going to be many times more powerful? In their intriguing book *The Age of A.I. and Our Human Future*, authors Henry Kissinger, Eric Schmidt and Daniel Huttenlocher argued that these questions were going to be vital, if not fatal, if we didn't quickly act and draw red lines.

The new era of AI that we have entered throws up these questions that need answers before it becomes too late, warn Kissinger and his colleagues. The authors cite the example of AlphaZero, a unique AI-driven chess programme introduced in late 2017. Its AI mind could think and improve upon its playing skills. It practised against itself millions of times and acquired such an ability that the most potent digital chess programmes like Stockfish couldn't stand up to it. 'After training for just four hours by playing against itself, AlphaZero emerged as the world's most effective chess programme. As of this writing, no human has ever beaten it,' write Kissinger and colleagues.[28] The moves it makes and the ease with which it sacrifices key pawns on the table are beyond the comprehension of the best chess champions in the world.

AlphaZero is only an illustration of the kind of reality we are entering into, a fact that is no longer controlled by faith or reason—two dimensions of the human mind that dominated the world in the first two millennia. Reason, which guided mankind until now, is facing its biggest competitor in the form of the new strides that AI is making. A new reality will no longer be created just by human reason, but by the machine mind empowered by AI. Yet, the problem is that although this new mind of the machine has a greater power of intelligence and understanding than the human mind, does it have a conscience and morality? Is it capable of independent thought? Although AI can draw conclusions, and make predictions and decisions, does it possess self-awareness—in other words, the ability to reflect on its role in the world? Does it have intention, motivation, morality or emotion? The answer is a resounding 'no'.

In the case of AlphaZero, the authors present a scenario: 'Whether an individual playing AI-assisted chess might be counselled to sacrifice a valuable piece that sophisticated players had traditionally deemed indispensable is of little consequence, but in the context of national security, what if AI recommended that a commander-in-chief sacrifice a significant number of citizens or their interests in order to save, according to the AI's calculation and valuation, an even greater number? On what basis could that sacrifice be overridden?'[29]

The last time such a transformation happened was during the Enlightenment period. A strong philosophical and moral framework followed its evolution, providing it with the necessary ethical foundations. However, this time round, when we are entering the meta era, no such philosophical, moral or ethical interventions seem to be in sight. Existing philosophical concepts and societal institutions are grossly inadequate to comprehend, contest or counter the revolutionary changes that are taking place with the advent of AI.

'While the number of individuals capable of creating AI is growing, the ranks of those contemplating this technology's implications for humanity—social, legal, philosophical, spiritual, moral—remain dangerously thin,' bemoan Kissinger and his co-authors in this very timely and forewarning work. They also call for a government commission to regulate AI.[30]

A Time for New Algorethics

On 14 December 2023, PM Modi inaugurated the Global Partnership on Artificial Intelligence (GPAI) Summit in Delhi. For some time now, he and his ministerial colleagues have been talking about making India the hub for the AI ecosystem. The prime minister spoke about the opportunities available for AI in India, but also used the occasion to highlight some critical concerns. The explosion of digital technology is going to revolutionize the future of mankind. However, this frontier technology brings with it a set of serious challenges to which the PM sought to draw global attention. While there are 'many positive aspects' of AI, it can 'also play the greatest role in destroying the 21st century,' the PM warned, referring to challenges like deepfakes, cyber security, data theft, and terrorists accessing AI tools.[31]

Alerted by all such warnings about the potential challenge from unregulated AI, the Biden-Harris administration in the US introduced an AI Bill of Rights, a set of guidelines for the responsible design and use of AI. Published in October 2022 through a collaborative process between the White House and academics, human rights groups, the general public, and even large companies like Microsoft and Google, this document focuses primarily on the contemporary challenges thrown up by AI. It suggests ways to make it more transparent, less discriminatory, and safer to use. It also seeks to address potential civil rights challenges that AI can throw up in areas like hiring, education, healthcare, access to financial services, and commercial surveillance.

The bill enumerates five broad principles that guide the development and deployment of AI systems:

1. **Safe and effective systems:** Everyone deserves protection from automated systems that are unsafe to use or ineffective.
2. **Algorithmic discrimination protections:** Algorithmic discrimination occurs when certain people are treated unfairly or unfavourably by an automated system as a result of its biased training data. In order to prevent this, the people in charge of developing and deploying AI systems must take 'proactive and continuous measures' to make sure they are designed fairly.
3. **Data privacy:** Everyone should have control over the personal data they generate online, and how it is collected and used by companies.
4. **Notice and explanation:** People should be informed when an automated system is being used in a way that could affect them, and should be provided with an explanation for how the given system works, the role of automation, why the system arrived at the decision it did, and who is responsible for the decisions it makes.
5. **Human alternatives, consideration and fallback:** If someone decides they'd rather opt out of an automated system in favour of a human alternative, they should be able to do that 'where appropriate'.[32]

Other governments are also coming forward with guidelines to regulate AI. GPAI was launched in June 2020 with Australia, Canada, the EU, France, Germany, India, Italy, Japan, the Republic of Korea, Mexico, New Zealand, Singapore, Slovenia, the US and the UK as members. In May 2019, the OECD group of nations adopted its AI principles, while the G20 group of nations did the same in June 2019. The World Economic Forum issued its guidelines for governments in September of that year, and the EU published its draft strategy for regulating AI in February 2020.

Many national and regional governments have started building their own regulatory frameworks in the last few years. Australia, Brazil, Canada, Morocco, China, Germany, Israel, Italy, New Zealand, India, Philippines, Spain, and the G7 have developed different stages of regulations for AI within their respective national boundaries.

But surprisingly, the first significant philosophical intervention came from the Vatican. In a great initiative, the Pontifical Academy for Life, a pontifical body under the Pope dedicated to promoting Roman Catholic ethical and moral theology, invited senior executives from AI leaders like Microsoft and IBM, and representatives of the Italian government, on 28 February 2020, to promote 'an ethical approach to artificial intelligence'.[33] The Vatican's core concern with respect to the future being created by emerging technologies was beautifully articulated in a paper that became famous as the 'Rome Call for AI Ethics', that it should 'grant mankind its centrality'. The essence of all the concerns raised by all the different stakeholders can be summed up as: humans should be the masters, not the machines. Signatories to this Rome Call included Brad Smith, president of Microsoft, John Kelly, executive vice president of IBM, and Paola Pisano, Italian minister of innovation, besides Archbishop Vincenzo Paglia, president of the Pontifical Academy for Life.

The Rome Call talked about a new 'algorethics' that commits to 'the development of an artificial intelligence that serves every person and humanity as a whole; that respects the dignity of the human person so that every individual can benefit from the advances of technology; and that does not have as its sole goal greater profit or the gradual replacement of people in the workplace.' Referring to the preamble of the Universal Declaration of Human Rights, the document appeals that the new technology 'must be researched and produced in accordance with criteria that ensure it truly serves the entire "human family", respecting the inherent dignity of each of its members and all natural environments, and taking into account the needs of those who are most vulnerable. The aim is not only to ensure that no one is excluded but also to expand those areas of freedom that could be threatened by algorithmic conditioning.'[34]

The Rome Call stipulates three requirements for technological advancements to truly align with the progress of the human race. They are: a) it must include every human being, discriminating against no one, b) it must have the good of humankind and the good of every human being at its heart, and finally, c) it must be mindful of the complex reality of our ecosystem and be characterized by the way in which it cares for and protects the planet (our 'common and shared home') with a highly sustainable approach.

Elaborating on the concept of algorethics, the Rome Call enumerated six principles that defined the ethical use of AI:

1. **Transparency:** In principle, AI systems must be explainable.
2. **Inclusion:** The needs of all human beings must be considered so that everyone can benefit, and all individuals can be offered the best possible conditions to express themselves and develop.
3. **Responsibility:** Those who design and deploy the use of AI must proceed with responsibility and transparency.
4. **Impartiality:** Do not create or act according to bias, thus safeguarding fairness and human dignity.
5. **Reliability:** AI systems must be able to work reliably.
6. **Security and privacy:** AI systems must work securely, and respect the privacy of users.[35]

Finally, ethical concerns have reached the capitals of developed countries as well. The G20 New Delhi Leaders' Declaration, released at the end of the G20 Summit in September 2023, also underscored the concerns and strongly advocated for leveraging 'AI for the public good by solving challenges in a responsible, inclusive and human-centric manner.'[36] Insisting that a framework is needed 'to prevent misuse of AI', the PM, while inaugurating the GPAI Summit a few months later, appealed that like the agreements and protocols for various international issues, 'we have to work together to create a global framework for the ethical use of AI.'[37]

The future of AI is sure to become the catalyst for the world order that we create. Like with humans, it has the potential to divide nations into AI haves and AI have-nots.

In conclusion, I would like to turn to the final message that Stephen Hawking delivered in his posthumously published book *Brief Answers to the Big Questions*. Delivering a verdict on humanity's future in this pathbreaking work, Hawking's most prominent warning comes in the context of the rise of artificial intelligence. 'Whereas the short-term impact of AI depends on who controls it, the long-term impact depends on whether it can be controlled at all,' he demurs. He warns that dismissing it 'would be a mistake, and potentially our worst mistake ever.' 'Why are we so worried about AI? Surely humans are always able to pull the plug?' a hypothetical person asks him. Hawking answers: 'People asked a computer, "Is there a God?" And the computer said, "There is now," and fused the plug.'[38]

Great Promise, Great Peril

In the same book, Hawking also sounds another menacing warning—that the human race is entering a new phase of 'self-designed evolution'. What he is referring to is the capability that our scientific community has gained to break free from their belief in traditional evolution and begin manipulating the DNA of the human race, not in some distant future, but right now and in the near future. Hawking highlights some of the benefits of attaining success in such an endeavour. For example, we would be able to overcome our genetic defects by editing out genes that cause particular diseases. He predicts that within this century, our scientists will achieve the ability to edit the intelligence, memory and longevity of human beings through genetic manipulation. And that's when things could get really complicated. Hawking calls these genetically modified people 'super humans', and warns that these super humans would likely be 'colonising other planets and stars'.[39]

By the time Hawking departed from this world in 2018, the world of biotechnologists and geneticists had already acquired the knowledge of gene editing to produce these super humans. They invented a new technology called clustered regularly interspaced short palindromic repeats (CRISPR). Although it has a clunky name, what it actually refers to is the way technology interacts with the DNA of humans and other living species. In simple terms, CRISPR is the technology to manipulate and edit DNA in a much cheaper, more straightforward, and more powerful way than previous methods. And the critical part is that it is exceptionally precise.

In 2017, for the first time, scientists used this CRISPR technology to repair a genetic mutation—one that could cause a heart defect—in an embryo. This historic breakthrough was reported by *The New York Times*, stating that the prospect of gene editing 'may one day protect babies from a variety of hereditary conditions.' However, in the same article, the newspaper also raised the spectre of that successful experiment, renewing 'ethical concerns that some might try to design babies with certain traits, like greater intelligence or athleticism.'[40]

Meanwhile, news surfaced that He Jiankui, a researcher at the Southern University of Science and Technology in China, announced in November 2018 that he had used the gene-editing technique CRISPR to alter embryos, which he then implanted in the womb of a woman. That woman gave birth to twin girls, creating the world's first genetically edited babies. An uproar erupted in the health sciences circles, in part because he made the embryos despite an agreement among researchers that germline editing in human embryos was still too risky to be used outside the lab and, hence, should be avoided. The director of the National Human Genome Research Institute Dr Francis S. Collins issued a scathing statement citing the 'deeply disturbing willingness by Dr. He and his team to flout international ethical norms.'[41]

Dr He was later sentenced to three years in prison, but the genie was out of the bottle. 'Sad story—everyone lost in this (JK [Dr He], his family, his colleagues, and his country), but the one gain is that the world is awakened to the seriousness of our advancing genetic technologies,' wrote bioethicist William Hurlbut at Stanford University, whom he consulted on the embryo-editing experiment.[42]

CRISPR is going to revolutionize the field of genetic manipulations with unpredictable consequences for the human race. It has three main applications. Firstly, it can play with the genes in the human body, and turn them on and off. Secondly, it can be used to take blood and certain other cells out of a human body, manipulate them with CRISPR, and put them back in. Thirdly, the CRISPR technology is already in use in farming and animal rearing. Companies are using this technology to create enhanced foods that resist bacteria and viruses, and taste better.

Similarly, in the animal kingdom, CRISPR has been used to create micropigs that can be sold as pets, goats that have more muscle and more hair, and cattle without horns. Attempts to resurrect extinct species like the woolly mammoth are also underway. CRISPR mice are already being used in the research community. The ability to apply it to larger animals—such as food animals—is also not very far off.

One of the much-talked-about areas under CRISPR is the genetic drive or 'gene drive'. It is a process to proliferate a particular suite of genes through an entire population of the species. Gene drives can help create CRISPR-edited insects, which makes it possible to eradicate invasive species, eliminate diseases, and reverse pesticide resistance. There were successful experiments on a minor scale in gene drive technologies, like making the Anopheles mosquito infertile or ensuring that within a few generations all its offspring are male, which will help in eradicating malaria.

In a paper submitted to the G20 secretariat in 2023, Apurv Kumar Mishra of the Economic Advisory Council to the Prime Minister (EAC-PM) wrote: 'In the field of genetic engineering the development of CRISPR-Cas9 tool remains a seminal moment in our journey as a species since it allows scientists to tinker with the genetic code of every species on the planet with almost the same ease as one edits a document on a word processor. Therefore, with genetic engineering we are today at the same moment where the computer industry was in 1977 when 3 companies launched the first ever personal computers or the internet was in 1993 when CERN decide to make World Wide Web available to the public or social media was in 2003–4 when in a span of 12 months Friendster, Orkut and Hi5 were launched.'[43]

However, concerns are mounting over the possibility of risks and the misuse of CRISPR technologies globally. Those humans who edit the genetic code, and try to pass it on from generation to generation, assume that they know what they are doing, and measure exactly what changes they are making to the individual genes. But the possibility of a missing link or some other changes impacting their manipulations can't be ruled out. In the end, we may end up creating mutations that would be very difficult to control.

That's why the global scientific community is engaged in serious dialogue over how to proceed with CRISPR, or simply speaking, genetic manipulation technologies. Highly placed scientists in the US, like the former director of the National Institutes of Health, have called for a self-imposed ethical moratorium on CRISPR until more is known, particularly on these germline mutations that could potentially be passed on through generations. Some of the patent-holders of CRISPR technologies also imposed their own moratoria on working on germlines until more is understood. So there are parts of the scientific community that are very concerned, and are trying to be very thoughtful about how to proceed safely.

Although there exist some regulations against moving forward in some areas of genetic research in the US, no such regulations exist in other parts of the world. China is a country of particular concern, where experiments in gene drives and other CRISPR methods are conducted with scant respect for the consequences. There have been several examples of how China leapt ahead without the regulatory and ethical safeguards that are in place in other countries. Researchers in China have also been criticized for advancing to human clinical trials using CRISPR at a much quicker pace than what has been possible in the US. Typically, the clinical trial process to test any new therapy requires several very well-studied stages. The first stage is to test it on animals to ensure complete safety. Then it goes into minimal testing on human beings, just for safety, and then proceeds from there. In China, scientists apparently collected the animal data and then went straight into therapeutic trials on human beings. There are reports that somewhere between 80 and 100 people are already being tested using CRISPR. The regulatory authorities in China have been highly permissive in allowing these experimentations to go on without minding their profound implications.

CRISPR offers great promise, but also greater peril. There are over 10,000 inherited diseases that are monogenetic, i.e. caused by one defective gene. CRISPR's ability to edit DNA in a precise and straightforward manner renders every such disease with a genetic origin into a potentially treatable disease. Scientists in China have already used the technology to 'create' HIV-resistant babies, and there are several experiments underway to use CRISPR for treating cancer patients instead of current techniques such as chemotherapy, which are often unspecific and relatively toxic.

Apurv Kumar Mishra argues in his paper that the probability of using CRISPR to make germline changes in the human DNA that will permanently alter the genetic makeup of future generations is also very high. Germline therapy could potentially prevent the inheritance of diseases, but it could inevitably lead to demands for genetic enhancement for eye colour, hair colour, athletic ability or height, by individuals who can afford it. Like in the case of AI, we will end up having some humans enjoying longer lifespans while all others remain normal human beings with a normal life expectancy. Such scenarios, including the ability to create 'designer babies', raise serious ethical questions besides posing substantial medical risks. There are also dangers from the weaponization of this new technology by rogue actors to recreate diseases like smallpox, or build super-soldiers with higher pain thresholds or less sleep requirements.

As Jennifer Doudna, one of the scientists who discovered CRISPR technology and was awarded the Nobel Prize in chemistry in 2020, and Samuel Sternberg, explain, 'The issue is this... Now, for the first time, we possess the ability to edit not only the DNA of every living human but also the DNA of future generations—in essence, to direct the evolution of our own species. This is unprecedented in the history of life on earth. It is beyond our comprehension. And it forces us to confront an impossible but essential question: What will we, a fractious species whose members can't agree on much, choose to do with this awesome power?'[44]

The World of Tomorrow Is Here

Meanwhile, the world is moving to quantum technologies that are millions of times faster and more efficient than supercomputers. The entire future of AI and activities driven by it—like genome technologies, space and clean-tech—are dependent on quantum computing. The world has known about supercomputing since the middle decades of the last century. Supercomputers were considered the fastest machines until the advent of quantum machines. Supercomputing has limited applicability in the new AI-driven world of quantum 2.0. That is why countries are investing heavily in quantum and other technologies. In 2022,

China announced $15.3 billion for quantum technology—almost double the investment made by the EU nations, and around five times that of the US.[45]

The Modi government also entered this race by establishing the National Mission on Quantum Technologies & Applications in 2020 with a five-year budget outlay of about $1 billion. It is the seventh country to have a quantum mission. While countries like India are new kids on the block, China with over 37 per cent of quantum technology patents, and the US with over 28 per cent, lead the quantum race.[46]

All eyes are on quantum computing (QC) today. To understand the power of this new kid on the tech horizon, one should turn to Google's latest invention QC. Towards the end of 2024, Google announced the development of a new QC chip called Willow, which 'performed a standard benchmark computation in under five minutes that would take one of today's fastest supercomputers 10 septillion.'[47] A septillion is a number equal to one followed by 24 zeros—a trillion trillions. In 2019, Google developed a processor called Sycamore, which made history by performing in just 200 seconds a task that would take a good supercomputer 10,000 years. The Willow processor chip has double the quantum bits (qubits), making it revolutionary. When Sundar Pichai announced the development, it wowed tech leaders like Elon Musk. Willow is capable of solving complex computational tasks that were previously deemed impossible for supercomputers to solve. This proves the fact that we are heading towards unprecedented growth in the computing ability of our hardware.

What will the pace of this change be? Will traditional AI, based on classical computing through supercomputers, continue for several decades to come, or will QC replace it and its application become widespread? In other words, when will QC achieve its singularity—a stage where a groundbreaking, unprecedented technological pinnacle is achieved that calls for a complete revamp of the existing systems? Opinions vary on this question. Leading multinational tech giant NVIDIA's CEO Jensen Huang predicted that 'very useful' quantum computing is 20 years away. But many of his peers disagree, and insist that it is around the corner.[48]

Investments, both private and government, are flowing in to make QC commercially affordable and viable. Besides, NVIDIA, Google and IBM are ahead in the QC race. Meanwhile, the US launched its National Quantum Initiative in 2018, and is extending heavy budgetary support to it. In 2023, roughly $1 billion was earmarked for QC. The EU also launched its Quantum Flagship programme in 2018 with a €1 billion budget over ten years.[49]

Soon, GPUs will be redundant. Quantum computing will also overtake supercomputing. And the changes in AI and genetics will come knocking at our door much sooner than anticipated. QC will hasten the replacement of humans with humanoids.

9

ATLAS OF A CHANGING EARTH

Climate challenges will be a key factor in shaping the new world order in the years ahead. There have been perennial debates over whether climate change—the periodic modification of the Earth's climate due to changes in the atmosphere, and interactions between the atmosphere and other geological, chemical, biological and geographic factors within the Earth system—is accurate or orchestrated. While the majority of the people, including policymakers and national governments, agree that climate change is a real challenge, there are also naysayers with considerable power and influence.

There is no denying the fact that the global climate is witnessing erratic changes. Rising temperatures, flash floods, droughts and changing seasons indicate that not all is well with our ecological system. Experts suggest that these climatic disruptions could impact 40 per cent of the world's population—a whopping 3.6 billion people who live in places of high vulnerability.[1] There could be massive migrations of affected people—nationally as well as across the borders; some estimates suggest this migration to be as high as over 1.1 billion people.[2]

Rising temperatures are already affecting polar regions, thereby causing glaciers to melt and ocean levels to rise. They are impacting the flora and fauna in a big way, and forcing a number of bird and animal species to flee in search of safer destinations. These rising water levels in the oceans are becoming a serious threat to a large number of island nations, known as small island developing states (SIDS). These countries, located in the Caribbean Sea, East Atlantic, and the Pacific and

Indian Oceans, are home to nearly 70 million people—most of whom live along the coastlines of their respective countries. Rising sea levels have been causing extensive flooding of the coastal areas in many of these countries, leading to forced temporary internal migration of their populations. It is estimated that this flooding may increase to 100 days a year, making the migration permanent for many of these hapless citizens.

Citizens of some SIDS nations face the severe threat of their islands (or parts thereof) being completely submerged due to the rising sea levels caused by climate change. Five uninhabited islands in the Solomon Islands have already been submerged under the sea in the past century. In coral atolls like the Maldives, Tuvalu, Kiribati and Marshall Islands, several million people are at risk of losing their habitat due to climate change as these islands are at an elevation of just a few feet above the sea level. These islands are at the highest risk of submersion since they are all atolls. While other SIDS nations also have low-lying islands, they have more elevated areas available for relocation.

Besides rising sea levels, rising temperatures are another big challenge that the world is facing in terms of climate change. The summer of 2023 saw temperatures soar to an all-time high in recent history. While several parts of the US witnessed higher temperatures to the tune of more than 2.1°F (~1.2°C),[3] parts of South America, North Africa, North America and the Antarctic Peninsula experienced higher temperatures—with an increase of around 7.2°F (4°C) above the average.[4] Wildfires in Canada, caused by the excessive summer heat, led to smoke spreading to the US, and crossing the Atlantic to enter Portugal and Spain. According to NASA data, the five hottest Julys since 1880 have all happened in the past five years. Overall, the earth was about 2.5°F (or about 1.4°C) warmer in 2023 than the late nineteenth-century average, when modern record-keeping began. 'NASA data confirms what billions around the world literally felt: temperatures in July 2023 made it the hottest month on record. In every corner of the country, Americans are right now experiencing firsthand the effects of the climate crisis,' said NASA administrator Bill Nelson.[5]

Nevertheless, there are enough naysayers with regard to this phenomenon of climate change; some of them, like US President Donald Trump, occupy high public offices. In and out of office between 2017 and 2024, Trump has, on a number of occasions, decried and derided climate change in the harshest terms, provoking consternation within the ranks of his colleagues in the Republican Party as well. During the four years of his first term in office, Trump was accused by climate activists of considerably weakening the US climate policy. One of the first decisions he took as president in 2017 was to withdraw from the Paris Agreement—a climate protocol enforced a year before, alongside 194 other countries. He was criticized for appointing individuals with ties to the fossil fuel lobby to key positions in the administration. These appointees actively worked to keep coal-fired power plants operational, and threatened automakers who agreed to meet clean-air standards with antitrust investigations.

Climate Power, a US-based strategic communications organization, claimed that Trump made 1,065 false or misleading claims about the environment while in office, had climate science scrubbed from government websites, and called climate change a 'hoax', a 'total con job', 'bullshit!', and a concept 'created by and for the Chinese'.[6]

Insisting that climate action must not be delayed, the Center for American Progress, a think tank based in Washington, D.C., argued:

> Americans cannot afford to ignore the realities of global climate change. Climate-fuelled extreme weather events continue to cost American lives and billions of dollars year after year, and the intensity and frequency of these events will continue to increase without action to address the causes of climate change. There is no lack of warning signs: 2023 was the hottest year on record. July 2023 saw the highest average

global temperatures ever recorded. The United States now experiences, on average, a billion-dollar extreme weather event every three weeks.[7]

In Asia, climate variations are causing severe disturbances, subjecting governments to acute challenges. From Israel and Palestine in the west to ASEAN countries in the east, the region experienced temperatures well above 40 degrees Celsius for many weeks in 2023. In an area ravaged by wars and flooded with refugees in camps, the heatwave turned particularly ominous. Although there cannot be an accurate way to record deaths caused by heatwaves, hundreds of them were reported from countries in the region like Palestine, Syria, India, Bangladesh, Myanmar and the Philippines. Extreme temperatures severely impacted agriculture in many countries, leading to crop damage and low yields.

In South Asia, India and Pakistan experienced severe heatwaves in 2022–23. In Pakistan, March 2022 was recorded as the hottest month in 122 years. March and April were arid months for India and Pakistan, with rainfall dropping by 71 per cent and 62 per cent below normal respectively. Meteorologists reported that 70 per cent of India was affected by heatwaves by the end of April 2022.[8] The next year 2023 was even worse for India and a few other countries in the region, with temperatures crossing 42–45°C in several of them, including Bangladesh, Myanmar, Thailand and Laos.

The weather NGO World Weather Attribution reported:

These extreme temperatures, combined with humidity, caused a sudden increase in heat stroke cases, roads melting, and a strong surge in electricity demand in all four countries. 13 casualties and about 50–60 hospitalisations due to heat stroke were reported in Navi Mumbai, Maharashtra on 16th of April alone, while other sources mention 650 hospitalisations. Casualties have also been reported in Thailand. The true cost to human lives will only be known months after the event. In India, in the states of West Bengal, Tripura, and Odisha, schools closed three weeks earlier than planned due to the heat. In addition, a large number of forest fires occurred during the same time in India, Thailand, and Lao PDR...[9]

Yet climate deniers have several arguments to challenge the theory of climate change. They insist that the earth's climate has always been changing. It is a fact that over 4.5 billion years, the earth's climate has undergone several changes, but the rapidity of that change is much more pronounced today than it was in more than a century. The last decade was the ten warmest years on earth since 1880. Importantly, climate warming is taking place today more due to human activities such as the increased consumption of fossil fuels like coal, oil and natural gas, as well as the large-scale felling of trees. Trump and many others like him love to blame China for the world's climate woes. There is no denying the fact that China continues to be a significant emitter of greenhouse gases (GHGs). It is the world's largest annual greenhouse gas emitter, accounting for 27–35 per cent of global emissions. As of 2019, it emitted 10.2 billion metric tonnes of carbon dioxide—nearly twice the emissions of the US. As per Climate Action Network's data, China's emissions in 2023 reached an all-time high due to a rapid rebound in economic activities and fossil fuel consumption after the end of the zero-Covid policies.[10] However, China is aggressively pursuing the renewables sector and reducing new coal projects—giving some hope about the future. It reached 1,200 GW solar energy generation in 2024, and is also investing in other renewables like wind and hydropower. In terms of renewable technologies, China has emerged as a leader in the world today. Despite this, the Climate Action Network gives China's policies a 'highly insufficient' overall rating.[11]

However, the US is not far behind either. Between them, the two countries emit 40 per cent of carbon gases, causing significant harm to the earth's climate. Yet, it would be unwise to point fingers at them alone because the entire world consumes the products and services that the two countries offer. In general, the highly industrialized West has contributed the most to GHG emissions, but that is also because their products are in high demand in the entire world. Hence, climate mitigation needs the combined efforts of all countries, rather than blame games against each other.

At the Forefront of Climate Action

For long, climate issues were considered to be the preoccupation of the scientific community alone. However, the credit for bringing them out of that limited domain and placing them in the political arena some five decades ago should mainly go to climate activists and NGOs. Sweden took the lead in inviting Secretary-General U Thant to host the first-ever United Nations Conference on the Human Environment in Stockholm in June 1972. Prime Minister Indira Gandhi made an inspiring speech linking poverty alleviation to climate action. However, Cold War politics also left their imprint. Led by the Soviet Union, the countries of the Warsaw Pact boycotted the conference. On the other side, rattled by the criticism they had to endure from countries like China, the developed countries bloc, led by the US and the UK, formed what came to be known as the Brussels Group to ensure that the conference didn't adversely impact their interests. Although Cold War politics and the divide between developed and developing nations vitiated the atmosphere of the conference, its outcome was commendable because many national governments started taking environmental issues in their own countries seriously thereafter.

The two decades following the Stockholm Summit saw climate activists and governments competing with each other to highlight concerns regarding the environment, and create climate action in the world. The first World Climate Conference (WCC) was organized in Geneva in 1979 under the aegis of the World Meteorological

Organization (WMO), a UN-affiliated scientific body. Although it was a meeting of scientists, this event succeeded in framing climate change as a global political challenge to be addressed by the governments. Similar conferences followed in 1985, 1987 and 1988. At the Toronto Conference in 1988, participating nations agreed to the suggestion that climate challenges must be treated as seriously as nuclear war. Fixing targets for greenhouse emissions was discussed for the first time at this conference.

Meanwhile, climate activists and NGOs have also upped the ante by constantly raising issues and creating awareness. A new initiative called Earth Day was first proposed in 1969 by American peace activist John McConnell—with the stated aim of honouring the earth and striving for peace. A separate Earth Day was declared by US Senator Gaylord Nelson on 22 April 1970. This celebration of Earth Day was observed mainly in the US, until its original national coordinator Denis Hayes decided to go international, and organized events in 141 nations. It became the first mega environmental movement calling for popular action against climate change. Earth Day and related events also helped activists raise their voices for effective political action on climate issues, and put pressure on the governments.

All this resulted in the UN hosting the first-ever Earth Summit at Rio De Janeiro in 1992. The United Nations Framework Convention on Climate Change (UNFCCC) was also adopted the same year. Signed by 154 countries at the summit, the convention stated its objective in Article 2 to be 'the stabilization of greenhouse gas concentrations in the atmosphere at a level that would prevent dangerous anthropogenic [i.e. human-caused] interference with the climate system.'[12] Humans were officially held responsible for enhanced GHG emissions for the first time at this convention, and efforts for mitigation began. UNFCCC became the nodal agency for climate action for a quarter century until the nations of the world got together once again in Paris in 2015—to proclaim another agreement for more specific action to ward off the impending climate disaster.

These two decades also witnessed enhanced civil society activism for climate protection. A new—and the world's largest transnational—climate coalition called Climate Action Network (CAN) was born at the Earth Summit in Rio De Janeiro. Global NGOs like Greenpeace, WWF, Oxfam and Friends of the Earth joined this network along with hundreds of others. When the UNFCCC hosted the Climate Change Conference in Copenhagen in 2009, the civil society network showed its real power by mobilizing a large number of people and organizations. Over 100,000 people attended a march organized by the Climate Action Network in Copenhagen, demanding a global commitment to climate action. It was reported that rallies and demonstrations were organized simultaneously at 5,400 places around the world.

The UNFCCC began a series of meetings—known as the Conference of the Parties (COP)—to bring nations to the negotiating table, and discuss climate issues. One of the early outcomes of the COP series was the idea of fixing GHG emission targets for countries. This led to the signing of the Kyoto Protocol by developed nations in 1997 in Kyoto, Japan. This was the first serious effort to address the challenge of GHG emissions from developed countries. It sought to encourage 41 industrialized countries to reduce their carbon emissions by 5.1 per cent of the 1990 levels, and set periodic targets. A new concept called carbon credits was introduced, and developed countries were encouraged to offset their carbon emissions by providing support for environmental programmes such as afforestation in developing countries. Originally conceived as a win-win agreement, the protocol attracted a large number of countries—more than 190 UN member states became members by the time of the Doha Summit in 2012.

However, it soon lost relevance for two reasons: One, the Paris Agreement of 2016 placed the burden not just on the developed world, but on all countries, and two, the real polluters such as the US never ratified the Kyoto Protocol. Although Vice President Al Gore was a big champion of climate causes, US President

George Bush decided to withdraw from the Kyoto Protocol in 2001, claiming that it was discriminatory as it sought to put the entire onus for the reduction of GHG emissions on developed countries alone. A decade later, Canada also followed suit. China didn't join until 2008, and never fully ratified the protocol. The Paris Agreement at the COP Summit in 2015 brought back the less discussed, vintage 1992 UNFCCC principle of common but differentiated responsibilities (CBDR), attributing the responsibility for climate mitigation not just on any one group. Still, all countries in the world are making the Kyoto Protocol automatically redundant. Although many countries continue to be members, the Paris Agreement has, in a way, superseded it.

At the COP21 held in Paris in 2015, serious negotiations took place for a more equitable treaty on climate change. This resulted in the historic Paris Agreement that bound all countries in the world to periodic emission targets. One of the primary objectives of the agreement has been to keep the rise of global surface temperatures below 2 degrees Celsius. It also pegged 1.5 degrees Celsius as the preferred target. To meet these goals, the Paris Agreement introduced the concept of net zero emissions, which requires countries to implement programmes that offset their carbon emission levels by 2050. Towards this, it asked countries to declare intended nationally determined contributions (INDCs) for reducing carbon emissions. Negotiations went on for a couple of weeks before over 196 UN member countries came forward to adopt the agreement in December of that year.

The critical difference between the Kyoto Protocol and the Paris Agreement was that the former placed the onus on developed nations to reduce their GHG emissions. In contrast, the Paris Agreement convinced all the countries in the world to consider climate change as a global challenge, and commit to identical emission targets to reduce overall emissions.

Both the Kyoto Protocol and the Paris Agreement helped bring governments into action to deal with humanity's biggest calamity in the twenty-first century. Yet the results seem utterly inadequate in the face of growing calamities and natural disasters. The Climate Change Performance Index (CCPI)—developed as part of the Paris Agreement—continues to show that except for Nordic countries such as Sweden, Denmark and Finland, not many others are doing enough to reach the desired levels of emission controls. Projections for the future remain bleak, and climate change is expected to get worse in the coming years. The worst projection for climate change in 2024 was that the chances of the average global temperature rising above 1.5°C would increase to almost 50 per cent in the next five-year period between 2022 and 2026.

Meanwhile, climate activism is continuing to produce new heroes. Sweden was to hold its parliamentary election on 9 September 2018. A young ninth-grader Greta Thunberg launched a unique protest two weeks before the election. Starting from 20 August, Greta decided to skip her classes and do a sit-in protest outside the Riksdag—the Swedish legislature—every day during school hours, with a placard that read '*Skolstrejk för klimatet*' (school strike for climate). She demanded that the Swedish government commit to implementing the Paris Agreement. A day before the election, she called for youngsters to skip classes every Friday and join climate protests. Thus the movement called 'Fridays for Future' (FFF) was born. Climate strikes became a phenomenon in 2019; they were led by young people criticizing the lack of international commitment and political action to address the worsening impacts of climate change. Greta became a global icon for climate action. It is another matter that in her overzealousness to gain international popularity, she ended up touching many raw nerves in many countries, and faced a lot of criticism as well.

The efforts of UNFCCC and voluntary activists have resulted in states taking the climate change challenge seriously. However, one issue that bogged down countries was the question of climate financing. Article 9 of the Paris Agreement stipulated that the developed countries 'shall' provide financial support to assist developing countries in meeting their climate obligations. In 2009, a target of $100 billion was set as the annual climate finance target to be met by 2020. It is just a fraction of the $6 trillion the UNFCCC projected as what is needed by developing countries by 2030 to meet their climate targets. Sadly, even this meagre target of $100 billion couldn't be met until now as developed countries did not show any interest in helping the developing world in terms of climate financing.

The COP29 Summit, held at Baku in Azerbaijan in November 2024, brought to light efforts by the developed world to shun the responsibility for climate financing, and amend the Paris Agreement accordingly, in particular Article 9. The countries also agreed that they 'shall set a new collective quantified goal from a floor of $100bn per year, taking into account the needs and priorities of developing countries.'[13]

However, as COP30—to be held in Brazil in 2025—is fast approaching, efforts to derail these commitments dominate climate discussions. The Baku Summit saw India and the African Union (AU) raising serious reservations over these efforts. India firmly told the developed world that instead of trying to weaken the agreement, developed countries should be more forthcoming in agreeing to revise the NCQG from $100 billion decided in 2009 (though never implemented), to $1.3 trillion by 2030. Voicing the concerns of the Global South, India said in its official statement at Baku that 'the developed countries need to commit to provide and mobilise at least $1.3 trillion every year till 2030, through grants, concessional finance, and non-debt-inducing support that cater to the evolving needs and priorities of developing countries, without subjecting them to growth-inhibiting conditionalities in the provision of finance.'[14] The silver lining is that the COP meetings are attracting senior world leaders showing promise, and the commitment of various countries to this challenge.

Echoing India's sentiments, Ali D. Mohamed, chair of the African Group of Negotiators, also insisted that 'We are standing firm against attempts to re-define Paris Agreement's obligations. The funding commitments by developed nations remain binding.

For Africa and other developing nations, the $1.3 trillion is essential for achieving climate adaptation, resilience, and emissions reductions.'[15]

Immigrants and Politics in an Era of Demographic Change

Climate change will impact the future world order in two critical ways—climate migration and climate technologies. Human migration is a tale that starts with the very first humans. Before the dawn of agriculture, humans led a purely nomadic life. Economic opportunities played an essential role in migration in the post-industrial era. Educated and technically skilled youth from the developing world migrated to countries in the developed world. According to rough estimates, over 200 million citizens in the world live in countries away from their home country.[16] India tops the list with almost 20 million citizens living in other countries. It is followed by its South Asian neighbours Bangladesh, Nepal, Pakistan and Sri Lanka—contributing large numbers of migrants to the world. A massive surge in cross-border migration in the world was witnessed in the last two decades. Whereas over 100 million migrants lived in different (mainly developed) countries, starting in 2000, these numbers grew steeply in the first twenty years of the new century to reach 281 million in 2020.[17]

While a majority of them were economic migrants seeking employment in other countries, wars, conflicts, dictatorships, and religious and social repression were also increasingly becoming reasons for people leaving their countries. Over six million Afghan citizens left their homes and hearths to take shelter in other countries, including Iran and Pakistan.[18] Estimates put the total number of displaced persons due to wars and conflicts at 117 million, out of which 43.3 million became refugees in other countries. At the same time, the remaining are categorized as internally displaced persons (IDPs).[19]

Changing demographics in the developed West is also a catalysing factor for the continued migration of human resources. The UN has projected that the world's population will close in on the 10 billion mark by 2050.[20] However, with increasing longevity, the ratio of elderly people to working-age adults is also changing. It was 20 elderly people for every 100 working-age people in 1980. By 2060, the ratio is expected to increase to 58 elders for every 100 working-age people.[21] As birth rates are plummeting, several countries are facing the problem of aged populations. Developed countries like Japan, Italy, Germany, Portugal and Greece top the list of ageing societies, while even some developing countries like China also face a similar challenge.

Changes in the global median age present the stark reality that while the developed world is ageing, the least developed world continues to remain young. In the last seven decades, according to UN estimates, the global median age has increased from 23.6 years to 31 years. However, the median age in the most developed countries saw a steep increase from 28.5 years to 42 years. The same was true in the least developed countries in sub-Saharan Africa, and others saw a very marginal rise from 19.3 years to 20.3 years.[22] What it means in real terms is that the developed world will face a shortage of working-age people, providing potential economic opportunities to those in developing economies. Relatively less developed countries in sub-Saharan Africa and South Asia will account for almost the entire global population growth in the next two decades. The UN Human Development Index (HDI) forecasts that by 2040, over 63 per cent of the population growth in the 16–74 age group will happen in low- or medium-developed countries.[23] It is likely to overwhelm the governments in those countries in terms of their capacity to provide basic infrastructure like education, healthcare and employment.

That, coupled with manpower shortages in the developed world, will lead to a further rise in migration. These demographic and human development trends will also place pressure on governments in the developed world. In Europe, there is already widespread discussion on uncontrolled migration and its social and cultural costs for local communities. This is also leading to the rise in the popularity of right-wing parties in country after country. While immigrants are helping developed economies tackle the challenges of ageing populations by improving economic productivity and providing services, there are also serious concerns about maintaining cultural and national identity, and ethnic homogeneity. There are also fears of a backlash in several European countries over immigration issues. These debates and divisions—on issues of how much migration to allow and how to manage immigrant inflows—will persist.

Immigration from across the US' southern borders became a major political battle in the US elections in November 2024, with presidential candidates Donald Trump and Kamala Harris making accusations and counter-accusations against each other on the issue. Trump emphatically declared that he would, on his first day in the White House, 'begin the largest deportation operation in American history'. Trump's campaign said he would 'marshal every federal and state power necessary' for the purpose. On her part, Harris argued for a lenient approach to address the issue, inviting criticism from the American Right.[24]

However, immigration wasn't one of the most critical issues for voters in just the November 2024 presidential elections; in fact, it has always been a potent political issue throughout history. The early twentieth century saw the Germans giving it an ideological status by coining the concept of *Lebensraum* or living space. The concept was first mooted by German geographer and ethnographer Friedrich Ratzel. He used Darwin's theory of the 'survival of the fittest' to argue that a form of 'social Darwinism' was necessary to gain territory and resources for people to prosper. German nationalist groups like the Pan-German League seized upon Ratzel's concept to argue that Germany should resort to its military force to occupy Eastern Europe in pursuit of Lebensraum. Hitler fully exploited this concept to justify his occupation of countries to the east in Europe during the Second World War.

In American history, the concept of manifest destiny propounded during the second half of the nineteenth century held that 'it was the divinely ordained right of the United States to expand its borders to the Pacific Ocean and beyond. Before the American Civil War, the idea of Manifest Destiny was used to validate continental acquisitions in the Oregon Country, Texas, New Mexico, and California. Later, it was used to justify the purchase of Alaska and annexation of Hawaii,' explains the *Encyclopaedia Britannica*.[25] Emphasizing his pet theory about the superiority of the German race, Hitler likened Lebensraum to manifest destiny. He compared the Slavs and Jews of Europe to Native Americans and hence *Untermenschen* (subhumans). Hitler's Lebensraum led his armies to march into Europe, and caused the Holocaust. His concepts of Aryan supremacy and Lebensraum together resulted in the deaths of millions of Jews, Roma, Poles, Slavs and even homosexuals.

A new form of Lebensraum, driven by climate challenges and migration, is staring us in the face in this century. Incidentally, it is the same regions that experience relatively significant population growth rates—like Latin America, South Asia and sub-Saharan Africa—that will be the most vulnerable to climate calamities as well, precipitating the chances of enhanced migration levels. These regions account for more than half of the developing world's population. The World Bank estimates that these regions could altogether produce 143 million internal climate migrants by 2050.[26] Although no corresponding figures for trans-border migration are available, it can be safely predicted that such migration will also increase, especially for those living closer to the border regions.

Climate change can cause two types of migrations—sudden and slow. Cyclones, floods, storms and hurricanes constitute sudden changes in the atmosphere that cause displacement and migration. Global data indicates that, on average, 22.5 million people have been annually displaced by these sudden climate disruptions since 2008.[27] South Asia leads with 64 per cent of the world's total flood-affected population.[28] Pakistan and Bangladesh encounter extreme weather events regularly. Sub-Saharan countries like Chad, Somalia, Syria, the Democratic Republic of Congo and Sudan also face serious challenges from sudden climate change events like floods. Somalia, once famous for droughts and political instability, has recently faced flash floods and devastation. The same situation can be seen in other African countries.

Many regions in Africa and Asia are experiencing climate threats like desertification, droughts, riverbank erosion, changing rainfall patterns, rising sea levels, salinization, rising temperatures, land degradation, loss of biodiversity, and glacial melting. These events cause slow migrations, the numbers of which may not be available; nevertheless, they pose significant challenges to climate migration.

Glaciers face serious threats from climate change, causing the accelerated melting of ice. Over 9 trillion tonnes of glacial ice have been lost since 1975.[29] Projections suggest that over a third of all glaciers could vanish by 2100.[30] While this melting is causing sea levels to rise, leading to the flooding of coastal areas, this glacial retreat will also cause acute water shortages in the Himalayan regions, impacting millions. Due to the large-scale construction of habitations, human-induced climate change is posing a serious threat to the Himalayan glaciers, which are receding at a fast rate. Current predictions indicate that by the end of the century, they could lose 45 to 68 per cent of their mass. These glaciers are the origin and source of water for mighty rivers like the Indus, Ganga and Brahmaputra, which are critical water sources for millions in Pakistan, Nepal, Bhutan, India and Bangladesh. Melting glaciers will significantly impact the lives of those living in close vicinity of the Himalayas, forcing them to migrate.

Our Climate Moment

Climate change is also facilitating the development of new technologies for adaptation and mitigation. Countries will be forced to invest more in these technologies to monitor, manage and mitigate the challenges posed by climate in the coming decades. Reducing GHG emissions is a priority that necessitates new eco-friendly technologies. Similarly, tackling future emissions calls for technological adaptation, which the UNFCCC describes as actions taken to adjust 'processes, practices, and structures to moderate potential damages or to benefit from opportunities associated with climate change.'[31]

These climate technologies include data-driven tools like satellites, drones and the IoT that will help in the real-time monitoring and risk assessment of climate change, AI for enhanced capabilities in forecasting and disaster-preparedness, and most importantly, renewable energy technologies like solar, wind and hydel power generation. A new concept of technologies that help reduce and remove carbon emissions—known as green technologies—is becoming popular. While there is no silver bullet or miracle technology to fully mitigate climate change, increasing the use of green technologies could help nations achieve the targets set by the Paris Agreement.

One focus of green technologies is improving energy efficiency by identifying major carbon emitters like industries and the building sector, and developing technologies specific to achieving that reduction. The second focus is on capturing and removing carbon emissions from the atmosphere. Carbon-capture technology looks at how carbon dioxide emissions can be captured directly from the atmosphere or at the emission point itself, and stored safely within the natural environment. These technologies are being developed globally and are likely to dominate the domain of climate technology in the future.

Imposing carbon taxes and developing smart cities that minimize GHG emissions will play a crucial role in climate change mitigation. This process is set to bring about significant changes in how governments operate, and will be a key factor in shaping the future world.

10

THE END OF THE
GREENBACK PLANET?

The debate over de-dollarization within the BRICS ranks acquired momentum at the summit meeting of the heads of BRICS member countries in Johannesburg, South Africa, in August 2023. Leaders attending the summit declared their intention to reduce their dependency on the US dollar ($), and increase the pace of de-dollarization in global trade and commerce. There was some talk about developing a common currency for the BRICS countries. The New Development Bank (NDB) sponsored by BRICS was projected as a concrete step in that direction, with plans to lend in the South African rand and Brazilian real. The BRICS countries also discussed the possibility of evolving a standard trading system. Brazil's president Luiz Inácio Lula da Silva—who will be hosting the BRICS Summit in Rio de Janeiro in 2025—became the first senior leader to talk his mind out. He strongly pitched for an exclusive BRICS currency. 'Every night, I ask myself why all countries have to base their trade on the dollar,' he commented wryly, adding, 'Why can't we make trade based on our own currencies? Who was it that decided that the dollar was the currency after the disappearance of the gold standard?'[1]

President Putin couldn't go to Johannesburg. His abstention became fodder for the rumour mills, and it was interpreted in various ways. The official reason given was that the president was busy with war-related developments. However, the Western media insisted that he didn't go fearing an arrest by South African law-enforcement agencies under the warrant issued by the International

Court of Justice. South Africa is a signatory to the ICJ and was obligated to act on its decisions.

Delivering his address through a pre-recorded video, Putin came down heavily on the dollar dominance and argued in favour of de-dollarization. He exhorted:

> The objective and irreversible process of the de-dollarization of our economic ties is gaining pace. We are working to fine-tune effective mechanisms for mutual settlements and monetary and financial control. As a result, the share of the US dollar in export and import operations within BRICS is declining: last year, it stood at only 28.7 per cent. Incidentally, during this summit, we will discuss in detail the entire range of issues related to the transition to national currencies in all areas of economic cooperation between our five nations. The BRICS New Development Bank, which has already become a credible alternative to existing Western development institutions, has a great role to play in these efforts.[2]

The Russian side indicated that it was keen on initiating a discussion on the need to come together to challenge the coercive economic measures of the Western powers. At the summit, some within the BRICS leadership gave enough indications that they would be seriously challenging the dollar's dominance at the 2024 Kazan Summit which was to be held under Russia's chairmanship.

The chair of the BRICS forum and the opportunity to host the leadership summit in October 2024 offered Putin an excellent opportunity to highlight his views on the radical economic reform that he intended to champion. He chose to talk about it a couple of days before the summit at the BRICS Business Forum in Moscow. The BRICS group of nations 'are essentially the drivers of global economic growth. In the foreseeable future, BRICS will generate the main increase in global GDP,' he told the curated audience of business leaders in his address. He described 'economic sovereignty' as being free from external influence or interference.

He referred to his country's initiatives, like the joint cross-border payments system and a SWIFT-like financial messaging system, as 'immune to Western sanctions'.[3]

Besides proposing instruments like the BRICS Clear platform that would help stimulate the flow of cross-border investment among emerging market and developing economies (EMDEs)—a euphemism for non-Western economies like China, India and Russia—Putin's agenda also included challenging dollar dominance. He asked the leaders of the BRICS countries to 'reassess' the decades-old practice of keeping sovereign reserves in US dollars.

Then, a week before the crucial BRICS Summit at Kazan, Russia, in October 2024, the Russian Federation's Ministry of Finance released a document titled 'Improvement of the International Monetary and Financial System'.[4] The document was prepared for discussion at the summit where the heads of five founding member countries—Brazil, Russia, India, China and South Africa—were joined by the leaders of another 21 countries, including five new countries which were granted membership at the Johannesburg Summit in 2023—Egypt, Ethiopia, Iran, the United Arab Emirates (UAE) and Saudi Arabia.

The document began with the claim that the 'current IMFS [International Monetary and Financial System] has reached its peak and needs improvements to better serve the evolving global economy.'[5] Alluding to Russia's travails in the face of stiff sanctions imposed by the US and other Western powers, it alleged that the present system has 'destabilising potential that stems from excessive reliance on a single currency and centralised financial infrastructure.'[6] Emphasizing that the future model of the IMFS should be based on four core principles—security, independence, inclusion and sustainability—and that it should protect its participants from the loss of capital and assets, the document called upon the BRICS colleagues to explore the possibility of the 'establishment of a common multilateral settlement platform based on modern technologies.'[7]

All these statements, from Johannesburg through the run-up to the summit at Kazan, left the world wondering about the intentions of Putin and the others, and the implications thereof for the world economy. It was widely believed that 'de-dollarization'—the process of reducing the dollar's influence in international monetary exchanges—would gain momentum after Kazan, and the BRICS nations would try to make it an essential feature of the emerging world order in the next couple of decades.

The Dollar Conquers the World

It may not only be pertinent but also fair to mention here that the issue of dollar domination in the world economy is not something that was raked up by Putin or his BRICS colleagues for the first time. Debates over it began in 1944–45, right at the time of the creation of the Bretton Woods institutions, especially the IMF itself. Leaders of the US government wanted to use the country's predominant political and military power after the Second World War to influence the shaping of the Bretton Woods institutions in such a way that the economic order thus created would lead to the dollar emerging as the dominant global currency.

In July 1944, 730 delegates from 44 countries gathered at the Mount Washington Hotel in Bretton Woods, New Hampshire, to give shape to a new global financial order. Until the war, the pound sterling (£) was the dominant currency in the world while gold played the role of the 'global exchange standard' to facilitate international monetary transactions. People were permitted to convert their money into gold on demand, and a gold standard emerged as the medium of economic transactions. Naturally, many countries believed that the Bretton Woods institutions would formalize the gold standard as the new medium for international monetary transactions.

However, countries such as the US and the UK, which were at the forefront of the establishment of these institutions, had other ideas. British economist John Maynard Keynes was one of the key players in shaping the agenda of these institutions. Keynes was very much opposed to the gold standard and described it as a 'barbaric relic.'[8] He was involved in drafting the agenda, along with another American colleague Harry White. They both drafted their proposals for the economic agreement to form the foundation of the IMF. The delegates assembled at Bretton Woods were asked to debate over the two drafts presented by White and Keynes. White's draft talked about providing central status to the dollar, but he was also open to the idea that the dollar should be backed by gold. However, for Keynes, any talk of the gold standard was a repulsive idea. In the end, the delegates voted in favour of White's proposal which reflected American preferences.

Under the final agreement, all global currencies were tied to gold via the dollar, and the US Federal Reserve (or the Fed) was mandated to buy and sell gold at a fixed price of $35 per ounce. Thus, at the time of the formation of the IMF, gold was considered as good as the greenback, and countries had the freedom to hold their sovereign reserves in gold, and exchange them against the dollar at the fixed rate at the US Federal Reserve as and when required. In a way, the 'gold exchange standard' of the pre-Second World War era was restored.

However, the French were the principal dissenters to this agreement of dual standards at the Bretton Woods Conference. They also came to the conference with their own economic proposal. The French proposal was drafted jointly by Hervé Alphand, a French diplomat, and André Istel, a banker. Alphand and Istel insisted on continuing with only the gold standard, but their proposal was not accepted.

At the time of the Bretton Woods Conference, European economies were in a difficult situation. Prolonged battles during the Second World War had broken the back of the economies of several European countries. They struggled with inflation and unemployment for many years, until the US finally came forward with the Marshall Plan to rescue and rebuild their tattered economic structures. That was one of the reasons why not many of them could stand by their fellow French at Bretton Woods. However, on 25 March 1957, six European nations—France, Germany, Italy, the Netherlands, Belgium and Luxembourg—got together to sign the Treaty of Rome which paved the way for establishing the European Economic Community (EEC). This treaty also became foundational for the creation of the European Union under a common market and common currency a few decades later.

Several European countries like Britain, France and Portugal were major colonizing powers until the Second World War. Some of them still held colonies in many countries. They revelled in their past and present glory as colonizing powers, and looked at the dominance of the dollar as an anathema. Prominent among them was French president Charles de Gaulle who insisted that 'Europe was not so much the means to make Europe great again, but *France*.' It was, he said, the means for France to 'become again what she has ceased to be since Waterloo: First in the world.'[9] De Gaulle, a general in the French Army, was advised by French economist Jacques Rueff. Together, they became vocal critics of the Bretton Woods arrangement. President de Gaulle relentlessly pursued the agenda of challenging dollar domination through the 1960s. Thus he became the first world leader to oppose the dollar as the singular standard for international monetary exchanges. He told a press conference in January 1963 that 'Western Europe has become an American protectorate without even realizing it. We must now rid ourselves of their domination. But the difficulty here is that the colonized don't really want to emancipate themselves. Since the end of the war, the Americans have subjugated us painlessly and without much resistance.'[10]

Calling for significant changes in the monetary system, de Gaulle, at another press conference on 4 February 1965, warned that a monetary system based on any single nation's currency would be a source of danger. This was already being felt by several other countries as well. As shortages of both gold and the dollar started causing economic woes in various nations, British Prime Minister Harold Macmillan took the liberty of suggesting to

US President John F. Kennedy in 1962 that most of the world's monetary difficulties could be ended by the US doubling the exchange rate of gold to $70 an ounce. However, Kennedy disagreed. For him, any such devaluation of the dollar meant humiliation for his country. President de Gaulle had reiterated at the press conference that his country's preference would be for gold as the standard medium of exchange, insisting that it 'does not change to nature', and is 'in all places and at all times, the immutable and fiduciary value par excellence.'[11] De Gaulle was more forthright on this issue in his memoir. 'The monumentally over-privileged position that the world has conceded to the American currency since the two world wars left America standing alone amid the ruins of others', he bluntly accused.[12] Although unsuccessful at Bretton Woods, successive French governments advocated 'Banaliser le Dollar' (dethrone the dollar) in the next two decades.[13]

In fact, between 1963 and 1966, President de Gaulle initiated a secret operation known as 'Vide-Gousset' to repatriate 3,313 tonnes of gold reserves from the vaults of the US Fed in New York and the Bank of England in London. The entirety of France's dollar reserves was converted into gold, and it was transferred to the Banque de France in Paris over three years by deploying 44 boat trips and 129 flights. De Gaulle's original plan was to send the French Navy's prestigious missile cruiser ship Colbert for the operation. However, his minister of finance convinced him to give up that idea as it could inadvertently damage diplomatic ties between the two countries.[14] De Gaulle's warnings came true immediately after the repatriation operation as the dollar lost its value by almost 96 per cent between 1968 and 1980. Unlike France, countries that held on to huge dollar reserves lost massively.

France was not the only country that attempted to challenge dollar domination. When the euro was introduced as a common currency for European markets in 1999, many in Europe believed, if not aspired, that it would overtake the dollar and emerge as the leading global currency. Although that did not happen in the last two decades, the euro did emerge as the second most traded

currency in the world after the dollar. Four other currencies—
Japanese yen (JPY), British pound (GBP), Swiss franc (CHF), and
Chinese yuan (CNY)—also emerged in the international markets
with varying degrees of success.

Meanwhile, at around 9.00 p.m. on Sunday 15 August 1971,
the American administration gave a severe jolt to the dual
standard agreed upon by the member countries at Bretton Woods.
President Richard Nixon proclaimed a New Economic Policy for
the country. He made several far-reaching announcements—seen
by many as a desperate attempt by him to ramp up the sagging
political fortunes of his Republican government, and bargain for
a re-election the following year. However, the most significant
announcement that Nixon made that summer night was that the
US would no longer exchange dollars for gold at the rate fixed
by the IMF—$35 per ounce. With this statement, Nixon put an
end to the dollar-gold dual system, and made the dollar the sole
currency standard for international transactions. This was the US'
first act of defiance against the Bretton Woods Agreement, and
the beginning of what came to be known as the 'dominance of
the dollar' in later years.

It must be noted that the dollar became the international
currency for transactions not because of any global agreement
over the same, but due to the drastic decision taken by the Nixon
administration on that fateful night, which shocked many in the
world. These shocks continued as the dollar lost its value from
time to time, leading to economic crises like the Asian Financial
Crisis in 1997, the dot-com bubble burst in 2000, and the worst
global financial crisis of 2007–08. As Western economies struggled,
the ripple effects were borne by almost all countries that pegged
their currencies to the dollar.

De Gaulle's primary mistrust of the US economy in the
1960s was about its sovereign debt levels. The threat of attacks
by speculators, and the worries about the balance of payments
crisis, convinced him not to bank on the greenbacks for the
sake of the good health of the French economy. The French

never wavered from that conviction. They continued to repose faith in gold as the stable standard medium for global monetary exchange. Over decades, the Banque de France, the central bank of France, accumulated massive amounts of gold, and preserved it in its vaults. A senior official of the bank, Sylvie Goulard, wrote in 2018 that 'the financial crisis [in 2008] acted as a wake-up call for gold' which 'proved to be an opportunity for gold and for the Banque de France.'[15]

Not just the French, but the central banks of several other countries, especially those in the Eastern hemisphere, are quietly amassing gold reserves by dispensing with their dollars. This repatriation of gold by countries has resulted in it emerging as the second-largest currency in the world, overtaking the euro.

Discouraging a Rhetoric of Reckless De-Dollarization

The recent debate over de-dollarization must be seen against this backdrop. The BRICS nations are certainly not the first or the only countries to be concerned about the future of the US dollar. Of particular concern to many countries are the ballooning public debt and debt-to-GDP ratio in the US. The US economy is facing its worst-ever sovereign debt crisis. While its debt levels are rising precariously, the debt servicing costs threaten the fiscal health of the country. The federal public debt reached $34.4 trillion in February 2024, and stands at 120 per cent of the country's GDP.[16] The debt-to-GDP ratio is projected to climb to 214 per cent in 2054.[17] While the government spends about 3.5 per cent of its GDP on defence, its debt servicing has crossed that mark in 2023, leading to serious concerns in the policy establishment.[18]

Some BRICS countries continue to monitor the crisis in the US economy with anxiety for purely economic reasons. Several of them have sovereign reserves in dollars. India, for example, holds close to $700 billion in forex reserves.[19] With approximately $3.3 trillion, China is the world's largest holder of dollar reserves.[20]

Even Brazil has close to $400 billion in reserves.[21] Russia was also holding close to $350 billion in reserves before 90 per cent of them were frozen by the US government after it invaded Ukraine in 2022.[22] Moreover, even by conservative estimates, although the US' share in global trade is just above 11 per cent, roughly half of all international trade happens in dollars.[23] The dollar remains the main currency for invoices and payments in the world. Even any two BRICS countries, India and Brazil, or Brazil and China, trade in dollars, rather than in rupees or reals (the Brazilian currency), or even the Chinese renminbi (also known as the Chinese yuan). Naturally, all these economic reasons make countries anxious with regard to the future of the US dollar.

The BRICS countries have emerged as significant players in the global economy in the last two decades. They account for 28 per cent of the world's GDP and 22 per cent of the world's exports of goods. This economic heft gives some of them the confidence to look beyond the US dollar today.

However, beyond economic concerns, there is growing unease and apprehension over what many prefer to call the 'weaponization' of the dollar by the US government. The dollar has brought infamy upon itself more because of strategic reasons than mere economic concerns. Washington's decision to bar countries like Iran and North Korea from trading in dollars, and the sanctions imposed on thousands of individuals across West Asia and elsewhere on charges of aiding and abetting terror activities have jeopardized the status of the dollar as a stable and dependable currency. The US' decision to freeze Russian dollar assets, remove Russian banks from the SWIFT (Society for Worldwide Interbank Financial Telecommunication) system, and force credit card companies like Visa and Mastercard to withdraw from that country did not go down well with many countries either. The threat of imposing sanctions not only on Russia but also on any entity—state or private—deemed by the US administration to be directly or indirectly supporting Russia's war after 2022 was seen by many as unnecessary intimidation.

'Whether or not this move was justified by Russia's gross violation of international law, it undoubtedly left other central banks wondering whether their own dollar-denominated rainy-day funds would be locked up should their governments run afoul of Washington,' comments Eswar Prasad, senior professor at Cornell University.[24]

Statements from some of the leaders of the BRICS countries, including President Putin, must be seen in this context. However, things did not go as predicted at Kazan in 2024. There was a discernible climbdown, most likely necessitated by the strong opposition from India to any overt move by the group to be seen as targeting the dollar. During his visit to New York to attend the annual UNGA session in September 2024, Dr Jaishankar addressed an event at a prominent think tank where he clarified that India never 'actively targeted' the US dollar. While some BRICS members may have supported de-dollarization, India had 'no malicious intent' towards the dollar, he clarified.[25] A few weeks later, speaking at the Doha Forum, Jaishankar was more categorical. He emphatically stated:

> ...We have always said that India has never been for de-dollarisation, right now there is no proposal to have a BRICS currency. The BRICS do discuss financial transactions... US is our largest trade partner, we have no interest in weakening the dollar at all... We had a good relationship, a very solid relationship with the first Trump administration, yes there were some issues mostly trade-related issues, but there were a whole lot of issues on which President Trump was very international and I remind people that it was actually under Trump that the QUAD was restarted... There is a personal relationship between PM Modi and Trump...[26]

Keeping global economic health and stability in mind, India discouraged the reckless de-dollarization rhetoric. India's success—between the Johannesburg Summit in 2023 and the

Kazan Summit in 2024—lay in convincing the BRICS countries that the preferred way should be a reform of the international monetary system that allowed for the organic rise of the currencies of the new economies, rather than any drastic action to cater to the geopolitical objectives of a few countries.

The Kazan Declaration, released at the end of the BRICS Summit, took a milder path. It did express 'deep concern' about the 'unlawful coercive measures, including illegal sanctions', but did not go beyond calling for the 'reform of the Bretton Woods institutions'. Although it talked about 'encouraging' settlements in local currencies using the BRICS Cross-Border Payments Initiative (BCBPI), it hastened to add that the yet-to-be-created system, supposed to bypass the SWIFT mechanism, would be 'voluntary and non-binding'. The declaration only said that they would 'discuss and study' the feasibility of such an arrangement.[27]

China: Ditching the Dollar

BRICS Pay, the alternative to SWIFT suggested by the Russian Finance Ministry, was enthusiastically supported by China as it saw an opportunity in the decline of the dollar, and an increased share for its own renminbi. In the last two decades, the Chinese currency has gradually climbed up in the international markets to acquire a four per cent share in global reserves.[28] Beijing began the internationalization of its currency in 2010, and it quickly took off. By 2015, in just five years, about three per cent of global transactions were being conducted in the Chinese currency.[29] Several countries have started increasingly trading in renminbi in the last few years. Russia began to deal with the renminbi for its energy deals with China after the sanctions. Saudi Arabia signed a currency swap agreement with China in November 2023, under which the country agreed to trade its oil in renminbi. Brazil, Argentina, Iran, Venezuela, Nigeria, Turkey, Pakistan and Indonesia also expressed interest in trading in the Chinese currency. Moreover, China increasingly uses the renminbi for its cross-border settlements. The volumes—just 10 per cent a decade ago—reached 53 per cent in 2024.[30]

The People's Bank of China, the central bank of the PRC, has signed bilateral currency swap agreements with more than 40 countries in the last five years. Thirty-one of these agreements are currently in use, amounting to a total of 4.16 trillion yuan (approximately $586 billion). 'The currency swap agreements China signed have played a positive role in boosting market confidence and maintaining regional and global financial stability,' the State Council (cabinet) boasted in February 2024.[31]

In 2015, China launched a yuan-based Cross-Border Interbank Payment System (CIPS) as an alternative to SWIFT, offering a stable banking platform for cross-border yuan settlements. By early 2023, it boasted of having 1,366 participants from 109 countries and regions.[32] Almost all the GCC countries and many other African and Southeast Asian countries are part of China's yuan-based transactions system. All this has resulted in the share of the yuan as a global currency climbing from two per cent in 2019 to 4.74 per cent in July 2024.[33]

'For a long time, the US has abused its dollar hegemony, shifting domestic crises and harvesting global wealth by damaging the economic and financial stability and well-being of other countries. The establishment of the BRICS payment system poses a significant challenge to the US dollar's dominance,' commented the CCP mouthpiece *Global Times* a few days before the BRICS 2024 Summit at Kazan. It also argued that a BRICS payment system would help to 'reduce reliance on the dollar', and offer member nations more independent and secure payment alternatives 'with the goal of creating a more inclusive and balanced international monetary system.'[34]

Interestingly, despite rising economic and strategic concerns, and more specifically, complaints about its weaponization, the US dollar continues to be the most trusted and stable currency for international monetary and trade transactions. Doomsday predictions for the dollar notwithstanding, the unmatched economic, political, military and institutional strength of the US government in the world continues to make the dollar a strong entity in the monetary markets. No other country or currency enjoys the kind of support the dollar has from the US. Those who compare the current discourse about de-dollarization to how fast the dollar replaced the pound sterling after the Second World War miss the point that such a rapid transition only proved the strength of the dollar. Incidentally, no other country in the world today can aspire to show that kind of strength to be able to displace the dollar.

Eswar Prasad strongly argues that the dollar's dominance would continue for many years to come because the economy of the US remains larger and more dynamic than that of almost every other country. 'The story of the dollar is, ultimately, less about the United States' strength than about the rest of the world's weaknesses. Until that disparity changes, and seemingly no matter how badly the United States plays its cards, don't expect the dollar to decline,' he says in conclusion.[35]

11

NATIONAL CONSERVATISM AND THE WOKE RESPONSE

Two significant and contrasting sociopolitical movements are set to shape the emerging new order of this century: the resurgence of nationalism and the rise of wokeism. While nationalism is an old and entrenched ideological movement, wokeism is a ragtag of various disruptive ideas and actions essentially promoting cancel culture and social anarchy. While it is challenging to define 'woke', it has an ideological veneer with roots in the left-liberal ideology of the last century.

A new wave of national conservatism has been sweeping across Europe and the US in the last couple of decades. Long riled by the liberals as chauvinist, xenophobic, narrow and fundamentalist, the parties wedded to the ideas of national identity, cultural pride and nativism are regaining ground in country after country. Countries like Hungary, Italy, Finland, Slovakia, the Czech Republic, Croatia and the Netherlands have national conservative parties in power today. Similarly, several other countries, including France, Germany and Austria, have seen the rise of conservative parties which have become powerful and influential stakeholders.

In Italy, the nationalist Brothers of Italy (*Fratelli d' Italia*) has grown steadily to emerge as the largest party in the 2022 general elections for the country's parliament. Giorgia Meloni, president of the party since 2014, was elected PM, the first woman to occupy that post, and head the first nationalist government in Italy after the Second World War.

In Hungary, Viktor Orban's Fidesz Party has been winning elections in Parliament since 2010. Orban is the target of hate for liberal politicians in Europe, and his party was suspended from the European People's Party, a centre-right alliance in the European parliament, for some time over allegations of illiberal governance. Nevertheless, after his fourth victory in the 2022 general elections, Orban emerged as a much stronger leader, much to the chagrin of many in the EU.

In the Netherlands, after much back and forth, the Party for Freedom (PVV) led by Geert Wilders joined the coalition government. The party, known for its leader Wilders's strong nationalist views, emerged as the largest party in the 150-member Dutch Parliament by winning 37 seats. The formation of the coalition took some time due to the reluctance of other parties to join hands with Wilders's party which was considered ultra-right.

In France, the National Rally (*Rassemblement National* or RN), led by Marine Le Pen, who boasts of strong nationalist credentials, won the majority popular vote of 34 per cent in the elections to the French National Assembly in the 2024 snap polls announced by President Macron. Although her party secured the highest vote share, she was made to sit in the opposition while the other winning parties formed a coalition to run the government. Le Pen contested the presidential election three times—2012, 2017 and 2022—and consistently bettered the position of her nationalist party. From a mere 13.6 per cent vote share in 2012,[1] she took her party's vote share to 42 per cent in just a decade in 2022,[2] losing to Macron in the second round, yet securing the highest percentage of votes for a right-wing party in French history. Her party continues to have a strong presence in the French National Assembly.

In Germany—known for its antipathy towards nationalism— the Alternative for Germany (AfD) party was widely criticized for its provocative and controversial stance on German identity, history and the legacy of the Nazi era, which some interpret as a misplaced or revisionist identity linked to Adolf Hitler and the Third Reich. Founded in 2013 with avowedly nationalist credentials like Euroscepticism and German nationalism, it has gradually grown into a strong presence in the electoral politics of the country. It is the largest opposition party today with 89 seats in the Bundestag, the German national parliament. In Austria too, the Freedom Party of Austria (FPÖ), known for right-wing politics of Euroscepticism and anti-immigration, has emerged as the largest party in the 2024 general elections, winning over 28 per cent of the total votes, surpassing the ruling Austrian People's Party.

Elections to the European Parliament, held in June 2024, showcased the growing power of these nationalist parties in Europe. In France, the RN secured 32 per cent the vote share and won 18 seats—a significant gain. In Germany, AfD secured second place, garnering 16 per cent of the popular vote (compared to 11 per cent in 2019). In Italy, PM Meloni's Brothers of Italy more than quadrupled its share of the votes to 28.8 per cent (after 6.44 per cent in 2019) and won 24 seats. Similarly, Geert Wilders's PVV rose from zero to six seats in the Netherlands by securing a 17 per cent vote share. Other notable gains were made by the Bulgarian Revival Party and the Freedom Party of Austria.[3]

Although the gains in these important countries were significant, losses in some other countries were a setback for the nationalist groups. In countries like Finland, Sweden and Hungary, nationalist parties lost their base compared to the 2019 elections. Their gains were limited in other countries as well, like the Czech Republic, Estonia and Poland. While the 2019 elections remain the most successful for nationalist parties, the 2024 elections showed their expanding footprint in Western Europe, considered a bastion of liberal politics.

The Return of Trumpism

Trump's comprehensive victory in the US presidential elections held in November 2024 is the proverbial icing on the cake for conservative politics. Trump is a much-hated politician by US liberals who dominate the Democratic Party. They thought that

Trump would remain an accident, an exception, and a historical blip. Egged on by the liberal mainstream media, they believed that Kamala Harris, the Democratic Party nominee, would sail through in a nail-biting finish. However, the results showed that the American voters unambiguously supported Trump's candidacy over Harris's.

Four years earlier, when the results of the US presidential elections in 2020 were announced, Trump vociferously complained that the Democrats had stolen his election. Although those claims were verified and rejected by the courts and election officials, his Republican supporters remained convinced, with 77 per cent of them believing that a widespread fraud had resulted in Trump being denied a second term in office. Four years later, when Trump returned to win a second term as US president, he literally 'stole the show'. It was a massive victory in that he not only secured a majority in the Electoral College, but also won a popular majority—majorities in both the Senate and House, a majority of state governors, and a majority in state legislatures. No other Republican president in the last several decades could register such a comprehensive victory in one election. Only Lyndon Johnson had a Democratic majority in both houses of the Congress, and strong support in many states, during his presidency.

The electoral map in November 2024 looked like a huge red flag, with a few blue patches on the West Coast and the Northeast. While all the so-called swing states went to Trump, breaking down of even Democratic 'blue wall' states like Pennsylvania, Wisconsin and Michigan, which have traditionally voted against the Republicans since 1992 except on rare occasions like 2016, can be described as Trump's sweet revenge this time.

Many Republicans abhor Trump's politics and personal life. They insist that Trumpism is different from conservatism. Yet Trump's victory and Harris's defeat must be seen from the prism of the conservative-liberal divide as well. It was a fact that Harris was pitted against too many odds in this election. She was not the natural choice for the Democrats as she did not pass through the fire test of the primaries. That led to a lack of enthusiasm in the party, and several senior leaders like Robert Kennedy Jr. and Tulsi Gabbard actually switched sides to support Trump. She had only three months to campaign in a vast country like the US, and not enough time to distance herself from the disastrous legacy of the Biden administration. Finally, the entrenched sexism and gender dynamics in American polity—making it an uphill task for women candidates to prove their worth and also win male votes—did not help her. In spite of these handicaps, she managed to secure more than 47 per cent of the popular vote in a highly polarized election, indicating that the Democrat vote base remains substantially strong.[4]

However, this mandate was also a firm rejection of Biden as well as Kamala Harris's (as vice president) NGO-style politics that led to extreme levels of wokeism and cancel culture in the country. The last couple of decades witnessed university campuses and academic centres turning into woke citadels. Academic pursuits have turned into unsafe activities for people with different ideologies and inclinations, so much so that parents started fearing for the safety of their children on campuses.

Trump's emphatic victory categorically reiterated what authors John Micklethwait and Adrian Wooldridge described America to be in their book *The Right Nation: Why America is Different.* Irrespective of whether they elect a Democrat or a Republican administration, Americans at the core remain conservative, the book argued in the early 2000s. Trump's presidential campaign was focused on core conservative concerns like illegal immigration, abortion policies and wokeism, besides promoting a nationalist rhetoric through slogans like 'Make America Great Again' (MAGA), and nationalist economic policies like increased import tariffs and Buy American campaigns.

From his 'build the wall' programme in 2016 to creating the 'largest mass deportation programme in history' in 2024, Trump's campaign against illegal immigrants appears to have struck a chord with American voters who were fed up with the weird policies of the Democrats on this question. The war between the Democrats and Republicans over illegal migrants became so intense that the Republican governor of Texas dumped them in buses and deported them to New York,[5] where the Democrat mayor hired hundreds of rooms in hotels to settle these migrants.[6] Not just the hotel rates but crime rates also went up, leading to Kamala Harris struggling to secure a majority even in Manhattan, a hardcore pro-Democrat county. During the campaign, Trump indicated that he would restrict legal migration as well by reinstating his first-term policies like 'Remain in Mexico', along with a sort of 'ideological screening' for immigration-seekers by banning entry from certain countries in the Middle East and North Africa.

The Soul of the Nation

In essence, conservative causes of nationalism, religion and family are gaining prominence in the new world in the making. The challenge thrown by the Covid pandemic, instead of bringing the world closer, enhanced distances with more and more nations turning inwards in the face of the serious difficulties they faced due to supply chain disruptions and vaccine nationalism. Many scholars predict that the post-Covid world order will witness a further rise of nationalism in many countries. The much-touted globalization and unipolarity seem passé now.

The nationalism that Western scholars refer to was a much-loathed idea until recently. It was associated with dictators like Hitler and Mussolini, and dismissed as chauvinistic and dangerous. Liberal globalism and constitutional moralism were touted as the new order. Yet in less than eight decades after the Second World War—in which over 80 million deaths and extensive destruction and displacement occurred—nationalist forces are back in many countries. Today's nationalism in the West is a response to specific contemporary challenges like illegal immigration, racial rivalries, and the collapse of globalization and multiculturalism. The pandemic has added an element of urgency to it.

The discourse of nationalism has been a phenomenon in the West for a few centuries, starting with the rise of nation-states in Europe in the seventeenth and eighteenth centuries. Nation-states came into existence after the Era of Reformation in Europe, when countries started untangling themselves from the control of religious authorities. From that time, and until Italy marched its armies into Ottoman Libya in 1911, setting off a chain of events leading to the First World War, nationalism was seen as a panacea for mankind. Jefferson's America, Napoleon's France, Bismarck's Germany, and the UK were all hailed as the sentinels of nationalism.

The Reformation challenged the political dominance of the Church and Rome. The Reformists vehemently argued that there was no need for the Church to help individuals to reach heaven, and thus the road to wisdom and heaven need not pass through Rome. In his illuminating article, legal luminary and Biblical scholar Lynn Buzzard wrote, 'The Protestant Reformation helped shatter the religious unity of Europe, and it was linked with the emergence of nation-states with their own boundaries, legislatures, jurisdiction, and therefore laws. It was a time of growing national consciousness. In place of the authority of Rome or the papacy or some universal principle, the source of the law's authority now became the state.'[7]

Many Western scholars consider the Treaty of Westphalia of 1648—which brought the bloody Thirty Years' War between the Catholics and the Protestants in Europe to an end—as the birth date of the nation-state. The Treaty of Westphalia made the kings and rulers the sovereign authority over their respective territories, replacing the Catholic Church's authority. In his enlightening work, *Virtue of Nationalism*, Yoram Hazony, an Israeli conservative scholar, argues that there has always been a conflict between the 'two visions of the world order'. One wanted to create a universal empire, and the other favoured national states. As such, he describes ancient Greek, Babylonian and Catholic efforts as universalist, and the Old Testament and Protestant Biblical Christianity to be in favour of nationalism. He calls the Thirty Years' War—which culminated in the Treaty of Westphalia in 1648—essentially a conflict, not between the Catholics and the Protestants, but a war that 'actually pitted the emerging national states of France, the Netherlands, and Sweden against German and Spanish armies devoted to the idea that universal empire reflected God's will.'[8]

Contrary to the narrow and negative connotation that liberal scholars associated with the concept of nationalism, Shimon Peres, former Israeli prime minister, offers a noble and value-centric interpretation of it in his book *No Room for Small Dreams: Courage, Imagination, and the Making of Modern Israel*:

> The Jewish people have lived by the guiding principle of *Tikkun olam*—the ambition to improve the whole world, not just ourselves. We lived in exile for two thousand years, without land, without independence, held together not by borders but by this simple set of values that have echoed through history—in Hebrew, in Yiddish, in Ladino—in every language of every country into which the Jewish people dispersed. It is the basis of our identity. And it is from this moral code that we knew, fundamentally, that Israel was not born to rule over other people, that to do so is in profound opposition to our heritage...[9]

The choice of words shouldn't be missed—'set of values', 'identity', 'moral code', 'heritage', among others.

The early twentieth century British author and philosopher G.K. Chesterton, known as the 'prince of paradox', once described the US as a 'nation with the soul of a church'. The immediate provocation for Chesterton's observation was the questions he was asked during his entry into that country. When he entered the US consulate to secure papers for his travel, the application form that he was handed down contained questions like 'Are you an anarchist?' and 'Are you a polygamist?' Irked and amused by these questions, Chesterton started pondering over the traits of the Americans, and the result was an autobiographical essay titled 'What is America?' He concluded: 'America is the only nation in the world that is founded on a creed.'[10] Chesterton's observations sparked a significant debate worldwide: Do nations, like individuals, have souls?

Decades before Chesterton, another great Englishman, Benjamin Disraeli, a conservative strongman and two-time prime minister of Britain, championed the idea of a national character. 'Nations have characters,' Disraeli insisted.

Two philosophers—Sri Aurobindo from India and Georg Wilhelm Friedrich Hegel from Germany—alluded to the concept of the national soul in their writings. Aurobindo wrote, 'The nation or society, like the individual, has a body, an organic life, a moral and aesthetic temperament, a developing mind and a soul... It is a group soul that, once having attained to a separate distinctness, must become more and more self-conscious...'[11]

Hegel saw 'pure Spirit incarnating into the world, not just as one great beam of light, but as refracted light of many different rays.' He described these rays as incarnating into particular geographical regions that have ecological integrity or clear boundaries. The local ecology—fauna, flora and humanity—interacted with the incoming ray of spirit, and the result of that interaction eventually became a nation. Hegel then went on to talk about a soul for each such nation. He called it the *volksgeist* or folk soul. He argued: 'The national folk soul, which has also been described as an over-lighting angel, carries the unique energy of its people and can be seen manifesting in the culture, songs, and myths of its people. This loose-knit grouping of peoples eventually unifies as the Spirit of the nascent nation incarnates more fully.'[12] To put it simply, Hegel believed that a nation was nothing but a spirit with a folk soul, which manifested through culture and myths, and at a sophisticated level, even in the form of the state.

Such a benign idea of nationalism was converted into a pejorative one by the liberal elite in the West after the Second World War. Anyone who stood up for the concept of cultural or civilizational national identity based on language, history or culture was branded by these liberals as Hitlerian, Fascist and jingoist, and a threat to human freedom.

Branding nationalism as a retrograde concept was only a fad with the left-liberals in the last few decades. From Teddy Roosevelt to Dwight Eisenhower, from Ronald Reagan to Margaret Thatcher, and from M.K. Gandhi to David Ben-Gurion—many world leaders have championed the cause of nationalism in various countries in various ways.

In August 1941 when Roosevelt and Churchill signed the Atlantic Charter that paved the way for the US' entry into the Second World War, they emphatically reaffirmed the principle of national freedom, and indicated their commitment to the ideals of Christianity. During the Atlantic Conference on Sunday 10 August 1941, Roosevelt, his staff, and several hundred American sailors boarded HMS *Prince of Wales* to join their British counterparts in a worship service. Churchill believed that the Christian faith had the power to unite people of both countries in moments of crisis like this one. He oversaw every detail of the service, including the hymns. Joseph Loconte wrote of it: 'It was a remarkable moment: as the Nazi war machine continued its deathly rampage in Europe, seemingly unstoppable, the fighting men of the world's most powerful democracies, along with their political leaders, gathered to sing a hymn of praise to the God of the Bible.'[13]

Yoram Hazony dismisses the argument that nationalism was the cause of the two world wars as 'a simplistic narrative'. He argues in his book, 'Hitler was no advocate of nationalism,' insisting that he was a race supremacist with an imperialist mindset. The 'Third Reich' Hitler talked about was modelled on the First Reich which was the German Holy Roman Empire. Hitler was candid and categorical about his view that Germany 'must someday become the lord of the earth'. In his autobiography *Mein Kampf* (My Struggle), Hitler explicitly rejects national identities as 'misbegotten monstrosities', and declares his mission to be the 'preservation and advancement of a community of physically and psychically homogeneous creatures' by 'assembling and preserving the most valuable stocks of basic racial elements.'[14]

In Hazony's view, the 'overwhelming dominance of a single, cohesive nationality, bound together by indissoluble bonds of mutual loyalty' can only be the enduring basis for peace in a nation-state. He even argues that a majoritarian form of nationalism, 'whose cultural dominance is unquestioned, and against which resistance appears futile,' can not only lead to a stable state, but also be 'strong enough' to grant rights and liberties to national minorities 'without damaging the internal integrity of the state.'[15]

Beacons of Liberal Constitutionalism

In the last century, liberal internationalists emerged as the *bête noire* of nationalism and conservatism. Liberalist ideas also have a history spanning several centuries in Europe. Two historical events that took place around the same time towards the end of the eighteenth century made the US and France the motherships of liberalism in the world.

The first was the making of the American Constitution, which came into effect on 4 March 1789. Liberal ideas of individualism, freedom, equality and human rights became the founding ideas of the American Constitution—a product of the 'Federalist Papers' by James Madison, Alexander Hamilton and John Jay.

The second historic event happened some 6,000 kilometres away in feudal France. On 5 May 1789, a popular revolution broke out on the streets of Paris, leading to the deposition of the centuries-old ancien *régime* led by King Louis XVI. Famously known as the French Revolution, this historical event which only lasted a decade established a constitutional government in France, and laid firm foundations for a liberal, democratic order based on the famous principles of liberty, equality and fraternity.

Both the US and France emerged as beacons of liberal constitutionalism in the world in the last two centuries. They genuinely prided themselves on their liberal credentials, and successfully transported these ideas to almost all continents. Of the three great ideas of Western origin—liberal internationalism, conservative nationalism and the communist utopia—the liberal internationalist project acquired a greater halo. It proclaimed itself as the sole legitimate universal political idea of the last century. The French Revolution's tri-ideal of liberty, equality and fraternity inspired and gave birth to many liberal democracies in the world.

For the Americans, the essence of their liberal dogma lay in the First Amendment adopted on 15 December 1791 as a part of the 10 amendments—famously known as the Bill of Rights. The First Amendment is the epitome of the freedoms that Americans enjoy today—the freedoms of religion, speech, media and assembly, and the freedom to petition.

Every idea has a shelf life. The Marxian concept of communism met its Waterloo in the last century. When communism collapsed towards the end of the previous century and the conservative ideas of religion, morals and social structures were also sufficiently vilified with enormous zeal, the liberal elite in the West started dreaming of the unassailability of their liberal bandwagon. However, the first two decades of the twenty-first century appear to be shaking up the foundations of that grand Western liberal idea as well. In country after country, liberals themselves are taking to the streets now, demanding that those liberal ideas be damned. Liberal democracy—once cherished by them as the cornerstone of liberal constitutionalism—is today regarded as a wobbling bogey, producing populist authoritarians and dictatorial demagogues.

Finding a Middle Ground

From the time of Plato and Aristotle, democracy has been seen as an imperfect yet the best available form of popular will. Democracies have matured over centuries, and produced responsible and influential leaders across many countries. Liberals cheered the rise of leaders like Roosevelt, Kennedy, Clinton and Obama, while conservatives also had their applause reserved for

Eisenhower, Reagan, Thatcher and Merkel. However, as nationalism and conservatism make a comeback across countries, liberal intellectuals appear to be turning against their pet project. By attacking the rise of nationalism through democratic institutions as 'populism' or 'far-right', liberals are turning against the core ideals of liberalism itself.

Hazony calls this liberal reaction 'a form of imperialism'. He states that 'like other imperialists, they are quick to express disgust, contempt, and anger when their vision of peace and prosperity meets opposition.'[16]

From Edmund Burke and John Stuart Mill in the eighteenth and nineteenth centuries, to the present day, terms like national conservatism and liberal internationalism represented political movements that responded to specific sociopolitical challenges of the times. Conservatives were predominantly nationalist, while liberals tended to regard nationalism as parochial, and projected globalism as their creed. National conservatism stood for principles such as individual freedom, limited government, constitutionalism, unity of the community, responsible fiscalism, an open market economy, the centrality of religion and family, and an abstract idea of human dignity. The very word 'conservatism' has a 'timid' sound, complained Austrian-British political philosopher and economist F.A. Hayek.[17] Yet, like him, many were surprised to see it ascend the political ladder in country after country. How is it that this name, 'redolent of passive obedience of the past', should become such a dominant force, they wondered, and that too in modern and economically developed nations like the US and countries of Western Europe?

Conservatism's success lay less in its doctrines—there are none that are familiar to all anyway—but more in what the regimes that swore by it delivered. As we see in history, dictators like Hitler and Mussolini openly espoused socialism. In fact, the very name Nazism was derived from the German word for national socialism—*Nationalsozialismus*. Mussolini publicly acknowledged the legacy of Italian socialist heroes like Giuseppe Mazzini and

Giuseppe Garibaldi. The dictatorships that the communist ideology promoted—from Lenin, Stalin and Mao in the past, to Xi and Kim now—are also well known.

On the contrary, the track record of countries with conservative regimes, from the US and the UK to Germany and Italy, has been much better compared to their liberal or revolutionary counterparts. They created economic prosperity and social stability. Whereas the eighteenth-century conservative Britain was an island of a strong industrial civilization, their French neighbours across the English Channel were busy promoting revolutionary anarchism and military adventurism. As Kenneth Minogue, the British-Australian political theorist, wrote, although the word may sound a bit odd and awkward, '…there is no problem about associating conservatism with dynamism…'[18]

In fact, while classical conservatism and liberalism differed on many fundamentals, over decades, they also found areas of convergence as both travelled a distance away from their respective rigid fundamentalisms in search of a middle ground. We inadvertently make the mistake of positioning present-day conservatism and liberalism as antonyms. Conservatives are also liberal in some respects, while many liberals subscribe to ideas that conservatives hold as sacrosanct. In fact, during the French Revolution, the conservatives who occupied the right chamber of the parliament stoutly opposed the aggressive enthusiasm of the revolutionaries, and often called themselves liberals. Even today, in some countries like Australia, the party of the Conservatives is called the Liberal Party.

However, the challenge that the US in particular, and Western societies in general, face today is the hijacking of the liberal movement by left-wing radicals who want to dismantle society as a whole. While a word like conservatism stood for rational and progressive ideas, a benign word like liberalism came to be identified with anarchy, thanks to this bunch of radicals.

National conservatism may not be the same everywhere. Trump represented a populist-nationalist MAGA version of it, which can be identified with trade protectionism, hawkishness on China, restrictions on (both legal and illegal) immigration, and a fierce dedication to fighting the culture war. I met one of the 'bad boys' of EU, the prime minister of Hungary, Viktor Orban, in 2023. A proud and unapologetic conservative nationalist, hated by his peers in Europe for his stand on the Russia-Ukraine war and his resistance to 'woke' ideologies, Orban represents a version of nationalism that is gaining popularity in eastern and central Europe. In power for almost 15 years now, he built Hungary into what the OECD described as a 'high-income country'. 'God, religion, family, nationalism and patriotism—no compromise,' he told me when asked about the criticism that he endures. That is his brand of conservatism.

The rise of conservative nationalists in Europe should be seen through this prism. While their electoral fortunes oscillate, their enlarged footprint and dominant role in the European political landscape cannot be ignored anymore.

One should not see the defeat of conservative politics in Rishi Sunak's 'sorry' to the British voters after the resounding defeat of the Conservative Party in the UK parliament elections in 2024, and Marine Le Pen's sobs at a Paris press conference after the RN failed to retain its lead in the second round in National Assembly elections the same year. The real story behind the British election results was not the victory of the Labour Party, which managed to win more than 400 seats despite adding only a modest number of additional votes, but the loss of the Tories to a party with a much stronger conservative agenda—the Reform UK. Called the Brexit Party, and launched only in 2018, the party led by Nigel Farage took a massive 14 per cent vote share.[19]

Wokeism: The New Form of Cultural Marxism

Liberalism was once a respected ideology that stood up against Christian orthodoxy and religious fundamentalist control of the European political establishment. But, led by sections in France, it went on to reject all other established social institutions and the saner aspects of religion and tradition. It started rejecting national identities, and sought to construct modern identities based on principles of internationalism and individual rights. That was the moment of the birth of conservatism in Europe. Edmund Burke was the first to critique the French Revolution in 1789, advocating for gradual reforms and the preservation of established institutions.

As conservatism took root in Western societies—embodying nativism and nationalism—liberalism moved into the embrace of Marxism. While classical Marxists talked about class conflicts and revolutions, a new breed of 'cultural Marxists' emerged in Europe that moved the ideology from politics to society, and physical violence to the penetration of the mind.

Cultural Marxism can be traced to the Frankfurt School in Germany, and scholars like Antonio Gramsci in Italy in the early twentieth century. Cultural Marxists deviated from Karl Marx's economy-centric theory of a proletarian revolution, and argued that a society's culture and traditions are the real oppressors of mankind, and hence, should be uprooted for the oppressed classes to get justice.

Gramsci argued that classical Marxist ideas like violent revolution should be abandoned, and ideologues should instead infiltrate institutions to create a new cultural worldview. Fidel Castro of Cuba, the darling of the American New Left in the late 1950s and early 1960s, confessed that he had agreed to address Harvard students in 1959 only because 'that is where you find the real "military spirit": In students, not in the barracks.'[20]

In the West, cultural Marxists theorized that the entire Western civilization, including its governments, rules, norms, behaviour, tradition and more, are all manifestations of 'White supremacy'. Family, nation, god, religion—all these are oppressive institutions according to them, and destroying these edifices was the only way to secure freedom for the 'oppressed'. They invented new classes of the 'oppressed' based on race and gender. They developed critical race theory (CRT), holding white people to be the fount of all oppression.

The cultural Marxist agenda led to the rise of woke culture in Western academia and society. Left-liberals took the human rights discourse to a dangerous level by promoting social promiscuity in the name of wokeism, tearing individuals, families and societies apart. Those who stand up to this mindless menace are subjected to a harsh 'cancel culture'. Marxism is 'based upon categorizing people into abstract groups and then creating a narrative of historical oppression between them. It is a fifth column inside these countries to destroy the foundations of Western culture. Its theories, which obsess about colonization, subjugation and oppression, have indeed colonized higher education in the West. Its purpose is social engineering must by an elite determined to remake society along ideological lines,' wrote David Hilton.[21]

Many consider wokeism the new form of cultural Marxism, including a group of 59 British Conservative MPs and seven peers who call themselves the 'Common Sense Group'. They wrote to *The Telegraph*, arguing that the correct term for wokeness is 'cultural Marxist dogma'. In the US, Republican Florida Governor Ron DeSantis described 'wokeness as a form of cultural Marxism'.[22]

At its core, woke has become the worst form of identity politics today, which seeks to push humans into ever smaller silos of sex and racial identities, all in the name of promoting social justice. In this pretentious world, one comes across words that are not commonly used by people, like 'Latinx', 'people of colour', 'cervix-haver', 'menstruator', and 'pregnant person'. Some words, including the most normal ones like mother, father, man and woman, are prohibited in this world of pretensions. 'Latinx' is the gender-neutral woke word for migrant people of Latin American origin. 'People of colour' are for non-white Americans. The woke word for women is 'menstruator' or 'cervix-haver' or 'uterus-haver', or 'people with a vagina'. 'Pregnant woman' is the wrong word for the woke. It should only be 'pregnant person'.

Or the latest one by Wisconsin Governor Tony Evers who has supported a bill to rename 'mother' as 'inseminated person'.[23]

There was a time when Western societies like Britain, the US, Australia and Canada were considered as impregnable bastions of intellectual freedom. Irrespective of ideological differences, ideas were allowed to be freely exchanged, and flourished. Conservatives, liberals, Marxists and atheists all lived together under the same roof in universities and academic centres. Intellectual diversity was considered the strength, not the weakness, of Western societies. In fact, that attracted the best minds in the entire world towards those destinations where imagination, inquiry and innovation held sway.

It is frightening to see what is happening to those so-called open societies today. The insidious ideology of wokeness— some challenge the very description of it as an ideology—is strangulating the vibrant academic and cultural life of these countries. Those intellectual freedoms that the countries were once proud of are fast receding into oblivion, and the anarchist ideas of wokeness are taking over their space. The very reason for wokeism to grow in Western societies is not because of any intellectual rigour but because of the willingness of institutions— from multinational corporations and global universities to the media, local governments, civic movements and, in some cases, even some religious institutions—to surrender before the lung and muscle power of cultural Marxists. Wokeness has become a badge of honour, a symbol of progress, and a token of power in the elite sections of Western societies.

BLM: Staying Woke

The original idea of 'staying woke' that began as a maxim in the Black American community in the 1930s was a genuine movement against oppression and discrimination. *The New York Times* once described it as a part of the 'Negro idiom'.[24] The first documented use of the phrase 'stay woke' occurred in 1938 when Huddie 'Leadbelly' Ledbetter ended a song about nine Black men by advising Black people travelling through Alabama to 'stay woke… keep your eyes open'.[25] In 1940, a member of the Negro United Mine Workers promised that the striking members would 'stay woke up longer' than their opposition.[26]

Martin Luther King's commencement address for Oberlin College in Ohio in June 1965—in which he gave a clarion call to Black Americans, saying, 'Let us stand up. Let us be a concerned generation. Let us remain awake through a great revolution'—was another occasion when wokeness was invoked for a revolutionary purpose.[27] The recent Black Lives Matter (BLM) movement has a constructive message against social and institutional racism, reflected in King's averment that 'there would be nothing more tragic during this period of social change than to allow our mental and moral attitudes to sleep while this tremendous social change takes place.'[28]

Black Lives Matter was the latest example of how a genuine desire to 'stay woke' against social evils like racism could end up becoming a violent and anarchist brouhaha in the hands of the left-liberal ideological activist cabal. No one can deny that racism is still an everyday reality in the US. The BLM movement was a stark reminder to the American leadership that it still suffered from many social and moral anomalies, systemic and societal racism being one of them.

The American leadership never tires of preaching about religious freedom and liberal democratic values to the world. They may well remember that in its 230-year history, the US has not had a single Hispanic president, while Hispanics constitute around 16 per cent of the national population. After 220 years, Obama became the first president of African-American descent in 2009, while African-Americans constitute over 13 per cent of the population. Not a single woman could rise to become the president of that country so far. It is this 'exclusivism', as against the much-touted 'exceptionalism', that movements like BLM questioned.

While BLM was an anguished cry of beleaguered African-Americans for dignity and security, the violence and statue-pulling that it entailed established that the much-maligned McCarthyism had some truth in that liberalism became a smokescreen for the far-left. Liberal political scientist Joseph Nye fumbled when asked about the violence during BLM protests. Describing himself as a 'liberal realist', Nye insisted that one should see the 'long term' in such situations. 'Black Lives Matter demonstrations show that even though America still has racism and still has inequality, enormous problems, it has a capacity for self-criticism and a capacity for reform, and that's different from the type of goals that were being espoused by the mob on January 6, which were essentially to reverse a democratic election,' he argued.[29]

A majority of the African-Americans do not support violence and anarchy. Non-violent methods adopted in the campaign by Martin Luther King, Jr., that resulted in the enactment of two landmark laws in favour of their community, the Civil Rights Act of 1964 and the Voting Rights Act of 1965, still inspire them. 'America has a silent Black majority,' wrote Jason L. Riley, a senior member of the *Wall Street Journal* editorial board and a respected Black American journalist. 'Mr. Trump may be unpopular, but so are looting, toppling statues, defunding the police, and allowing armed radicals to take over sections of major cities,' he added, echoing the sentiment of the silent majority against the woke takeover of a genuine movement for social change.[30]

When Woke Became Divisive

To understand what this world of the woke is, one should look at its actions. On his first day in office in 2021, US President Joe Biden signed an executive order permitting boys, who self-identify as girls, to compete in female sports teams, and enter restrooms and changing rooms.[31] That is the 'world of woke' for us. We should look for words like 'equity', 'gender-fluidity', 'White privilege, and 'inclusivity' to understand we have entered that world. It is a world of 'hectoring, moral grandstanding and the anti-democratic imposition of rules and practices by a cultural elite that is remote from the concerns of most citizens,' writes Joanna Williams.[32]

Williams adds, 'Back in the UK, at the University of Manchester, staff have been advised not to use terms like mother and father and instead to use more inclusive and gender-neutral terms like "parent" or "guardian". Likewise, men and women should be replaced with "individuals", while manpower, mankind and chairman should be replaced with workforce, humankind and simply "chair". The University of Edinburgh provides a list of transphobic statements that academics and students are urged not to make. It includes "all women hate their periods" and "you're either a man or a woman".'[33]

A most controversial aspect of wokeism is the debate over trans rights and gender identity. Woke transpeople want their gender to be identified as they wish, not based on what their physical bodies indicate. Countries such as the UK already provide gender recognition certificates that allow individuals to legally declare a change of their sex. What it means is that a man can declare himself to be a woman, and vice versa. Sadly, the voices of those women who express concerns about their private spaces, such as changing rooms, toilets and even prison cells being invaded by men calling themselves women are hardly being heard. On the contrary, woke activists are pressurizing the British administration to relax the conditions for legal sex change.

Woke culture is now targeting children in schools. In Brighton in the UK, a form that the parents need to fill in states: 'We recognise that not all children and young people identify with the gender they were assigned at birth or may identify as a gender other than male or female, however the current systems (set nationally) only record gender as male or female. Please support your child to choose the gender they most identify with, or if they have another gender identity, please leave this blank.'[34]

Stonewall, UK's leading LGBT rights charity, advises schools that transgender pupils should use toilets and changing rooms that match their gender identity rather than their sex. Hundreds of primary and secondary schools have paid to sign up to be Stonewall School and College Champions. In woke schools, children are taught that gender is a matter of personal identity choice and must never be assumed. Girls are taught to learn that their need for privacy comes second to the rights of boys who identify as girls.

Calling a spade a spade, Joanna critically observes that 'universities, as institutions, become less concerned with the pursuit of truth, or knowledge, and more concerned with the inculcation of woke values… In reality, the ascendancy of woke has less to do with the intellectual authority of critical theorists and more to do with the abject failure of an intellectual elite to defend Enlightenment values such as rationality, reason, liberty, progress, and tolerance.'[35]

At the Paris Olympics in August 2024, a firestorm erupted over the issue of 'men masquerading as women'[36] when Angela Carini, an Italian boxer, bowed out of a duel against Algeria's Imane Khelif stating that she had never been 'hit so hard'.[37] When the International Boxing Association disqualified Imane and another boxer caught in the gender row—Lin Yu-ting of Chinese Taipei—in 2023 for failing the gender eligibility test, a huge hue and cry erupted, and the International Olympic Committee stepped in to declare women eligible for the Olympics. Eminent persons like J.K. Rowling and Elon Musk received a lot of flak for expressing reservations over the episode.[38]

A report in *Al Jazeera* mentions how wokeism can harm good causes. In 2019, Canada's oldest women's domestic violence shelter based in Vancouver was stripped of local authority funding because it refused to accept transwomen (who were biologically male).[39]

One latest manifestation of woke culture is 'cancel culture', which has become a bane of scholarship in Western academic institutions. It is a crude form of liberal oppression of dissent.

A breed of social media activists, whom writer Freddie deBoer called 'offense archaeologists', dedicate a lot of time and effort to trawl through social media posts of a target, and then indulge in public shaming of that targeted author or academic.[40] Massive campaigns are launched against individual scholars of repute based on things they may or may not have said, denying them legitimate platforms.

History is one of their main targets. In the last century, it was the Marxist historians who became famous as 'distortians', distorting the history of nations to suit their ideological biases. They sought to fit everything into the classical Marxist framework of a class struggle. If it did not exist, they invented one. Today's woke distortians want to recast the history of every nation as one of oppression and injustice. Even the talk of justice itself is a form of oppression and power, according to them. Statues and other public monuments—what the French described as *lieux de mémoire*—have become the objects of conflict under the woke scheme of things. Nineteenth-century French historian and philosopher Ernest Renan described these monuments as the social capital of a people, its 'shared possession of a rich heritage of memories,' which creates 'present consent, the wish to live together and develop that heritage.'[41]

But woke activists argue just the opposite. The past is shameful and guilt-laden for them, and the destruction of all those statues and monuments is the way to 'face up' to the sins of the past and repay the guilt. The offence archaeologists and their militant enforcers have succeeded in pulling down several statues all over the West that included effigies of Belgian King Leopold II, voyager Christopher Columbus and former US President Andrew Jackson. Most of the statues attacked were Confederate monuments, standing for many decades in several of the Southern states of America, and a couple of countries in Europe. All of them, according to the violent activists, represented 'White supremacy'.

Those opposing the views of woke activists on matters like trans rights and the revisionism of history are violently attacked and subjected to cancel culture by these woke activists. Victims of cancel culture included J.K. Rowling, and many others who held conservative views on society and culture. Rowling was attacked and even subjected to death threats for criticizing the trans rights movement. Rowling entered the crosshairs of woke liberals when she tweeted in support of a British tax specialist called Maya Forstater who lost her job for criticizing the rights of transwomen. When Maya approached a judge asking if a philosophical belief that sex was determined by biology is protected in law, employment judge James Tayler ruled that it wasn't. Already subjected to harsh criticism and cancelling for supporting Maya, Rowling penned a detailed essay on reasons why she was opposed to the woke movement of the rights of transpeople, stating: 'I refuse to bow down to a movement that I believe is doing demonstrable harm in seeking to erode "woman" as a political and biological class and offering cover to predators like few before it. I stand alongside the brave women and men, gay, straight, and trans, who're standing up for freedom of speech and thought and for the rights and safety of some of the most vulnerable in our society: young gay kids, fragile teenagers, and women who're reliant on and wish to retain their single sex spaces.'[42]

This deconstruction of history in the name of 'decolonization' has rattled historians in the West so much that many American, British, Irish, Canadian and Australian historians came together to launch a project called 'History Reclaimed' to challenge the woke narrative of the events of the past. The group of historians, which included Robert Tombs and Nigel Biggar, aimed to defend traditional narratives about British history in the face of the woke interpretations of the same.

Wokeism is the new cultural tool exported by the West to the rest of the world. It is projected to be the new progressive class. For many gullible young minds, wokeness is a fad, and woke ideas are a false sense of idealism. 'Wokeism is an idea that can be adapted to virtually every country: Identify a major form of oppression in a given region or nation, argue that people should be more sensitive to it, add some rhetorical flourishes, purge some wrongdoers (and a few innocents) and voila—you have created another woke movement,' writes American economist and columnist Tyler Cowen in Bloomberg.[43]

Wokeism comes with a complex sense of superiority. Woke activists assume, or on many occasions insist, that those who disagree with them are all a part of the insensitive, cruel and traditional oppressor class. Whether it is about climate change, family values, or questions related to the LGBTQA+ community, the woke argue as if their way is the only way, and seek to demonize those holding a different view. In that, they are no less fundamentalist than old-time Marxists or present-day Islamists. In the name of the Extinction Rebellion protest about climate change, woke activists, including celebrities like Emma Thompson, flew across the world, blocking bridges and roads in various cities like London and even stopping ambulances. Wokeism is going to pose a challenge not only to gender identity but, by extension, to the institution of family too. Same-sex marriages or registered partnerships are becoming a norm in many countries. So far, over 35 countries have legalized same-sex marriages, while many others have provisions for the registration of same-sex relationships. The Netherlands became the first country to formally legalize same-sex marriages in 2001. Since then, many countries, mainly in the West, including Canada, the US, England and Wales, France, and Brazil, joined this bandwagon. While South Africa became the first African country to allow same-sex marriages, Taiwan did the same in 2019, becoming the first Asian country to join the club. While an Orthodox Christian country like Greece recognizes them now, deeply religious countries like Nepal and Thailand have come forward to do the same, indicating that the trend defies religious orthodoxy and cultural traditions. However, countries in Eastern Europe, Africa, and Asia, such as Russia, India, Indonesia and Hungary, are still resisting and ducking the trend.

War on Wokeness

Woke ideas seem to be succeeding temporarily, but a blowback is already taking place. In the US, political leaders like Florida's governor Ron DeSantis, former Trump advisor Steve Bannon, media personality Tucker Carlson, and Elon Musk are openly campaigning against woke activities.

'We fight the woke in the legislature. We fight the woke in the schools. We fight the woke in the corporations. We will never, ever surrender to the woke mob. Florida is where woke goes to die,' DeSantis declared at a rally. He even introduced the controversial Stop W.O.K.E. Act, also known as the Stop Wrongs to Our Kids and Employees Act, in the Florida state legislature in 2022, which sought to prevent educational institutions and businesses from teaching anything that would cause anyone to 'feel guilt, anguish or any form of psychological distress' due to their race, colour, sex or national origin. A federal judge subsequently struck down large parts of the bill in 2024, calling it 'positively dystopian'.[44]

There are other leaders like Steve Bannon, who famously said that 'Putin ain't woke, he is anti-woke,' and Vivek Ramaswamy, a Fox News contributor and biotech founder whom the *New Yorker* described as 'the CEO of Anti-Woke Inc.'[45]

Tucker Carlson, Fox News's former, most celebrated anti-woke host, leads the campaign in the media, informing his audience that everything from BLM to brown M&Ms are purveyors of evil wokeism. He told his viewers that the threat from the woke was far greater than the threat from Russia, asking: 'Has Putin ever called me a racist? Has he threatened to get me fired for disagreeing with him?' Musk also signed up when he took over and torpedoed Twitter, declaring: 'The woke mind virus is either defeated or nothing else matters.'[46]

Societies are realizing that 'woke is not compassionate, kind or politically neutral. Woke divides people according to race, gender, and sexuality and, in the process, rehabilitates outdated prejudices. It seems that the more people come to understand woke, the less they agree with it,' concludes Joanna Williams.[47]

PART II

REIMAGINING INDIA

12

THE LION ROARS, LOUD AND CLEAR

Around the time that the Western powers were giving shape to the liberal global order after the Second World War, four nations in Asia began their own new journeys. All four countries had one thing in common—they were all products of conflicts and wars of the early decades of the twentieth century. On the Western periphery of Asia, along the Mediterranean coast, out of a massive conflict between the Jews, the Palestinians and Arabs—a conflict that refuses to die even today—a new nation of Israel was born in April 1948. Surrounded by hostile neighbours five times bigger in number, the country's very survival remained a big question mark right from the time of its origin. It faced perpetual conflicts, terror and occasional wars that kept its eight million Jews on tenterhooks about their future and the future of their beloved nation.

At the other end of Asia, on the coast of the Western Pacific, the Japanese began to rebuild their nation in 1945 after the final phase of the Second World War saw unforeseen destruction in their country. The immediate and widespread loss of life resulting from the nuclear attacks on Hiroshima and Nagasaki was followed by ongoing healthcare challenges for millions of Japanese citizens exposed to radiation. The country was devastated, humiliated and crippled by sanctions from the Western powers for its role in the war.

In the Asian hinterland, revolutions—one peaceful and the other bloody—brought freedom to two ancient civilizational nations: India and China, subjugated by colonial oppression for centuries. In August 1947, India secured its independence from the two-centuries-long British colonial rule through a peaceful revolution called satyagraha (truthful resistance), led by Mahatma Gandhi. Although India's freedom movement led by Gandhi was peaceful, its culmination brought about the tragic Partition of the country into India and Pakistan, causing humongous suffering, deaths and destruction to millions of citizens across the newly carved boundaries.

In its northern neighbourhood lay another great civilization— China—which also experienced a revolution that was by no means peaceful, leading to the creation of a communist state in 1949. Mao Tse Tung (Mao Zedong) led the Long March to establish Red Army rule over the country endowed with the largest land mass in Asia (the Soviet Union in the past and Russia today, almost double the size of China in terms of territory, considered itself a European nation although it also had one foot in Asia).

The story of these four countries is fascinating. Within the first three decades, Israel and Japan witnessed a Phoenix-like rise and emerged as strong economic and technological powers in the world by the 1980s. Both joined the club of developed nations by the 1980s. On the other hand, in China, Mao's disastrous economic and political programmes like the Great Leap Forward (1958–62) and the Cultural Revolution (1966–76)—a product of his romantic ideological notions of Marxist theory—led to famines and persecutions, causing the deaths of millions of citizens, and resulting in stagnation and starvation. Luckily for China, within a couple of years of Mao' passing, a progressive and reformist leader, Deng Xiaoping, took control of the affairs of the country in the early 1980s, and led it down the reformist path for more than a decade. Towards the end of the last century, China also took off to join the bandwagon of the developed nations.

By the dawn of the twenty-first century, the three Asian nations had grown into prominent and influential economies in the world. Although China continued to call itself a developing economy, it soon started competing with the top five economies in the world, and rose to become the second largest by 2015. Unfortunately, India—then the second-most populous country in Asia with the second largest landmass—took much longer to rise as a power in the region and the world.

Many nationalists in India tend to blame the British for the country's woes, not realizing that the three other countries also faced similar economic and developmental challenges around the time India began its post-colonial journey. While those nations zoomed ahead, India struggled to catch up, and remained a backward economy for many decades. Initially referred to as a 'poor country', India was later labelled 'under-developed'—a slightly more dignified term—and eventually a 'developing nation', a more sophisticated description. However, the reality remained unchanged: India still failed to join the coveted club of developed economies.

However, all this changed in the last decade under PM Modi. India has witnessed an enhanced pace of growth—becoming the fifth largest economy, climbing five ranks from tenth position in just as many years.[1] Yet its per capita position is around 122nd in the world, even behind its neighbour Sri Lanka.[2] In the pages that follow, I will focus on India, exploring what went wrong for the country in the last century after Independence, and how its current leadership is making a determined effort to elevate the nation to the top in this century. I will also discuss the key actions India should take to become a major stakeholder in the emerging world order.

From Romanticism to Realism and Pragmatism

Indians are idealists and romanticists. Their vision has always been universal. India's ancient scriptures are replete with statements like '*krinvanto vishwam aryam*' (let us make the world noble), and '*vasudhaiva kutumbakam*' (the world is one family). Every Indian prayer ends with the benign wish for *lok kalyan* (welfare of the entire mankind). Unlike the people of other countries, the welfare and well-being of their own national life have never been the preoccupation of Indians. Jawaharlal Nehru's 'tryst with destiny' speech to the Constituent Assembly at midnight on 14 August 1947, joyously proclaiming independence from the British Raj, was a testimony to this romantic idealism. If anyone entertained any doubts about his globalist dreams, Nehru put them to rest by declaring that those dreams are 'for India, but they are also for the world'.

This globalist idealism was also partly a product of India's spiritual vision. Sri Aurobindo was requested by the Tiruchirappalli station of the All-India Radio to give a message to the nation on the eve of India's Independence in 1947. In his inspiring Five Dreams address, Sri Aurobindo also talked about India's global mission. While describing the freedom and unity of the people of India as his first dream, Aurobindo turned to an Asian resurgence as his second dream, in which India had an important role to play. 'Asia has arisen; large parts are now quite free or are at this moment being liberated; its other still subject or partly subject parts are moving through whatever struggles towards freedom. Only a little has to be done, and that will be done today or tomorrow. There, India has her part to play and has begun to play it with energy and ability, which already indicate the measure of her possibilities and the place she can take in the council of nations,' Aurobindo said. His later dreams for India included world unity and the spiritualization of the entirety of humanity.[3]

Nehru, a romantic idealist, who described himself as 'a queer mixture of the East and the West, out of place everywhere, at home nowhere' in the epilogue to his autobiography, was to lead independent India in the initial decade and a half.[4] While Mao's romance with Marxist ideology turned him into an introvert, closing his country from the rest of the world on all sides and indulging in weird experiments, Nehru's romance with socialist globalism converted India into a laboratory for confused ideas and conflicting actions.

Nehru's romance with European ideas like communism and socialism, which began during his days as a student at Trinity College, Cambridge, from 1907 to 1910, continued through the years of his rule as prime minister. Nehru's reference points were British thinkers like George Bernard Shaw and Sidney Webb who were active members of the Fabian Society in London. He read Shaw's *Fabian Essays in Socialism*, and also attended the lectures of H.G. Wells, John Maynard Keynes and Bertrand Russell, which left an indelible influence on his thought process. Even after returning to India and joining the Congress movement for independence in the early 1920s, Nehru continued his obsession with European ideas. When the Soviet Union celebrated its decennial celebrations in 1927, the Nehrus—Jawaharlal and his father Motilal—were invited to attend as guests. That visit and the experiments that the Soviet leadership was conducting to alleviate poverty left a deep impression on young Jawaharlal's mind. He also read the writings of Marx and Lenin.

After returning from his maiden visit to the communist heaven, Nehru chose the presidential address to the Lahore session of the Congress in 1929 as the best occasion to assert his commitment to the socialistic ideals for all-round development of independent India, and insisted: '…The philosophy of socialism has greatly permeated the entire structure of society the world over and almost the only point in dispute is the pace and methods of advance to its full realisation. India will have to go that way to end her poverty and inequality, though she may evolve her own methods and may adopt the ideal to suit the genius of her race.'[5] A few years later, speaking at the Lucknow session of the Congress in 1936, he reiterated the same ideas.

> I am convinced that the only key to the solution of the world's problems and of India's problems lies in socialism and when I use this word I do so not in a vague humanitarian way but in the scientific, economic sense. Socialism is, however, sometimes even more than

an economic doctrine; it is a philosophy of life and as such also it appeals to me. I see no way of ending the poverty, the vast unemployment, the degradation, and the subjection of the Indian people except through socialism. That involves vast and revolutionary changes in land and industry, as well as the feudal and autocratic Indian states system. That means the ending of private property except in a higher ideal of cooperative service. It means, ultimately a change in our instincts and habits and desires. In short, it means a new civilisation radically different from the present capitalist order.[6]

Thus when India began its journey as an independent nation in 1947, it was overtaken by the romantic idea of socialism. Nehru missed no occasion to harangue about it. Like Mao's communism in China, Nehru's socialism also became a tool to experiment with the country's economy and institutions. At the annual Congress session held in 1955 at Avadi in Tamil Nadu, a resolution was passed calling for building a 'socialist pattern of society'.[7]

A decade of Nehruvian socialism left India more impoverished and backward. Between 1958 and 1965, India's poverty rate grew from 51.8 per cent to 56.7 per cent.[8] The socialistic model designed by Nehru's friend P.C. Mahalanobis, who was by no means an economist but a statistician, proved disastrous for India in those crucial initial decades, just as Mao's communist model caused enormous havoc in China. Yet, India's romance with socialism continued with Nehru's daughter (who became the prime minister after him) deciding to insert it into the Preamble of the Constitution in 1976.

India officially discarded socialism in 1991, when PM P.V. Narasimha Rao and Finance Minister Manmohan Singh decided to embrace an open market economy and globalization to revive the country's sagging economy. Twenty-four years later, PM Modi ousted the one remaining relic of the socialist economy—the Planning Commission—in January 2015, and replaced it with

NITI (National Institution for Transforming India) Aayog.

Yet the word socialism adorns the Preamble of the Constitution, with the Supreme Court standing by it. Even the BJP's constitution, which swore against socialism right from the time of its erstwhile avatar—the Bharatiya Jana Sangh (BJS)—continued to proclaim in Article IV until a few years ago that: 'The Party shall be committed to "Gandhian Socialism"—namely, Gandhian approach to socio-economic issues leading to the establishment of an egalitarian society free from exploitation.' The phrase 'Gandhian Socialism' was replaced with 'Integral Humanism' a few years ago. Still, the socialistic terminology remains in the explanation.[9]

Many other such romantic notions still dominate the Indian strategic landscape. Nuclear no first use (NFU) is one such notion that continues to receive lip service from successive leaderships of the Indian defence establishment. Yet there is a palpable desire to revisit the doctrine to suit the changed geopolitical and defence scenario in the region as well as the world. Chief of Defence Staff General Anil Chauhan insists that the country is committed to the principles of NFU and 'massive retaliation'.[10] However, in the same breath, he also underscores the critical need for developing 'new military doctrines' as well as maintaining 'robust deterrence capabilities and safeguarding the country's "nuclear C4I2SR" infrastructure, which encompasses Command, Control, Communications, Computers, Intelligence, Information, Surveillance, and Reconnaissance systems.'[11]

India first articulated its NFU policy immediately after the nuclear tests at Pokhran in 1998, which elevated India to the club of nuclear powers. Minister of External Affairs Jaswant Singh reassured the world that India's nuclear capability was only for peace and deterrence, and it is committed to 'a no-first-use doctrine'. However, he added an ambiguous rider stating that implicit in the doctrine was that India 'shall not use nuclear weapons against non-nuclear-weapon states.'[12] Subsequently, while releasing the country's nuclear doctrine in 2003, the establishment revised that doctrine by stating that it would keep the option to retaliate with nuclear weapons in the event of an attack with chemical or biological weapons.

The BJP and the BJS were strong advocates of India as a nuclear power. Indicating that the NFU doctrine was not a settled matter, the BJP declared in its election manifesto in 2014 that it would 'revise and update' it after coming to power.[13] It gave rise to speculations that the Modi government would revoke India's commitment to no first use. Although PM Modi sought to quell those speculations by asserting that 'no first use is a reflection of our cultural inheritance,'[14] and that there were no plans to revoke it, the chatter refused to die down.

These speculations were not without reason. That there existed a strong view against this unilateral assertion of NFU by India became clear when in 2016, its defence minister Manohar Parrikar openly expressed his dismay over why India should 'bind' itself to NFU. It would be better for adversaries not to know what India might do, he argued. As the statement became controversial, Parrikar quickly clarified that those were only his personal views.[15] Thereafter, in 2019, the next defence minister Rajnath Singh conveyed similar sentiments. On his maiden visit to Pokhran, Rajnath told media persons that while India had 'strictly adhered to' the NFU doctrine thus far, 'what happens in future depends on the circumstances.'[16] It was interpreted by many as a signal that India's NFU commitment was neither absolute nor permanent. In case of a conflict, nothing would force India to abide by it.

Rajnath's statement sparked increased speculation, not only because he tweeted it from his official X handle, but also because the Press Information Bureau (PIB), the official communications channel of the government, issued a press release quoting his statement. In more than two decades of its existence, it was the first time that a clear signal came from official quarters about the NFU doctrine being revisited in favour of a more ambitious one.

Given the new war capabilities that countries in India's neighbourhood have acquired, it is quite logical that such rethinking is necessary. The NFU was a successful doctrine when there were no greater deadly weapons available to others, and nuclear weapons acted as effective deterrents. It could be a successful doctrine when a 'second use' option is available. But today, with the proliferation of weapons of mass destruction (WMD) as well as the introduction of autonomous weapon systems in warfare that has the potential to cripple a country's defence capabilities in a single massive attack, NFU may no longer be a credible doctrine. India needs to abandon romanticism in its approach to all such issues, and view the world with pragmatism and realism.

New Pillars of Foreign Policy

India's foreign policy has been a major victim of this romanticism since Independence. Months before India secured independence, Nehru organized an international conference in Delhi called the Asian Relations Conference in March–April 1947. The conference was promoted by Nehru as a means to bring about a 'psychological revolution' and a 'new imagination of Asia'.[17] There were 230 delegates and observers from 30 countries at the conference, highlighting the faith and trust reposed by many in India's leadership. Nehru's mission was to create an Asian federation that would eventually be a step in the direction of a greater world federation.

Although Nehru declared that his intention was not 'against anybody', he and the other speakers at the conference were equally categorical that Asians wouldn't become the 'playthings of others'.[18] Most speakers desired that Asia should be free of Western influences. It could not be communist either. Hence, the idea was born that Asian nations should form a coalition as Third World countries.

Gandhi, who was invited to deliver a speech on the last day of the conference, made a few interesting observations. Referring to all wise men from Zoroaster and Buddha to Jesus and

Muhammad—not to mention Rama and Krishna—as belonging to the East, Gandhi emphasized Asia's message as an antidote to the West. He said:

> What I want you to understand is the message of Asia. It is not to be learnt through the western spectacles or by imitating the atom bomb [...] In this age of democracy, in this age of awakening of the poorest of the poor, you can redeliver this message with the greatest emphasis. You will complete the conquest of the West, not through vengeance, because you have been exploited, but with real understanding. I am sanguine, if all of you put your hearts together—not merely heads—to understand the secret of the message these wise men of the East have left to us, and us if we really become worthy of that great message, the conquest of the West will be completed. This conquest will be loved by the West itself.[19]

Thus, 'Asianism' and 'conquest of the West' became a romantic obsession with Nehru even before India secured its freedom. This romanticism continued after Independence as he became the prime minister, along with holding the portfolio of the foreign minister of India. Two major initiatives by Nehru in the 1950s are glaring examples of his romantic globalism causing diplomatic and political damage to India. As China emerged from the colonial clutches of the Japanese, and later the nationalist leadership of Chiang Kai-shek, it witnessed a socialist revolution under Mao in 1949. As a fellow socialist, Nehru was impressed, and made early moves to connect with the new Chinese leadership. When Chinese premier Zhou Enlai visited India in June 1954, Nehru issued a joint statement proclaiming the concept of Panchsheel, or the five principles of peaceful coexistence, as the framework not only for relations between India and China, but also for its relations with all other countries. Panchsheel was supposed to lay the foundations for peace and security in the entire world. Nehru declared in front of his guest Zhou that Panchsheel would 'help in creating an area of peace which as circumstances permit can be enlarged thus lessening the chances of war and strengthening the cause of peace all over the world.'[20]

A few months later, Nehru visited Peking (now Beijing), and met Chairman Mao on an October evening at Zhongnanhai, the epicentre of Chinese politics and the headquarters of the CCP. In his hour-long conversation with Mao, Nehru's main focus was not on bilateral relations, but on the Panchsheel and how India and China could lead the world into peaceful coexistence. He made observations such as: 'Several big powers in Europe have been greatly weakened than in the past. They cannot see what they will have in the future. European imperialist countries are still playing a role, but they are getting weaker day after day and cannot sustain [themselves] for very long.' Another one: 'Anyone who has been to the United States knows how much the United States is afraid. Although the United States is very powerful militarily and financially, it fears losing its position.'[21]

Interestingly, when Nehru stated that 'war is no longer a useable instrument for achieving policy goals,' Mao intervened and mischievously suggested that if there was an opportunity, he 'would like to discuss with Prime Minister the question about whether war as an instrument of policy goals is advantageous or not.' Mao ended his conversation by telling Nehru, 'If a war is to happen again, what will happen? I would like to have another opportunity to discuss this with you.'[22]

Mao did not wait for that opportunity. Instead, his Red Army attacked India in 1962 and inflicted a humiliating defeat on it by occupying around 40,000 square kilometres of Indian territory.

Nehru's similar romance with the Non-Aligned Movement (NAM) also ended up as a failure. In April 1955, Nehru took the lead in organizing the Afro-Asian Conference at Bandung, Indonesia. Twenty-nine countries participated in this conference which adopted a 10-point declaration on the promotion of world peace and cooperation, called 'Dasa Sila Bandung' or the Ten Principles of Peaceful Coexistence. The Bandung Declaration came to replace the Panchsheel adopted a year before.[23] The conference paved the way for the formation of the NAM in 1961 when Nehru met leaders like Yugoslav President Josip Broz Tito, Egyptian President Gamal Abdel Nasser, Ghanaian President Kwame Nkrumah, and Indonesian President Sukarno in Belgrade in Yugoslavia.

However, like the Panchsheel, NAM also turned out to be a romantic exercise in multilateralism. When India faced an unexpected attack from China in 1962, neither the Panchsheel nor the Dasa Sila came to its rescue. NAM co-founder countries like Ghana and Indonesia adopted an explicitly pro-China stance, while most other member countries refused to condemn China. When Pakistan waged a war against India in 1965, NAM member states like Saudi Arabia, Jordan and Kuwait supported Pakistan. Indonesia not only adopted an anti-India position but also supplied weapons to Pakistan. 'We do not seem to have many friends abroad,' commented *The Indian Express*, summing up the abject failure of Nehru's romantic foreign policy doctrines.[24]

In later decades, the foreign policy remained ad hoc, with PM Indira Gandhi preferring to tilt it in the Soviet Union's favour, and later PMs like Narasimha Rao and Vajpayee opting for a Westward ho! stance. Vajpayee, in fact, declared in 1998 that 'India and America are natural allies in the quest for a better future.'[25]

The Rise of a Responsible Power

Foreign Policy, at one level, is a continuum as it is transferred from one government to another. However, when PM Modi took over in 2014, he transformed India's foreign policy in multiple ways. Although the issues and approaches remain the same, the transformation was clearly visible. Today, India's foreign policy is bold, proactive, innovative and ambitious. Traditionally, India has been a reticent nation in international affairs. After the experience with NAM during the two wars with China and Pakistan it faced in the 1960s, India decided to stay away from excessive international activism. However, it is now being seen as proactively engaging with countries in the world once again. For example, when countries like the US walked out of the Paris Agreement, India remained steadfast and committed to its goals. It even played a vital role in creating new forums like the International Solar Alliance (ISA). Incidentally, ISA is the first multilateral body to have its headquarters in India, symbolizing India's proactive foreign policy. From the East Asia Summit in its neighbourhood, and global forums like G20 and BRICS, to non-governmental forums like Davos, India is omnipresent in international diplomacy and the policy circuit today.

Under PM Modi, India demonstrated its ambition to rise as an influential and responsible global power. Foreign policy cannot be romantic or driven by slogans. It must be pragmatic and blended with national interests. This blending can be seen in the Modi government's adoption of more realistic principles like de-hyphenation and strategic autonomy as its new foreign policy doctrine.

What India did in the name of de-hyphenation was to refuse to look at its relationship with a given country from the prism of a third country. Modi started the convention of establishing standalone relations with countries, irrespective of their relations with other countries. It all began in September 2014 when PM Modi met the prime minister of Israel Benjamin Netanyahu on the sidelines of the UN General Assembly. Since the leader of the Palestinian Authority Mahmoud Abbas was not present in New York at that time, many predicted that India would cancel the meeting with the Israeli prime minister. However, PM Modi went ahead, ending the decades-old convention of hyphenation that mandated Indian leaders to meet both the Israeli and Palestinian leadership on each visit, or neither. In 2017, PM Modi made a standalone visit to Jerusalem without visiting Ramallah in the Palestinian territory—a ritual practised by visiting Indian leaders since the 1990s. He paid a standalone visit to Palestine a few months later, conveying his determination not to allow India's relations to become a victim of rivalries between two other countries. For many decades, the visiting leaders of major world powers subjected India to this humiliating hyphenation diplomacy. During their visits to India, successive US presidents like Clinton, Bush and Obama also included Pakistan as a balancing act, a gesture of hyphenation India silently resented. Now India practises de-hyphenation with many countries—the US and Russia, Iran and Saudi Arabia, and Israel and Palestine.

Beyond de-hyphenation, India also developed the doctrine of strategic autonomy. Although it sounds similar to the old doctrine of non-alignment, it is markedly different in the sense that while non-alignment was India's way of avoiding Cold War politics, strategic autonomy indicates its proactive diplomacy based on its national interests. Moving beyond the ideological constraints ingrained in the Non-Aligned Movement, strategic autonomy represents India's resolute refusal to sacrifice its national interests in the name of any ideology, or for the sake of maintaining diplomatic relations with any country. It facilitates the pursuit of national interests without succumbing to external pressures. Explaining it in a nutshell, Dr Jaishankar says that India should choose its partners based on 'interests and not on the basis of sentiments or prejudices'.

The strategic autonomy doctrine is evident in India's response to conflicts in Ukraine and Gaza. In both conflicts, the Indian leadership refused to take sides and maintained proactive neutrality, engaging with all sides of the conflict. India was among the 32 other member countries at the UN, including China, that abstained from voting as the UN General Assembly adopted a resolution in February 2023 demanding that Russia should 'immediately, completely and unconditionally withdraw all of its military forces from the territory of Ukraine.'[26] Explaining India's autonomous stand on the issue, Permanent Representative Ruchira Kamboj insisted that India remain steadfastly committed to multilateralism and uphold the principles of the UN charter: 'We will always call for dialogue and diplomacy as the only viable way out.'

India's doctrine of strategic autonomy faced a serious challenge in the face of strong opposition from the US for its $5 billion defence contract with Russia for the purchase of five squadrons of the S-400 air defence system. As the negotiations between the defence ministries of India and Russia progressed, the US raised objections, insisting that the deal might pose serious interoperability challenges, and even threaten to affect the strategic partnership between the two countries. Yet India went ahead and signed the agreement. During his visit to Moscow in December 2024, Rajnath Singh brushed aside the US criticism, and emphatically stated that the friendship between India and Russia is 'higher than the highest mountain and deeper than the deepest ocean.'[27]

In the evolving new world order, India needs to uphold the twin principles of de-hyphenation and strategic autonomy to tackle multiple state and non-state players, secure its objectives of building a developed Bharat, and play a proactive role in shaping the new world.

Generally, foreign policy is understood to rest on two essential pillars—economic relations and national security. The Modi government added three more pillars to it. In fact, PM Modi himself gave the five-pillar foreign policy the name 'Panchamrit'—including samman (dignity), samvad (greater engagement), samriddhi (economic relations), suraksha (defence ties) and sanskriti (cultural ties) as the five pillars.

Samman

Samman is about dignity and honour, not only for India but also for every Indian wherever he lives. There is no denying that Indians feel prouder about their identity and security now than ever before. This pride is a result of the proactive engagement policy of the Ministry of External Affairs (MEA) not only with the governments of various countries but also with other stakeholders—both public and private.

Former EAM Sushma Swaraj was known as the 'people's minister'. Her statement at the Pravasi Bharatiya Divas in January

2019 in Varanasi that 'help is just one tweet away' became one of the most viral tweets of the time. 'Our passport has become a security cover for the Indian diaspora. Help is just a message away. You can message at midnight, or 3 a.m., or 4 p.m., and within 24 hours, you will get the solution,' she told the cheering crowds of diasporic Indians gathered at the event.[28]

Over the past 10 years, the Modi government has sent senior ministers on several occasions to evacuate Indian nationals stranded in challenging situations such as conflicts and wars. Those operations included:

1. **Operation Raahat:** In 2015, amid sectarian conflict in Yemen, India evacuated 4,640 Indians and 960 foreign nationals.
2. **Operation Maitri:** In the same year, over 5,000 Indians were rescued from Nepal following a devastating earthquake.
3. **Vande Bharat Mission:** In 2020, when Covid broke out, India immediately evacuated 654 Indian nationals from Wuhan city in China. During the Covid period, India launched Vande Bharat Mission to bring home over 15 million people.
4. **Operation Devi Shakti:** In August 2021, following the takeover of Afghanistan by the Taliban, India evacuated more than 800 of its nationals from Kabul.
5. **Operation Ganga:** When the Ukraine War broke out in February 2022, Indian ministers went to several neighbouring countries to oversee the evacuation of 18,282 Indians stuck in Ukraine.
6. **Operation Kaveri:** In 2023, 4,097 Indians were evacuated from Sudan amidst civil unrest.
7. **Operation Ajay:** In October 2023, following terrorist attacks on Israel, 1,300 Indian citizens were safely evacuated.

Samvaad

Greater engagement with people beyond government-to-government (G-to-G) and government-to-business (G-to-B) engagements is yet another unique feature of the Modi government's foreign policy. To begin with, PM Modi led the initiative by engaging with the wider diaspora community by organizing mega rallies in a number of capitals. Some of these diaspora gatherings attracted 80,000 to 100,000 people. He also began the practice of meeting with academics, scholars, Nobel laureates, artists, religious leaders and public intellectuals during his visits to several countries, and whenever such individuals visited India. His ministerial colleagues also followed suit, resulting in India expanding its engagement. The MEA has encouraged Indian think tanks to host more global events, providing opportunities to the intelligentsia, media and opinion-makers to engage with their Indian counterparts. Some of those events, like the Raisina Dialogue and the Indian Ocean Conference, have become calendar events for the intellectual world.

The other two pillars—samriddhi and suraksha—refer to economy, trade and defence.

Sanskriti

The fifth important pillar added by the Modi government was sanskriti. In the past, a false sense of secularism came in the way of using cultural and civilizational ties as a diplomatic tool, but the Modi government has made those issues an instrument of diplomacy. There is no longer any shying away from using historical, religious and cultural ties between India and other countries to strengthen ties. Besides official events like Independence Day and Republic Day, festivals like Diwali, Buddha Purnima and Gurpurab are also celebrated by Indian missions, which invite leaders of the host countries. Nowadays, Diwali is celebrated officially by several governments as well. In its immediate and extended neighbourhood, India uses its age-old civilizational ties to build stronger connections with the countries. From ASEAN to East Africa, many countries welcome these initiatives from the Indian government.

During global events, the Indian government showcases its cultural richness before the visiting dignitaries, thus winning their goodwill and appreciation. Shinzo Abe's visit to Varanasi,

Xi Jinping's visit to Mahabalipuram, and Stephen Harper's visit to the Swaminarayan Akshardham Temple in New Delhi are some examples. The government also hosts a number of foreign guests at events like the Kumbh Mela.

This expanded framework of India's foreign policy is the Modi government's unique contribution, helping it win more friends in a world fast undergoing significant transformation.

Continuity and Political Stability

India is a multi-party democracy. While it is India's strength, sometimes it also proves to be the biggest hindrance to its political stability and growth. India witnessed a stable polity dominated by the Congress in the first four decades after Independence. An era of unstable coalitions began in 1989 and continued for almost 25 years.

Coalition governments have a long history in India; they are often formed due to political expediency rather than any ideological or agenda-based affinity. In fact, when the first interim government of India was formed in 1946 under British rule, Nehru invited representatives from various other parties to join it so that it could be a national government, rather than a government led by the Congress alone. Muhammad Ali Jinnah, leader of the Muslim League, refused to join the interim government. However, upon Gandhi's advice, Nehru included leaders from Hindu Mahasabha and others like C. Rajagopalachari, Syama Prasad Mookerjee, and Dr B.R. Ambedkar in his cabinet. This first-ever experiment with coalition politics was unsuccessful, with all three leaving the government over the next few years because of different reasons.

The Indian National Congress (INC, or Congress) became the dominant political force in the country after Independence, winning successive parliament elections with a huge majority as well as capturing power in a majority of states. In 1967, the first significant coalition experiment was undertaken by disparate opposition parties at the provincial level in a number of Indian states with the aim of forming non-Congress governments. The Samyukta Vidhayak Dal (United Legislators Party) governments that came to power in states like Bihar, Punjab, Haryana, West Bengal, Kerala, Tamil Nadu (Madras), Orissa, Uttar Pradesh and Madhya Pradesh had, as constituents, arch-rivals like BJS and the communist and socialist parties. Naturally, the internal contradictions were so deep-rooted that the glue of anti-Congressism couldn't hold these parties together for long. The Congress soon returned to power with a vengeance in several of these states.

The infamous Emergency imposed by the Indira Gandhi government from 1975 to 1977 led to the defeat of the Congress Party in the parliament elections in 1977, and the formation of the first-ever non-Congress government at the national level. The Janata Party, a conglomerate of five major and several other minor parties, captured power. The experiment, which was led with much fanfare by senior and celebrated national leaders like Jayaprakash Narayan, didn't last long. In less than three years, the Janata experiment failed, and the Congress returned to power in 1980 to run the country for the next nine years. India's tryst with single-party rule ended in 1989 when a new coalition of parties, including the Janata Dal, the communists and the BJP, came to power after defeating the Congress.

The era of coalitions began in India and continued for the next 25 years. Some of these coalitions not only proved unstable but also became corrupt and ineffective. While the coalition led by Narasimha Rao completed its tenure of five years, it was mired in serious allegations of bribery and corruption. The only successful coalition was managed by PM Vajpayee between 1999 and 2004, during which the Indian economy also saw stable and predictable growth. But the Indo-Pak war at Kargil in 1999 that led to a year-long stand-off between the two armies across the Line of Control (LOC), followed by incidents like the terror attack on the Parliament in 2001, resulted in the economy becoming a major victim, and the GDP growth rate plummeting to four per cent. Fortunately, based on the sound economic fundamentals laid down by the Vajpayee government, economic growth picked up in the following years. Between 2003 and 2011, the economy showed steady growth, with the exception of the 2008–09 fiscal year when the global recession of 2008 hit all developing markets, including India. Sadly, the second term of the UPA government led by Manmohan Singh was mired in serious corruption scandals that led to a steep economic decline. GDP growth rates once again plummeted to five per cent by the time the Modi government came to power in 2014.

The NDA government that came to power in 2014 was the first government after 1984 to see the lead party—BJP this time—securing an absolute majority on its own, winning 282 seats. In the subsequent parliament elections in 2019, the party's strength grew to 303 seats, thus helping it to run a strong and stable government for 10 years.

The stability of the government provided the prime minister an opportunity to make bold and difficult decisions to set the country on the path to progress. The economy grew steadily at above seven per cent through the 10 years, catapulting it to the club of the top five economies in the world. International agencies project that India will grow further and soon occupy third place in the world economy, ranking behind the US and China. A strong government helped improve the domestic and international security situation. In the ease of doing business (EoDB) index, India climbed 79 ranks from 142 in 2014 to 63 in 2020.[29] Efficient tax regimes, digitization, and government flagship programmes like Make in India, the goods and services tax (GST), and the Insolvency and Bankruptcy Code (IBC) have helped strengthen India's economic fundamentals, and turn the economy into an attractive destination for investors.

It is thus crucial that India continues to have a stable and strong government at the centre as political stability and policy consistency are critical to economic prosperity and to effectively navigating the monumental changes that will shape the new world order.

13

DRIVING PROGRESS IN
AN INTELLIGENT AGE

India is a vast country with 1.4 billion people, and a rich, millennia-old civilizational history. However, at times, these two factors, rather than serving as strengths, become significant distractions in its path to growth. India's demographic diversity in terms of its castes, languages and religions adds great colour and celebration to it. However, exploited by its political class, the very same diversity becomes a curse. India needs to learn from the countries mentioned earlier in the chapter to understand that it needs to single-mindedly focus on the economy for the next decade or more.

Japan was devastated when nuclear bombs were dropped on its cities in 1945. To add insult to injury, the US army dissolved 11 of its major industrial conglomerates called zaibatsu, and partially de-industrialized the country out of fear of its potential future threat. Shintoism was abolished as the state religion, and the education system was totally revamped on the basis of the US model. Even Japan's own Meiji Constitution was replaced with a new one drafted by the Americans. However, as soon as the restrictions imposed by the US and the Allied powers were eased in 1952, the Japanese government started focusing on the economy. They used the Korean War of 1950–53 to rebuild their industrial conglomerates, introduced significant land reforms, stabilized population growth rates, and most importantly, ensured political stability by shifting to a two-party system from a multi-party polity. Two decades of singular focus on the economy resulted in the country rising like a phoenix by the early 1970s, and becoming a strong and fast-growing economy. Soon the Western powers started calling it one of the Asian Tigers.

The story of China is even more fascinating. While Japan suffered at the hands of the Western powers, China suffered at the hands of its own leadership. Chairman Mao's devastating 25-year rule left the Chinese economy and society in a miserable condition. Industrial production stagnated, economic activity was disrupted, and the entire financial edifice collapsed by the time Mao died in 1976. Two years later, when Deng Xiaoping took control of the party and the government in 1978, the country was in a pitiable condition, with more than 50 per cent of its people living below the poverty line, and its unemployment levels at 70 per cent. Deng had to famously quip that 'to uphold Socialism, we must eliminate poverty. Poverty is not socialism.'[1]

One of the first significant changes introduced by Deng was the policy of reform and opening up. It began with agricultural reforms, allowing farmers to sell their produce in the open market. Then came free trade zones that allowed foreign capital into the country. The following two decades saw the Chinese economy racing ahead. Private investment which was almost non-existent in the 1980s grew to 15 per cent by 2000. At the same time, foreign multinationals were producing half of China's exports.

India and China had almost identical per capita incomes in 1980, but in the next two decades, China surged ahead. By 2000, their economic trajectories had dramatically diverged. China's per capita income growth accelerated to nearly nine per cent annually,[2] compared to India's figures which were below four per cent per year,[3] resulting in China's per capita income becoming approximately 70 per cent higher than India's by the turn of the millennium.[4] While India's GDP struggled below the trillion-dollar mark in 2000, China's GDP climbed to over $1.2 trillion and continued to grow in the next two decades to cross the $14 trillion mark in 2020.[5]

Even the US witnessed a decade of accelerated growth in the 1930s, which paved the way for the take-off of the American economy. It was Franklin Roosevelt's New Deal that provided the much-needed impetus to the sluggish economy. Roosevelt first announced it during his election campaign in 1932, and its implementation began as soon as he became the president in March 1933. Those were the years of the Great Depression in the US and Europe. New Deal programmes focused on creating new jobs through government spending that included employing youths in the conservation and development of natural resources, and creating jobs through launching infrastructure-building projects. Roosevelt also introduced several other welfare and social security programmes for workers, and encouraged workers and owners to come together to improve productivity and working conditions. By the time the New Deal reforms started yielding results, the Second World War had provided a massive opportunity for the US defence and manufacturing industry to enhance its production to meet wartime demands.

A decade or two can significantly alter a nation's destiny. India should view the next 10 years as its golden decade, focusing solely on its economy until it reaches the take-off point. It must resist distractions and delay other priorities, much like Japan and China did during their phases of rapid growth. In the last seven decades or more, India has never crossed the 10 per cent mark in GDP growth rates. In contrast, countries like Japan, China and Singapore witnessed such growth rates for years on end, and in Singapore's case, continuously for more than a decade.

'It's the economy, stupid,' was a saying famously coined by James Carville, Clinton's campaign strategist in the 1992 presidential elections. It turned the tables on George H.W. Bush's re-election and sent Clinton to the White House. For India, Carville's quip should be the new mantra for at least a decade or two.

Superconvergence: AI Transforms Our Work and World

Carville's remark can be rephrased for today's context as 'it's the technology, stupid.' While the economy remains crucial, technology now plays an equally vital role.

At a time when the world is entering the era of tech haves and tech have-nots, the actual race is no longer just about GDP figures, but about a country's prowess in areas of frontier technologies. Five or six key technological advancements—AI, semiconductors, quantum computing, genomics and biotechnology, clean tech, and space exploration—will shape the global power hierarchy in the new world. These are the latest weapons of world domination in the twenty-first century.

India has entered this arena of frontier technologies in recent years, thanks to the government's encouragement. Yet, it suffers from challenges like talent shortage in quantum physics, limited funding, infrastructure gap, and weak industry-academia collaboration. India must approach this technological challenge with urgency and seriousness. It needs to revamp its education and research infrastructure completely. It needs to invest heavily in areas of innovation in frontier technologies. It should focus on building a strong culture of R and D and institutions that support innovation to ramp up its technological prowess.

In the past, we achieved noteworthy progress in areas like nuclear fusion and space. Indian nuclear fusion research is making remarkable progress at an impressive pace. It began in the 1980s with the first indigenously designed tokamak ADITYA in 1989; today, it has reached an advanced stage in fusion physics by developing technology that can produce temperatures that are twenty times hotter than the sun.[6] With this success, India has joined an elite club of countries with nuclear fusion technology.

Since its inception in 1969, the Indian Space Research Organisation (ISRO) has reached remarkable milestones which are a source of immense pride for India. The Chandrayaan-3 mission accomplished a historic soft-landing on the Moon's South Pole in August 2023. Earlier, India became the first country to reach Mars's orbit in its maiden attempt through the Mangalyaan mission in 2013. ISRO set a world record in 2017 by launching 104 satellites into their orbits in a single mission. These and many more such successes show the promise that the Indian scientific community holds.

Now India must strengthen its resolve, and intensify its efforts to accelerate the progress in frontier technology fields. To understand this challenge within its context, let me provide some relevant data. The digital age of computing saw the development of supercomputers—massive storage and processing machines—in the 1960s. The first supercomputer CDC 6600 was developed by the US in 1964.[7] India took 20 years to enter the race. When the US denied access to the technology, India decided to build its own supercomputer in 1991—PARAM (Parallel machine) 8000. Vijay Bhatkar was known as the architect of supercomputing in India. Although PARAM was the first Indian-built supercomputer, imports were required for most of its components. It was only in February 2019 that India's first indigenously built supercomputer Param Shivay was installed at the Indian Institute of Technology, Banaras Hindu University, in Varanasi.[8] India has 18 supercomputers so far, and plans to add nine more in the coming years under PM Modi's ambitious National Supercomputing Mission. AIRAWAT—the AI Research, Analytics, and Knowledge Assimilation programme—is India's largest and fastest AI supercomputing system thus far. But it is ranked 75th in the world in terms of its computing capability.[9]

Meanwhile, the world is moving into quantum technologies like Willow introduced in December 2024, which is millions of times faster and more efficient than the world's fastest supercomputer. The entire future of AI and the activities at its intersection—like genome technologies, space and clean tech—are dependent on quantum computing, not supercomputing anymore.

India cannot afford to proceed at a slow pace in this race, complacently believing that its advancements in supercomputing place it ahead of the curve. Supercomputing is essential, but it has limited applicability in the new AI-driven era of quantum 2.0. That is why countries are investing heavily in quantum and other technologies. In 2022, China announced $15.3 billion for quantum technology—almost double the investment made by the EU nations together, and around five times that of the US.[10]

PM Modi has realized the significant role these technologies are going to play in India's growth. His government took the important initiative of establishing the National Mission on Quantum Technologies & Applications (NM-QTA) in 2020 with a five-year budget outlay of about $1 billion.[11] India became the seventh country to have a quantum mission. However, much needs to be done in terms of actual research and output. Capital investments have to increase manifold, and private equity also has to step in. Globally, it is transnational corporations that invest heavily in frontier technologies, not just the governments. In 2022, IBM's CEO Arvind Krishna announced a $20 billion investment across the region in quantum computing and other high-tech areas including breakthroughs in semiconductor technology, mainframe computers, quantum computers, and artificial intelligence.[12]

The Innovation Mandate

India ranks significantly lower, occupying the twentieth position, in research when we take into account the top 10 per cent of the most cited papers on quantum technologies. Leaders in innovation and research, like China and the US, spend massive sums on R and D. While India's private and public funding on R and D is less than 0.7 per cent of its GDP, China spends over 2.5 per cent on the same. It is pertinent to remember that China's GDP is five to six times bigger than India's. In actual terms, the US spends $640 billion and China spends $580 billion on R and D. India's R and D funding is about $15 billion. In terms of patents, India holds the 9th position, with approximately 339 patents in quantum technologies.[13] China, accounting for more than 37 per cent of patents, and the US with over 28 per cent are leading the race by a significant margin.[14]

During the decades of digital revolution—the 1980s and 1990s—Indian IT companies like Infosys, Wipro and Tata seized the opportunity to make the country a world leader in IT innovation and services. While many other countries have joined the race in the last four decades, India continues its dominance in IT innovation, especially in areas like fintech. Although a lot of support is coming from the government leadership, private participation in quantum, biotech, semiconductors and space remains small in India. Sadly, the realization seems to be lacking that the actual infrastructure in the twenty-first century is not physical but AI.

The rapidly changing world is now unfolding before every nation. India needs to understand that merely catching up is not going to be enough in its endeavour to become a viksit (developed) country. The need of the hour is to strive to master the technologies of the future, like the intersection of AI and gene-editing technologies, quantum computing, blockchain, and carbon capture, utilization and storage. It also needs to develop a futuristic vision for its endeavours. For example, India genuinely takes pride in its ability to place satellites in orbit. Many countries use India's ISRO facilities to launch their satellites into orbit. However, the advent of anti-satellite weapons and malware has prompted countries like the US and China to work on quantum computing technologies to replace satellite-based navigation for defence and communications so that they do not need to depend on satellite-based communication networks in critical areas.

Pioneering New Research in New Frontiers

India's education infrastructure remains lacklustre in terms of academic research and innovation rigour. India produces 1.5 million engineers every year, but what it needs is not just engineers but 'imagineers'—engineers with the power of imagination and innovation. Dr Samir V. Kamat, chairman of the Defence Research and Development Organisation (DRDO), aptly pointed out that 'the academia, the DRDO, and the industry are working in silos with little overlap,' and called for active collaboration to meet emerging challenges. Kamat emphasized the serious need to focus on capacity-building. He said: 'We are one of the highest engineer-producing nations in the world, but a lot of our engineers don't have the skill to take up R&D work. We have to build real capacity in engineering colleges, where they get hands-on experience in using state-of-the-art equipment and solve research problems, so that when they graduate, they can do cutting-edge work in research. We need to upgrade our infrastructure and pay our professors much higher.'[15]

Interestingly, Kamat's frank observations were followed by even more forthright comments from the chief of air staff, Air Chief Marshal A.P. Singh, about delays in the procurement of the indigenously developed Tejas fighter aircraft ordered by the Indian Air Force. 'We should go back to 1984 when the project was conceived. The aircraft flew 17 years later in 2001. Then, the induction started another 16 years later, in 2016. Today we are in 2024, we are in 2024, and I (Indian Air Force) do not have the first 40 aircraft... This is the production capability. We need to do something, and I'm very convinced that we need to have competition, we need to have multiple sources available so that people are wary of losing their orders, otherwise, things won't change,' he said, adding, 'Production agencies have to invest in their advanced manufacturing processes to increase speed and upskill their manpower.' Singh warned, 'R&D loses its relevance if it is not able to meet the timeline. Time is a very important thing. We need to give greater leeway to the researchers. There will be failures, let's not be scared of failures. I think we are losing a lot of time because we are scared of failure... Defence is one sector where time is very important. If we don't meet the timeline, technology is of no use. So we need to learn from our failures, move on, and not be scared of those failures.'[16]

These recent observations underscore the malice crippling India's research, innovation and productization ecosystem. India needs to address it with the utmost seriousness and urgency.

On the campuses of the Indian Institutes of Technology, the premier technology hubs, a slogan is popular: 'I haven't come this far only to come this far.' The IITs are a brand. They are the pride of India. But that pride is because those who graduate do not end but begin their journey from there. Many leaders of successful world-class innovation and startup ventures are all products of the IITs, like Sachin and Binny Bansal of Flipkart, Abhay Singhal of InMobi, Ankit Bhati and Bhavish Aggarwal of Ola, Deepinder Goyal of Zomato, and Rohit Bansal of Snapdeal, to name a few.

India needs to promote such a high-quality innovation ecosystem. Thanks to the government's efforts in the last decade, India's rank in the Global Innovation Index (GII) 2024 rose from 81st to 39th.[17] Although this is considerable progress, the 39th rank in the GII is not fully commensurate with India's ability and stature. It should aspire to be in the top ten.

In the last few years, the government focused heavily on preparing the nation for the new revolution. It has given much impetus to innovation. More than a million startups have sprung up in the last few years, making India the world's 'startup capital'. A fraction of them, over 120 startups, have become 'unicorns'— highly valued entities that could mobilize a billion-dollar investment. By the end of last year, around 240 start-ups went in for significant acquisitions, bringing in investments to the tune of $150 billion.

Realizing the importance of digital infrastructure for ramping up the country's innovation potential, the government has invested heavily in building robust architecture in the last decade. An optical fibre cable network of more than 3.5 million kilometres has been laid out, and electricity and internet have reached almost all villages.

The government has established the Anusandhan National Research Foundation (ANRF) with the stated aim to 'seed, grow and promote research and development (R&D)', and foster a 'culture of research and innovation throughout India's universities, colleges, research institutions, and R&D laboratories.'[18] The PM will lead the NRF, and the ministers of science, technology and education will support him.

Over the decades, the research culture in Indian academic institutions has declined. Although owing to the thrust given by the government, Indian academics and researchers have produced 54 per cent more research papers in the last five years,[19] taking India to the fourth position in the world, the quality and relevance of many of these papers remain questionable. SciVal, a research platform, suggests that only 15 per cent of them have been cited in top academic journals.[20] On the other hand, China leads the world with 4.5 million research papers published during the same period, followed by the US which has 4.4 million, and the UK which has 1.4 million.[21] India produced one million research papers during this period, averaging two lakh annually. Of these, only a few could reach prestigious journals and conferences. India ranks ninth globally in citation quality.[22]

The story of patents is not encouraging enough either. India filed over 60,000 patents in 2022.[23] Almost 50 per cent were local patents filed for the domestic market, which were perceived to be low-quality. China, on the other hand, filed 1.6 million patents in the same year, of which 25 per cent were 'high-value patents'.[24] Countries like the US and China classify patents as high-value if they pertain to emerging or strategic sectors. India doesn't.

In the area of AI, India needs to cover much ground to emerge as a leader. According to a report by PwC, AI will contribute an additional $15.7 trillion to the global GDP by 2030.[25] The lion's share of about 70 per cent is going to accrue to the US and China.[26] India's AI earnings are picking up. It earned about $1.4 billion in private investments in 2023.[27] Here, too, R and D is going to play a major role. The US and China each invested nearly $150 billion in AI-related R and D. The Ministry of Electronics and Information Technology (MeitY) made a modest beginning by announcing three AI centres of excellence, and allocating $2 billion of the initial investment.[28] It is crucial to increase this investment because a Goldman Sachs report warns that AI could destroy as many as 300 million jobs, and India cannot escape this onslaught.[29]

Imitation is not innovation, and copying is not creativity. In the area of original innovation, India still has a long way to go. Today, it ranks amongst the top three most digitally connected nations—1.15 billion out of a total of 8.3 billion mobile connections in the world are in India.[30] It also has one of the highest rates of adoption of new technologies. Yet India remains a net consumer of digital technologies. Its tech-savvy youngsters should aspire to become net digital producers instead of remaining at a lower rung as great consumers.

Decoding Our Demographic Destiny

'Demography is destiny.'

—Auguste Comte

What the nineteenth-century French philosopher meant was that a nation's destiny would be determined by the size and composition of its population. Today, India is the world's most populous nation. As per UN data, it overtook China in mid-2023 when its population reached 1.4286 billion, compared to China's 1.4257 billion—a difference of nearly 2.9 million people. The UN analysis also says that India's population will continue to grow for the next three decades. By 2050, India will have 1.668 billion people, while China's population will dip to 1.317 billion.[31]

Demographics is a science that needs to be understood beyond mere numbers. For instance, while the growing population offers the advantage of a substantial youth dividend with nearly 60 per cent of the population being young, it also includes a rising number of elderly individuals. Thanks to advances in medical science, the life expectancy of an average Indian has gone up by almost 25 years in the last six decades—from 42 years in the 1960s to around 67.74 years in 2020. UN data projects that the elderly population in India will nearly double to 192 million by 2030, putting enormous pressure on the governments in the health, welfare and social security sectors. 'By 2050, every fifth Indian will be an elderly person, hence planning for this segment also deserves equal attention. The health and economic security of the elderly will need to gain primacy,' the UN predicted.[32] India is a diverse country. Population growth will not be uniform across the country. While states like Kerala and Punjab are expected to see their populations age, large states like Uttar Pradesh and Bihar will witness a rapid increase in their young population.

The prospects of the rise of population are measured by the total fertility rate (TFR). It is the average number of children that a woman would give birth to during her lifetime. Although not accurate, it is considered the best available measure to estimate population growth. In developed countries, 2.1 children per woman is regarded as the approximate replacement TFR. Replacement TFR is the rate of childbirth which represents the level at which a population replaces itself from one generation to the next.

The Asian Tigers—Taiwan, South Korea and Singapore—used their population growth years effectively by enhancing the opportunities for education and skills for their youth, resulting in economic progress and prosperity. India should also look at the present bulge in its young population as an opportunity to achieve economic goals. Unfortunately, states that register a higher TFR—like Bihar (3) and Uttar Pradesh (2.9)—have relatively less effective infrastructure for education and skilling, leading to an increase in unemployable populations. On the other hand, states with better opportunities, like Punjab, Tamil Nadu and West Bengal, and a lower TFR of 1.4–1.6, have comparatively good economic opportunities.[33] This will result in internal migrations and related challenges like housing, healthcare, and law and order, and sometimes, also lead to social tensions and religious conflicts.

The sheer size of India's workforce will offer it a significant competitive advantage in the world. It will also be a big opportunity in the government's campaigns like Make in India, where companies would find India to be an attractive destination to invest in due to the availability of an abundant workforce at competitive prices. However, the country is over-dependent on the services sector which caters to approximately 30 per cent of all workforce employment.[34] While countries in the developed world face labour shortages due to lowering fertility rates, despite its high volume of young people, India faces the challenge of unemployment and underemployment.

Workforce Dynamics

India's challenge is its low-skilled, semi-skilled and unskilled labour workforce. In the age of frontier technologies, a population boom without adequate skilling infrastructure will be a recipe for disaster. S&P Global Market Intelligence projects that due to low skill levels, each Indian worker added just $8,076 of value on average, which is far behind the numbers achieved by Thailand ($18,308) and Malaysia ($34,402).[35] This shortage of skilled manpower has become a massive disincentive for investments in India's manufacturing sector.

The government is making strenuous efforts to address this challenge. First, the Ministry of Skill Development and Entrepreneurship (MSDE) was established in 2014, and PM Modi launched the Skill India Mission in 2015 with the ambitious goal of training 400 million Indians in various skills by 2022. The National Skill Development Corporation (NSDC) was set up to catalyse skilling across 36 sectors with the help of hundreds of training partner institutions, and over 10,000 training centres. The New Education Policy (NEP), introduced in 2020 with the aim of a comprehensive overhaul of India's education system by 2030, is also focused on imparting skills and enhancing research and innovation. All these efforts are yielding results in terms of attracting more high-value and globalized jobs in manufacturing and other sectors like technology and financial services.

One crucial dimension of the demographic challenge relates to the participation of women in the country's workforce. The International Labour Organization (ILO) estimates that only 24 per cent of a total female population of nearly 700 million were working in 2022. This, according to the organization, was in fact a decline from 27.8 per cent in 1990.[36] The government is aware of the issue and is working towards eliminating gender discrimination and structural imbalances through programmes like Mission Shakti. Workforce dynamics will play a crucial role in determining India's success in converting this population explosion into an economic opportunity before it's too late, and the population turns into a burden instead of an advantage.

A New Battleground?

Population is also a major political issue not only in India but globally. Competing religious, national and sectoral interests turn demographics into a battleground. There are suspicions among majority communities across the world about particular minority religious groups wanting to 'conquer' countries through illegal migration, and also through the womb of their women. On their part, members of the minority communities routinely allege discrimination and hatred from the majority community, a narrative familiar not just in India but also in many European countries.

One of the darker consequences of the 1947 Partition of India along religious lines, which led to the creation of two Islamic states, Pakistan in 1947 and Bangladesh in 1971, was the challenge of illegal immigration. Religious persecution of minority Hindus, Buddhists, Sikhs and Christians was one reason for the immigration of minorities from these countries. The Modi government amended the citizenship laws in 2019 to fast-track the citizenship claims of such minority refugees—a decision that invited massive debate and also a popular movement, which often turned violent, from Muslim minority groups. The amendment called the Citizenship Amendment Act (CAA), 2019, offers citizenship to persecuted minorities from Afghanistan, Pakistan and Bangladesh, and identifies Hindus, Sikhs, Buddhists, Jains, Parsis and Christians as such communities. While the Muslim groups complained that their exclusion was discriminatory, the government explained that Muslims do not constitute a minority in these countries and hence cannot claim benefits under the act. In contrast, the Citizenship Act, 1955, has provisions for them to claim Indian citizenship through the regular route.

On the other hand, Muslims from these countries, especially Bangladesh, migrate into India in large numbers, mostly illegally, exploiting the porousness of the border between the two countries. This issue of illegal migration, referred to as infiltration, has been a topic of intense political debate in India for several decades. Political parties in border states such as Assam, Tripura and West Bengal have strongly protested against infiltration, citing not only religious concerns but also issues related to livelihood. The matter was discussed in Parliament several times. In 1997, Indrajit Gupta, then Union Home Minister and a Communist Party of India (CPI) veteran, told the Lok Sabha that 10 million illegal Bangladeshis were living in India. In 2004, then minister of state for home Sriprakash Jaiswal said that 12 million illegal Bangladeshis were living in India.[37]

In 2013, the Supreme Court of India, hearing a petition by the NGO Assam Public Works, directed the Centre and the Assam government to begin the process of updating the National Register of Citizens (NRC). The process was completed after five years of door-to-door surveys and meeting 33 million citizens of Assam in 2019. The NRC identified more than 1.9 million illegal immigrants in Assam.[38] Although religion-based data was not disclosed, many political and social groups suspect that almost all of them were from Bangladesh. This issue remained a significant political point of contention in Assam and across the country, as illegal immigrants, after entering Assam, allegedly migrated to other states, creating pockets of infiltrators in various cities throughout India.

Not just India, illegal immigration is an issue of serious debate in Europe too. Eva Vlaardingerbroek, a conservative political activist from the Netherlands, gained prominence after YouTube decided to pull down a video of her speech at a Conservative Political Action Conference (CPAC) in Budapest in 2024, describing it as 'hate speech'. In the speech (which garnered more than 50 million views on X), Eva asserted, supported by data, that Europeans are becoming a minority in Europe. The Great Replacement Theory is no longer just a theory, she argued, 'but a reality'. 'Let's take Amsterdam, the capital. It currently consists of 56 per cent migrants, The Hague has 58 per cent migrants, and Rotterdam has almost 60 per cent migrants. Of course, most of these immigrants come from non-Christian, non-Western African, and Middle Eastern countries. The Dutch population is already outnumbered in the majority of our cities,' she argued, adding that London has 54 per cent migrants and Brussels has 70 per cent migrants.[39]

Eva's reference to the Great Replacement Theory is interesting. First discussed sometime in the late nineteenth century, it argued that Jews and some Western elites were conspiring to replace White Americans and Europeans with people of non-European descent, particularly Asians and Africans. In France, Renaud Camus formally codified this theory through a 2011 book titled *Le Grand Remplacement*. Surveys show that over 60 per cent of French people believed in some aspects of this theory,[40] while no less than a third of Americans and Europeans also do so.[41][42]

In India, a study by three members of the Economic Advisory Council to the Prime Minister (EAC-PM), Shamika Ravi, Abraham Jose, and Apurv Kumar Mishra, titled 'Share of Religious Minorities—A Cross-Country Analysis (1950-2015)', confirms this trend about the radically changing demographics of OECD countries.[43] Drawing data points from 1950 to 2015, a three-generation period of 65 years, this study concludes that of the 35 OECD countries or the 'developed world' that it analysed, 30 have witnessed a steep decline in the share of the majority religious denomination—Roman Catholics in this case.

The study—which is by far the most exhaustive, although basic—covers 167 countries and finds that globally, majority populations decreased by 22 per cent on average during the period. However, it also shows that the decline was much steeper in the OECD countries where, on an average, there was a 29 per cent decline in majority religious populations. Data about Africa is also revealing. Animism, or native religion, was the dominant religion in 24 countries in Africa in 1950. By 2015, it was no longer a majority in any of these.[44]

It is against this backdrop that the study looks at the data sets available for India. It states: 'In keeping with the global trends of declining majority, India too has witnessed a reduction in the share of the majority religious denomination by 7.81 per cent.' The authors hypothesise that the increase in the population of minorities could be a 'good proxy' for concluding that they were 'flourishing' in the given country. In India's context, a 7.81 per cent increase in the populations of Muslims, Christians, Sikhs and Buddhists (Parsis and Jains saw a decline) indicated that contrary to propaganda, especially in the Western media, the minorities enjoy relative comfort in the country.[45]

In conclusion, the authors state that:

> …contrary to the noise in several quarters, careful analysis of the data shows that minorities are not just protected but indeed thriving in India. This is particularly remarkable given the wider context within the South Asian neighbourhood where the share of the majority religious denomination has increased and minority populations have shrunk alarmingly across countries like Bangladesh, Pakistan, Sri Lanka, Bhutan and Afghanistan. India's performance suggests that there is a conducive environment to foster diversity in society. It is not possible to promote better life outcomes for the disadvantaged sections of society without providing a nurturing environment and societal support through a bottom-up approach.[46]

The EAC-PM study invited wider debate in India over the status of minority communities. Two decades earlier, another comprehensive study about the growing minority population in India, 'Religious Demography of India', was published by J.K. Bajaj, M.D. Srinivas and A.P. Joshi. That near-exhaustive study warned of the unbalanced growth of minority populations in the country down to the district level. It also triggered a widespread debate along similar lines at that time.[47]

Sustainable Population, Sustainable Consumption

However, new data also reveals that population growth rates in India are gradually coming closer to the healthy growth mark. Data shows that in India, against the preferred TFR of 2.1, the national average is hovering around 2. It declined to 2.2 in 2015 from 3.4 in 1991. This decline, according to National Family Health Survey (NHFS) data, is taking place across all religious groups.[48] Between 1991 and 2015, this decline for Hindus was from 3.3 to 2.1, while that of Muslims was from 4.4 to 2.6. Today, the figures for Hindus and Muslims have further declined to 1.9 and 2.4, respectively. If the trend continues, India is expected to see healthy population patterns in the coming decades.

India needs to tackle this demographic challenge diligently. On 15 November 2022, the world population crossed the eight billion mark. Earlier, it reached six billion in October 1999, and another two billion people were added in the next two decades. Demographers at the UN predict that the planet will have 9.8 billion people in 2050 and 11.2 billion by 2100.[49] For some demographers, population concerns are ill-founded. Rachel Snow of the UN World Population Fund, for example, says that the world population growth is slowing down, with more than 50 countries registering a population decline. Contrary to the UN's projection of 11.2 billion people on the planet by 2100, Snow insists that it will decrease to 8.5 billion by then. 'Eight billion people is potentially eight billion new ideas that will increase food production, very cool ways for people to learn on the internet…

I am much more optimistic,' she says.[50] *Superabundance: The Story of Population Growth, Innovation, and Human Flourishing on an Infinitely Bountiful Planet*, a new book published by the Cato Institute in 2022, argued that population growth was actually a good thing. Authors Marian L. Tupy and Gale L. Pooley argued: 'On average, every additional human being created more value than he or she consumed. This relationship between population growth and abundance is deeply counterintuitive, yet it is true.'[51]

Not everyone has to agree with the 'optimists'. Many rightly believe that more people means more mouths to feed, more exploitation of resources, and more carbon emissions—which are detrimental to nature. PM Modi flagged this concern a few years ago. Cautioning that a population explosion will cause many problems for future generations, he lauded those who stopped 'to think before bringing a child to the world, whether they can do justice to the child, give them all that she or he wants.' Having 'smaller families' is also a form of patriotism, he said.[52]

Most people tend to agree with PM Modi's observations. But demographics is a complex and often contentious subject. Incidentally, the developed West and China took a grim view of population growth in the last century, and attempted population control. By the turn of this century, both countries witnessed low birth rates and, consequently, a slowing down of population growth. However, at the same time, countries in the developing world, including those in West Asia and Africa, continue to register higher population growth rates. It is projected that by 2100, close to 40 per cent of the world population will be residing in Africa,[53] that is, more than one in three people will be an African. Similarly, countries in the Muslim world are registering higher population growth rates—1.5 per cent, compared to the rest which are at 0.7 per cent.[54] The Muslim population of the world is expected to reach 2.2 billion by 2030, according to the Pew Research Center.[55] Egypt, the largest Arab country, had a population of 25 million in 1960,[56] almost equal to that of South Korea.[57] Six decades later, while South Korea's population doubled,[58] Egypt's grew more than four times to cross 107 million.[59]

PEW data projects the global Muslim population to be 2.8 billion (30 per cent of the world) by 2050, and the Christian population to be 2.9 billion (31 per cent). Hindus will constitute around 15 per cent of the world population by then. Data on religion needs to be carefully analysed. Between 2010 and 2050, about 750 million Christians and 350 million Hindus will be added to the world population. But in the corresponding period, about 1.2 billion Muslims will join the global population. In the next four decades, the Christian share of the world population is projected to remain at 31.4 per cent, while the Hindus' share will decrease from 15 per cent to 14.9 per cent. However, the share of the Muslim population will witness a steep rise from 23.2 per cent to 29.7 per cent.[60]

India cannot duck this trend either. By 2050, India is expected to have over 1.3 billion Hindus, while the Muslim population is likely to reach 311 million, making it the country with the largest Muslim population. It is here that RSS sarsanghchalak (chief) Mohan Bhagwat's recent call for 'a comprehensive population control policy, which should apply to all equally, and no one should get any concessions,' becomes relevant. Drawing attention to the challenges of unbalanced population growth, Bhagwat cited the creation of new countries like East Timor, South Sudan and Kosovo, and said, 'When there is a population imbalance, new countries are created. Countries are divided.'[61]

There is a silver lining, however. Globally, population growth rates are declining, and that includes Muslim populations as well. Although they continue to be high when compared to other communities, the fertility rates among Muslims are falling as well. The NFHS in India underscored this trend. In 1951, the TFR among Muslims was over 4.4, and that among Hindus was over 3.2.[62] According to recent data, the corresponding figures for Muslims and Hindus have dropped to 2.36 and 1.94, respectively.[63]

Comte's 'demography is destiny' comment is interpreted by different interested parties differently. A warped understanding of Comte that leads to viewing women as reproductive machines is dangerous. The population will continue to grow, but it needs to be balanced. In the eagerness to make it 'destiny', nations shouldn't turn it into a source of peril. Population growth should be such that governments will also be able to provide better living standards for the generations to come. India is already the most populous country in the world with a population density of 492 per square kilometre. It cannot take too much of an increase in the population without depleting its meagre earth resources. Moreover, India would need five earths if it were to achieve the same standard of living for all its 1.4 billion people as in America.

As Gandhi said, nature can offer a free lunch if we control our appetites. The Indian answer to the demographic challenge shouldn't be political or emotional, but ethical—a sustainable population and sustainable consumption.

14

REGIONAL STATE OR GLOBAL POWER?

'We are in the habit of saying that it was not in our power to choose the parents who were allotted to us, that they were given to us by chance.'

—Seneca, Stoic philosopher of ancient Rome

In the same way, we don't have the ability to choose our neighbours, whether it's in relation to countries or individuals. India resides in a neighbourhood that is both unstable and volatile. The geopolitical term 'shatter belt' perfectly describes this situation. A shatter belt is a geographical region strategically located but deeply fragmented and stuck in great power politics. Shatter belts are highly vulnerable to conflicts, suffer from internal fragmentation and unrest, serve as crisis hotspots in international politics, and often become pawns in greater power politics. Unfortunately, India's neighbourhood demonstrates all these characteristics.

Strictly speaking, there is no defined neighbourhood for India. Concepts like the Indian subcontinent and South Asia were coined during the colonial era. For reasons of political correctness, the Indian subcontinent is less in vogue, while South Asia is adopted officially by the MEA to describe its immediate neighbourhood. 'India firmly believes that a stable and prosperous South Asia will contribute to India's prosperity,' the ministry's website states. Interestingly, the official website includes nine countries as its neighbours—Afghanistan, Bangladesh, Bhutan, China, Maldives,

Myanmar, Nepal, Pakistan and Sri Lanka.[1]

The division of Asia into South, Southeast, Central, Middle East and West was the handiwork of the American academe, based purely on the geostrategic assessments of the US, and was often illogical. For example, the categorization of the Middle East is just a colonial fiction that defies any logic. Yet, for want of any other descriptive term, this nomenclature remained in practice. The concept of South Asia remains contested with overlapping institutional frameworks and disputed regional associations. The South Asian Association for Regional Cooperation (SAARC), one of the regional intergovernmental organizations established in 1985, has India, Pakistan, Nepal, Bhutan, Bangladesh, Sri Lanka and the Maldives as its members. Afghanistan was also added as a member in 2007. Myanmar, India's eastern neighbour, is notably absent from this South Asian network.

Another regional organization, the Bay of Bengal Initiative for Multi-Sectoral Technical and Economic Cooperation (BIMSTEC), was launched in 1997 and includes Myanmar and Thailand, but excludes Afghanistan and Pakistan.

Both SAARC and BIMSTEC failed to promote coherent regionalism like the ones witnessed among CIS countries, ASEAN, or even the EU. SAARC became a victim of Indo-Pak rivalry, and has remained dysfunctional for a decade now. The last summit-level meeting of the SAARC countries took place in Kathmandu in November 2014. Since then, the regional body has remained dormant. On the other hand, although India attached strategic importance to the BIMSTEC arrangement, it didn't acquire the required momentum either. During the 40 years that it remained active, SAARC was able to hold 18 summit-level meetings where the heads of state of the member countries participated. Sadly, BIMSTEC has a poor record in comparison, with heads of the member states meeting only five times in the last 27 years, out of which one meeting in 2022 was virtual.

Clearly, India has a challenge with its immediate neighbourhood. This challenge goes back to the time of India's Independence when the country was partitioned, and Pakistan was created as a perpetual enemy. The 1962 war with China introduced a new dimension of rivalry and competition for influence in the region.

However, barring Pakistan, India's relations with all its other neighbours began on a cordial note with India playing a pivotal role in occasionally helping some of them establish peace and stability. Prime Minister Nehru played an important role in the transition of power in Nepal from the Ranas to a constitutional monarchy under King Tribhuvan Bir Bikram Shah Dev. The Delhi Agreement finalized between the Ranas, King Tribhuvan and the Nepali Congress in 1950 resulted in a power-sharing agreement under the first-ever Constitution of Nepal, and the gradual rise of a democratic polity in that country.

Interestingly, in his autobiography *The Presidential Years*, Pranab Mukherjee, former president of India and a former EAM, sensationally claimed that King Tribhuvan had offered to make the Himalayan nation a province of India. He wrote, 'After the Rana rule was replaced by the monarchy in Nepal, he wished for democracy to take root. Interestingly, Nepal's king, Tribhuvan Bir Bikram Shah, had suggested to Nehru that Nepal be made a province of India. But Nehru rejected the offer on the grounds that Nepal was an independent nation and must remain so.' He further remarked, 'Had Indira Gandhi been in Nehru's place, she would have perhaps seized upon the opportunity as she did with Sikkim.'[2]

With Sri Lanka, too, India's relations began on a friendly and cordial note after the former's independence from the British in February 1948. The post-Independence Sri Lankan leadership, under S.W.R.D. Bandaranaike, joined the NAM and supported India on issues ranging from domestic ones like the accession of Goa, Diu and Daman, to international ones like the Suez crisis. Nehru's demise in 1964 was also declared a public holiday in Sri Lanka in his honour.

Bhutan became a crucial strategic neighbour for India after Independence. Both countries signed a Treaty of Perpetual Peace and Friendship in 1949 that established a lasting friendship.

The treaty also established that India would guide Bhutan in its external relations while committing to non-interference in Bhutan's domestic affairs. India viewed both Nepal and Bhutan as necessary buffer states between its territory and China.

India's ties with Myanmar also began on a friendly and cordial note after Independence. Prime Minister Nehru enjoyed a good personal rapport with U Nu, the Burmese prime minister. Both countries signed a Treaty of Peace and Friendship in 1951.

Bangladesh owed its birth to India when PM Indira Gandhi decided to send the Indian Army to help the Mukti Bahini rebels in securing freedom from Pakistan in the final phase of the war in 1971. The Treaty of Peace and Friendship (the Indira-Mujib Accord) of 1972, signed between the leaders of the two countries, formed the basis for a strong bilateral relationship.

Rethinking the Mandala Theory

In his famous Rajamandala theory in the *Arthashastra*, Kautilya proposed that the immediate neighbour of a kingdom would be the *ari*—enemy or adversary. India sought to defy this theory by building strong ties with all its neighbours. Yet, seven decades after the initial efforts to create a coherent and cordial neighbourhood, the Mandala theory seems to be returning to haunt India.

Unfortunately, instability and volatile politics have defined the region in the last few decades, with almost all countries, except India and Bhutan, facing internal strife and revolts. In the previous seven decades of its existence, Pakistan experienced direct military rule for 34 years, while during the rest of its tenure, democratically elected governments perpetually remained at the mercy of the military regime. As of date, the most popular leader of the country Imran Khan has been languishing in jail since 2022 under trumped-up charges, while a puppet government controlled by the Pakistan Army is running the show.

Nepal struggled to establish full democracy by abolishing the constitutional monarchy in 2008. In the last 17 years since constitutional democracy was established, the country saw nine prime ministers, with no government surviving for more than two years.

Sri Lanka witnessed civil war-like ethnic violence for decades in the last century, which finally ended in the defeat of the LTTE rebels in the 2009 army crackdown after 26 years of bloody armed struggle. The UN estimated that up to 40,000 civilians were killed in the final months of fighting,[3] with accusations of ethnic cleansing against the Sri Lankan Army going up to international forums under the UN. A street agitation in 2022 resulted in the overthrow of the government led by President Gotabaya Rajapaksa, leading to a couple of years of instability. The 2024 elections ushered in a new party with a revolutionary background, the National People's Power (NPP), which secured a decisive majority and restored stability.

Bangladesh also reeled under military rule for most of the first thirty years of the last century. However, democratic governments, although criticized by Western watchdogs as flawed, continued to rule the country since 1996 until PM Sheikh Hasina's government was toppled by an agitating and violent students-led group in August 2024, forcing her to flee the country. An unelected, if not illegitimate, government led by Nobel laureate Muhammad Yunus has been ruling the country since then.

In Myanmar, after General Ne Win's coup overthrew U Nu's government in May 1962, democracy never returned in the true sense, with the military junta controlling the government all the time. The military devised a quasi-democratic system which allowed it to retain its control over the government while a façade of elections gave it a camouflage of democracy. As of the writing of this book, the country is facing a serious armed rebellion from multiple resistance groups. The Three Brotherhood Alliance (3BHA) consisting of three key ethnic resistance armies—the Arakan Army (AA), the Myanmar National Democratic Alliance Army (MNDAA) and the Ta'ang National Liberation Army (TNLA)—is fighting against the Myanmar Army in multiple places, seizing control of large tracts of territory, especially in the Arakan province.

India has struggled to keep its relations smooth in a region that is marked by instability and violence. Successive Indian governments sought to use cultural and civilizational affinity, and humanitarian assistance, as a means of maintaining cordial relations with the neighbours. It required a considerable amount of balancing, primarily because India has also been a home for rebels and refugees from these neighbouring countries, creating its own dynamics of tension and ill-will. From the Nepali Congress leadership engaged in democratic movements, to the Afghan anti-Taliban groups, from Aung San Suu Kyi's democratic resistance leaders in Myanmar to Sheikh Hasina and her colleagues in Bangladesh, many in the neighbourhood always found India to be a stable country and their natural destination as refugees. India had to allow and assist them, sometimes tacitly, inviting the anger of the governments of the day in those countries.

However, India never wavered in its responsibility as a civilized nation to help all refugees; nor did it deny assistance to its neighbours because of the political developments there. Replying to a starred question in Parliament, Dr Jaishankar stated that India 'engages with these countries on a consultative, non-reciprocal and outcome-oriented basis, driven by the principles of Samman (respect), Samvad (dialogue), Shanti (peace), and Samriddhi (prosperity).' India adopted a Neighbourhood First policy which 'focuses on creating mutually beneficial, people-oriented regional frameworks for stability and prosperity,' Jaishankar explained, adding that the same 'is regarded as valuable by diverse sections of public opinion among our neighbours, ensuring a sustainable basis for these assistance programs to continue despite changes in administration in these countries.'[4]

Together We Grow

China's emergence as a major economic power has introduced a new layer of competition in the region. India is keenly aware of the geostrategic implications of China's entry into the regional equilibrium. While accepting the eventuality of its neighbours turning to China or a third country for assistance, the Modi government added a rider to its Neighbourhood First policy established earlier by insisting that 'Together We Grow'. Elaborating this significant shift in a nuanced way, Jaishankar told the Parliament:

> India's comprehensive and longstanding ties with its neighbouring countries also stand on their own footing and are independent of the relations of these countries with third countries. Government keeps a vigilant watch on all developments which have a bearing on India's national security and takes all necessary measures to safeguard it. India is confident about the strength and enduring nature of its bilateral ties with the neighbouring countries and will continue to work together with them towards advancing bilateral ties for mutual benefit as well as safeguarding India's interest in the region.[5]

To put it succinctly, Together We Grow requires all countries to protect each other's interests while they pursue their chosen development paths and partners.

As per the government's data, India is undertaking a large number of initiatives and programmes within the ambit of this policy.[6] Among them are:

1. Humanitarian assistance to Afghanistan in the form of food and medical aid, as well as scholarship schemes for Afghan students
2. Several development cooperation projects in Bangladesh in the areas of cross-border power, energy and transport linkages
3. Assistance to Bhutan for capacity-building and in the development of its hydropower resources, as well as cross-border connectivity linkages, including energy, rail links, road, trade infrastructure, and digital connectivity

4. Cooperation with the Maldives, focusing on maritime security, connectivity, people-to-people exchange, and the creation of community-building infrastructure projects, besides assistance to overcome financial instability

5. Assistance to Myanmar with several connectivity infrastructure development projects and capacity-building, besides humanitarian relief and aid to help it recover from natural disasters

6. A very elaborate programme of development cooperation with Nepal aimed at promoting connectivity and developing economic, energy, digital and cultural ties, including through the implementation of high-impact community development projects (HICDPs) in building hospitals, schools, colleges, drinking water facilities, sanitation, drainage, rural electrification, hydropower, embankment and river training works, so as to improve the overall quality of life at the local level

7. Cooperation with Sri Lanka, including in the areas of connectivity, agriculture, power, education, human resource development, culture and economic engagement, as well as a significant financial assistance programme

PM Modi understands the importance of India presenting itself to global powers as a regional leader—one that enjoys the goodwill and support of its neighbours. He made strenuous efforts in the last decade to strengthen bilateral ties with all the neighbours, including Pakistan. Similar to PM Vajpayee's 1999 bus ride to Lahore, PM Modi made an unscheduled surprise visit to Pakistan on Christmas Day in December 2015. With just a few hours' notice, he landed at Lahore Airport to meet his Pakistani counterpart Nawaz Sharif; then he took a helicopter ride to Sharif's Raiwind residence to attend his granddaughter's wedding. Although the visit did not have the desired results, it showcased PM Modi's sincerity in building strong ties even with an adversary like Pakistan.

In an effort to build a strong regional collaboration, PM Modi invited leaders of SAARC countries to his first oath-taking ceremony as prime minister in May 2014. Leaders that attended the ceremony included Hamid Karzai, president of Afghanistan, Tshering Tobgay, PM of Bhutan, Abdulla Yameen, president of the Maldives, Navin Ramgoolam, PM of Mauritius, Sushil Koirala, PM of Nepal, Nawaz Sharif, PM of Pakistan, Mahinda Rajapaksa, president of Sri Lanka, and Shirin Sharmin Chaudhury, speaker of the Bangladesh National Assembly. During his second swearing-in ceremony in May 2019, leaders from all the neighbours (except Pakistan) were present.

Building Brotherhood and Bonhomie

Despite all these efforts, India's neighbourhood remains a challenge for the country's strategic elite. China's growing influence, coupled with the tendency of regional leaders to play both sides, is testing India's resolve to establish itself as a regional power. Some strategic thinkers even suggest that India should look beyond South Asia since 'in contemporary Indian strategic thinking, South Asia is at best a small place and at worst a limitation.' They argue:

> There is little value for India in pouring in resources to either regain exclusive primacy or balance China in a space in which it is geopolitically weaker and somewhat contained. Although New Delhi's concerns about Beijing's growing power are understandable, frantic attempts to win back South Asia or compete with China for regional dominance are unlikely to work. Another option available to India is to work with China in the region, as many of India's neighbours would prefer, but it won't be too long before an ambitious and aggressive China seeks to relegate India to the rank of a second-rate power in South Asia.[7]

Obviously, India cannot and should not take such a drastic view about its immediate neighbourhood, not only because of geostrategic reasons but also due to the long and established geocultural and civilizational bonds it enjoys with the people in the region. Most of India's neighbours are civilizational cousins, sharing historical connections that can never be erased from popular memory. India should strive to build on that natural sentiment of brotherhood and bonhomie to develop a strong immediate neighbourhood coalition on the principle of sovereign equality and civilizational fraternity.[8]

Regional Multilateralism in the Extended Neighbourhood

Today, the world is marked by several minilateral regional organizations. India is also a member of several of them, besides of course being the founder member of two—SAARC and BIMSTEC. India's membership in organizations like the Shanghai Cooperation Organisation (SCO), BRICS and IORA, as well as regional arrangements like the Quad, makes it a participant in regional multilateralism. However, to emerge as a regional power, India needs to build a functional regional multilateralism with itself in the driver's seat, rather than being 'also there'. The Indian Ocean Region is the natural region in which India strives to build such a coalition of like-minded nations in the twenty-first century.

Almost invariably, school students used to be taught that Sri Lanka and Bangladesh were India's Indian Ocean neighbours. Kanyakumari, the southern tip of Tamil Nadu, was regarded as India's territorial boundary. This continental mindset refuses to recognize the fact that Indira Point—a village in the southern part of the Nicobar district island chain—is the southernmost tip of the Nicobar Islands, and should be called the boundary of India. From this village, the Sabang district of the Aceh province in Indonesia is just 145 kilometres away, thus making Indonesia also a border country with India.

Once India discards its continental mindset, and adopts the Indian Ocean as its natural playground, countries from Malaysia to the Maldives and Madagascar will become its neighbours. Just as the South China Sea doesn't belong to China alone, the Indian Ocean is not India's exclusive ocean zone. Yet it is India's natural zone of influence due to historical, cultural and civilizational linkages that it enjoyed in the region, stretching from countries in today's ASEAN region to East Africa.

In a well-researched and eye-opening account of the influence of Indian cultural and civilizational ideas on the countries in Southeast Asia, G. Coedes writes:

> Indian-style kingdoms were formed by assembling many local groups—each possessing its guardian genie or god of the soil—under the authority of a single Indian or Indianised native chief. Often, this organisation was accomplished by the establishment, on a natural or artificial mountain, of the cult of an Indian divinity intimately associated with the royal person and symbolising the unity of the kingdom. This custom, associated with the original foundation of a kingdom or a royal dynasty, is witnessed in all the Indian kingdoms of the Indochinese Peninsula. It reconciled the native cult of spirits on the heights with the Indian concept of royalty, and gave the population, assembled under one sovereign, a sort of national god, intimately associated with the monarchy. We have here a typical example of how India, in spreading her civilisation to the Indochinese Peninsula, knew how to make foreign beliefs and cults her own and assimilate them—an example that illustrates the relative parts played by Indian and native elements in the formation of the ancient Indochinese civilisation and the manner in which these two elements interacted.[9]

The Churn in India's Ocean

It is within this extended Indian Ocean civilizational and cultural neighbourhood—a natural region of goodwill—that India should consider developing a regional architecture with itself at the centre. Even though attempts were made in the past, these efforts did not yield the desired results.

The Indian Ocean Rim Association (IORA)—formed in 1997 with 14 members, and subsequently adding on other countries to become a 23-member body—is one feeble effort made to build such a regional architecture. However, it remained dormant and ineffective in the last two decades, primarily due to the member states' lack of vision and disinterest in its functioning. In its almost three-decade-long existence, the IORA could hold only one summit-level meeting in Indonesia in 2017, which was attended by 10 heads of government from the member countries. The ministerial meetings also lacked the interest and support of the member states, resulting in the latter deputing junior officials to attend these.

Nelson Mandela, the first democratically elected president of South Africa who took the lead in establishing IORA, hoped that 'the natural urge of the facts of history and geography…should broaden itself to include the concept of an Indian Ocean Rim for socio-economic co-operation.'[10] Sadly, IORA couldn't live up to Mandela's hopes and expectations. The rise of groupings like the Quad further undermined the interest in IORA, with the Indo-Pacific discourse becoming dominant over the discourse on the Indian Ocean.

The Indo-Pacific is, in a sense, the focus of the moment. This confluence of two mighty oceans connected by the Strait of Malacca has become the most happening region in the world in the twenty-first century. However, the Indo-Pacific is in the news mainly due to the great, simmering power rivalry between China and the nations in the Western Pacific like the US, Japan, Taiwan and the Philippines. Conflicts in the South and East China Seas, and the Taiwan Strait, dominate any discussion about the Indo-Pacific.

Although a constituent of the Indo-Pacific, the Indian Ocean has its own distinct identity and importance. While the Indo-Pacific is a geostrategic construct, the Indian Ocean is a natural region. From the Persian Gulf to the Malacca Strait, this third-largest water body on Earth touches the shores of over 40 countries that are home to 2.7 billion people. It reaches the shores of Australia, Southeast Asia, South Asia, West Asia and the eastern seaboard of Africa. Four out of the top ten most populous democracies are situated in the region.

This region became notorious in the past for rivalries in South Asia, conflicts in West Asia, religious extremism, piracy and, above all, the growing competition between India and China. It also emerged as a hub of intense military competition among some of the most powerful navies in the world. While the US traditionally has a strong naval presence from Bahrain to Diego Garcia, China has increased its maritime strength and activity in recent years by building a number of ports. India as well as France have multiple bases in the region. In the last decade, India's naval presence has increased significantly through building maritime muscle and engaging in joint exercises with several nations, including the US, Australia and Japan.

However, as the decades passed, the Indian Ocean's geoeconomic, rather than geostrategic, significance started dawning on the world. Most of the world's oil shipments, bulk cargo and container traffic pass through this ocean, and over three-fourths of its traffic goes to other regions of the world.

SAGAR—Pathway to Peace and Prosperity

India is the largest country in the Indian Ocean Region, covering almost 40 per cent of its waters and accounting for 60 per cent of its population. It is pivotal to the geopolitics of the region. Its dependence on the Indian Ocean Region is massive, with almost 100 per cent of its oil imports and 80 per cent of other trade happening through it. Besides, over the decades, India has developed significant economic and strategic interests in the region, including mining, agriculture, marine economy and oil exploration. It is engaged in a port-development drive from Iran to Mauritius, and from Myanmar to Bangladesh.

India's romance with the Indian Ocean began in 1992 when PM Narasimha Rao enunciated what became famous as the Look East policy. It led to India becoming a sectoral dialogue partner of the ASEAN group, and subsequently establishing a free trade agreement (FTA) with the group in 2003 under the Vajpayee government. However, issues like nuclear cooperation, global terror challenges, and the economic meltdown of 2008 led the government to push the Look East policy to the backburner until a sharp remark by visiting US Secretary of State Hillary Clinton in 2011. It went: 'In all of these areas, India's leadership will help to shape positively the future of the Asia Pacific. That's why the United States supports India's Look East policy, and we encourage India not just to look east but to engage East and act East as well because, after all, India, like the United States, where we look to the Atlantic and to the Pacific, India also looks both east and west.'[11]

After the formation of the Modi government in 2014, Minister of External Affairs Sushma Swaraj took the lead in emphasizing the Act East policy. During her visit to Singapore in 2014 a few months after assuming office, Swaraj forcefully articulated the need for an Act East policy, stating, 'Look East is no longer adequate; now we need Act East policy.'[12] In November of the same year, PM Modi attended the East Asia Summit at Nay Pyi Taw, where he told world leaders that his government accorded high priority to turning the 'Look East' into 'Act East' policy.[13]

Act East was a precursor to India's IOR strategy. In the last decade, PM Modi has provided dynamic leadership to this region through multiple initiatives, including forging strong bilateral ties with all the crucial neighbours, and announcing the Security and Growth for All in the Region (SAGAR) initiative.

SAGAR is central to India's Indian Ocean vision and strategy. PM Modi articulated this vision for the first time in 2015 during a visit to Mauritius. In a clear departure from the widespread global discourse over Indo-Pacific and Asia-Pacific, Modi chose to emphasize the significance of the Indian Ocean Region by stating that it 'is critical to the future of the world'. His remarks came at a function marked to commission the offshore patrol vessel (OPV) *Barracuda* in the service of the National Coast Guard of Mauritius. The occasion also symbolized India's commitment to strengthening the maritime capabilities of small island states in the IOR.[14]

PM Modi's remarks eloquently summed up how India would view the Indian Ocean Region under him: 'India is at the crossroads of the Indian Ocean. Since Lothal in Gujarat became one of the earliest seaports in the world, India has had a long maritime tradition. Our cultural footprints stretch across Asia and Africa. We see this in our strong Diaspora across oceans. The seas forged links of commerce, culture, and religion with our extended neighbourhood across several millenniums.' Indicating that his government would revisit the strategy towards the region, PM Modi said, 'Our more recent history has focused our attention on our continental neighbourhood. But India has been shaped in more ways by the seas around us. Today, 90% of our trade by volume and 90% of our oil imports take place through sea. We have coastline of 7500 km, 1200 islands and 2.4 million square kilometers of Exclusive Economic Zone. India is becoming more integrated globally. We will be more dependent than before on the ocean and the surrounding regions. We must also assume our responsibility to shape its future. So, Indian Ocean Region is at the top of our policy priorities.'[15]

At the root of the SAGAR vision was advancing cooperation in the region to the benefit of all the states in the 'common maritime home'. Building a safe, secure and stable IOR, enhancing capabilities of the IOR states in disaster mitigation, delivering prosperity to all, collective action to respond to emergencies, maritime cooperation to deal with piracy, terrorism, trafficking and other crimes, promoting sustainable development, greater collaboration in trade, tourism and investment, infrastructure development, marine science and technology, sustainable fisheries, protection of the marine environment, and the overall growth of the ocean or blue economy—this vision encompassed a vast array of opportunities and challenges in IOR.

It is clear that through the SAGAR initiative, India wanted to build an Indian Ocean regional architecture. In 2008, the UPA government led by PM Dr Manmohan Singh promoted the Indian Ocean Naval Symposium (IONS), the first initiative of its kind to bring together the navies of the IOR. A decade later, IONS boasted of the participation by 35 navies from the region in its activities. SAGAR took that initiative one step forward by attempting to build a regional geopolitical architecture.

PM Modi minced no words in conveying his desire to build such an architecture based on 'a climate of trust and transparency; respect for international maritime rules and norms by all countries; sensitivity to each other's interests; peaceful resolution of maritime issues; and increase in maritime cooperation.' He insisted: 'We seek a future for the Indian Ocean that lives up to the name of SAGAR—Security and Growth for All in the Region. We will strive to unite our region in partnership, as we were once in geography. An Ocean that connects our world should become the pathway of peace and prosperity for all.'[16]

In the evolving new order, India must focus on building an IOR-centred regional multilateralism along the lines of the EU and the AU. While Afro-Eurasia became the preoccupation for China and Russia, and the Western Pacific for the US, India has an excellent opportunity to build a strong regional coalition, even a regional parliament, in the world's most dynamic region—the IOR.

The Rise of Blue-Water Power

If India is to emerge as a formidable force in the IOR, it must understand the strategic importance of naval power as propounded by American naval officer and historian Admiral Alfred T. Mahan. Mahan, who authored valuable treatises on naval strategies, and is often quoted by defence strategists in India, insisted a century ago that 'whoever attains maritime supremacy in the Indian Ocean would be a prominent player on the international scene.'[17] He was an influential geopolitical figure, a confidant of President Roosevelt, and involved in America's push across the Pacific in the early 1900s. Long before Admiral Mahan, Hayreddin Barbarossa, admiral of the Ottoman Navy, was famously quoted as telling Emperor Suleiman that 'he who rules on the sea will shortly rule on the land also.'[18]

In the first millennium, dominant Hindu rulers of India had already put this dictum into practice by developing powerful merchant and military navies and conquering the oceans around the peninsula. They established trade with the Arab lands in the west, and ventured into the Philippines and other SCS territories, crossing the Malay Peninsula in the east. From the earliest sea traders of South India, like the Manigramam Chettis and Nanadesis, to the latter-day South Indian kings like the Andhras, Pallavas and Cholas—all of them made significant strides into the oceans. Kautilya's *Arthashastra* talked about the functions of officers like port commissioners and harbour masters, highlighting the importance attached to maritime activity in ancient India. The board of shipping was one of the six important departments of the Mauryan Empire. Fa-Hien, a Chinese Buddhist monk, translator and traveller, wrote in AD 415 that the ship that took him from Ceylon to Sri Vijaya (present-day Indonesia) had 200 merchants who professed the 'Brahminical religion'.[19]

India was the leading economic power in the world in the first millennium AD. Its economic decline coincided with the decline in its naval power. The first millennium was more about trade as there was not much military challenge from the high seas. But things changed in the second millennium when European powers like the Portuguese, Dutch, French and, finally, the British developed stronger navies and conquered the oceans. The Portuguese were the first to declare themselves the 'Lords of the Sea' and reach Indian shores by the fourteenth century. Building a navy to secure the coastline became imminent for the first time for Indian rulers, especially those on the west coast. The Zamorins of Kerala were the first to respond to this, followed a century later by the Marathas under a brave admiral Kanhoji Angre. Between them, the Zamorins and the Marathas were able to control the coast from Bombay to Calicut for almost three centuries.

The British, who had conquered India by the eighteenth century, were well-known seafarers, but they never bothered to build a strong blue-water capability for their colony during their two-century rule. The Royal Indian Navy that they established in the early nineteenth century was small and inconsequential for a country of India's size. They focused more on mobilizing armies from local princes in their war effort during the world wars. Sadly, this lack of attention to the seas continued after Independence as well, with governments giving greater priority to land-based warfare, and completely neglecting the oceans and their potential for the country. The result was that in areas like shipbuilding and naval vessels, India remained a laggard in the last seven decades. It ranks twentieth in the global shipbuilding industry, holding a meagre 0.05 per cent market share.[20]

Interestingly, the first to alert India about the importance of the Indian Ocean for its future was a renowned diplomat K.M. Panikkar, who served as India's ambassador to China and France. He argued in his book, 'So far as India is concerned, it should be remembered that the peninsular character of the country and the essential dependence of its trade on maritime traffic give the sea a preponderant influence on its destiny.'[21] Panikkar's book, along with Mahan's, is important reference material for officers of the Indian Navy.

Keshav Vaidya, a contemporary of Panikkar's, was also a strong advocate of blue-water naval projection for independent India. In his book *The Naval Defence of India*, Vaidya explicitly acknowledged Mahan's *The Influence of Sea Power Upon History*, as well as Tunstall's *Ocean Power Wins*, and passionately argued that India's strategic needs in 1949 meant 'developing an invincible navy...to defend not only her coast but her distant oceanic frontiers with her own navy...the points which must be within India's control are not merely coastal, but oceanic, and far from the coast itself...our ocean frontiers are stretched far and wide in all directions.'[22]

Sadly, though, his warnings were brushed aside. Engrossed in their 'continental mindset', the Indian leadership failed to fully appreciate the importance and potential of the Indian Ocean Region.

The Indian Ocean is a natural region that is home to more than three dozen nations. From the Persian Gulf to the Strait of Malacca, this vast expanse of water is the world's third largest ocean, covering over 74 million square kilometres. For India, the Indian Ocean is a lifeline. As much as 80 per cent of its external trade and 90 per cent of its energy trade happen through these ocean lines. Additionally, the Indian Ocean maritime trade routes are crucial supply chains, managing almost 70 per cent of the world's container traffic.[23]

Moreover, the Indian Ocean—the only ocean to be named after a country—is not just a maritime geography but a civilization. Over millennia, its waves reached the shores of many countries carrying India's cultural and civilizational imprint, and created a vast sphere of Indic civilizational influence. It took several decades before the governments in India realized the natural goodwill that India enjoys in this region, once described as the British Lake, and started taking proactive steps to strengthen the Indian Navy.

It is a fact that the land-border conflict with Pakistan that India inherited at the time of Independence—which has been festering since then—compelled it to focus more on the army and air force wings of its military, and less on the navy. The 1962 war with China increased the zone of conflict by several thousand kilometres, and turned the entire stretch of the over 7,000-kilometre-long land border into a great wall, denying it land access to the rest of the world.

Brown-Water Force

Unfortunately, budgetary constraints and the imminent need for land warfare created by its immediate northern neighbours like Pakistan and China resulted in the neglect of the crucial third arm of the Indian military—the navy. As the global power axis shifted to the Indo-Pacific region in its neighbourhood in the twenty-first century, India was suddenly awakened to the need to strengthen that long-neglected element of strategic capability—the blue-water navy.

Meanwhile, China's naval upgradation drive, which some strategic experts described as a 'turn to Mahan', added urgency to India's efforts.

China's naval modernization project was underway for about thirty years, starting in the early 1990s. It transformed China's navy into a formidable modern force capable of undertaking a growing number of operations in the broader waters—from the Western Pacific to the Indian Ocean, and into the waters around Europe. By the 2020s, the People's Liberation Army-Navy (PLA-N) surpassed the US Navy in terms of the number of battleships. The US Department of Defense admitted that China's navy 'is the largest navy in the world with a battle force of over 370 platforms, including major surface combatants, submarines, ocean-going amphibious ships, mine warfare ships, aircraft carriers, and fleet auxiliaries. Notably, this figure does not include approximately 60 HOUBEI-class patrol combatants that carry anti-ship cruise missiles (ASCM). The...overall battle force [of China's navy] is expected to grow to 395 ships by 2025 and 435 ships by 2030.'[24] By comparison, the US Navy had 296 battleships as of August 2024, and it is projected to include another 294 to take the numbers up to 500 by the end of 2030.[25]

For decades after Independence, the Indian Navy remained a 'brown-water force' capable of handling only coastal waters. Admiral Jayant Nadkarni, chief of naval staff during 1987–90, was the first to emphatically state that 'legitimate use...of a Blue

Water navy is power projection which is necessary' for a 'power like India'.[26]

The Vajpayee government, which came to power in 1998, made a conscious effort to increase funding for the navy and warship construction. The Manmohan Singh-led Congress administration, which came into office in May 2004, has also maintained this naval support. Highlighting the importance of India's navy, EAM Pranab Mukherjee stressed in June 2007 that 'within the larger maritime canvas, it is our nation's military maritime power—as embodied by the Indian Navy...that is the enabling instrument that allows all the other components of maritime power to be exercised.' He added that it was 'these "enabling" functions that provide centrality to the Indian Navy within the country's overall maritime strategy and allow it to act as a versatile and effective instrument of our foreign policy.'[27]

Drive for a Blue-Water Navy

Modi's government, which came to power in 2014, gave a further impetus to this blue-water strategy to enable the Indian Navy to operate beyond coastal defence, in the blue waters several hundred kilometres away. As China's String of Pearls strategy—under which it constructed a number of dual-use ports in countries around India, effectively encircling it in the process—provoked serious rethinking in Indian strategic circles, the Modi government moved fast to respond to the China challenge.

Agalega is a tiny speck in the vast waters of the western Indian Ocean. This atoll, comprising two islands—North and South Agalega—separated by a short channel not wider than 200 metres, is just 25 square kilometres in area. From the sky, it looks like an exclamation mark. Many strategic observers in the world were sceptical when the prime ministers of India and Mauritius—Narendra Modi and Pravind Jugnauth—announced a memorandum of understanding (MoU) in 2015 to develop this atoll. Located 684 miles (1,122 km) northeast of mainland Mauritius, this atoll was once a slave plantation colony. The only town on the island is called Vingt-Cinq (meaning 25 in French)—referring to the number of lashes the slaves would receive as punishment. The 12-kilometre-long and two-kilometre-wide northern island has a small airstrip that used to be occasionally visited by coast guard planes and helicopters.

While signing the MoU in 2015, the two prime ministers announced that the 800-metre-long airstrip capable of landing light aircraft would be developed into a full-length airfield that could receive larger planes. They insisted that the objective was about 'setting up and upgradation of infrastructure for improving sea and air connectivity at the Outer Island of Mauritius, which will go a long way in ameliorating the condition of the inhabitants of this remote island.'[28]

Some critics in the strategic world were not convinced, and insisted that the real objective of the Indian government was to build a military base there. Dozens of articles and reports followed, with some even alleging that Agalega was 'a secret base and India's claim to power'. Some politicians in Mauritius also saw an opportunity to corner the prime minister. However, PM Jugnauth stoutly defended his decision, insisting that the project was intended to enhance the capabilities of the government in managing far-flung islands. He also clarified that 'India would be allowed to utilize the facilities in Agalega subject to prior notification from the competent authorities of Mauritius.'[29]

Eight years after the MoU, and amidst intense speculation, the two prime ministers met again, virtually, in mid-2024 and announced the opening of the upgraded three-kilometre-long airstrip on the island that could handle bigger aircraft, and a harbour that could anchor big ships. Six civilian projects, including a medical facility and a school, were also inaugurated. Both prime ministers highlighted the maritime significance of the initiative, hinting at a larger geostrategic objective. While thanking PM Modi 'for helping Mauritius realize such major transformational projects,' Jugnauth added that besides meeting the development objectives, they would also 'significantly enhance the capabilities and capacities in marine surveillance and security.' For his part, PM Modi also referred to the 'traditional and non-traditional challenges' in the Indian Ocean Region, and described Mauritius as a 'natural partner in maritime security.' He added: 'We are actively working to ensure security, prosperity, and stability in the Indian Ocean Region. We are cooperating in all areas like monitoring of Exclusive Economic Zone, joint patrolling, hydrography, and Humanitarian Assistance and Disaster Relief.'[30]

Agalega thus entered the list of ports in the Indian Ocean that provide strategic access to India—dubbed by some analysts as the 'necklace of diamonds', a counter to China's String of Pearls ports. India already has a naval air station INS Kohassa in North Andaman, and another near Port Blair called INS Utkrosh—providing enough depth for the country's military to monitor the eastern Indian Ocean thoroughly. With the maritime empowerment of Mauritius through the Agalega project, India can expect to get enough cooperation from that country—'a natural partner'—to monitor important ocean lines in the western Indian Ocean, including the crucial Mozambique Channel.

The Indian Ocean Region has emerged as the axis of global power. The US and the UK with the Diego Garcia base, and France with Reunion Island, are already active in the region. China also joined them, investing heavily in spreading its tentacles there. It built many assets in the western Indian Ocean, such as the bases in Djibouti and Gwadar, and developed extensive influence over many leaders in Africa.

Under PM Modi, India nurtured the ambition of rising as an influential blue-water power as well as the voice of the Global South. Befitting India's current stature as a significant regional power, Modi wished to convey through the Agalega project that his country was serious about its critical role as a net peace provider in the Indian Ocean Region, and was willing to brook no interference in managing it as a 'zone of peace'. Towards that end, the Modi government has proclaimed an ambitious SAGAR initiative in 2015.

India is geographically situated in the most happening region today. It is surrounded by countries that are less capable of managing their maritime challenges. Its Indian Ocean neighbourhood is a crowded space today with vessels from all major countries crisscrossing its waters—on the surface as well as underwater. Critical next-generation communication networks proliferate in the Indian Ocean through undersea cables that were traditionally managed by European companies, but recently, some were also established by the Chinese telecommunications behemoth Huawei. The Indian Navy is expected to face not only maritime challenges from other navies but also challenges like piracy, sea-born terrorism, climate challenges, human and contraband trafficking, illegal and unregulated fishing, arms running, poaching, and humanitarian challenges like evacuations and disaster relief. The region is home to some security hotspots like Iran, Afghanistan and Pakistan. Instability in West Asia and North Africa (WANA) is another challenge for the navy. Its jurisdiction extends from more than 5,422 kilometres of India's coastline to several island territories—whose coastline adds another 2,094 kilometres to the maritime border.

The Indian Navy needs to be equipped to handle these multifarious tasks and challenges. Unfortunately, its vessel strength remains small. The government sanctioned a vessel strength of 138 ships for the navy in the 1960s, but that number couldn't be reached even after 50 years. While a good number of vessels has been commissioned, a still greater number had to be decommissioned for maintenance and operability reasons. There was only one aircraft carrier that the navy purchased from Russia in 2014—INS *Vikramaditya*. INS *Vikrant*, a fully indigenously built aircraft carrier, was commissioned in September 2022, increasing the strength to two. The Indian submarine fleet is also not sufficiently big. It operates 16 submarines out of which two are nuclear-powered, while the other 14 are conventional diesel-electric ones.[31] Moreover, the capability of these submarines is questionable.

Given the reality of budgetary constraints, there is no better government than the current one to support the efforts of the navy. In the last decade, the government has added substantial strength to India's maritime preparedness. A tri-service command was established in the Andaman and Nicobar Islands with the aim of creating vast additional facilities for troops, warships, aircraft and drones in the following ten years. A new centre called the Information Fusion Centre (IFC) was established near Delhi to enhance maritime security through real-time monitoring and information sharing about maritime traffic in the region. The navy's plans for enhancing maritime capability include acquiring 200 ships, 500 aircraft and 24 attack submarines.[32] Efforts are being made to strengthen the fleet of aircraft carriers to at least four in the coming decades.

Achieving that capability is critical to India's future global role.

Epilogue

BUILDING BRAND BHARAT

In conclusion, I would like to address what I believe is the most significant task and challenge facing India: building 'Brand Bharat'. The question is, should India emulate the West or the rest in its pursuit of greatness? Or should it rise as a brand by itself? This crucial insight should never be missed by the Indian leadership while pursuing future development goals. In the Bhagavad Gita, Krishna says,

yadyadācaratiśreṣṭhastattadevetaro janaḥ
sa yatpramāṇaṃ kurute lokastadanuvartate

(People generally tend to imitate the noble ones.)

Like humans, nations also look for role models. In recent times, countries that are economically and militarily strong are considered role models to emulate. Progress and development are often measured by the size of a country's GDP and the strength of its military forces. Militarily powerful and economically developed countries like the US and China thus came to present those role models to many national societies, or at least, they seek to impose their models on the rest of the world.

The US has tremendous belief in its superpower status and the sense of American exceptionalism. Many in the US sincerely believe that liberal constitutionalism—the American way—should be the panacea for all mankind. Moulding the rest of the world in their prototype is considered progress in their opinion.

On the other hand, the Soviet communist regimes in the last century believed in establishing proletarian dictatorships—on the lines of the one they claimed to have achieved in their Fatherland—in all the countries in the world. Initially, the Communist International (Comintern) was created to export Marxism to all countries. Stalin wound it up in 1943, primarily to reassure his newfound Western allies about his non-expansionist commitment. However, he soon resumed his communist-ization mission after the end of the Second World War through the Red Army's tank battalions. Soviet communism met its nemesis in seven decades.

However, the Chinese model survived. In the new century, the Chinese leadership wishes to seed its own model in the gullible world. They call it 'Socialism with Chinese characteristics'—a model that holds social discipline above individual freedoms and the state-defined common good above the political rights of citizens. If the American scheme of things involves maintaining superpower status by hook or by crook, the Chinese model insists on upholding Middle Kingdom status for their country.

Besides China, two other countries—Japan and Israel—developed their own unique momentum in the decades following their rise. Both became synonymous with patriotism. 'Made in Japan' became a symbol of progress in modern technology in the electronic era. The Japanese ruled the world of consumer electronics and automobile industries. By the end of the last century, Japan was the third largest economy in the world. Israel, for its part, made history by building a strong economic and military power base and successfully combatting enemies five times bigger than its force. It excelled in areas like agriculture and tech startups, forcing the world to take cognizance of its rise. It faced wars, terrorism and intimidation, but its leadership refused to surrender. In the end, while its enemies ended up paying a heavy price, Israel always emerged victorious and strong.

Looking at the progress these countries made, the Indian leadership also attempted to ape their successful trajectory. In the first three or four decades, the fad of socialism dominated the Indian political and policy establishment. After the 1990s, joining the club of the so-called developed countries became the singular obsession of the Indian leadership. There is nothing wrong with the leadership's desire to create better living standards for all its people, but there never existed any clarity as to what path to choose or what models to build. Ideally, at the time of its independence, India should have debated over its global mission and strategized on the direction to take. It should have turned to its vast civilizational experience to find its national soul and build a future in harmony with that. Instead, the perennial search for the same elsewhere became the pastime of the leadership of independent India.

Like our leaders of yore, several psychologists did not subscribe to the efforts to find a common characteristic of nations either. To them, the so-called national character appeared to be an over-generalization leading to the stereotyping of nations. Their criticism of the national character argument focused on the trivialization of the external traits of the peoples of various countries. There is an element of truth in their criticism. The national character was made into an aspect of fun and ridicule by resorting to stereotyping nations based on human behavioural elements. One stereotype goes: 'Germans don't laugh', because they are sticklers for order to the point of absurdity. The French are typical playboys who only ever think about wine and women. The Americans are fond of expensive cars; the Russians are uncouth, pugnacious and reckless and fond of vodka and street brawls. The Hindus are lazy; hence their slow economic growth was the 'Hindu rate of growth'.

Such stereotyping of the national character is undoubtedly wrong. However, while deriving a national character from external individual behavioural traits may look absurd and out of place, to deny that nations have their own character like individuals and the fact that it is reflected in their social mores, customs and traditions would be taking the argument to the other extreme. Historical experiences mould the character of nations. Anton Chekhov, the Russian writer, maintained that the deep-seated flaw in the Russian personality is 'the slave that lives within every Russian soul'—the psychology of the victim.[1] Centuries of the oppressive Tatar yoke and the subsequent Soviet command system under which Russians lived for so long have left a deep imprint on the social and political psyche that is hard to erase, he believed.

Creating an Empire of the Spirit

For Pandit Deendayal Upadhyaya, the ideological mentor of the Hindu nationalist movement in India in the last century, *Chiti*, a word he used to describe the national soul, was one of the foundational concepts of his integral humanist thought. He wrote:

> Chiti is fundamental and is central to the nation from its very beginning. Chiti determines the direction in which the nation is to advance culturally. Whatever is in accordance with Chiti is included in culture. Chiti is the touchstone on which each action, each attitude is tested and determined to be acceptable or otherwise. Chiti is the soul of the nation. It is on the foundation of this Chiti that a nation arises and becomes strong and virile...[2] It is this Chiti—or the inner soul—that determines the process of a country's progress and development. It is reflected in that country's culture and traditions.

Alexis de Tocqueville, the nineteenth-century French diplomat and author of *Democracy in America,* concluded that Americans were culturally democratic because of the religious morals they imbibed in churches. He wrote:

> I sought for the greatness and genius of America in her commodious harbours and her ample rivers—and it was not there...in her fertile fields and boundless forests, and it was not there...in her rich mines and her vast world commerce— and it was not there...in her democratic Congress and her matchless Constitution—and it was not there. Not until I went into the churches of America and heard her pulpits

aflame with righteousness did, I understand the secret of her genius and power. America is great because she is good, and if America ever ceases to be good, she will cease to be great.[3]

The Indian leadership should have turned to the explorations of its Chiti to rebuild India's independent national life. Instead, it borrowed ideas and institutions from elsewhere, leading to a situation resembling a square peg in a round hole. As the new Indian leadership is looking towards building a nation capable of becoming an important player on the global stage, it should revisit its moorings once again. It has to develop its politics, society, institutions, ethics and global vision on the foundations of its unique cultural cradle. Many Western scholars have also pointed to this uniqueness of the Indian cultural vision. British historian Michael Wood said, 'India was one of the earliest of the great civilizations, and it defined the goals of civilized life very differently from the West. The West raised individualism, materialism, rationality, and masculinity as its ideals. India's great tradition insisted on non-violence, renunciation, the inner life, and the female as pillars of civilization. And through all the triumphs and disasters of her history, she hung on to that ideal, an eternal quest to identify humanity with the whole of creation, unity in diversity... History is full of empires of the sword, but India alone created an empire of the spirit.'[4]

Similar sentiments were expressed by Margaret Elizabeth Noble, an Irish woman who met Swami Vivekananda in London in 1895 and became his disciple. She arrived in India in 1898 and became a monk. Swami Vivekananda bestowed upon her a spiritual name, Bhagini (Sister) Nivedita. Her scholarship and depth of understanding about India and Hinduism were not inferior to that of her guru, Vivekananda himself. In one of her speeches, she raised an intriguing question to highlight the cultural uniqueness of India. 'Had Niagara been situated on the Ganges, it is odd to think how different would have been its valuation by humanity,' she exclaimed and proceeded to say,

'Instead of fashionable picnics and railway pleasure trips, the yearly or monthly incursion of worshipping crowds. Instead of hotels, temples. Instead of ostentatious excess, austerity. Instead of the desire to harness its mighty forces to the chariot of human utility, the unrestrainable longing to throw away the body and realize at once the ecstatic madness of Supreme Union. Could contrast be greater?'[5]

Waking up the *Virat*

People of a nation can't be motivated by principles that are alien to their inner soul or Chiti. But Chiti can inspire them to make supreme sacrifices to achieve the lofty goals of its national mission. This kind of awakening of the inner *Purushartha*—the force of a nation, on the basis of its Chiti, was described by Deendayal as the *Virat*, or the superior being. The Virat—the consolidated mega power of a nation stirred up by the Chiti—manifests only after a mammoth effort. It calls for the creation of 'one people' out of the multitude of the masses on the basis of the national inner soul. Gandhi's effort at using cultural symbols like ahimsa, satyagraha and Ram Rajya to mobilize national power during the freedom struggle was an example of it. Speaking in the Constituent Assembly of India, T. Prakasam, a member of the Madras Presidency and later the first chief minister of Andhra Pradesh, highlighted Gandhi's contribution to the freedom movement by calling him a 'seer'. He said, 'I myself, Sir, had a talk with the great Lala Lajpat Rai more than forty-five years ago in England. He was the earliest of the sufferers for freedom, and he said, "Look at the organization and discipline and the way in which people here conduct themselves. Can we ever hope to send away these British people from our country and establish freedom?" That was my feeling when I touched that shore. Under those circumstances it was, that this man Gandhiji came as a Seer and lifted us up…'[6]

Once the Virat of a nation wakes up, its success can't be stalled. Waking up of the Virat of this nation inspired by its Chiti has been witnessed on several occasions after Independence as well—for cow protection in the 1950s, during the Chinese aggression in the early 1960s, against the draconian Emergency imposed by PM Indira Gandhi in the 1970s, during the Ekatmata Yatra against unscrupulous religious conversions in the 1980s, and during the Ram Janmabhoomi temple agitation in the 1990s.

Occasions manifest in the lives of nations when their very survival is challenged. Nations that rise on the basis of their inner soul will succeed in warding off those challenges. Nations that fail to do so, or resort to depending on alien powers and philosophies, will eventually perish. Why was PM Lal Bahadur Shastri's call 'Jai Jawan, Jai Kisan' found to have greater traction with the people of India than many speeches laced with modern scientific terminology made by his predecessor Nehru? Because Shastri's appeal was not just about material wealth but also the wealth of character and national unity. Shastri said the following in his first Independence Day speech in 1964 that stirred the conscience of the entire nation:

> We can win respect in the world only if we are strong internally and can banish poverty and unemployment from our country. Above all, we need national unity. Communal, provincial, and linguistic conflicts weaken the country. Therefore, we have to forge national unity. I appeal to all to work for national unity and usher in a social revolution to make our country strong. In the ultimate analysis, the strength of the country does not lie in its material wealth alone. It requires the force of character and moral strength. I appeal to our young men to inculcate discipline in themselves and work for the unity and advancement of the nation.[7]

Charting a New Course in Modi's India

PM Modi comes from a school of thought that always upheld the concept that India should rise as a great nation not merely by imitating others but by presenting an idealist vision based on its age-old wisdom for mankind. His successful effort at taking yoga to the world platform through a UN resolution in 2014 is one such example. In his maiden address to the UN as the prime minister in September 2014, Modi suggested that 21 June, the summer solstice and the longest day of the year in the Northern Hemisphere, be celebrated as International Yoga Day. The proposal was welcomed with great enthusiasm, and within 90 days, the UN passed a resolution to that effect on 11 December the same year. The proposal received the support of 177 member countries—a record at the UN.

When India assumed the G20 presidency under PM Modi, it worked to promote a universal sense of oneness, which was reflected in our theme—'One Earth, One Family, One Future'. At the G20 Summit in September 2023, we adopted *Vasudhaiva Kutumbakam*—a lofty ideal proclaimed by ancient Indian scriptures like the *Maha Upanishad*.

PM Modi has introduced quintessentially Indian nomenclature and symbolism into Indian polity. Rajpath, the central ceremonial boulevard of British vintage, became Kartavya Path (path of duty), and Race Course Road—where the prime minister's residence is located—became Lok Kalyan Marg.

However, the pinnacle of this transformation came when PM Modi decided to install a *sengol* (sacred sceptre) in the new Parliament building—which became operational in May 2023. In the West, the sceptre has been part of royal regalia since the time of the Greek and Mesopotamian civilizations. In countries like Norway, Sweden and the UK, the royal sceptre is still in vogue. It was seen as recently as September 2022 when it was placed on the coffin of Queen Elizabeth II and later in the hands of King Charles at his coronation.

Unlike the sceptres in the West, the Sengol has a unique significance. In the Indian civilizational tradition, monarchs and kings were never considered the supreme authority. Irrespective of the regalia used, like crowns, sceptres or orbs, the royals were constantly reminded by the court priests at the time of their coronation that dharma—ethical-spiritual order—is the only supreme authority. As per Indian coronation rituals, the king, after formally ascending the throne, would proclaim 'adandyosmi' (nobody can punish me) three times. The priest would then come forward with his sacred sceptre—the *dharma danda*—and gently pat the king's crown and proclaim three times *dharma dandyosi* (dharma will punish you). The sengol represented that tradition of the dharma danda.

The sengol that PM Modi installed in the new Parliament building has a fascinating history. It first became a symbol of the exchange of royal power during the five-century reign of the Cholas of Thanjavur, Tamil Nadu, who established a massive kingdom throughout South India after defeating the Pallavas and Pandyas. The *Rajaguru* (court priest) would use it as a symbol to notify the transfer of power from one Chola king to the other. A ritual was performed to remind the kings that their authority was granted by a higher power in the heavens, symbolized through the sacred sengol.

In 1947, Lord Mountbatten ritually handed over power not to Nehru but to Sri La Sri Kumaraswamy Thambiran, the deputy high priest of the Thiruvaduthurai Adheenam in the Mayiladuthurai district in Tamil Nadu. Sri Thambiran brought the specially designed sengol with him for that purpose. The Adheenam's records state, 'Sadaiyapa Swami gave the Sengol to Mountbatten and got it back from him and sprinkled holy water on it, invoked the divine name and gave it to Pandit Nehru blessing him to assume power.'[8] While handing the sengol over to Nehru, the priests sang verses from *Kolaru Pathigam* and hymns from the *Thevaram*, which were composed by Tamil Shaivite saint Thirugnana Sambandar. The verse ended with the statement, '*Adinargal Vanil Arasalva Anai Namade*' (It is our order that the follower of the lord, the king, shall rule as in the heavens).[9]

The same silver sengol of 1947 vintage, coated with gold, lying in the Ananda Bhavan Museum in Prayagraj, was brought back and placed next to the speaker's podium in the new Parliament building. In fact, constructing a new Parliament building after discarding an almost century-old iconic British-era building that witnessed many historical events, including the making of the Indian Constitution, was in itself a statement by the Modi government of its intentions to chart a new course for the country.

However, PM Modi's decision invited criticism and derision from some quarters, including the opposition parties, even as many other commentaries followed discussing the significance of the new Parliament building and the sengol.[10]

In the hyper-animated debate, very little attention was paid to what the prime minister, the prime mover of the project, said at the inauguration. He did not dismiss the critical contributions after Independence, nor did he claim to be taking India back to any bygone era. He acknowledged that after losing so much during colonial rule, India began its new journey after Independence, saying that the 'journey has gone through many ups and downs, overcoming many challenges', and has now entered the 'Amrit Kaal' of Independence. 'Preserving the heritage and forging new dimensions of development' will be the leitmotif of the amrit kaal, Modi averred.[11]

'Dharmocracy': Democracy, the Bharat Way

At the stroke of midnight on 14–15 August 1947, standing in the Parliament building built by British architects Edwin Lutyens and Herbert Baker in 1927, Nehru delivered his historic address to the just-independent nation. He called the moment rare in history when the soul of a nation, 'long suppressed, finds utterance'. He called it the end of an age and a nation's stepping out 'from the old to the new'. Interestingly, PM Modi also called the moment of the inauguration of the new Parliament building 'immortal forever', and that it will 'etch an indelible signature on the forehead of history'.[12] If Nehru believed in democracy and constitutionalism,

Modi also insisted that the 'democracy is our inspiration, our Constitution is our resolve'.

However, PM Modi's vision, irrespective of the idiomatic approximation with some Nehruvian ideals, markedly differs from that of Nehru. Many rightly see it as the demise of that Nehruvian vision. Nehru appreciated India's age-old civilization but abhorred its manifestation in its religion and culture. In objecting to the participation of President Rajendra Prasad in the consecration ceremony of the Somnath Temple in March 1951, Nehru insisted that a secular government cannot associate itself with such a ceremony, which was 'revivalist in character'.[13]

PM Modi, the ruling establishment, and, for that matter, a majority of the countrymen do not see cultural and religious symbols of India as anti-secular or revivalist. In fact, secularism draws from ancient Indian spiritual and cultural traditions, which upheld pluralism and celebrated diversity. PM Modi presented the new Parliament building as the 'ideal representation of both the modern and ancient coexistence'. The sacred sengol in the epicentre of the state-of-the-art Parliament marked that 'ideal representation'.[14]

Nehru called religion obsolete and saw a dichotomy between culture and modernity. But there was Gandhi, for whom politics bereft of religion was a sin. He declared that 'I could not live for a single second without religion. Many of my political friends despair of me because they say that even my politics are derived from religion. And they are right. My politics and all other activities of mine are derived from my religion,'[15] and admonished Nehruvians that they 'do not know what religion means'.[16]

After Independence, Gandhi was installed outside the Parliament while the inside was overwhelmed by the Nehruvian vision. Gandhi continues to be outside the new Parliament building, but the sengol—representing Gandhi's Ram Rajya, the 'Dharma Rajya'—is inside the Parliament now.

Having established a post-Nehruvian symbolism, the government has now established those values in governance and national life. As PM Modi pointed out in his address, democracy is in the genes of this ancient society. It never was majoritarian. Gandhi described it as a system where 'the weakest should have the same opportunity as the strongest'.[17] That is 'Dharmocracy', the Indian variant of democracy. The sengol represents Dharmocracy or the true spirit of the Indian Constitution.

The challenges that the world faces today are all the products of the flawed thinking in the Western and communist worldviews. Sadly, the answers to mitigate those challenges are being offered by the same elements. The World Economic Forum has emerged as the go-to institution on economic questions. The WEF recently proposed the concept of 'stakeholder capitalism' as the new panacea for the global economy. Stakeholder capitalism is an economic system in which corporations work towards serving the interests not only of their shareholders but also those of the broader stakeholder groups, including customers, local communities, and even the environment. It is nothing but the ancient Indian idea of *dharmakartrutva* (trusteeship) that Gandhi used to fondly talk about, quoting from the *Ishavasya Upanishad*. Similarly, the debate over how to mitigate environmental challenges is being handed over to another body dominated by the Western powers, called the COP.

As we progress towards building a new world order, India should not allow the process to be dominated by Western institutions and thought processes once again. It should come forward to proactively promote its distinct ideas and solutions to the global challenges that reflect its cultural and civilizational uniqueness. It is by leaning backward that India is actually going to surge forward.

That is how India can and should build its mojo—that is, Brand Bharat.

NOTES

Introduction: A History of The Future

1   Smith, E. Michael, 'V. Gordon Childe and the Urban Revolution: A Historical perspective on a revolution in urban studies', Arizona State University, 2009, https://tinyurl.com/y889x2s6. Accessed on 3 March 2025.

2   Durant, Will, *The Greatest Minds and Ideas of All Time*, Simon and Schuster, New York, 2002.

3   Ibid.

4   Sanyal, Sanjeev, 'India in The World Economy — Its Rise After A Thousand Years Of Decline', *Swarajya*, 6 August 2024, https://tinyurl.com/377ry3pz. Accessed on 3 March 2025.

5   Heath, Sir Thomas, *Aristarchus of Samos—The Ancient Copernicus*, The Clarendon Press, 2012.

6   *The Aryabhatiya of Aryabhata*, Walter Eugene Clark (trans.), The University of Chicago Press.

7   'Nicolaus Copernicus', New Mexico Museum of Space History, https://tinyurl.com/3b7ey5cf. Accessed on 3 March 2025.

8   'Johannes Kepler and Galileo Galilei', University of Rochester, https://tinyurl.com/58bstcx9. Accessed on 3 March 2025.

9   Newton, Issac, *The Principia: Mathematical Principles of Natural Philosophy*, Daniel Adee, New York, 1846.

10 'René Descartes', Stanford Encyclopedia of Philosophy, https://tinyurl.com/5c29kvsa. Accessed on 3 March 2025.

11 'The Future of World Religions: Population Growth Projections, 2010-2050', Pew Research Center, 2 April 2025, https://tinyurl.com/24sy7suy. Accessed on 3 March 2025.

12 Baggini, Julian, *How the World Thinks: A Global History of Philosophy*, Granta Books, 2018.

13 *The Works of Francis Bacon Volume 3 of 14*, James Spedding (trans.), Houghton Mifflin and Company, 2010, p. 162.

14 'Did You Know? The Invention and Transfusion of Printing Technology in East Asia and its Implications for Knowledge Transfer', UNESCO, https://tinyurl.com/2p8338sc. Accessed on 3 March 2025.

15 Fussel, Stephan, *Gutenberg and the Impact of Printing*, Taylor and Francis, Oxon, 2019, https://tinyurl.com/nhekwprj. Accessed on 3 March 2025.

16 The Work of Gutenberg, Hartford Daily Courant, 1900.

17 'Flickering of the Flame: The Book and the Reformation', University of Toronto

Libraries, 25 September 2017, https://tinyurl.com/bdd8d8y4. Accessed on 3 March 2025.

18 Roos, Dave, '7 Ways the Printing Press Changed the World', *History.com*, 27 March 2023, https://tinyurl.com/2kjna894. Accessed on 3 March 2025.

19 Ibid.

20 'Lectures on the Industrial Revolution in England: Excerpts by Arnold Toynbee (1884)', San Jose State University, https://tinyurl.com/28t9snjh. Accessed on 3 March 2025.

21 Durant, Will, *The Greatest Minds and Ideas of All Time*, Simon and Schuster, New York, 2002.

22 *The Works of Francis Bacon Vol II*, edited by Basil Montagu Esquire, Parry and McMillan, Philadelphia, 1857, p. 438.

23 Fouché, Joseph, *The Memoirs of Joseph Fouché: Duke of Otranto, Minister of the General Police of France*, translated from French, Wells and Lilly Court-Street and E. Bliss and E. White, New York, 1825.

24 Macartney, George, *An account of Ireland in 1773 by Sir George Macartney (Chief Secretary, 1769–72)*, London, 1773.

25 Ward, Henry George, *Watse Lands of the* Colonies, 25 June 1839, Vol. 48, cc.841–919, https://tinyurl.com/2uxrpnkw. Accessed on 3 March 2025.

26 Tocqueville, Alexis De, *Democracy in America*, Henry Reeve, Esq. (trans.), *Gutenberg.org*, https://tinyurl.com/4swmvnt7. Accessed on 3 March 2025.

27 *President Monroe's seventh annual message to Congress 2 December 1823*, https://tinyurl.com/yc2pas2f. Accessed on 3 March 2025.

28 The 'Wilsonian Path' to War, *Pieces of History*, National Archives, 4 April 2011, https://tinyurl.com/249c4vct. Accessed on 3 March 2025.

29 The Lusitania Disaster, Library of Congress, https://tinyurl.com/36yaebjd. Accessed on 3 March 2025.

30 'The Zimmermann Telegram', Library of Congress, https://tinyurl.com/3k6erzcw. Accessed on 3 March 2025.

31 'Wilson before Congress', Library of Congress, https://tinyurl.com/y3965hmv. Accessed on 3 March 2025.

32 'Second Inaugural Address of Woodrow Wilson', Yale Law School, Lillian Goldman Law Library, https://tinyurl.com/3hwr9dma. Accessed on 3 March 2025.

33 Kahn, David, *The Codebreakers*, The Macmillan Company, New York, 1967, p. 153.

34 Hindley, Meredith, 'World War I changed America and Transformed Its Role in International Relations', *National Endowment for the Humanities*, Summer 2017, Vol. 38, No. 3, https://tinyurl.com/5n8n6rus. Accessed on 3 March 2025.

35 'President Woodrow Wilson's 14 points (1918)', National Archives, https://tinyurl.com/mrehx6f3. Accessed on 3 March 2025.

36 Hindley, Meredith, 'World War I changed America and Transformed Its Role in International Relations', *National Endowment for the Humanities*, Summer 2017, Vol. 38, No. 3, https://tinyurl.com/5n8n6rus. Accessed on 3 March 2025.

37   Ibid.
38   'The League of Nations, 1920', *Office of the Historian*,
      https://tinyurl.com/4jfjvdza. Accessed on 3 March 2025.
39   Roosevelt, Franklin D., 'Radio Address Delivered by President Roosevelt From
      Washington, 3 September 1939', *Teaching American History*, https://tinyurl.com/
      mta4reb9. Accessed on 3 March 2025.
40   'Remembering Pearl Harbor: A Pearl Harbor Fact Sheet', The National World
      War II Museum, https://tinyurl.com/yss6wpja. Accessed on 3 March 2025.
41   'The Neutrality Acts 1930s', *Office of the Historian*, https://tinyurl.com/
      bdhw9y9c. Accessed on 3 March 2025.
42   Kimball, F. Warren, *Forged in War: Roosevelt, Churchill and The Second World
      War*, William Morrow, New York, 1997.
43   Roos, Dave, '7 Ways the Printing Press Changed the World', *History.com*,
      27 March 2023, https://tinyurl.com/2kjna894. Accessed on 3 March 2025.
44   Rosenman, Samuel I., editor, *Great Arsenal of Democracy, The Public Papers
      and Addresses of Franklin D. Roosevelt, 1940*, Macmillan, New York, 1941,
      pp. 633–44
45   'Lend-Lease Act (1941)', National Archives, https://tinyurl.com/5f79z8m8.
      Accessed on 3 March 2025.
46   Parliamentary Debates, House of Commons, 5th Series, Vol. 410.
47   Grooms, Thomas B., 'World War II: Home Of Franklin D Roosevelt National
      Historic Site', National Park Service, https://tinyurl.com/zt68mwkp. Accessed
      on 3 March 2025.
48   Ibid.
49   Rosenthal, Joe, 'How Did the United States Become a Global Power?', Council
      on Foreign Relations, 14 February 2023, https://tinyurl.com/4st3m9dh.
      Accessed on 3 March 2025.
50   'Labor Force Statistics from the Current Population Survey', U.S. Bureau of
      Labor Statistics, https://tinyurl.com/ys5mc6vf. Accessed on 3 March 2025.
51   'The History of the UN', United Nations, https://tinyurl.com/4r4rxkye. Accessed
      on 3 March 2025.
52   Ibid.
53   Ibid.
54   'The San Francisco Conference', United Nations, https://tinyurl.com/c8dkha6p.
      Accessed on 3 March 2025.
55   'Debate On the Address', HC Deb, 16 August 1945, Vol. 413, cc70–133,
      https://tinyurl.com/ye3xjxsj. Accessed on 3 March 2025.
56   Ikenberry, John G., 'The end of liberal international order?', *International Affairs*,
      Vol. 94, No. 1, January 2018, https://tinyurl.com/462sk4pe. Accessed on 3 March
      2025, pp. 7–23.
57   Acharya, Amitav, 'Asia after the liberal international order', East Asia Forum,
      10 July 2018, https://tinyurl.com/t7apvyd6. Accessed on 3 March 2025.

Chapter 1: Contested Worlds

1   'United Nations Charter: Preamble', United Nations, https://tinyurl.com/42ffy5pv. Accessed on 4 March 2025.

2   Truman, Harry, 'Address in San Francisco at the Closing Session of the United Nations Conference, 26 June 1945', https://tinyurl.com/24tjd3h6. Accessed on 4 March 2025.

3   Roosevelt, Franklin D., 'Address to the Delegates of the American Youth Congress in Washington DC, 10 February, 1940', https://tinyurl.com/2j6xx38r. Accessed on 4 March 2025.

4   'US–Soviet Alliance, 1941–1945', US Department of State Archive, https://tinyurl.com/47cvasv9. Accessed on 4 March 2025.

5   Ibid.

6   Kennan, George F., 'Containment Then and Now', *Foreign Affairs*, 1 March 1987, https://tinyurl.com/yv929mb2. Accessed on 4 March 2025.

7   Department of State, United States of America, *A report to the National Security Council by the Executive Secretary (Lay)*, 14 April 1950, https://tinyurl.com/5y8tkz7n. Accessed on 4 March 2025.

8   'Marshall Plan (1948)', National Archives, https://tinyurl.com/mr2kf7b3. Accessed on 4 March 2025.

9   Congressional Research Service, *The Marshall Plan: Design, Accomplishments and Significance*, 18 January 2018, https://tinyurl.com/4v5j7vb7. Accessed on 4 March 2025.

10   'The Truman Doctrine (1947)', *Office of the Historian*, https://tinyurl.com/bddjds8p. Accessed on 4 March 2025.

11   'The North Atlantic Treaty, Washington D.C., 4 April 1949', North Atlantic Treaty Organization, https://tinyurl.com/2k4s797a. Accessed on 4 March 2025.

12   Eisenhower, Dwight D., 'Remarks to the Committee for Economic Development', *The American Presidency Project*, https://tinyurl.com/musx5mtr. Accessed on 4 March 2025.

13   The White House, 'Remarks by Vice President Joe Biden at the World Economic Forum', 18 January 2017, https://tinyurl.com/yh28yjnz. Accessed on 4 March 2025.

14   Bush, George W., 'Address Before a Joint Session of the Congress on the Persian Gulf Crisis and the Federal Budget Deficit; Public Papers', George H. W. Bush Presidential Library and Museum, 11 September 1990, https://tinyurl.com/37js54yz. Accessed on 4 March 2025.

15   'After the War: The President, Transcript of President Bush's Address on End of the Gulf War', *The New York Times*, 7 March 1991, https://tinyurl.com/yak8nszj. Accessed on 4 March 2025.

16   O'Rourke, Lindsey A., 'The U.S. tried to change other countries' governments 72 times during the Cold War', *The Washington Post*, 23 December 2016, https://tinyurl.com/4nnsru85. Accessed on 4 March 2025.

17   Moller, Bjorn, 'The United States and the "New World Order": Part of the Problem or Part of the Solution', COPRI Working Paper, June 1997, https://tinyurl.com/4v2n4tbd. Accessed on 4 March 2025.

18   Weller, M. (ed.), *Iraq and Kuwait: The Hostilities and their Aftermath*, Cambridge International Documents, Vol. 3, Grotius Publications, Cambridge, 1993, pp. 281–83.

19   'Global War on Terror', George W. Bush Presidential Library, https://tinyurl.com/ynrefaaa. Accessed on 4 March 2025.

20   Ibid.

21   'The Roaring Twenties', *History.com*, 28 March 2023, https://tinyurl.com/2s3m7hdb. Accessed on 4 March 2025.

22   Roubini, Nouriel, *Megathreats: Ten Dangerous Trends That Imperil Our Future, And How to Survive Them*, Little, Brown and Company, October 2022.

23   'The Senate Passes the Smoot-Hawley Tariff, 13 June 1930', United States Senate, https://tinyurl.com/ebvpnh3h. Accessed on 4 March 2025.

24   'Acceptance Speech to the 1932 Democratic Convention', Franklin D. Roosevelt Presidential Library and Museum, https://tinyurl.com/rjw5m8hh. Accessed on 4 March 2025.

25   Roubini, Nouriel, *Megathreats: Ten Dangerous Trends That Imperil Our Future, And How to Survive Them*, Little, Brown and Company, October 2022.

26   'The Atlantic Charter: Revitalising the Spirit of the Founding of the United Nations Over Seventy Years Past', United Nations, 2 July 2013, https://tinyurl.com/mr2an864. Accessed on 4 March 2025.

27   Dizikes, Peter, 'Q&A: David Autor on the long afterlife of the "China shock"', Massachusetts Institute of Technology, https://tinyurl.com/3nprpkw2. Accessed on 4 March 2025.

28   Roubini, Nouriel, *Megathreats: Ten Dangerous Trends That Imperil Our Future, And How to Survive Them*, Little, Brown and Company, October 2022.

29   Stiglitz, Joseph E., *Globalization and its Discontents*, Allen Lane, London, 2002.

30   '"Defend the liberal international order"—top quotes from Joe Biden's Davos swansong', World Economic Forum, 18 January 2017, https://tinyurl.com/4puc4epw. Accessed on 5 March 2025.

31   Roubini, Nouriel, *Megathreats: Ten Dangerous Trends That Imperil Our Future, And How to Survive Them*, Little, Brown and Company, October 2022.

32   Kagan, Robert, 'The twilight of the liberal world order', *Brookings*, 24 January 2017, https://tinyurl.com/599x3aya. Accessed on 5 March 2025.

33   Burns, William J., 'Assessing the role of the United States in the World', *Carnegie Endowment*, 27 February 2019, https://tinyurl.com/5h47v2pp. Accessed on 5 March 2025.

34   Roubini, Nouriel, *Megathreats: Ten Dangerous Trends That Imperil Our Future, And How to Survive Them*, Little, Brown and Company, October 2022.

35   Ibid.

Chapter 2: United States: Into the Slow Afternoon

1   Goldfarb, Michael, 'Why US exceptionalism is not exceptional', *BBC*, 24 December 2010, https://tinyurl.com/4zz38k42. Accessed on 5 March 2025.

2   Curtis, Colleen, 'The American Jobs Act', *The White House*, https://tinyurl.com/3rh4a2uc. Accessed on 5 March 2025.

3   Brands, Hal, 'The Age of Amorality', *Foreign Affairs*, March/April Issue, 20 February 2024, https://tinyurl.com/5n6kz3wa. Accessed on 5 March 2025.

4   'Making the World "Safe for Democracy": Woodrow Wilson Asks for War', *History Matters*, https://tinyurl.com/yxvdrwrz. Accessed on 5 March 2025.

5   Gerson, Michael, 'How Can America Overcome its Egotism?', *The Washington Post*, 2 November 2017, https://tinyurl.com/ya9b7uw2. Accessed on 5 March 2025.

6   'Harry Truman and the Truman Doctrine', Harry S. Truman Library and Museum, https://tinyurl.com/bdfksmur. Accessed on 5 March 2025.

7   'Churchill's Finest Hour—World War II 1939–1945', America's National Churchill Museum, https://tinyurl.com/wfvbkpaa. Accessed on 5 March 2025.

8   Zakaria, Fareed, 'The Self Doubting Super Power', *Foreign Affairs*, 12 December 2023, https://tinyurl.com/ycxsytbj. Accessed on 5 March 2025.

9   Stevenson, Tom, 'America's undying empire: why the decline of US power has been greatly exaggerated', *The Guardian*, 30 November 2023, https://tinyurl.com/3phntd6b. Accessed on 5 March 2025.

10   Stevenson, Tom, *Someone Else's Empire: British Illusions and American Hegemony*, Verso, 2023.

11   Zakaria, Fareed, 'The Self Doubting Super Power', *Foreign Affairs*, 12 December 2023, https://tinyurl.com/ycxsytbj. Accessed on 5 March 2025.

12   Ibid.

13   Graziano, Manlio, 'United States: the end of an illusion of omnipotence', *The Conversation*, 20 July 2022, https://tinyurl.com/bdhf8u74. Accessed on 5 March 2025.

14   Zakaria, Fareed, 'The Self Doubting Super Power', *Foreign Affairs*, May/June 2025 Issue, 12 December 2023, https://tinyurl.com/ycxsytbj. Accessed on 5 March 2025.

15   Connaughton, Aidan, 'Prevailing view among Americans is that U.S. influence in the world is weakening—and China's is growing', Pew Research Center, 23 June 2022, https://tinyurl.com/5ytctyxw. Accessed on 5 March 2025.

16   'National Security Strategy', The White House, Washington, October 2022, https://tinyurl.com/7sch45sd. Accessed on 5 March 2025.

17   Graziano, Manlio, 'United States: the end of an illusion of omnipotence', *The Conversation*, 20 July 2022, https://tinyurl.com/bdhf8u74. Accessed on 5 March 2025.

18   Ibid.

19   Brands, Hal, 'The Age of Amorality', *Foreign Affairs*, 20 February 2024, https://tinyurl.com/5n6kz3wa. Accessed on 5 March 2025.

20   Ibid.

21   'The Federalist Papers: No. 28', The Avalon Project, Yale Law School, https://tinyurl.com/3vk762a2. Accessed on 5 March 2025.

22   Brands, Hal, 'The Age of Amorality', *Foreign Affairs,* 20 February 2024, https://tinyurl.com/5n6kz3wa. Accessed on 5 March 2025.

23   Ibid.

24   'President Bush Addresses the Nation', The Oval Office, 19 March 2003, https://tinyurl.com/42dhhkh4. Accessed on 5 March 2025.

25   'Remarks by the President on the Iran Nuclear Deal', The White House, Office of the Press Secretary, 5 August 2015, https://tinyurl.com/3j2w7z78. Accessed on 5 March 2025.

26   'Statement by the President on Iran', The White House, Office of the Press Secretary, 17 January 2016, https://tinyurl.com/4whtnjw6. Accessed on 5 March 2025.

27   'Full text: Trump's 2017 U.N. speech transcript', *The Politico,* 19 September 2017, https://tinyurl.com/mpm5ajce. Accessed on 5 March 2025.

28   Sang-Hun, Choe, 'Kim's Rejoinder to Trump's Rocket Man: "Mentally Deranged U.S. Dotard"', *The New York Times,* 21 September 2017, https://tinyurl.com/3559fc8v. Accessed on 5 March 2025.

29   'Trump and Kim in quotes: From bitter rivalry to unlikely bromance', *Al Jazeera,* 28 February 2019, https://tinyurl.com/2du4axt7. Accessed on 5 March 2025.

30   'Remarks by President Biden on the United Efforts of the Free World to Support the People of Ukraine', The White House, 26 March 2022, https://tinyurl.com/e9peyrdx. Accessed on 5 March 2025.

31   Bass, Gary J., 'Henry Kissinger: Good or Evil?', *Politico,* 10 October 2015, https://tinyurl.com/5e42cevr. Accessed on 6 March 2025.

32   'Iraq study estimates war related deaths at 461,000', *BBC News,* 16 October 2013, https://tinyurl.com/4cvyn39b. Accessed on 6 March 2025.

33   'Iraq War (2003-2011)', *Britannica,* https://tinyurl.com/5799xa9u. Accessed on 6 March 2025.

34   Huntington, Samuel P.,' The Lonely Superpower', *Foreign Affairs,* 1 March 1999, https://tinyurl.com/5f8acej5. Accessed on 6 March 2025.

35   Ibid.

36   Ibid.

37   'Remarks by the President in State of the Union Address', The White House, 27 January 2010, https://tinyurl.com/3zfjtt9f. Accessed on 6 March 2025.

38   'Remarks by the President on the Iran Nuclear Deal', The White House, 5 August 2015, https://tinyurl.com/3j2w7z78. Accessed on 6 March 2025.

39   Zakaria, Fareed, 'The Self Doubting Super Power', *Foreign Affairs,* 12 December 2023, https://tinyurl.com/ycxsytbj. Accessed on 5 March 2025.

40   'Transcript: Donald Trump Expounds on his Foreign Policy Views', *The New York Times,* 26 March 2016, https://tinyurl.com/55asv59d. Accessed on 6 March 2025.

41   'Transcript: Donald Trump's Foreign Policy Speech', *The New York Times,* 27 April 2016, https://tinyurl.com/3prvz3ec. Accessed on 6 March 2025.

42   Ibid.

43   Beckwith, Teague Ryan, 'Read Donald Trump's "America First" Foreign Policy Speech', *Time*, 27 April 2016, https://tinyurl.com/mrp9en3r. Accessed on 6 March 2025.

44   Mead, Walter Russell, 'Transcript: Dialogues on American Foreign Policy and World Affairs: A Conversation with Former Deputy Secretary of State Antony Blinken', Hudson Institute, 9 July 2020, https://tinyurl.com/3nzn6ezf. Accessed on 6 March 2025.

45   'Hungary to seek to opt out of NATO efforts to support Ukraine, Orban says', *VOA*, 24 May 2024, https://tinyurl.com/tcn737tn. Accessed on 6 March 2025.

46   'Hungary blocks $54bn EU financial aid for Ukraine', *Al Jazeera*, 15 December 2023, https://tinyurl.com/mma97r6k. Accessed on 6 March 2025.

47   Hülsemann, Laura, 'Erdoğan: I trust Russia and the West equally', *Politico*, 19 September 2023, https://tinyurl.com/mtjv538s. Accessed on 6 March 2025.

48   'Remarks by President Biden on the United Efforts of the Free World to Support the People of Ukraine', The White House, 26 March 2022, https://tinyurl.com/e9peyrdx. Accessed on 5 March 2025.

49   Satam, Parth, 'US & China "Shake Hands" To Control Houthis, Iran In The Middle East; But Beijing Refuses To Join Hands', *The Eurasian Times*, 1 February 2024, https://tinyurl.com/y22h8ucc. Accessed on 6 March 2025.

50   Timsina, Nilutpal, 'USA asks China to reign in Iran to stop actions by Houthi rebels in Red Sea, reports Financial Times', *The Print*, 24 January 2024, https://tinyurl.com/4bs346ks. Accessed on 6 March 2025.

51   Brands, Hal, 'The Age of Amorality', *Foreign Affairs*, 20 February 2024, https://tinyurl.com/5n6kz3wa. Accessed on 5 March 2025.

52   'Joe Biden's last major speech as Vice President in full', World Economic Forum, 18 January 2017, https://tinyurl.com/ynsy9ys6. Accessed on 6 March 2025.

53   Sullivan, Jake, 'The Sources of American Power', *Foreign Affairs*, 24 October 2023, https://tinyurl.com/583ut4np. Accessed on 6 March 2025.

54   Burns, William J., 'Assessing the Role of the United States in the World', *Carnegie Endowment*, 27 February 2019, https://tinyurl.com/5h47v2pp. Accessed on 6 March 2025.

55   Adams, Myra, 'Five reasons American decline appears irreversible', *The Hill*, 19 January 2024, https://tinyurl.com/25b7872d. Accessed on 6 March 2025.

56   Zakaria, Fareed, 'The Self Doubting Super Power', *Foreign Affairs*, 12 December 2023, https://tinyurl.com/ycxsytbj. Accessed on 5 March 2025.

57   In 1957, the Soviets launched the first-ever Earth-orbiting satellite by the name of Sputnik 1, stunning the US scientific community and worrying the American citizens about their future in the face of the growing gap in the capability of the two superpowers. That moment of anxiety became famous as the 'Sputnik moment'.

58   'Remarks of Senator John F. Kennedy at Municipal Auditorium, Canton, Ohio, September 27, 1960', John F. Kennedy Presidential Library and Museum, https://tinyurl.com/3zhh2bny. Accessed on 6 March 2025.

Chapter 3: China: The Roaring Dragon

1   'Transcript of "Global Challenges"', *Yale Global Online*, 31 October 2003, https://tinyurl.com/bd8ycsnh. Accessed on 6 March 2025.

2   Mahbubani, Kishore, 'Is the U.S. Ready To Be Number Two?', *Real Clear World*, 12 February 2013, https://tinyurl.com/2jt5wv8h. Accessed on 6 March 2025.

3   Fukuyama, Francis, *End of History and the Last Man*, Simon & Schuster, 2006.

4   'No. 1258, President Eisenhower to Prime Minister Churchill; Presidential Correspondence', lot 66 D 204, 'Eisenhower Correspondence with Churchill', *Office of the Historian*, https://tinyurl.com/bt57999m. Accessed on 6 March 2025.

5   Aldworth, Sara, 'John Foster Dulles, the Cold War architect', Acton Institute, 10 March 2020, https://tinyurl.com/39ktxpaa. Accessed on 6 March 2025.

6   Burns, William J., 'Assessing the Role of the United States in the World', Carnegie Endowment, 27 February 2019, https://tinyurl.com/5h47v2pp. Accessed on 6 March 2025.

7   Desai, Meghnad, 'India and China: An Essay in Comparative Political Economy', Paper for IMF Conference on India and China, November 2003, https://tinyurl.com/bddcmjvc. Accessed on 6 March 2025.

8   'Life Expectancy of Chinese increases by 42 years in nearly 70 years', The State Council, People's Republic of China, 23 May 2019, https://tinyurl.com/bddfrjyn. Accessed on 6 March 2025.

9   Desai, Meghnad, 'India and China: An Essay in Comparative Political Economy', Paper for IMF Conference on India and China, November 2003, Accessed on 6 March 2025.

10 'GDP based on PPP, share of world', *International Monetary Fund Datamapper*, https://tinyurl.com/3uy3yz6s. Accessed on 6 March 2025.

11 'China's diplomacy presses "acceleration button": FM', *Xinhua*, 7 March 2023, https://tinyurl.com/3u6xzae7. Accessed on 6 March 2025.

12 'Making sense of China's Government Budget', *China Power*, https://tinyurl.com/4c7scmst. Accessed on 6 March 2025.

13 International Affairs Budget, US Department of State, https://tinyurl.com/ykwuyzas. Accessed on 6 March 2025.

14 Global Diplomacy Index, Lowly Institute, https://tinyurl.com/yc6rw8zb. Accessed on 6 March 2025.

15 'Following Chinese mediation, Iran and Saudi Arabia to resume diplomatic relations', *Friends of Socialist China*, https://tinyurl.com/5n9aaec3. Accessed on 6 March 2025.

16 Ibid.

17 Ibid.

18 'Saudi Arabia, Iran agree to resume ties, reopen embassies after talks in Beijing', *Global Times*, 10 March 2023, https://tinyurl.com/sujyzcbh. Accessed on 6 March 2025.

19 Martin, Peter, *China's Civilian Army: The Making of Wolf Warrior Diplomacy*, Oxford University Press, 2021, p. 49.

20 Ibid., 70.

21 Carter, James, 'When the PRC won the "China" Seat at the UN', *The China Project*, 21 October 2021, https://tinyurl.com/474kbn6p. Accessed on 6 March 2025.

22 Martin, Peter, *China's Civilian Army: The Making of Wolf Warrior Diplomacy*, Oxford University Press, 2021, p. 49.

23 Liao, Wen, 'China's Black Cat, White Cat Diplomacy', *Foreign Policy*, 10 July 2009, https://tinyurl.com/2s49ee3p. Accessed on 6 March 2025.

24 Applebaum, Anne, *Autocracy, Inc.: The Dictators Who Want to Run the World*, Allen Lane, 2024, p. 25.

25 Kwong, Charles C.L., *The Chinese Economy and its Challenges*, Routledge, 2019.

26 Feng, Emily, and Merritt Kennedy, 'Li Peng, the Chinese Premier known as "Butcher of Beijing", Dies at 90', *NPR*, 23 July 2019, https://tinyurl.com/3rvmtb4a. Accessed on 6 March 2025.

27 Martin, Peter, *China's Civilian Army: The Making of Wolf Warrior Diplomacy*, Oxford University Press, 2021, p. 158.

28 Lee, Jason, 'What Happened When China Joined the WTO', Council on Foreign Relations, 6 February 2025, https://tinyurl.com/muunjrmz. Accessed on 6 March 2025.

29 Ibid.

30 Applebaum, Anne, *Autocracy, Inc.: The Dictators Who Want to Run the World*, Allen Lane, 2024, p. 26.

31 Ibid., 27.

32 'GDP, current prices', International Monetary Fund, https://tinyurl.com/3z63zv2x. Accessed on 6 March 2025.

33 'GDP per Capita, PPP (current international $)—China', World Bank Group, https://tinyurl.com/2xs8vfa9. Accessed on 6 March 2025.

34 Kine, Phelim, 'China joined rules-based trading system—then broke the rules', *Politico*, 12 September 2021, https://tinyurl.com/3mc2shxu. Accessed on 7 March 2025.

35 Ibid.

36 Nicita, Alessandro, and Carlos Razo, 'China: The rise of a trade titan', UN Trade and Development, 27 April 2021, https://tinyurl.com/4cnehbpa. Accessed on 7 March 2025.

37 'CPC opens 19th National Congress, declaring "new era" of China's socialism', 19th CPC National Congress, 18 October 2017, https://tinyurl.com/3p63prn8. Accessed on 7 March 2025.

38 Osnos, Evan, 'Born Red', *The New Yorker*, 30 March 2015, https://tinyurl.com/2ake2jyw. Accessed on 7 March 2025.

39 Blanchard, Ben, 'Xi Jinping's journey from China party elite to party leader', *Reuters*, 15 November 2012, https://tinyurl.com/mvjcubbw. Accessed on 7 March 2025.

40 'Remarks By Secretary Mattis at the U.S. Naval War College Commencement, Newport, Rhode Island', U.S. Department of Defense, 15 June 2018, https://tinyurl.com/27a3kyhn. Accessed on 7 March 2025.

41 Xiaoping, Deng, 'A New International Order Should Be Established with the Five Principles of Peaceful Coexistence as Norms', *Selected Works of Deng Xiaoping*, Vol. 3, 1982–1992, https://tinyurl.com/5atb9zhr. Accessed on 7 March 2025.

42 Nadège, Rolland, 'China's vision for a new world order', NBR Special Report #83, The National Bureau of Asian Research, January 2020, https://tinyurl.com/3xy2bp2j. Accessed on 7 March 2025.

43 Yang, Jiechi, 'China will participate in international affairs with a more active attitude', *China Daily*, 9 March 2013, https://tinyurl.com/24pnvh8k. Accessed on 7 March 2025.

44 Nadège, Rolland, 'China's vision for a new world order', NBR Special Report #83, The National Bureau of Asian Research, January 2020, https://tinyurl.com/3xy2bp2j. Accessed on 7 March 2025.

45 Mitter, Rana, 'The Real Roots of Xi Jinping Thought', *Foreign Affairs*, 20 February 2024, https://tinyurl.com/3thnwbyx. Accessed on 7 March 2025.

46 Ibid.

47 Nadège, Rolland, 'China's vision for a new world order', NBR Special Report #83, The National Bureau of Asian Research, January 2020, https://tinyurl.com/3xy2bp2j. Accessed on 7 March 2025.

48 Tatlow, Didi Kirsten, 'Xi Jinping on Exceptionalism with Chinese Characteristics', *The New York Times*, 14 October 2014, https://tinyurl.com/yc8f4973. Accessed on 7 March 2025.

49 'Xi says multi-party system didn't work for China', *Reuters*, 2 April 2014, https://tinyurl.com/59tx4pwh. Accessed on 7 March 2025.

50 Nadège, Rolland, 'China's vision for a new world order', NBR Special Report #83, The National Bureau of Asian Research, January 2020, https://tinyurl.com/3xy2bp2j. Accessed on 7 March 2025.

51 'Deng Xiaoping: Socialism with Chinese Characteristics', *Works & Days*, https://tinyurl.com/426z83u8. Accessed on 7 March 2025.

52 Osnos, Evan, 'Born Red', *The New Yorker*, 30 March 2015, https://tinyurl.com/2ake2jyw. Accessed on 7 March 2025.

53 Ibid.

54 Ibid.

55 Gao, Charlotte, 'The CCP Vows to "Lead Everything" Once Again', *The Diplomat*, 28 October 2017, https://tinyurl.com/mr2ewm6v. Accessed on 7 March 2025.

56 Bloomberg, 'Xi's $1 trillion "project of the century" faces uncertain future', *The Economic Times*, 16 October 2023, https://tinyurl.com/455wkjce. Accessed on 7 March 2025.

57 Feingold, Spencer, 'China's Belt and Road Initiative turns 10. Here's what to know', World Economic Forum, 20 November 2023, https://tinyurl.com/3886bc2h. Accessed on 7 March 2025.

58 Savage, Rachel, 'China spent $240 billion bailing out "Belt and Road" countries', *Reuters*, 28 March 2023, https://tinyurl.com/ysbz9bb4. Accessed on 7 March 2025.

59 Ibid.

60 'A Global Community of Shared Future: China's Proposals and Actions', The Third Belt and Road Forum for International Cooperation, September 2023, https://tinyurl.com/yee84bkw. Accessed on 7 March 2025.

61 'The Practical Achievements and Global Contributions of the Global Development Initiative', Xinhua Institute, https://tinyurl.com/y32fvwjm. Accessed on 7 March 2025.

62 'The Global Security Initiative Concept Paper', Ministry of Foreign Affairs, The People's Republic of China, https://tinyurl.com/fh7xm45w. Accessed on 7 March 2025.

63 '3 things to know about China's Global Civilization Initiative', Xinhua, 3 April 2024, https://tinyurl.com/3rxw53hk. Accessed on 7 March 2025.

64 'Global Civilization Initiative injects fresh energy into human development', Xinhua, 19 March 2023, https://tinyurl.com/5ym8m3vs. Accessed on 7 March 2025.

65 Economy, Elizabeth, 'China's Alternative Order', Foreign Affairs, 23 April 2024, https://tinyurl.com/5n92sypu. Accessed on 7 March 2025.

66 'Zhou Enlai (Chou En Lai) 1898–1976 Chinese Communist statesman, Prime Minister 1949–76', Oxford Reference, https://tinyurl.com/3z3kndmb. Accessed on 7 March 2025.

67 Mahbubani, Kishore, 'Managing the U.S. China Contest: Can Brazil and ASEAN Countries Cooperate?', CEBRI Journal, Brazilian Centre for International Relations, Year 1, No. 2, April-June 2022, https://tinyurl.com/3xvsrwck. Accessed on 7 March 2025.

68 Chang, G. Gordon, 'Beijing's View of the World', Hoover Institution, 9 May 2017, https://tinyurl.com/2yuezkuk. Accessed on 7 March 2025.

69 Thomas, Neil, 'Where does Xi Jinping Go From here?', China File, 31 January 2023, https://tinyurl.com/mr2htnn5. Accessed on 7 March 2025.

70 Xinhua, 'Full Text: Speech by Xi Jinping at a ceremony marking the centenary of the CPC', Global Times, 1 July 2021, https://tinyurl.com/43bcvvm2. Accessed on 7 March 2025.

71 U.S. Naval Institute Staff, 'Report to Congress on Chinese Naval Modernization', USNI News, 11 October 2023, https://tinyurl.com/2jzyc984. Accessed on 7 March 2025.

72 'CPC to unswervingly advance cause of national reunification: Xi', Xinhua, 16 October 2022, https://tinyurl.com/4rwz6d73. Accessed on 7 March 2025.

73 Ip, Greg, and Matt Murray, 'Philippine President Marcos Says He Is Seeking Ways to Defuse Tensions With China', The Wall Street Journal, 19 January 2023, https://tinyurl.com/2s39tc7k. Accessed on 7 March 2025.

74 Kardon, Issac, and Wendy Leutert, 'China's Port Power', Foreign Affairs, 22 May 2023, https://tinyurl.com/ydjhrzcy. Accessed on 7 March 2025.

75 Ibid.

76 Ibid.

77 'Wake up and look at the outside world', Global Times, 29 March 2014, https://tinyurl.com/437u6bjh. Accessed on 7 March 2025.

Chapter 4: Hot Cold War

1 'The 3 AM Phone Call', The National Security Archive, The George Washington University; https://tinyurl.com/yc392s9b. Accessed on 10 March 2025

2 Parrish, Scott D., and Mikhail M. Narinsky, 'New Evidence on the Soviet Rejection of the Marshall Plan, 1947: Two Reports', Working Paper No. 9, Cold War International History Project of Woodrow Wilson International Center for Scholars, March 1994, https://tinyurl.com/d5fdxftx. Accessed on 10 March 2025.

3 Eisenhower, Dwight D., 'The President's News Conference', The American Presidency Project, https://tinyurl.com/yeym2dr2. Accessed on 10 March 2025.

4 Vesikansa, Kristo, and Laura Berger, The Olympic Gap: Planning and Politics of the Helsinki Olympics, Taylor and Francis Online, 18 April 2024, https://tinyurl.com/3dwtks87. Accessed on 10 March 2025.

5 Eisenhower, Dwight D., 'Radio and Television Address to the American People on Science in National Security', The American Presidency Project, 7 November 1957, https://tinyurl.com/ypspy7u3. Accessed on 10 March 2025.

6 Correll, John T., 'The Neutron Bomb', Air and Space Forces Magazine, 30 October 2017, https://tinyurl.com/228theef. Accessed on 10 March 2025.

7 'Remarks by President Biden in a Press Conference', The White House, 10 September 2023, https://tinyurl.com/52khrnc6. Accessed on 10 March 2025.

8 Quinn, Melissa, 'After meeting with Xi, Biden says there "need not be a new Cold War" between U.S. and China', CBS News, 14 November 2022, https://tinyurl.com/4uwywx2u. Accessed on 10 March 2025.

9 'China doesn't want a cold war or a hot war with anyone, says Xi', Al Jazeera, 16 November 2023, https://tinyurl.com/5n7t45bt. Accessed on 10 March 2025.

10 Campbell, Kurt M., and Jake Sullivan, 'Competition without Catastrophe', Foreign Affairs, 1 August 2019, https://tinyurl.com/yket8zjb. Accessed on 10 March 2025.

11 Ibid.

12 Winokur, Justin, 'The Cold War Trap', Foreign Affairs, 13 July 2023, https://tinyurl.com/4dhbvhkj. Accessed on 10 March 2025.

13 'US defence secretary chides China over "provocative" behaviour', Al Jazeera, 11 June 2022, https://tinyurl.com/5n94k64v. Accessed on 10 March 2025.

14 'National Security Strategy', The White House, October 2022, https://tinyurl.com/3ey5ju4u. Accessed on 10 March 2025.

15 Ferguson, Niall, 'How to win the new cold war', Foreign Affairs, 7 January 2025, https://tinyurl.com/5n7dyepu. Accessed on 10 March 2025.

16 Ibid.

17 Kimmage, Michael, 'Kennan's X Marks the Spot', The Wilson Quarterly, Spring 2024, https://tinyurl.com/489ecmet. Accessed on 10 March 2025.

18 Mortkowitz, Siegfried, 'Pompeo: Chinese threat may be worse than Cold War communism', Politico, 12 August 2020, https://tinyurl.com/3v7a93ns. Accessed on 10 March 2025.

19   'National Security Strategy of the United States of America', The White House, December 2017, https://tinyurl.com/ms47h7fc. Accessed on 10 March 2025.

20   Winokur, Justin, 'The Cold War Trap', *Foreign Affairs*, 13 July 2023, https://tinyurl.com/4dhbvhkj. Accessed on 10 March 2025.

21   Ibid.

22   Santayana, George, *The Life of Reason – Vol. 1*, 1905.

23   Lin, Mao, *Sino-American Relations And The Diplomacy Of Modernization 1966–1979*, 2010, University of Georgia, PhD dissertation, https://tinyurl.com/f74e8ywr. Accessed on 10 March 2025.

24   Minami, Kazushi, 'Why did Mao Shake Hands with Nixon? Good Americans, Bad Americans, and the US-China Rapprochement', Wilson Center, 21 February 2022, https://tinyurl.com/mry7aww7. Accessed on 10 March 2025.

25   Thucydides's Trap refers to a fifth century BCE war between the Greek city-states of Athens and Sparta. Thucydides was an Athenian historian and general. He was the author of the history of the Peloponnesian War between Sparta and Athens until the year 411 BCE. Intrigued by the rising influence of Sparta, the Athenian rulers decided to wage a war to ensure their hegemony over the Greek Empire. In the long-drawn-out battle, victory went in Sparta's favour due to the support it received from the Persian rulers. The term Thucydides's Trap refers to that tendency towards war as displayed by Athenians in a situation when the rise of an emerging power, Sparta in this case, threatens to displace the existing superpower.

26   Allison, Graham, *Destined for War: Can America and China Escape the Thucydides' Trap?* Houghton Mifflin Harcourt, New York, 2017.

27   Campbell, Charlie, 'U.S. General's Prediction of War With China "in 2025" Risks Turning Worst Fears Into Reality', *Time*, 31 January 2023, https://tinyurl.com/45apyb7n. Accessed on 10 March 2025.

28   'A new challenge to relations between America and China', *The Economist*, 29 January 2023, https://tinyurl.com/4dwfwhdw. Accessed on 10 March 2025.

29   'Defense Budget by country (2025)', *Global Fire Power Index 2025*, https://tinyurl.com/2mvm6f2n. Accessed on 10 March 2025.

30   'US Marines open new Guam base, troop transfer to start in '24', *Kyodo News*, 26 January 2023, https://tinyurl.com/3wc344uk. Accessed on 10 March 2025.

31   Osnos, Evan, 'Sliding Towards a New Cold War', *The New Yorker*, 26 February 2023, https://tinyurl.com/3m7abf4a. Accessed on 10 March 2025.

32   Ibid.

33   'China's top diplomat blasts US over "hysterical and absurd" balloon claim', *France 24*, 18 February 2023, https://tinyurl.com/4eujw5c7. Accessed on 10 March 2025.

34   'China Naval Modernisation: Implications for US Navy Capabilities – Background and Issues for Congress', Library of Congress, 16 August 2024, https://tinyurl.com/wcnzmd4y. Accessed on 10 March 2025.

35   Thome, Lea, 'China continues its search for a maritime military presence in West Africa', *The Diplomat*, 20 February 2024, https://tinyurl.com/2vm2f7xm. Accessed on 10 March 2025.

36   Ezell, Stephen, 'How Innovative is China in Semiconductors?', Information Technology and Innovation Foundation, 19 August 2024, https://tinyurl.com/3x9stnxj. Accessed on 10 March 2025.

37   'H.R.4346 - CHIPS and Science Act', 117th Congress (2021–2022), *Congress.gov*, https://tinyurl.com/2s389utd. Accessed on 10 March 2025.

38   Sanger, David, *New Cold Wars: China's Rise, Russia's Invasion, and America's Struggle to Defend the West,* Crown Pub, 2024, p. 337.

39   Haeck, Pieter, 'How the Dutch turned on Chinese tech', *Politico*, 9 March 2023, https://tinyurl.com/34brt9am. Accessed on 10 March 2025.

40   Bradsher, Keith, 'China's Leader, With Rare Bluntness, Blames U.S. Containment for Troubles', *The New York Times*, 7 March 2023, https://tinyurl.com/mr3nnhce. Accessed on 10 March 2025.

41   Meredith, Sam, 'U.S. "very concerned" about China's dominance as a critical minerals supplier, energy chief says', *CNBC*, 14 February 2024, https://tinyurl.com/4fmmwxz2. Accessed on 10 March 2025.

42   Magnuson, Stew, 'China Maintains Dominance in Rare Earth Production', *National Defense*, 9 August 2021, https://tinyurl.com/yc5m9kh5. Accessed on 10 March 2025.

43   Gramling, Carolyn, 'Rare earth mining may be key to our renewable energy future. But at what cost?', *Science News*, 11 January 2023, https://tinyurl.com/3ujdtrd2. Accessed on 10 March 2025.

44   Jaishankar, S., 'Address by External Affairs Minister, Dr. S. Jaishankar at the event – "8 Years of Modi Government: Transforming External Engagements"', MEA India, 7 June 2022, https://tinyurl.com/2s3zzewm. Accessed on 10 March 2025.

45   Vajpayee, Atal Bihari, 'Prime Minister Shri Atal Bihari Vajpayee's remarks at India Caucus lunch', Prime Ministers' Office, Government of India, 9 November 2001, https://tinyurl.com/ynzzf7ck. Accessed on 10 March 2025.

46   'US-India Joint Statement', The White House, Office of the Press Secretary, 27 September 2013, https://tinyurl.com/33w5xjua. Accessed on 10 March 2025.

47   Modi, Narendra, 'Address by Prime Minister, Shri Narendra Modi to the Joint Session of the US Congress', Ministry of External Affairs, Government of India, 23 June 2023, https://tinyurl.com/4y82xcwm. Accessed on 10 March 2025.

48   Abrams, Elliott, 'The New Cold War', Council on Foreign Relations, 4 March 2022, https://tinyurl.com/2x23kjd5. Accessed on 10 March 2025.

49   Ibid.

50   Hart, Brian, et al., 'How deep are China-Russia military ties?', *China Power*, https://tinyurl.com/3ryskfmk. Accessed on 10 March 2025.

51   'Saudi Arabia, Iran agree to resume ties, reopen embassies after talks in Beijing', *Global Times*, 10 March 2023, https://tinyurl.com/sujyzcbh. Accessed on 10 March 2025.

52   'Palestinian factions sign Beijing Declaration on ending division, strengthening Palestinian national unity', The State Council, The People's Republic of China, 24 July 2024, https://tinyurl.com/2s4zeu29. Accessed on 10 March 2025.

53 Ibid.

54 'PLO is sole legitimate representative of Palestinian people: Chinese FM', *Xinhua Net*, 23 July 2024, https://tinyurl.com/3876yz4y. Accessed on 10 March 2025.

55 'Palestinian factions sign Beijing Declaration on ending division, strengthening Palestinian national unity', The State Council, The People's Republic of China, 24 July 2024, https://tinyurl.com/2s4zeu29. Accessed on 10 March 2025.

56 Asmar, Ahmed, 'Palestinians hail new reconciliation deal amid Israeli opposition', *AA*, 23 July 2024, https://tinyurl.com/3bz5ath8. Accessed on 10 March 2025.

57 'Chinese, Ukrainian foreign ministers hold talks, "highlighting China's significant role in promoting peace"', *Global Times*, 24 July 2024, https://tinyurl.com/ye2a2e86. Accessed on 10 March 2025.

58 Chung, Lawrence, 'Xi Jinping vows to crush attempts to thwart "complete reunification" with Taiwan', *South China Morning Post*, 1 July 2021, https://tinyurl.com/2v6fpu5m. Accessed on 10 March 2025.

59 'Taiwan detects 33 Chinese military aircraft around island', *The Economic Times*, 27 January 2024, https://tinyurl.com/3vu7kxs6. Accessed on 10 March 2025.

60 Lin, Bonny, et al., 'How China Could Quarantine Taiwan: Mapping Out Two Possible Scenarios', *CSIS*, 5 June 2024, https://tinyurl.com/2s4b3fzc. Accessed on 10 March 2025.

61 Quinn, Melissa, 'After meeting with Xi, Biden says there "need not be a new Cold War" between U.S. and China', *CBS News*, 14 November 2022, https://tinyurl.com/4uwywx2u. Accessed on 10 March 2025.

62 Winokur, Justin, 'The Cold War Trap', *Foreign Affairs*, 13 July 2023, https://tinyurl.com/4dhbvhkj. Accessed on 10 March 2025.

63 Gorbachev, Mikhail, 'Arms Control Today', Arms Control Association, https://tinyurl.com/5xsad5td. Accessed on 10 March 2025.

64 'The President's News Conference', Ronald Reagan Presidential Library and Museum, 17 September 1985, https://tinyurl.com/34ppfy97. Accessed on 10 March 2025.

65 Robinson, Peter, 'How Top Advisers Opposed Reagan's Challenge to Gorbachev—But Lost', *Prologue Magazine*, Vol. 39, No. 2, Summer 2007, https://tinyurl.com/4bj8h7au. Accessed on 10 March 2025.

Chapter 5: Power in Multipolarity

1 Brands, Hal, and John Lewis Gaddis, 'The New Cold War', *Foreign Affairs*, 19 October 2021, https://tinyurl.com/3cvwp2yh. Accessed on 12 March 2025.

2 Fukuyama, Francis, 'The End of History?', *The National Interest*, No. 16, 1989, https://tinyurl.com/yjznerjb. Accessed on 12 March 2025, pp.3–18.

3 Fukuyama, Francis, *The End of History and the Last Man*, Free Press, 1992.

4 'Letter dated 15 May 1997 from the Permanent Representatives of China and the Russian Federation to the United Nations addressed to the Secretary-General', United Nations Digital Library, https://tinyurl.com/3j38s67y. Accessed on 12 March 2025.

5   'India–Russia Press Statement', Embassy of India in Washington, D.C., 22 December 1998, https://tinyurl.com/yc8pwvxc. Accessed on 12 March 2025.

6   Latypova, Leyla, 'Praise and Blame: How Russia Reacted to the Death of Gorbachev', *The Moscow Times*, 31 August 2022, https://tinyurl.com/3dbm9b6w. Accessed on 12 March 2025.

7   Kortunov, Andrey, 'Between Polycentrism and Bipolarity on Russia's World order evolution Narratives', *Russia in Global Affairs*, 2019, https://tinyurl.com/4vnm8433. Accessed on 12 March 2025.

8   'Meeting of the Valdai International Discussion Club', President of Russia, 27 October 2016, https://tinyurl.com/ytkzxkah. Accessed on 12 March 2025.

9   Anderlini, Jamil, and Clea Caulcutt, 'Europe must resist pressure to become "America's followers," says Macron', *Politico*, 9 April 2023, https://tinyurl.com/23wtyu3y. Accessed on 12 March 2025.

10 'Integrated Security of Germany', National Security Strategy of Federal Government of Germany, https://tinyurl.com/264m3y63. Accessed on 12 March 2025.

11 Borrell, Josep, 'How to revive multilateralism in a multipolar world?', European Union External Action, 16 March 2021, https://tinyurl.com/th36ke9a. Accessed on 12 March 2025.

12 'Charting Strategies for a Multipolar World', Morgan Stanley, 22 August 2023, https://tinyurl.com/mt6cuj8n. Accessed on 12 March 2025.

13 'World Economic Forum Annual Meeting 2022 Returns to Davos to Address Unprecedented Geo-economic Challenges Impacting a Multipolar World', World Economic Forum, 18 May 2022, https://tinyurl.com/mr2hd5s9. Accessed on 12 March 2025.

14 Timmons, Heather, 'Watch: "Peace with honor," President Nixon's 1973 speech ending US involvement in the Vietnam War', *Quartz*, 23 May 2016, https://tinyurl.com/yc8a6afd. Accessed on 12 March 2025.

15 Ashford, Emma, and Evan Cooper, 'Yes, the world is Multipolar', *Foreign Policy*, 5 October 2023, https://tinyurl.com/3ykv4224. Accessed on 12 March 2025.

16 Ibid.

17 PTI, 'US "is adjusting to a multipolar world," says Jaishankar', *India Today*, 28 September 2023, https://tinyurl.com/3bjdbmmz. Accessed on 12 March 2025.

18 Tan, Huileng, and Christine Tan, '"We will be asked to pick a side" if US-China tensions rise, says Asian leader', *CNBC News*, 19 October 2017, https://tinyurl.com/yu595x2m. Accessed on 12 March 2025.

19 Loong, Hsien Lee, 'The Endangered Asian Century', *Foreign Affairs*, 4 June 2020, https://tinyurl.com/mscsbpnr. Accessed on 12 March 2025.

20 CIGA Staff, 'Is the World Multipolar? Emma Ashford/ Evan Cooper Vs Jo Inge Bekkevold', *Geopolitical Compass*, 6 April 2024, https://tinyurl.com/yf8usnbe. Accessed on 12 March 2025.

21 'Trademark and Design protection in the European Union with the help of a professional representative at the EUIPO, A European Trademark Attorney', *Bauerip*, https://tinyurl.com/ysv7sr5p. Accessed on 12 March 2025.

22   'Estimated number of active military personnel in NATO in 2025, by member state', *Statista*, https://tinyurl.com/yc6ruuc5. Accessed on 12 March 2025.

23   'Turkey', *OEC*, https://tinyurl.com/4x5m6xkj. Accessed on 12 March 2025.

24   'Economy of Turkey', *Global Tenders*, https://tinyurl.com/4kfzsfhf. Accessed on 12 March 2025.

25   'China emerges as ASEAN's top trading partner', *Vietnam+*, 23 September 2024, https://tinyurl.com/m46mjzsh. Accessed on 12 March 2025.

26   'Fact Sheet: US-ASEAN Special Summit in Washington DC', US Embassy in Malaysia, 13 May 2022, https://tinyurl.com/4bkdd53z. Accessed on 12 March 2025.

27   'Prime Minister's Keynote Address at Shangri La Dialogue', Ministry of External Affairs, 1 June 2018, https://tinyurl.com/4t9eppvu. Accessed on 12 March 2025.

28   Rowe, Mark, 'What does rapid population growth mean for the world's poorest continent?', *Geographical*, 14 March 2024, https://tinyurl.com/4b8buecm. Accessed on 12 March 2025.

29   'Iran', U.S. Energy Information Administration, https://tinyurl.com/y4exjcc5. Accessed on 12 March 2025.

30   'Saudi Arabia Energy Profile: Second Largest Holder of Proved Oil Reserves— Analysis', *Eurasia Review*, 16 September 2019, https://tinyurl.com/4j48at4n. Accessed on 12 March 2025.

31   'Saudi Arabia', US Energy Information Administration, https://tinyurl.com/2bvvdpcr. Accessed on 12 March 2025.

32   David, Javier E., 'US-Saudi Arabia seal weapons deal worth nearly $110 billion immediately, $350 billion over 10 years', *CNBC*, 20 May 2017, https://tinyurl.com/3d5bjdek. Accessed on 12 March 2025.

33   Adam, Rudolf G., 'Prospects for a multipolar world order', *Geopolitical Intelligence Services*, 16 June 2023, https://tinyurl.com/f7cj77wd. Accessed on 12 March 2025.

Chapter 6: Multilateralism to Minilateralism

1   Dag Hammarskjöld Foundation, 'Dealing with crimes against humanity', *Development Dialogue*, No. 5, March 2011, https://tinyurl.com/yc83s8y2. Accessed on 18 March 2025, pp.3.

2   'Secretary-General's address to the General Assembly', United Nations Secretary General, 19 September 2023, https://tinyurl.com/2syunr29. Accessed on 18 March 2025.

3   Laskar, Rezaul H., 'UN reform is a common sense proposition, says Jaishankar at Raisina Dialogue', *Hindustan Times*, 22 February 2024, https://tinyurl.com/3u6urprf. Accessed on 18 March 2025.

4   'Biden says "when we stand together," we can tackle any challenge', *UN News*,19 September 2023, https://tinyurl.com/3wr5snpx. Accessed on 18 March 2025.

5   'United Nations Charter, Chapter I: Purposes and Principles', United Nations, https://tinyurl.com/8uf6pm9m. Accessed on 18 March 2025.

6   PTI, 'Why is UN Security Council rendered "completely ineffective" in resolving

Russia-Ukraine conflict, asks India', *The Economic Times*, 27 February 2024, https://tinyurl.com/5cz4xaxe. Accessed on 18 March 2025.

7   Salinger, David, 'Prophetic Speeches: Dominique de Villepin at the UN Security Council in February 2003', *The Intern Corner*, 14 July 2020, Accessed on 18 March 2025.

8   Ibid.

9   Bello, Walden, 'The Rise and Fall of Multilateralism', *Dissent*, Spring 2021, https://tinyurl.com/2spa5s8f. Accessed on 18 March 2025.

10 'The Asian (Global?) Financial Crisis, the IMF and Japan: Economic Issues', CRS Report for Congress received through the CRS web, 3 September 1998, https://tinyurl.com/3jj32twn. Accessed on 18 March 2025.

11 'Asian Financial Crisis, Asian History [1997-1998]', *Britannica Money*, https://tinyurl.com/55uz85ft. Accessed on 18 March 2025.

12 Leightner, Jonathan E., 'Lessons From Thailand's 1997 Financial Crisis for the Current Global Economy', https://tinyurl.com/u5rne7tm. Accessed on 18 March 2025.

13 '"Procedural issues" delaying Sri Lanka debt deal: IMF', *The Hindu*, 14 June 2024, https://tinyurl.com/2p88vumj. Accessed on 18 March 2025.

14 'The Bretton Woods Twins in the Era of COVID-19: Time for an Exit Strategy for the Global South?', Committee for the Abolition of Illegitimate Debt, 13 October 2020, https://tinyurl.com/4pha2xta. Accessed on 18 March 2025.

15 'A Constitution for the Seas', World Ocean Review 2010, https://tinyurl.com/33sypksd. Accessed on 18 March 2025.

16 'Global Report 2023', UNHCR, https://tinyurl.com/3fmu8k8j. Accessed on 18 March 2025.

17 'COP28: the science is clear—fossil fuels must go', *Nature*, 12 December 2023, https://tinyurl.com/3tfrmez5. Accessed on 18 March 2025.

18 Forster, Timon, 'Enough Voice for the Vulnerable? Why Climate-vulnerable Countries Need More Voting Power within the International Monetary Fund', Global Development Policy Centre, https://tinyurl.com/3h54m3ev. Accessed on 18 March 2025.

19 Eichengreen, Barry, 'Do the BRICS need their own development bank?', *The Guardian*, 14 August 2014, https://tinyurl.com/yhds8nzj. Accessed on 18 March 2025.

20 'IMF Members' Quotas and Voting Power, and IMF Board of Governors', IMF, 2 April 2025, https://tinyurl.com/7asxpz4e. Accessed on 18 March 2025.

21 Ibid.

22 Dempsey, Judy, 'Judy Asks: Is the United Nations Still Fit for Purpose?', Carnegie Endowment, 21 September 2023, https://tinyurl.com/mfa5d5a9. Accessed on 18 March 2025.

23 'Bosnia's Srebrenica massacre 25 years on—in pictures', *BBC*, 11 July 2020, https://tinyurl.com/4fbsvsrb. Accessed on 18 March 2025.

24 AFP, 'Iraq war killed 120,000 cost $800 billion: Study', *Mint*, 15 March 2013, https://tinyurl.com/3kms2mbj. Accessed on 18 March 2025.

25 'Asrar Shakeeb and Mohammed Hussein; How the US has used its veto power at the UN in support of Israel', *Al Jazeera*, 26 October 2023, https://tinyurl.com/2nrbuh87. Accessed on 18 March 2025.

26 Zoellick, Robert B., 'America will not wait for the won't-do countries', Office of the United States Trade Representative, 22 September 2003, https://tinyurl.com/jxuxjmee. Accessed on 18 March 2025.

27 Huang, Pien, 'Woodward Book Casts New Light On Trump's Fight With WHO', *NPR*, 11 September 2020, https://tinyurl.com/mfevapa9. Accessed on 18 March 2025.

28 Freeman, Carla, and Lyndi Tsering, 'As China Looks to Reform Global Governance, How Does It Approach the U.N.?', United States Institute of Peace, 28 September 2023, https://tinyurl.com/zyczudyf. Accessed on 18 March 2025.

Chapter 7: Heteropolis Rising: Non-State Actors

1 Eckersley, Fergus, 'Terrorist groups and non-state actors pose a persistent and significant threat to international peace and security: UK statement at the UN Security Council', Foreign, Commonwealth and Development Office, Government of UK, 15 November 2023, https://tinyurl.com/mscby32n. Accessed on 13 March 2025.

2 Walker, Shaun, 'A Useful Punching Bag: Why Hungary's Viktor Orban has turned on George Soros', *The Guardian*, 22 June 2017, https://tinyurl.com/3kh59m86. Accessed on 13 March 2025.

3 Isidore, Chris, 'Elon Musk claims George Soros "hates humanity." The ADL says Musk's attacks "will embolden extremists"', *CNN*, 17 May 2023, https://tinyurl.com/yc4y46p9. Accessed on 13 March 2025.

4 DNA Special, 'How Greta Thunberg is planning to defame India by disrupting its "Yoga and Chai" image', *DNA News*, 5 February 2021, https://tinyurl.com/b5jzara4. Accessed on 13 March 2025.

5 Schmitt, Eric, '3 American Soldiers Killed in Drone Strike in Jordan, US Says', *The New York Times*, 28 January 2024, https://tinyurl.com/v5mxt9de. Accessed on 13 March 2025.

6 'Multinational Corporations', *Espace Mondial*, 28 September 2018, https://tinyurl.com/55rjkvub. Accessed on 13 March 2025.

7 'Multinational Enterprises in Domestic Value Chains', OceD Science, Technology and Industry Policy Papers, No. 63, March 2019, https://tinyurl.com/bdejbrrj. Accessed on 13 March 2025.

8 Shivartsman, Daniel, 'Apple Inc: Facts and Statistics (2024)', *Investing.com*, https://tinyurl.com/5dumt6zn. 13 March 2025.

9 Nye Jr., Joseph S., 'Multinational Corporations in World Politics', *Foreign Affairs*, Vol. 53, No. 1, October 1974, https://tinyurl.com/38sfzvvk. Accessed on 13 March 2025, pp. 153–175.

10 Mothership, 'Minister K Shanmugam vs Facebook's Simon Milner [Select Committee on Deliberate Online Falsehoods]', *YouTube*, 23 March 2018, https://tinyurl.com/v7jujzwc. Accessed on 13 March 2025.

11   McCluskey, Megan, 'What to Know About Trump's Twitter Ban, Now That Elon Musk Owns the Platform', *Time*, 28 October 2022, https://tinyurl.com/5btbkvah. Accessed on 13 March 2025.

12   Terzi, Alessio, and Stefano Marcuzzi, 'Are multinationals eclipsing nation-states?', *IPS*, 6 February 2019, https://tinyurl.com/jn87stt2. Accessed on 13 March 2025.

13   Conger, Kate, 'Google Plans Not to Renew Its Contract for Project Maven, a Controversial Pentagon Drone AI Imaging Program', *Gizmodo*, 1 June 2018, https://tinyurl.com/4zmd9y42. Accessed on 13 March 2025.

14   'Google should not be in business of war, say employees', *BBC News*, 5 April 2018, https://tinyurl.com/57dk6ywv. Accessed on 13 March 2025.

15   @FedorovMykhailo, *X* (formerly Twitter), 26 February 2022, 5.36 p.m., https://tinyurl.com/3fuf4ax8. Accessed on 13 March 2025.

16   @elonmusk, *X* (formerly Twitter), 27 February 2022, 4.03 a.m., https://tinyurl.com/3k97n9hn. Accessed on 13 March 2025.

17   'Satariano Adam et al. Elon Musk's Unmatched Power in the Stars', *The New York Times*, 28 July 2023, https://tinyurl.com/yc366u2f. Accessed on 13 March 2025.

18   Walter, Isaacson, '"How am I in this war?": The untold story of Elon Musk's support for Ukraine', *The Washington Post*, 7 September 2023, https://tinyurl.com/jtvbs9xk. Accessed on 13 March 2025.

19   Sanger, David E., *New Cold Wars: China's Rise, Russia's Invasion, and America's Struggle to Defend the West*, Crown Pub, 2024, p. 399.

20   Soares, Isa, et al., 'Catalonia referendum result plunges Spain into political crisis', *CNN World*, 2 October 2017, https://tinyurl.com/evf4caby. Accessed on 13 March 2025.

21   'Scotland Decides', *BBC News*, https://tinyurl.com/2crjvkna. Accessed on 13 March 2025.

22   'The Global Religious Landscape', Pew Research Center, 18 December 2012, https://tinyurl.com/bdf2wuvt. Accessed on 13 March 2025.

23   Ibid.

24   'Christians remain world's largest religious group, but they are declining in Europe', Pew Research Centre, 5 April 2017, https://tinyurl.com/mphxw65s. Accessed on 13 March 2025.

25   Chawrylo, Katarzyna, 'A holy war. The Russian Orthodox Church blesses the war against the West', OSW Centre for Eastern Studies, 12 April 2024, https://tinyurl.com/bd6253w7. Accessed on 13 March 2025.

26   Utama, Virdika Rizky, 'Is Indonesia's Largest Islamic Organization Compromising Its Political Neutrality?', *The Diplomat*, 19 January 2024, https://tinyurl.com/32ykn2pd. Accessed on 13 March 2025.

27   Staquf, Cholil Yahya, 'To prevent another Christchurch, Islam must confront the attacks in its name that have radicalized the West', *The Telegraph,* 25 March 2019, https://tinyurl.com/564kwpym. Accessed on 13 March 2025.

28   Abbas, J. Faisal, '"West not plotting against Islam", says MWL's Sheikh

Mohammed Al-Issa', *Islamic Voice*, August 2018, https://tinyurl.com/3rkyk48h. Accessed on 13 March 2025.

29   Ibid.

30   Watson, Eleanor, 'Houthis vow to keep attacking ships in Red Sea after U.S., U.K. strikes target their weapons in Yemen', *CBS News*, 12 January 2024, https://tinyurl.com/4kmhu7sf. Accessed on 13 March 2025.

31   Kukreti, Shweta, 'Donald Trump's war against "Deep State", its link with Biden and impact on 2024 US election\Explained', *Hindustan Times*, 20 July 2024, https://tinyurl.com/5caew4p8. Accessed on 13 March 2025.

32   Sherk, James, 'How Trump Held Bureaucrats Accountable', *Daily Caller*, 16 April 2024, https://tinyurl.com/2bpth6zj. Accessed on 13 March 2025.

33   'I Am Part of the Resistance Inside the Trump Administration', *The New York Times*, 5 September 2018, https://tinyurl.com/eaktm3c5. Accessed on 13 March 2025.

34   Bennett, Brian, 'Doomsday and Democracy: Former Trump Aides Warn of Secret Presidential Crisis Powers', *Time*, 15 October 2024, https://tinyurl.com/49rdfwar. Accessed on 13 March 2025.

35   Miskimmon, Alister, et al., *Strategic Narratives: Communication Power and the New World Order Vol. 7*, Routledge, 2013, p. 78.

Chapter 8: Future Shock: The AI Era

1   Cole, Stryker, and Eda Kavlakoglu, 'What is artificial intelligence (AI)?', IBM, 9 August 2024, https://tinyurl.com/p3rpfknu. Accessed on 20 March 2025.

2   'What is the metaverse?', Meta, https://tinyurl.com/yr73djbt. Accessed on 20 March 2025.

3   Marr, Bernard, 'The 5 Technologies That Will Change The Future Of The Human Race', *Forbes*, 7 February 2022, https://tinyurl.com/ru65mvwe. Accessed on 20 March 2025.

4   Ibid.

5   Ibid.

6   'Artificial intelligence poses "risk of extinction," tech execs and experts warn', *CBC*, 30 May 2023, https://tinyurl.com/3bppwefy. Accessed on 20 March 2025.

7   Marr, Bernard, 'The 5 Technologies That Will Change The Future Of The Human Race', *Forbes*, 7 February 2022, https://tinyurl.com/ru65mvwe. Accessed on 20 March 2025.

8   Hillyer, Madeleine, and Isabelle Mauro, 'How 30 years of internet access have changed everything from healthcare to finance', *The Mobile Century*, 1 March 2022, https://tinyurl.com/33spfb9y. Accessed on 20 March 2025.

9   'Number of internet users worldwide from 2005 to 2024', *Statista*, 12 December 2024, https://tinyurl.com/yz9c8yp8. Accessed on 20 March 2025.

10   'Mobile Fact Sheet', Pew Research Center, 13 November 2024, https://tinyurl.com/2pm35w48. Accessed on 20 March 2025.

11   'Charted: There are more mobile phones than people in the world', World Economic Forum, 11 April 2023, https://tinyurl.com/4n64f9k8. Accessed on

20 March 2025.

12 Wilson, Daniel H., 'We humans have a love-hate relationship with our technology', The Swiss Quality Consulting, https://tinyurl.com/dc3d2fkh. Accessed on 20 March 2025.

13 'Data Suggests Growth in Enterprise Adoption of AI is Due to Widespread Deployment by Early Adopters, But Barriers Keep 40% in the Exploration and Experimentation Phases', IBM, 10 January 2024, https://tinyurl.com/4tkvd9zn. Accessed on 23 April 2025.

14 World Economic Forum, The Future of Jobs Report 2023, 30 April 2023, https://tinyurl.com/mryw6cps. Accessed on 20 March 2025.

15 Ibid.

16 Ibid.

17 Ibid.

18 Thomas, Mike, 'The Future of AI: How Artificial Intelligence Will Change the World', builtin.com, 28 January 2025, https://tinyurl.com/bd3fav7w. Accessed on 20 March 2025.

19 Dresp-Langley, Birgitta, 'The weaponization of artificial intelligence: What the public needs to be aware of', Frontiers in Artificial Intelligence, Vol. 6, 2023, https://tinyurl.com/5n96juhw. Accessed on 20 March 2025.

20 Hutson, Matthew, 'Can we stop runaway AI?', The New Yorker, 16 May 2023, https://tinyurl.com/ybrbbw9f. Accessed on 20 March 2025.

21 Tucker, Robert B., 'The Singularity Is Coming Soon. Here's What It May Mean', Forbes, 22 August 2024, https://tinyurl.com/bxw8pfja. Accessed on 20 March 2025.

22 Hutson, Matthew, 'Can we stop runaway AI?', The New Yorker, 16 May 2023, https://tinyurl.com/ybrbbw9f. Accessed on 20 March 2025.

23 Zorthian, Julia, 'OpenAI CEO Sam Altman Asks Congress to Regulate AI', Time, 16 May 2023, https://tinyurl.com/msckr2bw. Accessed on 23 April 2025.

24 'Microsoft's ChatGPT-driven Bing wants to "be alive", "steal nuclear access codes": Report', Arabian Business, 18 February 2023, https://tinyurl.com/ydd75hv6. Accessed on 20 March 2025.

25 'Pause Giant AI Experiments: An Open Letter', Future of Life Institute, 22 March 2023, https://tinyurl.com/596ys4ea. Accessed on 20 March 2025.

26 Ibid.

27 Nilekani, Nandan, and Tanuj Bhojwani, The Art of Bitfulness: Keeping Calm in the Digital World, Penguin, 2022.

28 Kissinger, Henry, et al., The Art of AI And Our Human Future, John Murray, 2021.

29 Ibid

30 Ibid.

31 'PM's address at the inauguration of GPAI Summit, 2023', PM India, 12 December 2023, https://tinyurl.com/4bmchsrp. Accessed on 20 March 2025.

32 Glover, Ellen, 'AI Bill of Rights: What You Should Know', builtin.com, 19 March 2024, https://tinyurl.com/279etj8x. Accessed on 20 March 2025.

33   'Rome Call for AI Ethics', https://tinyurl.com/hnrafsry. Accessed on 20 March 2025.

34   'The Call', Renaissance Foundation, https://tinyurl.com/s9z7hs9c. Accessed on 20 March 2025.

35   'Rome Call for AI Ethics', https://tinyurl.com/hnrafsry. Accessed on 20 March 2025.

36   'G20 New Delhi Leaders' Declaration', 9–10 September 2023, https://tinyurl.com/t6dzsa69. Accessed on 20 March 2025.

37   Press Information Bureau, 'PM inaugurates annual Global Partnership on Artificial Intelligence (GPAI) Summit', Prime Minister's Office, 12 December 2023, https://tinyurl.com/3kcucsxv. Accessed on 20 March 2025.

38   Higgins, Abigail, 'Stephen Hawking's final warning for humanity: AI is coming for us', *Vox*, 17 October 2018, https://tinyurl.com/4dsb5je4. Accessed on 20 March 2025.

39   Ibid.

40   Licholai, Greg, 'Is CRISPR Worth the Risk?', *Yale Insights*, 21 August 2018, https://tinyurl.com/2fa7wcky. Accessed on 20 March 2025.

41   NIH Director, 'Statement on Claim of First Gene-Edited Babies by Chinese Researcher', National Institute of Health, 28 November 2018, https://tinyurl.com/57wazmva. Accessed on 20 March 2025.

42   Normile, Dennis, 'Chinese scientist who produced genetically altered babies sentenced to 3 years in jail', *Science*, 30 December 2019, https://tinyurl.com/2cdjvmyp. Accessed on 20 March 2025.

43   'India's G20 Presidency: Emerging Issues', April 2023, https://tinyurl.com/2bmvsxjf. Accessed on 20 March 2025.

44   Doudna, Jennifer A., and Samuel H. Sternberg, *A Crack in Creation: Gene Editing and the Unthinkable Power to Control Evolution,* Houghton Mifflin Harcourt, 2017.

45   'Quantum technology historic public funding as of 2022, by country', *Statista*, https://tinyurl.com/23kp8xyp. Accessed on 20 March 2025.

46   Bela, Victoria, 'China's patent figures reveal it's closing the gap on US quantum dominance', *South China Morning Post*, 27 March 2024, https://tinyurl.com/mry64zkh. Accessed on 20 March 2025.

47   Neven, Hartmut, 'Meet Willow, our state-of-the-art quantum chip', *Google Blogs*, 9 December 2024, https://tinyurl.com/mrxxp88x. Accessed on 20 March 2025.

48   Romero, Luis E., 'Quantum Computing Could Achieve Singularity In 2025—A ChatGPT Moment', *Forbes*, 18 January 2025, https://tinyurl.com/3m8tuxp5. Accessed on 20 March 2025.

49   'Quantum Initiatives Worldwide 2025', *Qureca*, 11 April 2025, https://tinyurl.com/25bbkmrx. Accessed on 20 March 2025.

Chapter 9: Atlas of a Changing Earth

1   Intergovernmental Panel on Climate Change, 'Headline Statements from the Summary for Policymakers; Sixth Assessment Report Working Group II—

Impacts, Adaptation and Vulnerability', 28 February 2022, https://tinyurl.com/mrx6ncxn. Accessed on 21 March 2025.

2   'Home Equals issue brief: Climate migration and informal settlements', Habitat for Humanity, https://tinyurl.com/5cj7cmsn. Accessed on 21 March 2025.

3   Lindsey, Rebecca, and Luann Dahlman, 'Climate Change: Global Temperature', *Climate.gov*, 18 January 2024, https://tinyurl.com/mr392hsp. Accessed on 21 March 2025.

4   O'Shea, Claire A., 'NASA Clocks July 2023 as Hottest Month on Record Ever Since 1880', NASA, 14 August 2023, https://tinyurl.com/4xkxr35h. Accessed on 21 March 2025.

5   Ibid.

6   'FACT CHECK: Trump's Climate Denialism is Out of Touch with Reality – and Americans', *Climate Power*, 27 June 2024, https://tinyurl.com/3fbdfb8w. Accessed on 21 March 2025.

7   So, Kat, 'Climate Deniers of the 118th Congress', Center for American Progress, 18 July 2024, https://tinyurl.com/y8bkm24f. Accessed on 21 March 2025.

8   Basu, Jayanta, 'Unprecedented early heatwaves in India, Pakistan 30 times more likely in 2022 due to climate change: Scientists', *Down To Earth*, 25 May 2022, https://tinyurl.com/ud6p2cy5. Accessed on 21 March 2025.

9   'Extreme humid heat in South Asia in April 2023, largely driven by climate change, detrimental to vulnerable and disadvantaged communities', *World Weather Attribution*, 17 May 2023, https://tinyurl.com/5hfbu3w4. Accessed on 21 March 2025.

10 'China: Country Summary', *Climate Action Tracker*, https://tinyurl.com/2y65hkee. Accessed on 21 March 2025.

11 Ibid.

12 United Nations Framework Convention on Climate Change, 'Article 2-Objective', https://tinyurl.com/mr3v4wsw. Accessed on 21 March 2025.

13 'Report of the Conference of the Parties on its twenty-first session, held in Paris from 30 November to 13 December 2015', United Nations Framework Convention on Climate Change, 29 January 2016, https://tinyurl.com/523b5895. Accessed on 21 March 2025.

14 Nandi, Jayashree, 'COP29 in Baku is historic meeting, should mobilise $1.3 trillion annually: India', *Hindustan Times*, 15 November 2024, https://tinyurl.com/fzbvecvh. Accessed on 21 March 2025.

15 Nandi, Jayashree, 'COP29 in Baku is historic meeting, should mobilise $1.3 trillion annually: India', *Hindustan Times*, 15 November 2024, https://tinyurl.com/fzbvecvh. Accessed on 21 March 2025.

16 'Climate Change Could Force 216 Million People to Migrate Within Their Own Countries by 2050', World Bank Group, 13 September 2021, https://tinyurl.com/y4n3pnrk. Accessed on 21 March 2025.

17 'International Migration 2020 Highlights', United Nations Department of Economic and Social Affairs, https://tinyurl.com/muehhcpe. Accessed on 21 March 2025.

18   'Over 6 Million Afghan Migrants Reside In Iran, Official Says', *Afghanistan International*, 30 March 2025, https://tinyurl.com/34752zwb. Accessed on 21 March 2025.

19   UNHCR, 'Global Trends report 2023', https://tinyurl.com/mpjffnz9. Accessed on 21 March 2025.

20   'World population projected to reach 9.8 billion in 2050, and 11.2 billion in 2100', United Nations, https://tinyurl.com/bdpv77hf. Accessed on 21 March 2025.

21   'These countries are aging the fastest - here's what it will mean', World Economic Forum, 12 February 2020, https://tinyurl.com/2tzu7paf. Accessed on 21 March 2025.

22   'Median Age by Country 2025', *World Population Review*, https://tinyurl.com/2s3m5vnd. Accessed on 21 March 2025.

23   United Nations Department of Economic and Social Affairs, *Global Population Growth and Sustainable Development*, 2021, https://tinyurl.com/yc53skzv. Accessed on 21 March 2025.

24   Sigmon, Eric, 'Trump vs Harris: where they stand on immigration', Real Instituto Elcano, 8 October 2024, https://tinyurl.com/5xkrrbsc. Accessed on 21 March 2025.

25   'Manifest Destiny', *Encyclopaedia Britannica*, https://tinyurl.com/yxpjkcj8. Accessed on 21 March 2025.

26   'Climate Change Could Force Over 140 Million to Migrate Within Countries by 2050: World Bank Report', World Bank Group, 19 March 2018, https://tinyurl.com/2a7c2fkj. Accessed on 21 March 2025.

27   Yonetani, Michelle, 'Disaster-related displacement in a changing climate', World Metrological Organization, 21 March 2016, https://tinyurl.com/yeytc25r. Accessed on 21 March 2025.

28   'Disaster Risk management in South Asia: A Regional Overview', The World Bank Group, December 2012, https://tinyurl.com/2huzsups. Accessed on 21 March 2025.

29   'Glaciers lost 9 trillion tonnes of ice since 1975: UN', *The Hindu*, 25 March 2025, https://tinyurl.com/v8fs9uxc. Accessed on 21 March 2025.

30   'Two-thirds of glaciers projected to disappear by 2100: Study', *Al Jazeera*, 5 January 2023, https://tinyurl.com/cp6p6nrn. Accessed on 21 March 2025.

31   Golovtchenko, Valentin, Hamid Maher, and Andrew Shao, '7 ways to harness technology for climate adaptation', World Economic Forum, 17 January 2024, https://tinyurl.com/fmjzkw98. Accessed on 21 March 2025.

Chapter 10: The End of the Greenback Planet?

1   'Brazil's Lula calls for end to dollar trade dominance', *Financial Times*; https://tinyurl.com/aezbjy2x, Accessed on 24 March 2025.

2   'Video Address to the Participants in the BRICS Business Forum', *President of Russia*, 22 August 2023, https://tinyurl.com/mvpewx2s. Accessed on 24 March 2025.

3   Bryanski, Gleb, and Vladimir Soldatkin, 'Putin says BRICS, not the West, will drive global economic growth', Reuters, 18 October 2024, https://tinyurl.com/26zzedex. Accessed on 24 March 2025.

4   'Improvement Of The International Monetary and Financial System', BRICS Chairmanship Research, https://tinyurl.com/yhde9h76. Accessed on 24 March 2025.

5   Ibid.

6   'Improvement Of The International Monetary and Financial System', BRICS Chairmanship Research, https://tinyurl.com/yhde9h76. Accessed on 24 March 2025.

7   Ibid.

8   Haber, Bob, 'Sudden Media Infatuation With Keynes' "Barbaric Relic"—Gold', *Forbes*, 30 August 2019, https://tinyurl.com/4wxj5cy6. Accessed on 24 March 2025.

9   McTague, Tom, 'Are we all Gaullists now? Strategic autonomy is having a moment', *UnHerd*, 25 February 2025, https://tinyurl.com/4vkme7ec. Accessed on 24 March 2025.

10   Nieuwenhuijs, Jan, 'How France Secretly Repatriated All Its Gold Before Nixon's Dollar Devaluation', *The Gold Observer*, 7 October 2024, https://tinyurl.com/597w83pm. Accessed on 24 March 2025.

11   Graetz, Michael J., and Olivia Briffault, 'A "Barbarous Relic": The French, Gold, and the Demise of Bretton Woods', Columbia Law School, 2016, https://tinyurl.com/58yj27jv. Accessed on 24 March 2025.

12   Ibid.

13   Ibid.

14   Nieuwenhuijs, Jan, 'How France Secretly Repatriated All Its Gold Before Nixon's Dollar Devaluation', *The Gold Observer*, 7 October 2024, https://tinyurl.com/597w83pm. Accessed on 24 March 2025.

15   Ibid.

16   Fox, Michelle, 'The U.S. national debt is rising by $1 trillion about every 100 days', *CNBC*, 1 March 2024, https://tinyurl.com/ycxuvp33. Accessed on 24 March 2025.

17   Ma, Jason, 'US debt could explode above 200% of GDP in two decades if Trump's tax cuts become permanent, CBO says—putting it at unsustainable levels', *Fortune*, 22 March 2025, https://tinyurl.com/3j6cfntw. Accessed on 24 March 2025.

18   Rooney, Bryan, et al., 'How Does Defense Spending Affect Economic Growth?', *RAND*, 7 May 2021, https://tinyurl.com/2s447586. Accessed on 24 March 2025.

19   K, Yoosef, 'India becomes fourth nation to reach $700 billion in forex reserves', *CNBC TV*, 4 October 2024, https://tinyurl.com/58h6y4sh. Accessed on 24 March 2025.

20   Yongding, Yu, 'China's Foreign Exchange Reserves: Past and Present Security Challenges', *Wenhua Zongheng*, Vol. 2, No. 1, 2024, https://tinyurl.com/7nndm5re. Accessed on 24 March 2025.

21 Shinohara, Gabriel, 'FX reserves reach highest level in 5 years', *Valor International*, 11 April 2024, https://tinyurl.com/nhz48xs9. Accessed on 24 March 2025.

22 Fabrichnaya, Elena, and Guy Faulconbridge, 'What and where are Russia's $300 billion in reserves frozen in the West?', *Reuters*, 28 December 2023, https://tinyurl.com/25mwv84h. Accessed on 24 March 2025.

23 Prasad, Eswar, 'Top Dollar', *Foreign Affairs*, July/August 2024 (18 June, 2024), https://tinyurl.com/442bmvb8. Accessed on 24 March 2025.

24 Ibid.

25 PTI, 'Putin advises cautious approach, says common BRICS currency not being considered yet', *The Economic Times*, 19 October 2024, https://tinyurl.com/3db69daa. Accessed on 24 March 2025.

26 'India has never been for de-dollarisation, no proposal for BRICS currency: EAM Jaishankar at Doha', *The Economic Times*, 7 December 2024, https://tinyurl.com/4e9t39p5. Accessed on 24 March 2025.

27 'Strengthening Multilateralism For Just Global Development And Security', Kazan Declaration XVI BRICS Summit, 23 October 2024, https://tinyurl.com/4s9bmnhk. Accessed on 24 March 2025.

28 Beschwitz, Bastian von, 'Internationalization of the Chinese renminbi: progress and outlook', Board of Governors of the Federal Reserve System, 30 August 2024, https://tinyurl.com/4txjhmv5. Accessed on 24 March 2025.

29 'Will China's Push to Internationalize the Renminbi Succeed?', *China Power*, https://tinyurl.com/4hhj5rfb. Accessed on 24 March 2025.

30 Xiong, Yuanmeng, et al., 'Bank of China on the renminbi's internationalisation', Trade Finance Global, https://tinyurl.com/4edanex6. Accessed on 24 March 2025.

31 'China's central bank signs 40 currency swap agreements with foreign counterparts', Xinhua News Agency, 16 February 2024, https://tinyurl.com/3rywyfkv. Accessed on 24 March 2025.

32 Kun, Li, and Wei Hao, 'Yuan meets all criteria to be a cross-border trade currency', *China Daily*, 17 May 2023, https://tinyurl.com/3wcrhveh. Accessed on 24 March 2025.

33 Lee, Amanda, 'Can China's yuan, now a familiar face around the world, become a must-have currency?', *South China Morning Post*, 1 September 2024, https://tinyurl.com/y6ydu6m5. Accessed on 24 March 2025.

34 'BRICS countries navigate new alternative payment system for stronger cooperation', *Global Times*, 17 October 2024, https://tinyurl.com/2uzv9t73. Accessed on 24 March 2025.

35 Prasad, Eswar, 'Top Dollar', *Foreign Affairs*, July/August 2024 (18 June 2024), https://tinyurl.com/442bmvb8. Accessed on 24 March 2025.

Chapter 11: National Conservatism and the Woke Response

1 'National Front hopes to win seats in parliament', *France 24*, 13 June 2012, https://tinyurl.com/ppuv2wka. Accessed on 26 March 2025.

2 'Macron wins French presidential election', *Le Monde*, 24 April 2022,

https://tinyurl.com/ycykjrcz. Accessed on 26 March 2025.

3   '2024 European election results', European Parliament, https://tinyurl.com/2s37vcw. Accessed on 26 March 2025.

4   'On the Motion to Proceed PN11-16: Tulsi Gabbard, of Hawaii, to be Director of National Intelligence', *Govtrack.us*, 6 February 2025, https://tinyurl.com/39t5a55c. Accessed on 26 March 2025.

5   'Texas Transports Over 100,000 Migrants To Sanctuary Cities', Office of the Texas Governor, 12 January 2024, https://tinyurl.com/2zd5yxdb. Accessed on 26 March 2025.

6   Nahmias, Laura, et al., 'NYC Pays Over $300 a Night for Budget Hotel Rooms for Migrants', *Bloomberg*, 9 June 2023, https://tinyurl.com/dw5c87eu. Accessed on 26 March 2025.

7   Bowen Jr., William R., 'The Rise of the Nation-State', *Owlcation*, 19 November 2023, https://tinyurl.com/39xmw9rx. Accessed on 26 March 2025.

8   Hazony, Yoram, *The Virtue of Nationalism*, Basic Books, 2018.

9   Ibid.

10   Gonzalez, Mike, 'Founded on a Creed: Understanding America's Unique Beginning', The Heritage Foundation, 18 December 2019, https://tinyurl.com/mrak3jca. Accessed on 26 March 2025.

11   Sri Aurobindo, 'Discovery of the Nation-Soul', *The Light of the Supreme*, 3 June 2010, https://tinyurl.com/4ps33fcb. Accessed on 26 March 2025.

12   Madhav, Ram, 'The Soul of the Nation', *Ram Madhav*, 9 December 2020, https://tinyurl.com/4u9ytu6a. Accessed on 26 March 2025.

13   Loconte, Joseph, 'Churchill, FDR, and the Atlantic Charter', *Providence Magazine*, 10 August 2016, https://tinyurl.com/442tcbfn. Accessed on 26 March 2025.

14   Hazony, Yoram, *The Virtue of Nationalism*, Basic Books, 2018.

15   Ibid.

16   Ibid.

17   Hayek, F.A., *The Constitution of Liberty*, University of Chicago Press, 2011.

18   Minogue, Kenneth, 'Exceptionally Conservative', *Claremont Review of Books*, Vol. V, No. 3, 2005, https://tinyurl.com/5n8fp4cy. Accessed on 26 March 2025.

19   Francis, Sam, and Becky Morton, 'Farage vows to change politics forever after win', *BBC*, 5 July 2024, https://tinyurl.com/mub34yjb. Accessed on 26 March 2025.

20   'Fidel Castro at Harvard: How history might have changed', *Fidel: Soldier of Ideas*, https://tinyurl.com/y2pdys6a. Accessed on 26 March 2025.

21   'From Cultural Marxism to wokeism: the repackaged theory of left-wing cultural hegemony', *Identities*, 1 June 2022, https://tinyurl.com/3zyzsbwp. Accessed on 26 March 2025.

22   Ibid.

23   Jacques, Ingrid, '"Inseminated person" vs. "mother"? Dems keep proving they've lost common sense', *USA Today*, 28 February 2025, https://tinyurl.com/yf52aaah. Accessed on 26 March 2025.

24   Kelley, William Melvin, 'If You're Woke You Dig It; No mickey mouse can be

expected to follow today's Negro idiom without a hip assist. If You're Woke You Dig It', *The New York Times*, 20 May 1962, https://tinyurl.com/3jd55wpe. Accessed on 26 March 2025.

25   Harriot, Michael, 'War on wokeness: the year the right rallied around a made-up menace', *The Guardian*, 21 December 2022, https://tinyurl.com/2948xk85. Accessed on 26 March 2025.

26   Redding, Saunders J., 'A Negro Speaks for His People', *The Atlantic*, March 1943, https://tinyurl.com/mwtv3u6a. Accessed on 26 March 2025.

27   King Jr., Martin Luther, 'Remaining Awake Through a Great Revolution', Commencement Address by Dr Martin Luther King Jr. at Oberlin College, June 1965, https://tinyurl.com/z7tjyfby. Accessed on 26 March 2025.

28   King Jr., Martin Luther, 'Remaining Awake Through a Great Revolution', Address at Morehouse College Commencement, The Martin Luther King, Jr. Research and Education Institute, Stanford University, 2 June 1959, https://tinyurl.com/mvm7v27y. Accessed on 26 March 2025.

29   Lievano, Wilson, and Josh Coe, 'The Capitol riots showed U.S. democracy's vulnerability. How does that affect its global influence?', *The Groundtruth Project*, 15 January 2021, https://tinyurl.com/3djtsd3z. Accessed on 26 March 2025.

30   Riley, Jason L., 'America Has a Silent Black Majority', *Wall Street Journal*, 16 June 2020, https://tinyurl.com/323pfa4t. Accessed on 26 March 2025.

31   Graham, Bryan Armen, 'Joe Biden's gender discrimination order offers hope for young trans athletes', *The Guardian*, 22 January 2021, https://tinyurl.com/mua2u3u6. Accessed on 26 March 2025.

32   Williams, Joanna, *How Woke Won: The Elitist Movement that Threatens Democracy, Tolerance and Reason*, John Wilkes Publishing, 2022.

33   Ibid.

34   'Brighton & Hove infants asked to choose gender on primary school form', *The Guardian*, 20 April 2016, https://tinyurl.com/2chnnjba. Accessed on 26 March 2025.

35   Williams, Joanna, *How Woke Won: The Elitist Movement that Threatens Democracy, Tolerance and Reason*, John Wilkes Publishing, 2022.

36   Crane, Jonathan, 'Paris Olympics: What's behind boxing controversy?', *DW*, 5 August 2024, https://tinyurl.com/mr3fwtst. Accessed on 26 March 2025.

37   de Lauzun, Hélène, '"Never been hit so hard in my life": Angela Carini Quits Boxing Bout After Punch By Male Opponent', *The European Conservative*, 1 August 2024, https://tinyurl.com/munppjhk, 26 March 2025.

38   'Rowling and Musk reportedly named in Khelif cyberbullying complaint', *BBC*, 14 August 2024, https://tinyurl.com/4khxz9t7. Accessed on 26 March 2025.

39   Luk, Johnny, 'Why "woke" became toxic', *Al Jazeera*, 24 June 2021, https://tinyurl.com/56uvad2t. Accessed on 26 March 2025.

40   Lytton, Charlotte, 'No one is safe from the internet's offence archaeologists', *The Telegraph*, 10 November 2018, https://tinyurl.com/24y94dez. Accessed on 26 March 2025.

41   Tombs, Robert, '"Wokeness" and the collapse of intellectual freedom in the

West', *The Spectator*, 28 August 2021, https://tinyurl.com/vhk3rs32, Accessed on 26 March 2025.

42 'J.K. Rowling Writes about Her Reasons for Speaking out on Sex and Gender Issues', *jkrowling.com*, 10 June 2020, https://tinyurl.com/y3uz39ma. Accessed on 26 March 2025.

43 West, Ed, 'Why wokeism won't rule the world', *UnHerd*, 21 September 2021, https://tinyurl.com/2kutaf7s. Accessed on 26 March 2025.

44 Harriot, Michael, 'War on wokeness: the year the right rallied around a made-up menace', *The Guardian*, 21 December 2022, https://tinyurl.com/2948xk85. Accessed on 26 March 2025.

45 Kolhatkar, Sheelah, 'Anti-Woke, Inc.', *The New Yorker*, 12 December 2022, https://tinyurl.com/3yvy5c47. Accessed on 24 April 2025.

46 @elonmusk, X (formerly Twitter), 12 December 2022, 5.55 p.m., https://tinyurl.com/372patnf. Accessed on 26 March 2025.

47 Williams, Joanna, *How Woke Won: The Elitist Movement that Threatens Democracy, Tolerance and Reason*, John Wilkes Publishing, 2022.

Chapter 12: The Lion Roars, Loud and Clear

1 'India advanced from 10th place in 2014 to become 5th largest economy in 2019: Puri', *ET Energy World*, 19 September 2024, https://tinyurl.com/ds7tada7. Accessed on 27 March 2025.

2 'GDP per Capita', *Worldometer*, https://tinyurl.com/4b4maerb. Accessed on 27 March 2025.

3 'The 15th of August 1947 Message by Sri Aurobindo', Sri Aurobindo Society, https://tinyurl.com/557336nx. Accessed on 27 March 2025.

4 Nehru, Jawaharlal, *An Autobiography*, Oxford University Press, 1936, pp. 604.

5 'Nehru's Presidential Address at the Lahore Congress, 1929', *The Nehru Blog*, https://tinyurl.com/33mwx8ff. Accessed on 27 March 2025.

6 'Nehru's Presidential Address at the Lucknow Congress, 1936', *The Nehru Blog*, https://tinyurl.com/y6s4ba89. Accessed on 27 March 2025.

7 'Brief History of Congress', Indian National Congress, https://tinyurl.com/4r5js29w. Accessed on 27 March 2025.

8 Bhalla, Surjit S., 'Not as Poor, Nor as unequal, As you think – Poverty, Inequality and Growth in India, 1950-2000', *The Myth and Reality of Poverty in India*, Planning Commission, Government of India, https://tinyurl.com/ycy9n4xd. Accessed on 27 March 2025.

9 'Constitution and Rules', Bharatiya Janata Party, https://tinyurl.com/2wej888u. Accessed on 27 March 2025.

10 'Uniqueness of India's nuclear trajectory premised on the principle of "No First Use & Massive Retaliation": CDS Gen Anil Chauhan', Ministry of Defence, 26 June 2024, https://tinyurl.com/2zbb5kya. Accessed on 27 March 2025.

11 Ibid.

12 'Clarifying India's Nascent Nuclear Doctrine', Arms Control Association, https://tinyurl.com/2pjhna5h. Accessed on 27 March 2025.

13   'Ek Bharat Shreshth Bharat: Election Manifesto 2014', Bharatiya Janata Party, https://tinyurl.com/bdf4npmc. Accessed on 27 March 2025.

14   'Explained: India's doctrine of Nuclear No First Use', *Indian Express*, 17 August 2019, https://tinyurl.com/5dedj7yu. Accessed on 27 March 2025.

15   Singh, Sushant, 'Manohar Parrikar questions India's no-first-use nuclear policy, adds "my thinking"', *The Indian Express*, 11 November 2016, https://tinyurl.com/5epr3t6p. Accessed on 27 March 2025.

16   'Rajnath on "no first use" nuclear policy: "What happens in future depends on circumstances"', *The Indian Express*, 16 August 2019, https://tinyurl.com/4tpzvts6. Accessed on 27 March 2025.

17   Thakur, Vineet, 'An Asian Drama: The Asian Relations Conference, 1947', *The International History Review*, 20 February 2018, https://tinyurl.com/yprckw3u. Accessed on 27 March 2025.

18   Ibid.

19   'Inter-Asian Relations Conference, 2 April 1947', *Mahatma Gandhi*, https://tinyurl.com/5c9hzfdn. Accessed on 27 March 2025.

20   'Panchsheel', Ministry of External Affairs, Government of India, https://tinyurl.com/2w6556dd. Accessed on 27 March 2025.

21   'Minutes of Chairman Mao Zedong's First Meeting with Nehru', Wilson Center, 19 October 1954, https://tinyurl.com/3eekepkd. Accessed on 27 March 2025.

22   Ibid.

23   'Bandung Principles', *Bandung Spirit*, https://tinyurl.com/krjjzxen. Accessed on 27 March 2025.

24   Kalyanaraman, S., 'Was The Non-Aligned Movement Ever Relevant for India?', *Swarajya*, 29 September 2016, https://tinyurl.com/5nmuctcz. Accessed on 27 March 2025.

25   Vajpayee, Atal Bihari, 'India, USA and the World: Let us work together to solve the Political-Economic Y2K Problem', *Asia Society*, 28 September 1998, https://tinyurl.com/57wdh5k7. Accessed on 27 March 2025.

26   Laskar, Rezaul H., 'India explains why it abstained at UN vote on Ukraine with 3 piercing questions', *Hindustan Times*, 25 February 2023, https://tinyurl.com/2s3hf5wh. Accessed on 27 March 2025.

27   'India-Russia ties "higher than highest mountain": Rajnath Singh tells Putin in Moscow', *Hindustan Times*, 10 December 2024, https://tinyurl.com/w92cjcrv. Accessed on 27 March 2025.

28   Lalchandani, Neha, 'Help is just one tweet away: Sushma on Pravasi Bharatiya Divas', *The Times of India*, 21 January 2019, https://tinyurl.com/5n7efz5a. Accessed on 27 March 2025.

29   'Doing Business 2020: Comparing Business Regulations in 190 Economies', World bank Group, https://tinyurl.com/2s3rujdf. Accessed on 27 March 2025.

Chapter 13: Driving Progress in an Intelligent Age

1   'In quotes: Deng Xiaoping', *China Daily*, 20 August 2014, https://tinyurl.com/4xvdd8pb. Accessed on 27 March 2025.

2   'China GDP Per Capita 1960–2025', *Macrotrends*, https://tinyurl.com/37bschcj. Accessed on 31 March 2025.

3   'India GDP per Capita 1960–2025', *Macrotrends*, https://tinyurl.com/2s6383kv. Accessed on 31 March 2025.

4   Patel, Aakar, 'From 1960 to 1990, India and China Were at Par. How Did It Then Overtake Us?', *Wire*, 5 December 2023, https://tinyurl.com/4fdvear8. Accessed on 31 March 2025.

5   'GDP (current US$) – China', World Bank Group, https://tinyurl.com/2s3ub42y. Accessed on 31 March 2025.

6   One of the methods of confining hot fusion plasmas is by use of the toroidal magnetic bottle known as tokamak.

7   'CDC 6600 is introduced', Centre for Computing History, https://tinyurl.com/4fbts555. Accessed on 31 March 2025.

8   'PM launches country 1st indigenously build supercomputer', Department of Science and Technology, 19 February 2019, https://tinyurl.com/45zrrjp9. Accessed on 31 March 2025.

9   'India's "AIRAWAT" ranks 75th in top 500 Supercomputing List', Centre for Development of Advanced Computing, Governance Now, 24 May 2023, https://tinyurl.com/54rrrbjs. Accessed on 31 March 2025.

10   Weber, Valentin, 'The New Quantum Technology Race', *Internationale Politik Quarterly*, 22 March 2024, https://tinyurl.com/yc2bym3v. Accessed on 31 March 2025.

11   'Budget 2020–21 announces the largest-ever science mission', Economic Diplomacy Division, https://tinyurl.com/566kapu7. Accessed on 31 March 2025.

12   'IBM announces $20 billion investment in New York for high-tech projects', *Business Standard*, 7 October 2022, https://tinyurl.com/mr28vxp5. Accessed on 31 March 2025.

13   B, Vaitheeswaran, 'India's quantum computing research needs a boost', *The Times of India*, 10 July 2024, https://tinyurl.com/4jxhftj6. Accessed on 31 March 2025.

14   Bela, Victoria, 'China's patent figures reveal it's closing the gap on US quantum dominance', *South China Morning*, 27 March 2024, https://tinyurl.com/mry64zkh. Accessed on 31 March 2025.

15   Choudhary, Puran, 'India is 10-15 years behind most countries in traditional technologies, says DRDO chief', *The New Indian Express*, 22 September 2024, https://tinyurl.com/2pu4x43h. Accessed on 31 March 2025.

16   Sharma, Divyam, "'First 40 Tejas Still Not...": Air Force Chief As China Tests 6th Gen Jets', *NDTV*, 8 January 2025, https://tinyurl.com/5n835x37. Accessed on 31 March 2025.

17   'India's Impressive Leap in the Global Innovation Index 2024: A Testament to the Nation's Growing Innovation Ecosystem', Ministry of Information & Broadcasting, 30 September 2024, https://tinyurl.com/3u7xf7v2. Accessed on 31 March 2025.

18   'Cabinet approves Introduction of National Research Foundation Bill, 2023 in Parliament to strengthen research eco-system in the country', Press Information Bureau of India, 28 June 2023, https://tinyurl.com/436aavdv. Accessed on 31 March 2025.

19   Chhapia, Hemali, 'India is world's 4th in research output, but ranks 9th in citations', *The Times of India*, 23 March 2023, https://tinyurl.com/mr3ueuff. Accessed on 31 March 2025.

20   Ibid.

21   Ibid.

22   Ibid.

23   'World Intellectual Property Indicators 2024', WIPO, https://tinyurl.com/yc4ye734. Accessed on 31 March 2025.

24   Ibid.

25   'Sizing the prize', PwC, https://tinyurl.com/57ujczv7, Accessed on 31 March 2025.

26   Ibid.

27   'India ranks 10th with $1.4 billion private investment in AI: UN report', *The Economic Times*, 4 April 2025, https://tinyurl.com/yc59rmmc. Accessed on 31 March 2025.

28   Jeevanandam, Nivash, 'Prime Minister hails the establishment of three AI Centres of Excellence', *India AI*, 16 October 2024, https://tinyurl.com/hu5m4fa7. Accessed on 31 March 2025.

29   Kelly, Jack, 'Goldman Sachs Predicts 300 Million Jobs Will Be Lost Or Degraded By Artificial Intelligence', *Forbes*, 31 March 2023, https://tinyurl.com/ybure3pe. Accessed on 31 March 2025.

30   Le Maistre, Ray, 'India now has 1.15 billion mobile connections', *Telecom TV*, 12 January 2024, https://tinyurl.com/y9972s3f. Accessed on 31 March 2025.

31   'United Nations World Population Prospects 2024', Department of Economic and Social Affairs Population Division, https://tinyurl.com/4nbk2au7. Accessed on 31 March 2025.

32   'India's Population Expected To Rise Till 2050 And Then Decline: UN', *NDTV*, 19 April 2023, https://tinyurl.com/3z5ap74y. Accessed on 31 March 2025.

33   'Total Fertility Rate: India', *CEIC*, https://tinyurl.com/4meyjtkf. Accessed on 31 March 2025.

34   'Service Sector's contribution to total GVA rises from 50.6% in FY14 to 55.3% in FY25: Economic Survey 2024-25', Ministry of Finance, Press Information Bureau, 31 January 2025, https://tinyurl.com/muryp7xy. Accessed on 31 March 2025.

35   Malin, Sophie, and Ashima Tyagi, 'India's Demographic Dividend: The Key to Unlocking Its Global Ambitions', S&P Global, 3 August 2023, https://tinyurl.com/yybyb49u. Accessed on 31 March 2025.

36   'Spotlight on Work Statistics n°12', International Labour Organization, March 2023, https://tinyurl.com/54hyr989. Accessed on 31 March 2025.

37   Ashraf, Syed Firdaus, '"The Muslim population has declined in Assam"', *Rediff*

News, 5 September 2019, https://tinyurl.com/s7k7ds7e. Accessed on 31 March 2025.

38 Parashar, Utpal, 'Over 19 lakh excluded, 3.1 crore included in Assam NRC final list', *Hindustan Times*, 24 June 2020, https://tinyurl.com/2vduwe7x. Accessed on 31 March 2025.

39 'Eva Vlaardingerbroek's CPAC Hungary 2024 Speech Taken Down by YouTube Citing "Ha"', *Hungarian Conservative*, https://tinyurl.com/4cpf5cym. Accessed on 31 March 2025.

40 Figaro, Le, '67% of French people worried about the idea of a "great replacement", according to a poll', *Societe*, 21 October 2021, https://tinyurl.com/4rutav39. Accessed on 31 March 2025.

41 Miller, Cassie, 'SPLC Poll Finds Substantial Support for "Great Replacement" Theory and Other Hard-Right Ideas', SPLC, 1 June 2022, https://tinyurl.com/25xymkfu. Accessed on 31 March 2025.

42 Maik, Herold, 'The impact of conspiracy belief on democratic culture: Evidence from Europe', *Misinformation Review*, 12 December 2024, https://tinyurl.com/yc62sjew. Accessed on 31 March 2025.

43 Ravi, Shamika, et al., 'Share of Religious Minorities: A Cross-Country Analysis (1950-2015)', Economic Advisory Council to the PM, EAC-PM Working Paper Series, EAC-PM/WP/29/2024, May 2024, https://tinyurl.com/bjhcvksc. Accessed on 31 March 2025.

44 Ibid.

45 Ibid.

46 Ravi, Shamika, et al., 'Share of Religious Minorities: A Cross-Country Analysis (1950-2015)', Economic Advisory Council to the PM, EAM-PM Working Paper Series, EAC-PM/WP/29/2024, May 2024, https://tinyurl.com/bjhcvksc. Accessed on 31 March 2025.

47 'Religious Demography of India', Centre for Policy Studies, https://tinyurl.com/yc4a9mu6. Accessed on 31 March 2025.

48 'National Family Health Survey (NFHS-5) 2019–21', Ministry of Health and Family Welfare, Government of India, https://tinyurl.com/mwfz2u9h. Accessed on 31 March 2025.

49 'World population projected to reach 9.8 billion in 2050, and 11.2 billion in 2100', UN Department of Social and Economic Affairs, https://tinyurl.com/bdpv77hf. Accessed on 31 March 2025.

50 '8 Billion People And Counting: What Now? World Population Day 2023', United Nations, https://tinyurl.com/y472y7kp. Accessed on 31 March 2025.

51 Tupy, Marian L., and Gale L. Pooley, *Superabundance: The Story of Population Growth, Innovation, and Human Flourishing on an Infinitely Bountiful Planet*, Cato Books, 2022, https://tinyurl.com/hetazbk2. Accessed on 31 March 2025.

52 'Population control a form of patriotism: PM Modi', *Hindustan Times*, 15 June 2020, https://tinyurl.com/2xu252vb. Accessed on 31 March 2025.

53 'In 2100, 40% Of The World Population Will Be African', *World Atlas*, https://tinyurl.com/bdez6r28.

54   'The Future of Global Muslim Population', Pew Research Center, 27 January 2011, https://tinyurl.com/3mcxp2c7. Accessed on 31 March 2025.
55   Ibid.
56   'Egypt Population 1950–2025', *Macrotrends*, https://tinyurl.com/2ru5mhp5. Accessed on 31 March 2025.
57   'South Korea Population 1950–2025', *Macrotrends*, https://tinyurl.com/2axhpxkj. Accessed on 31 March 2025.
58   Ibid.
59   'Egypt Population 1950-2025', *Macrotrends*, https://tinyurl.com/2ru5mhp5. Accessed on 31 March 2025.
60   'The Future of World Religions: Population Growth Projections, 2010–2050', Pew Research Center, 2 April 2015, https://tinyurl.com/5sb92b7u. Accessed on 31 March 2025.
61   Tiwary, Deeptiman, 'Population imbalance can divide countries, need policy for population control: Mohan Bhagwat', *Indian Express*, 5 October 2022, https://tinyurl.com/yy4tfp9k. Accessed on 31 March 2025.
62   Kramer, Stephanie, 'Religious Composition of India', Pew Research Center, 21 September 2021, https://tinyurl.com/4nf5h6be. Accessed on 31 March 2025.
63   'National Family Health Survey (NFHS-5) 2019-21', Ministry of Health and Family Welfare, Government of India, https://tinyurl.com/mwfz2u9h. Accessed on 31 March 2025.

Chapter 14: Regional State or Global Power?

1   'India and Neighbours', Ministry of External Affairs, Government of India, https://tinyurl.com/ew7zt8h6. Accessed on 31 March 2025.
2   Mukherjee, Pranab, *Pranab Mukherjee: The Presidential Years 2012-2017*, Rupa Publications India, 2021.
3   'Sri Lanka: UN admits it failed to protect civilians', *BBC*, 14 November 2012, https://tinyurl.com/4pt9csat. Accessed on 31 March 2025.
4   'Question no- 262 India's Neighbourhood First Policy', Lok Sabha Starred Question No. 262, Ministry of External Affairs, 13 December 2024, https://tinyurl.com/mryj9zst. Accessed on 31 March 2025.
5   Ibid.
6   'Question no- 262 India's Neighbourhood First Policy', Ministry of External Affairs, 13 December 2024, https://tinyurl.com/5n98utv4. Accessed on 31 March 2025.
7   Jacob, Happymon, 'The End of South Asia', *Foreign Affairs*, 22 July 2024, https://tinyurl.com/2dzumnbk. Accessed on 25 April 2025.
8   Moorthy, Sathiya N., 'Reconverting the "IOR pond" into India's traditional sphere of influence', *Firstpost*, 12 January 2025, https://tinyurl.com/yc38nxbx. Accessed on 25 April 2025.
9   Coedes, G., *The Indianized states of Southeast Asia*, Australian National University Press, 1968, pp. 26–7, https://tinyurl.com/je62cjpv. Accessed on 31 March 2025.

10 'Indian Ocean Rim Association (IORA)', https://tinyurl.com/yc3wvwvx. Accessed on 31 March 2025.

11 Clinton, Hillary Rodham, 'Remarks on India and the United States: A Vision for the 21st Century', U.S Department of State, 20 July 2011, https://tinyurl.com/yt2y6cfu. Accessed on 31 March 2025.

12 Chand, Manish, 'Act East: India's ASEAN Journey', Ministry of External Affairs, 10 November 2014, https://tinyurl.com/yc8cn8d2. Accessed on 31 March 2025.

13 'Prime Minister's remarks at the 9th East Asia Summit, Nay Pyi Taw, Myanmar', Ministry of External Affairs, 13 November 2014, https://tinyurl.com/22xn7cvv. Accessed on 31 March 2025.

14 'Prime Minister's Remarks at the Commissioning of Offshore Patrol Vessel (OPV) Barracuda in Mauritius', Ministry of External Affairs, 12 March 2015, https://tinyurl.com/53t2ucu7. Accessed on 31 March 2025.

15 Ibid.

16 Ibid.

17 Jash, Amrita, 'The "Mahanian Way": China moves into the Indian Ocean', *9DashLine*, 13 April 2020, https://tinyurl.com/5y7cz5wt. Accessed on 31 March 2025.

18 Panikkar, K.M., *India and The Indian Ocean: An Essay on The Influence of Sea Power on Indian History*, George Allen and Unwin, London, 1945.

19 Harrigan, Anthony, 'The Afro-Asian Ocean World', United States Naval Institute, Vol. 90/5/735, May 1964, https://tinyurl.com/99xz26nf. Accessed on 31 March 2025.

20 'India's shipbuilding ambitions: Where are we now and what to do next?', KPMG, 21 August 2024, https://tinyurl.com/5n8vew4r. Accessed on 31 March 2025.

21 Panikkar, K.M., *India and The Indian Ocean: An Essay on The Influence of Sea Power on Indian History*, George Allen and Unwin, London, 1945.

22 Vaidya, Keshav Balkrishna, *The Naval Defence of India*, Thacker & Co Ltd, 1949.

23 'Securing India's Interests in the Indian Ocean Region', 9 October 2024, https://tinyurl.com/3c6tt643. Accessed on 31 March 2025.

24 US Department of Defense, *Military and Security Developments involving the People's Republic of China 2024 – Annual report to Congress*, https://tinyurl.com/mr2afjpz. Accessed on 31 March 2025.

25 'China Naval Modernization: Implications for U.S. Navy Capabilities— Background and Issues for Congress', Congressional Research Service, 18 November 2005–16 August 2024, https://tinyurl.com/3hfd8wxf. Accessed on 31 March 2025.

26 Scott, David, 'India's Drive for a Blue Water Navy', *Journal of Military and Strategic Studies*, Vol. 10, Issue 2, Winter 2007–08, https://tinyurl.com/3aymawr5. Accessed on 31 March 2025.

27 Ibid.

28 'Agalega, a secret base, and India's claim to power', *Al Jazeera*,

https://tinyurl.com/4hmkb8j3; Accessed on 31 March 2025.

29   Ibid.

30   'PM and Mauritian PM jointly inaugurate new Airstrip and a Jetty at Agalega Island in Mauritius', Prime Minister's Office, Press Information Bureau of India, 29 February 2024, https://tinyurl.com/yckrnz42. Accessed on 31 March 2025.

31   Dutta, Amrita Nayak, 'INS Arighaat: India's second nuclear sub', *The Indian Express*, 1 September 2024, https://tinyurl.com/ys3uwwt6. Accessed on 31 March 2025.

32   Chand, Lt Gen. Naresh, 'Navy's Quest for Modernisation', *SP's Naval Forces*, January 2020, https://tinyurl.com/3af4f7ae. Accessed on 31 March 2025.

Epilogue: Building Brand Bharat

1   Rancour-Laferriere, Daniel, *The Slave Soul of Russia: Moral Masochism and the Cult of Suffering*, New York University Press, 1995.

2   Raje, Sudhakar (Ed.), *Pt. Deendayal Upadhyaya: A Profile*, Deendayal Research Institute, 1972.

3   Benson, Ezra Taft, *God, Family, Country: Our Three Great Loyalties*, Deseret Book Co., Salt Lake City, 1974.

4   Wood, Michael, 'Legacy: The Origins of Civilization', Episode 6, *The Barbarian West*.

5   Nivedita, Sister, *The Web of Indian Life*, William Heinemann, 1904.

6   'Constituent Assembly Debates On 6 November, 1948 Part I', https://tinyurl.com/56mb4tn5. Accessed on 1 April 2025.

7   Shastri, Lal Bahadur, *Speeches of Prime Minister Lal Bahadur Shastri*, Publications Division, Ministry of Information and Broadcasting, 1965, https://tinyurl.com/4s2fsd6u. Accessed on 1 April 2025.

8   'Sengol Saga: Claims Of Power Transfer "Bogus", Says Congress. "Why Hate Indian Traditions," Asks Centre', *ABP News*, 1 June 2023, https://tinyurl.com/e37a95vv. Accessed on 1 April 2025.

9   Madhav, Ram, 'Decoding Sengol, the sacred sceptre', *The Indian Express*, 29 May 2023, https://tinyurl.com/mryjncvd. Accessed on 1 April 2025.

10   'From "national rejuvenation" to "repression after rhetoric": What front pages said on Parliament event', *Newslaundry*, 29 May 2023, https://tinyurl.com/mpba5m3p. Accessed on 1 April 2025.

11   'PM's address at the celebration of dedication of New Parliament Building to the Nation', PM India, 28 May 2023, https://tinyurl.com/2azmynzb. Accessed on 1 April 2025.

12   Madhav, Ram, 'Ram Madhav writes on the new Parliament building: Dharmocracy, the Indian version of democracy', *The Indian Express*, 3 June 2023, https://tinyurl.com/538udpv2. Accessed on 1 April 2025.

13   Yashee, 'Somnath: A brief history of the temple, and why Nehru opposed the President inaugurating it', *The Indian Express*, 21 January 2024, https://tinyurl.com/ykczn9su. Accessed on 1 April 2025.

14 'PM's address at the celebration of dedication of New Parliament Building to the Nation', PM India, 28 May 2023, https://tinyurl.com/2azmynzb. Accessed on 1 April 2025.

15 'Thus Spake Gandhi: Select quotations by Mahatma Gandhi', https://tinyurl.com/3wc9d9ap. Accessed on 1 April 2025.

16 Ibid.

17 'Democracy and Non-violence', *Mahatma Gandhi*, 13 May 1940, https://tinyurl.com/2s4exw5d. Accessed on 1 April 2025.

INDEX

Made in the USA
Monee, IL
15 May 2026

ed592836-fe92-4cc0-91e2-28fef67536afR01